Passionate About Photography
February and March 2017
Black and White Album

ISBN-13: 978-1544997599
ISBN-10: 1544997590

Author, Photographer, Publisher - Ian McKenzie
www.iansbooks.com

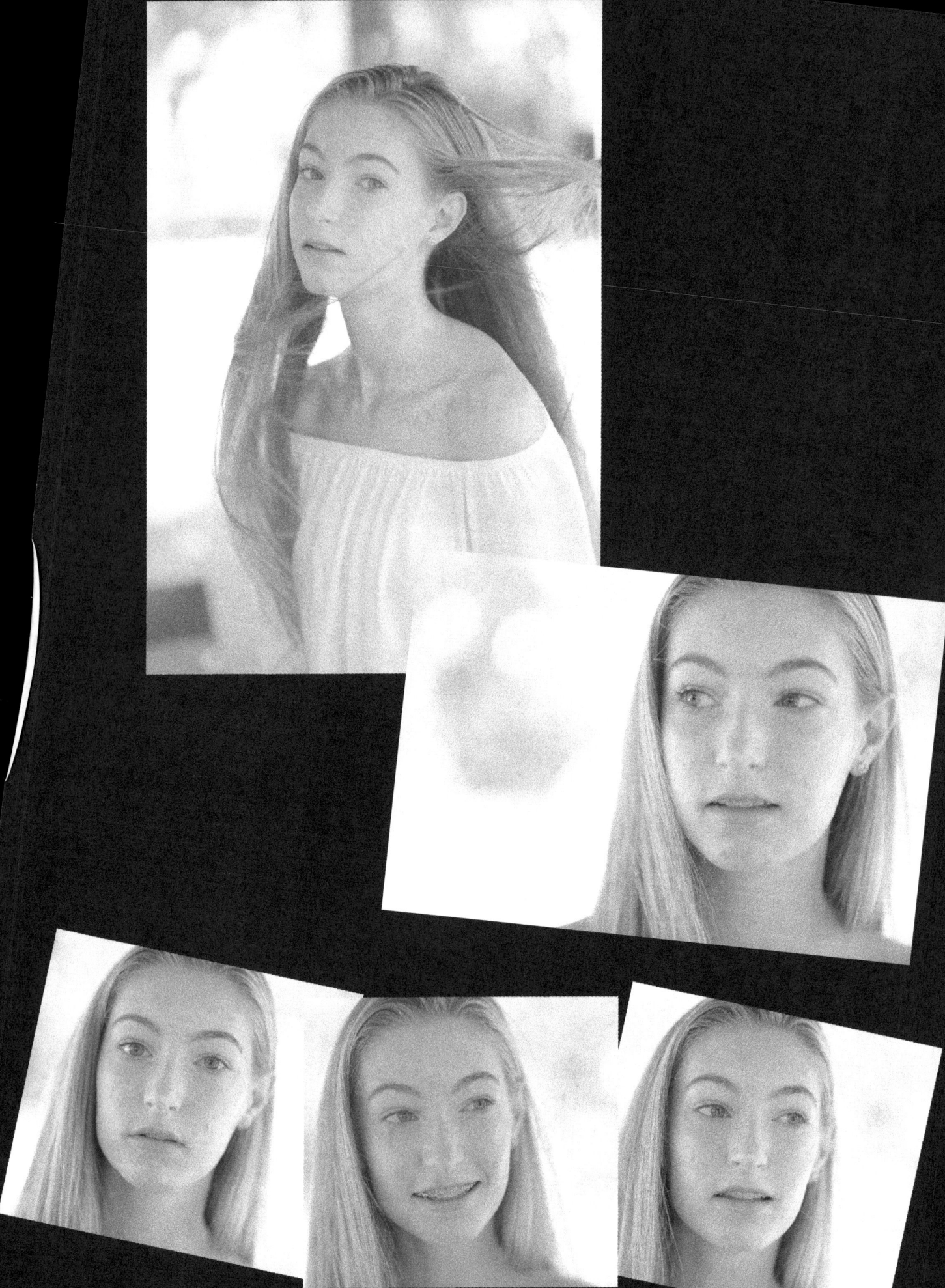

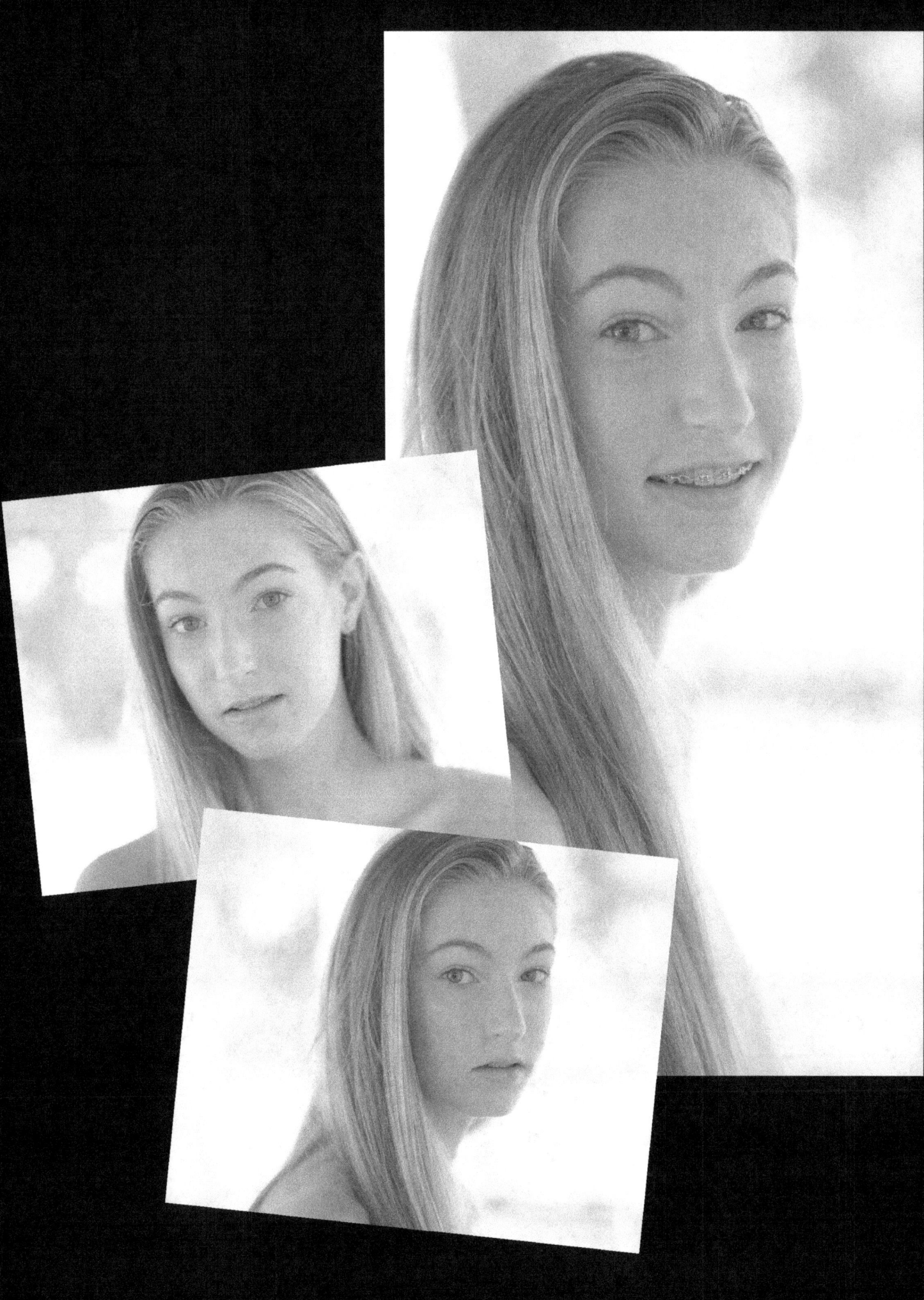

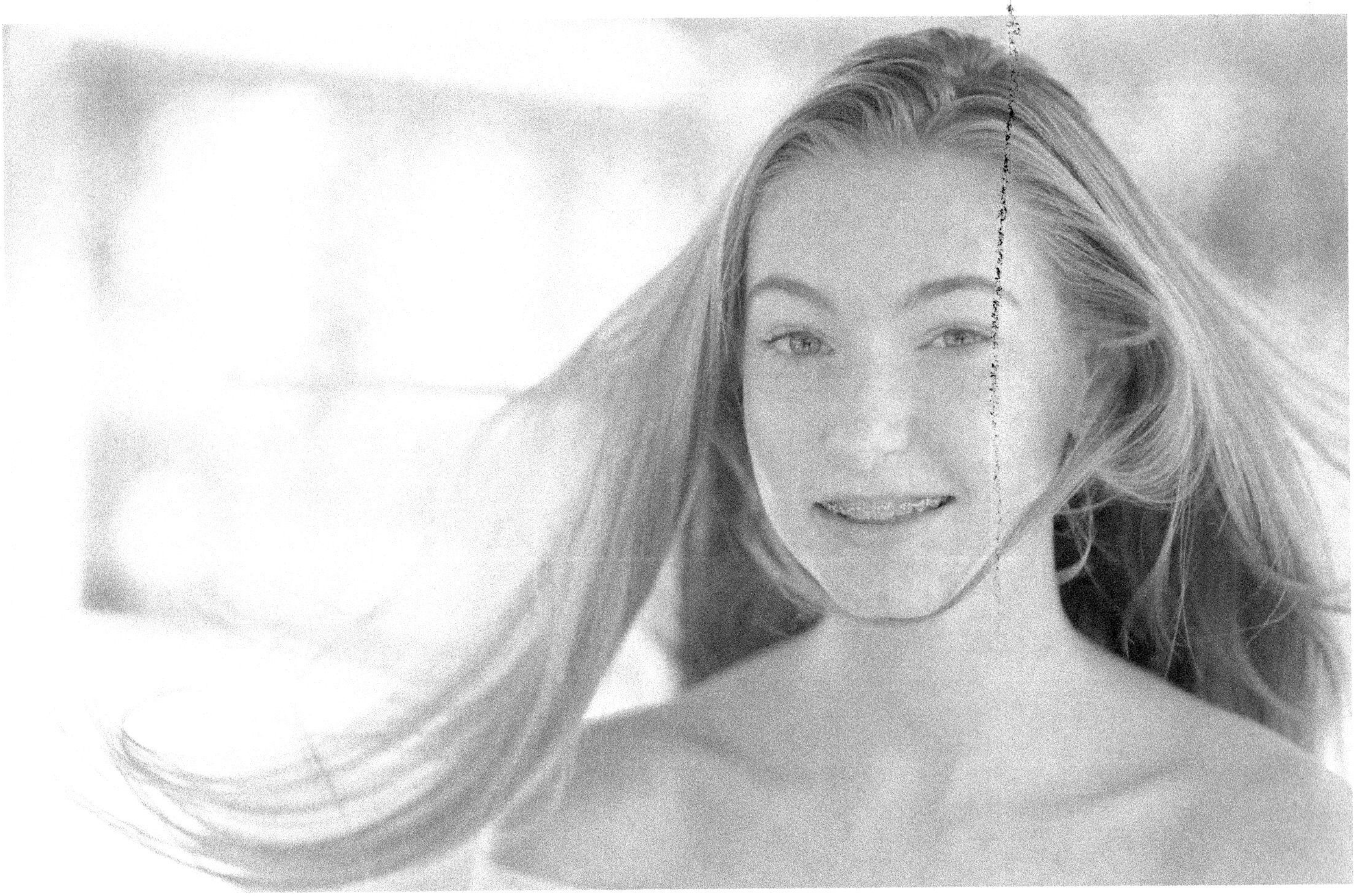

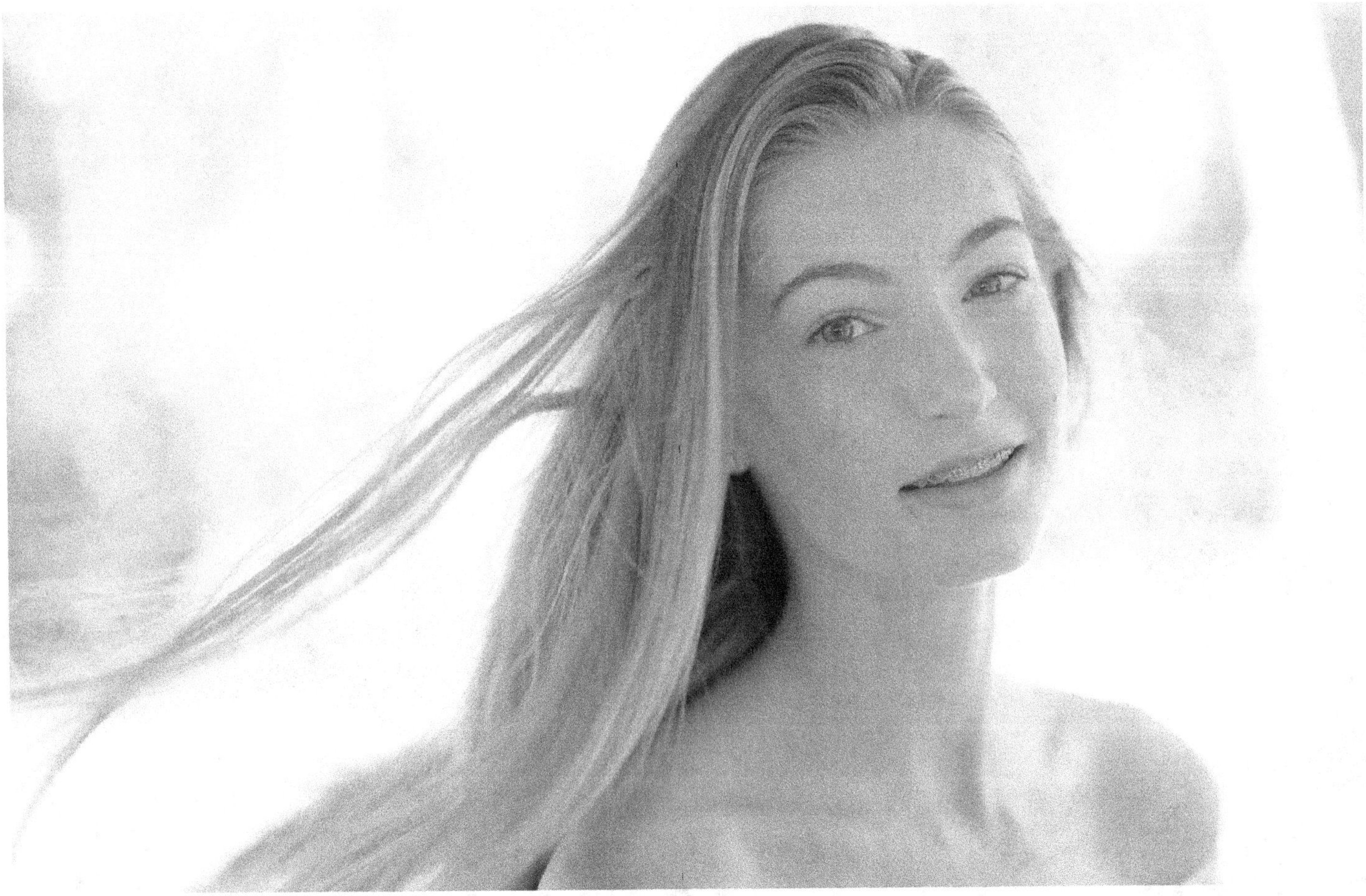

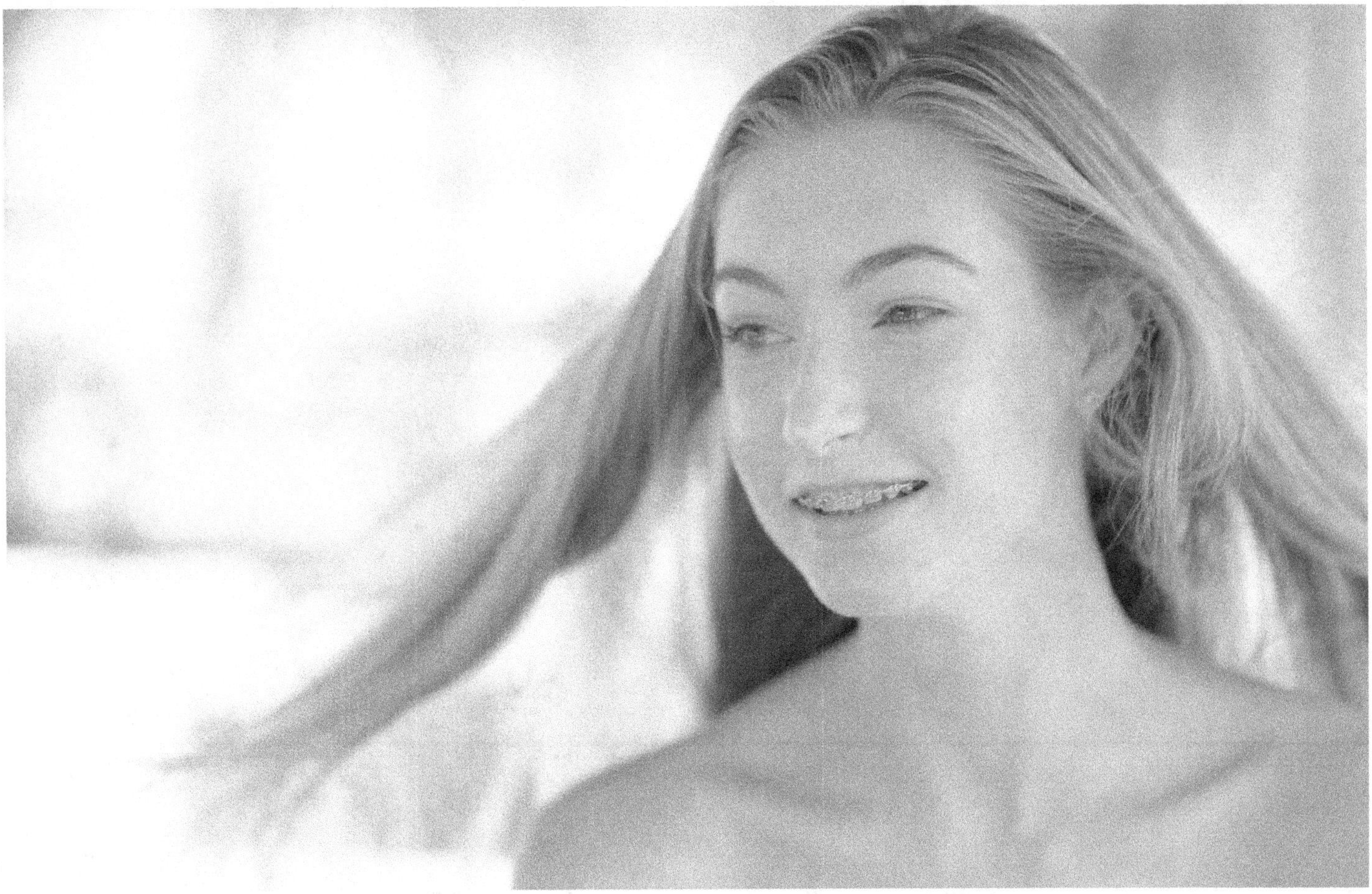

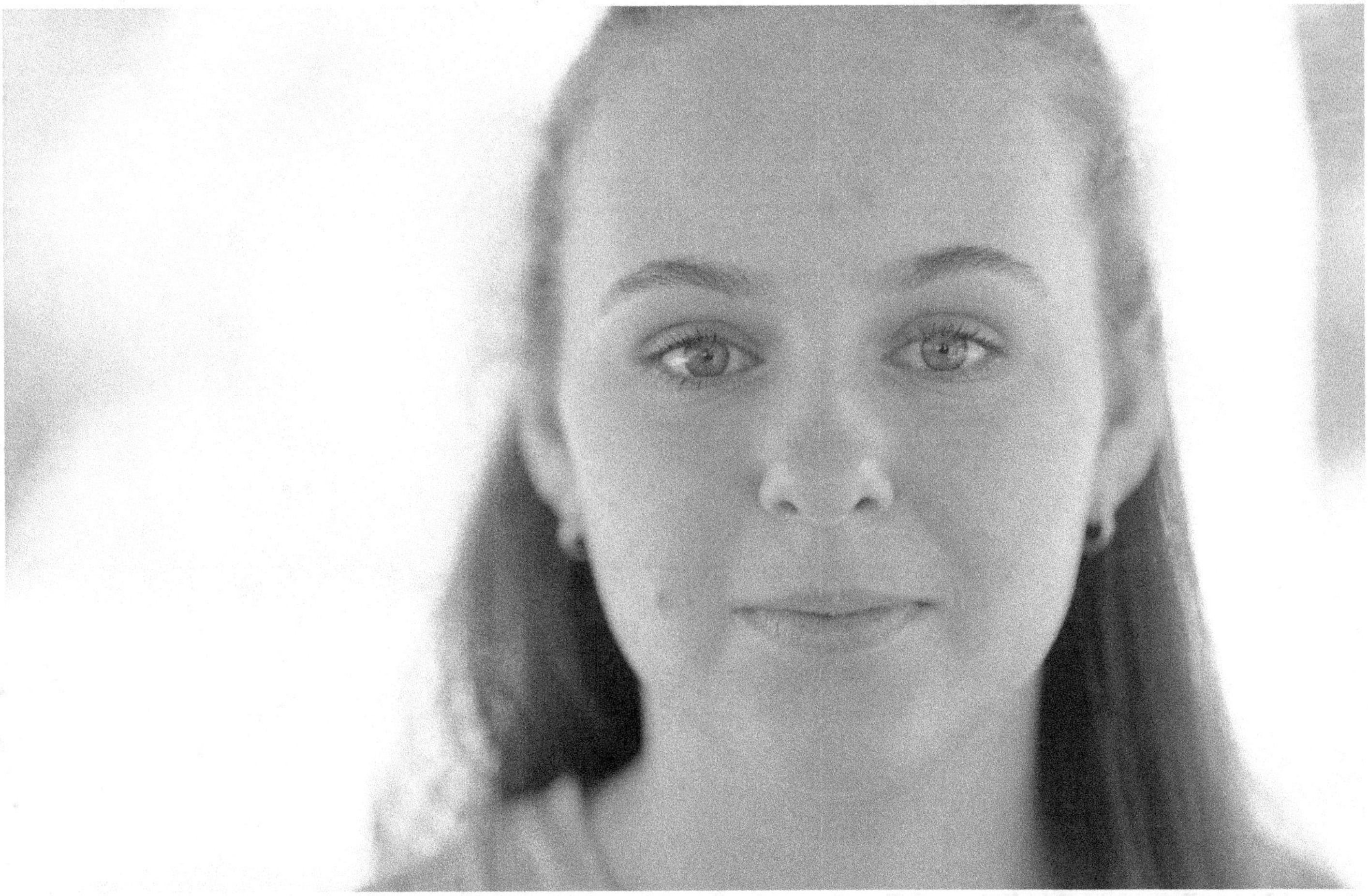

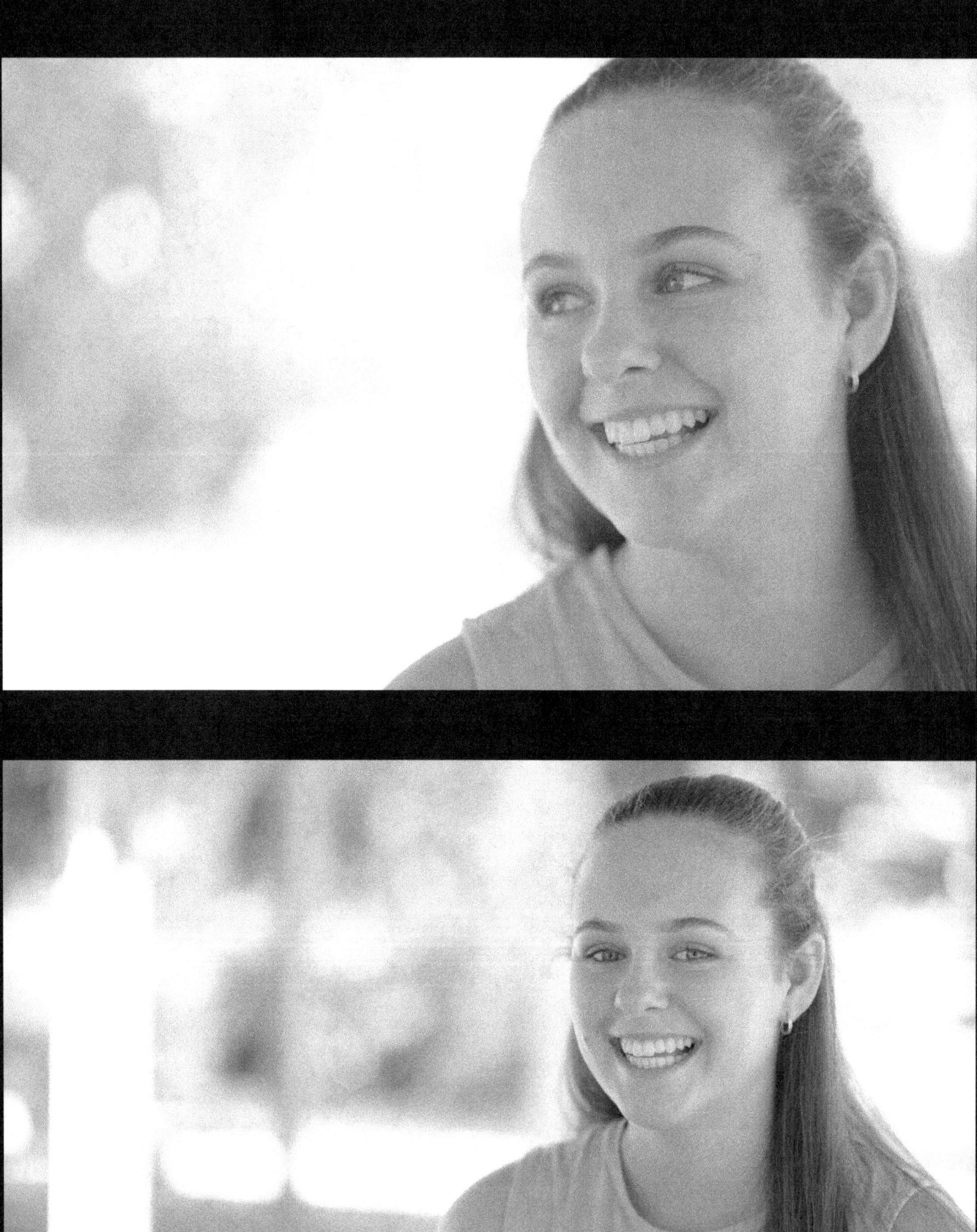

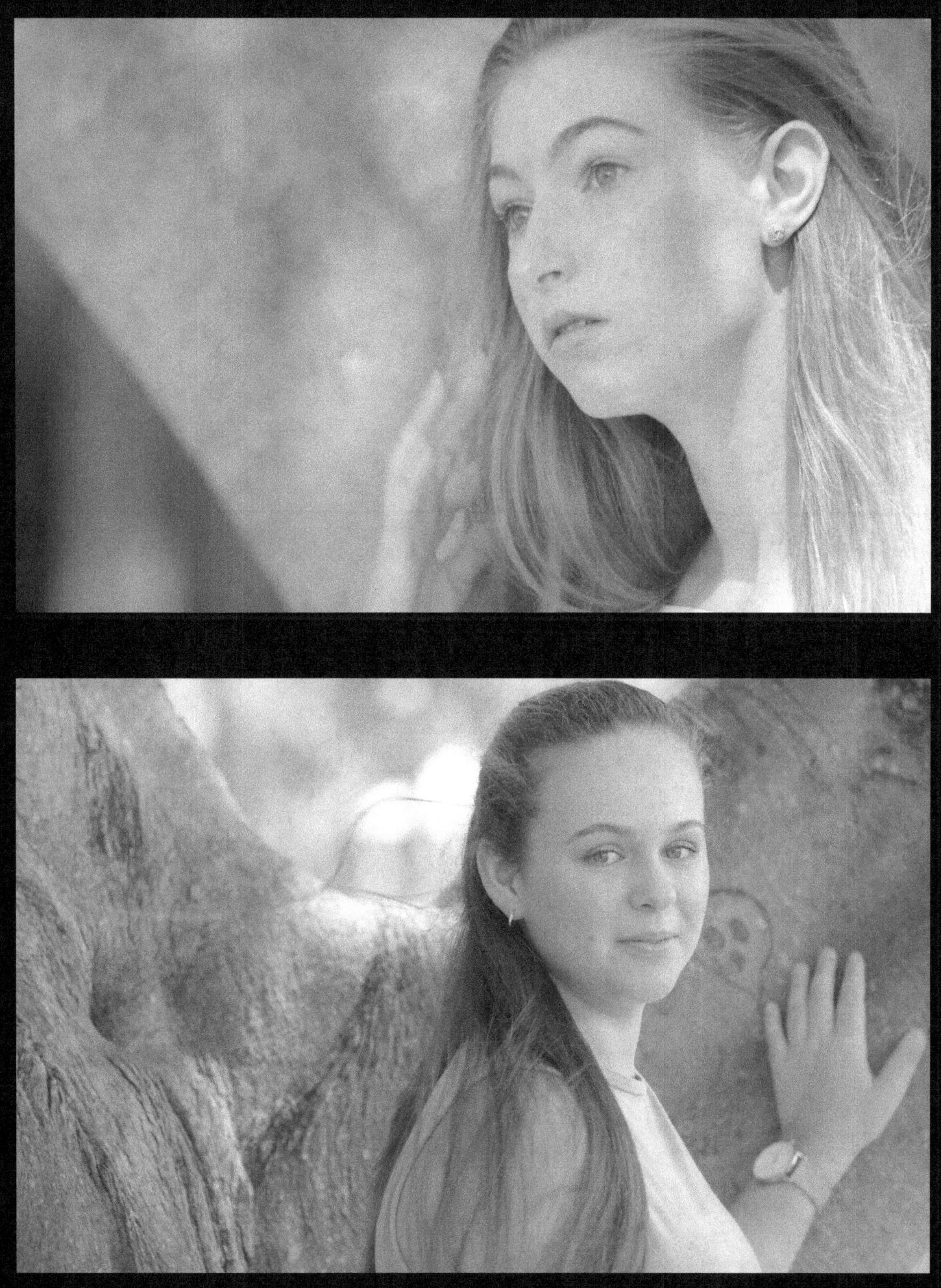

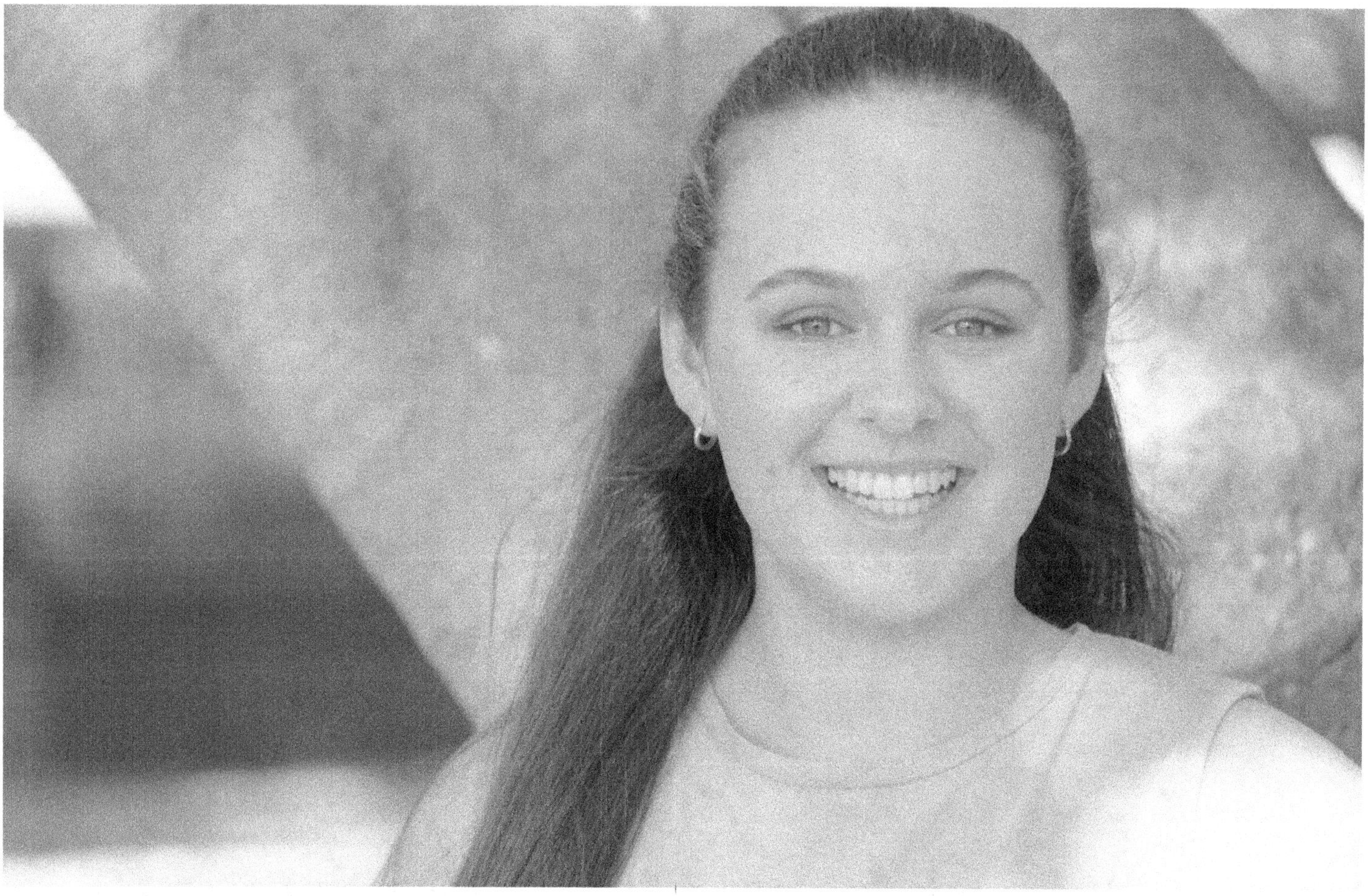

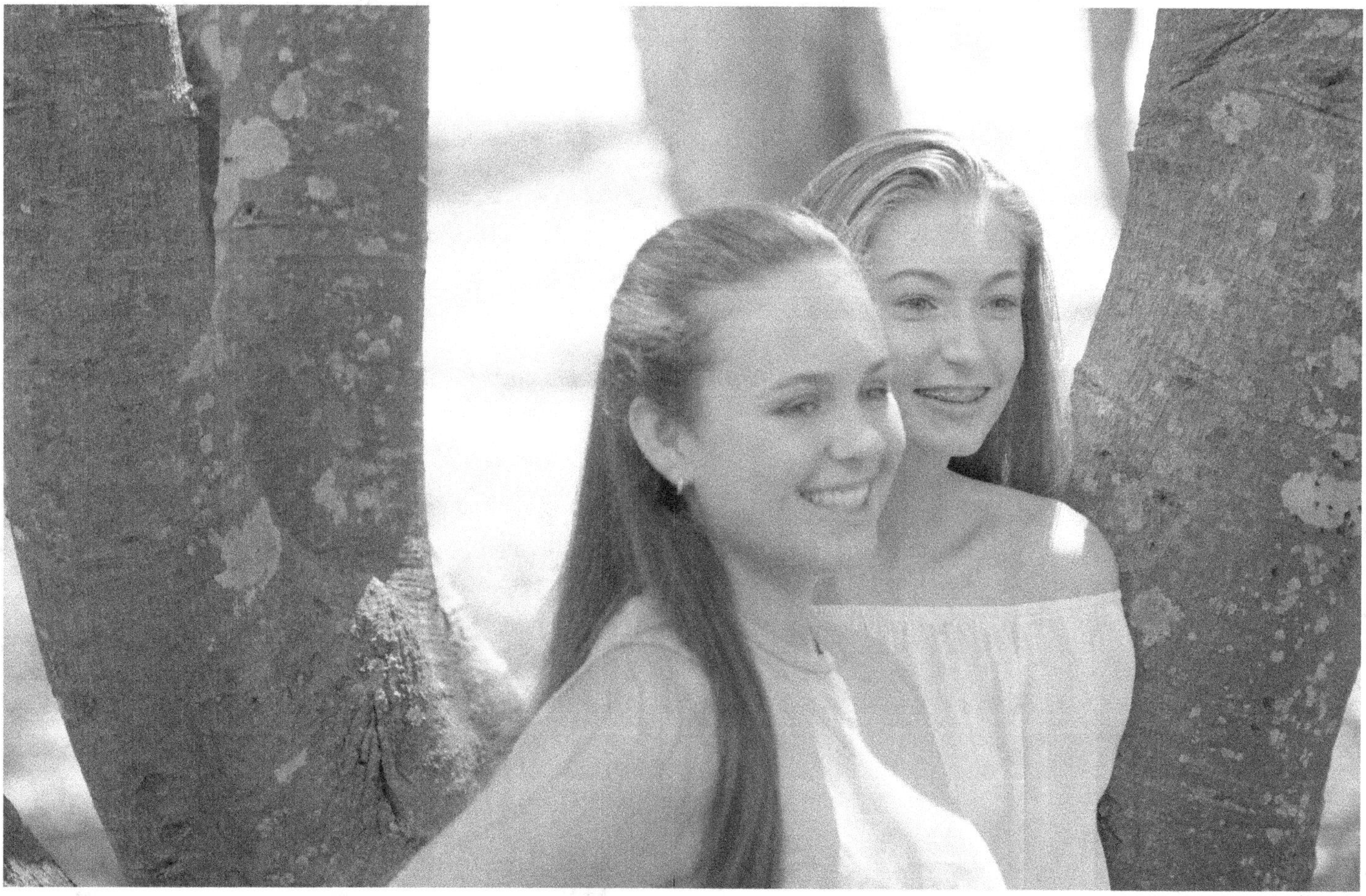

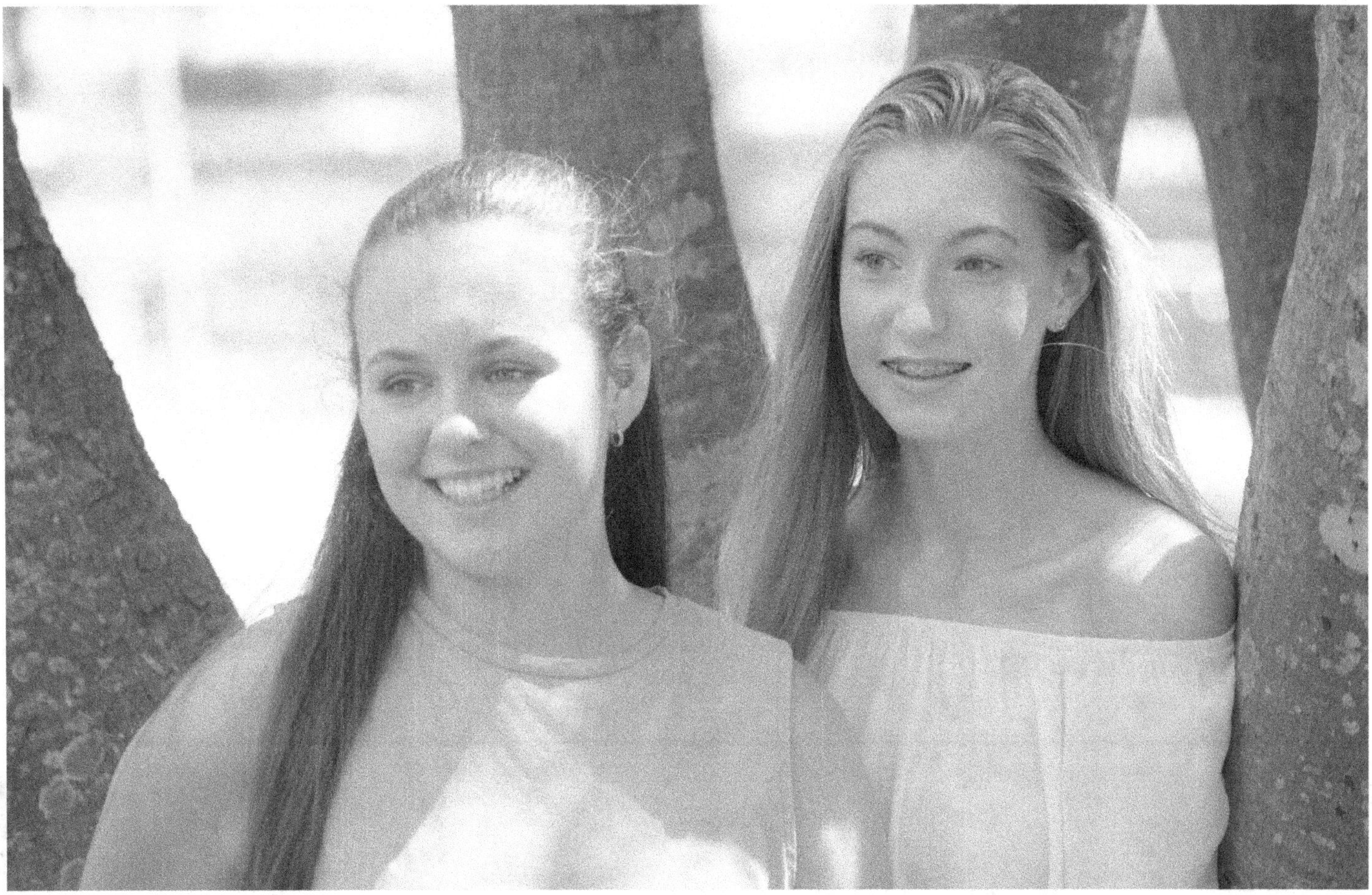

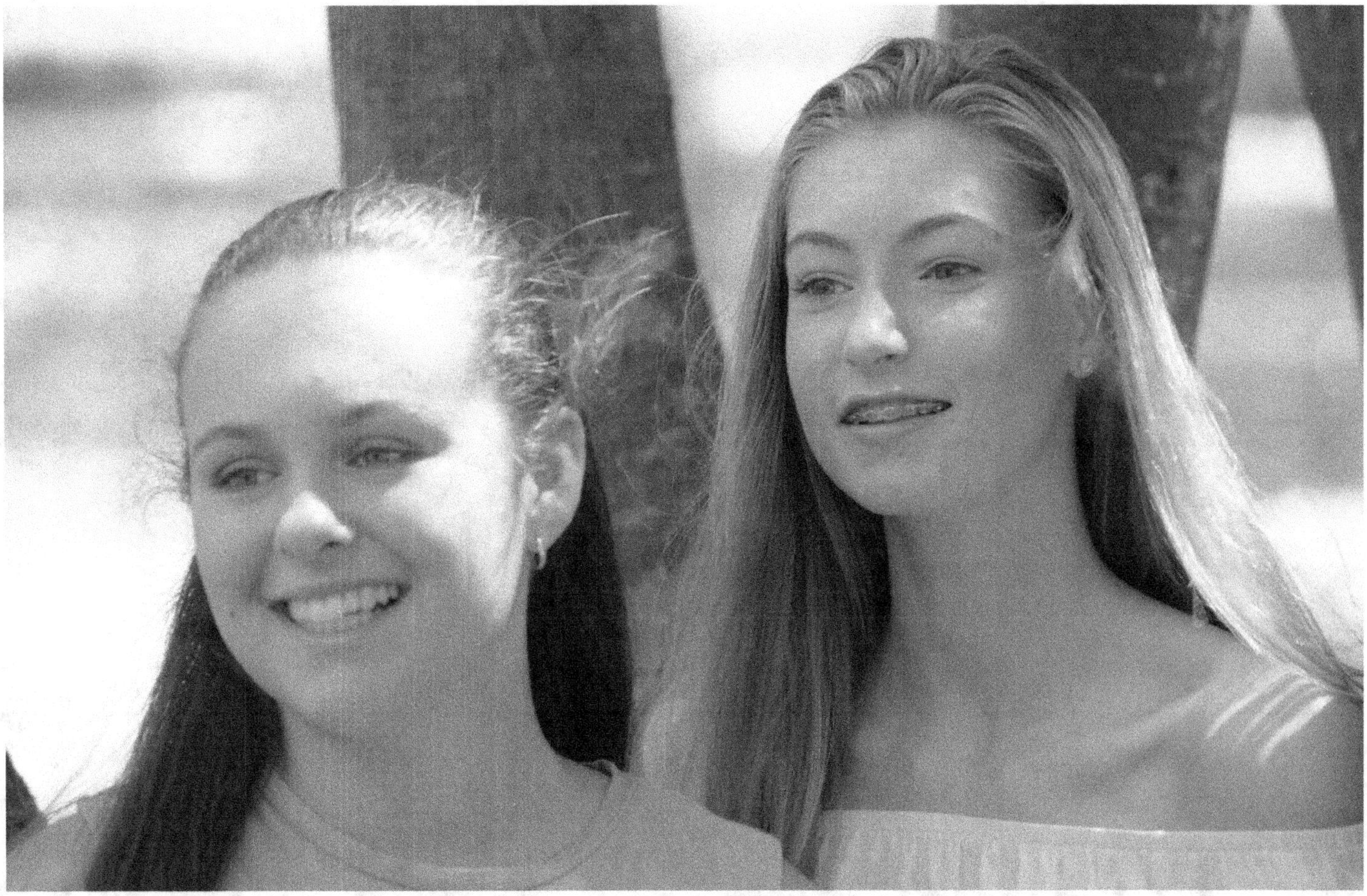

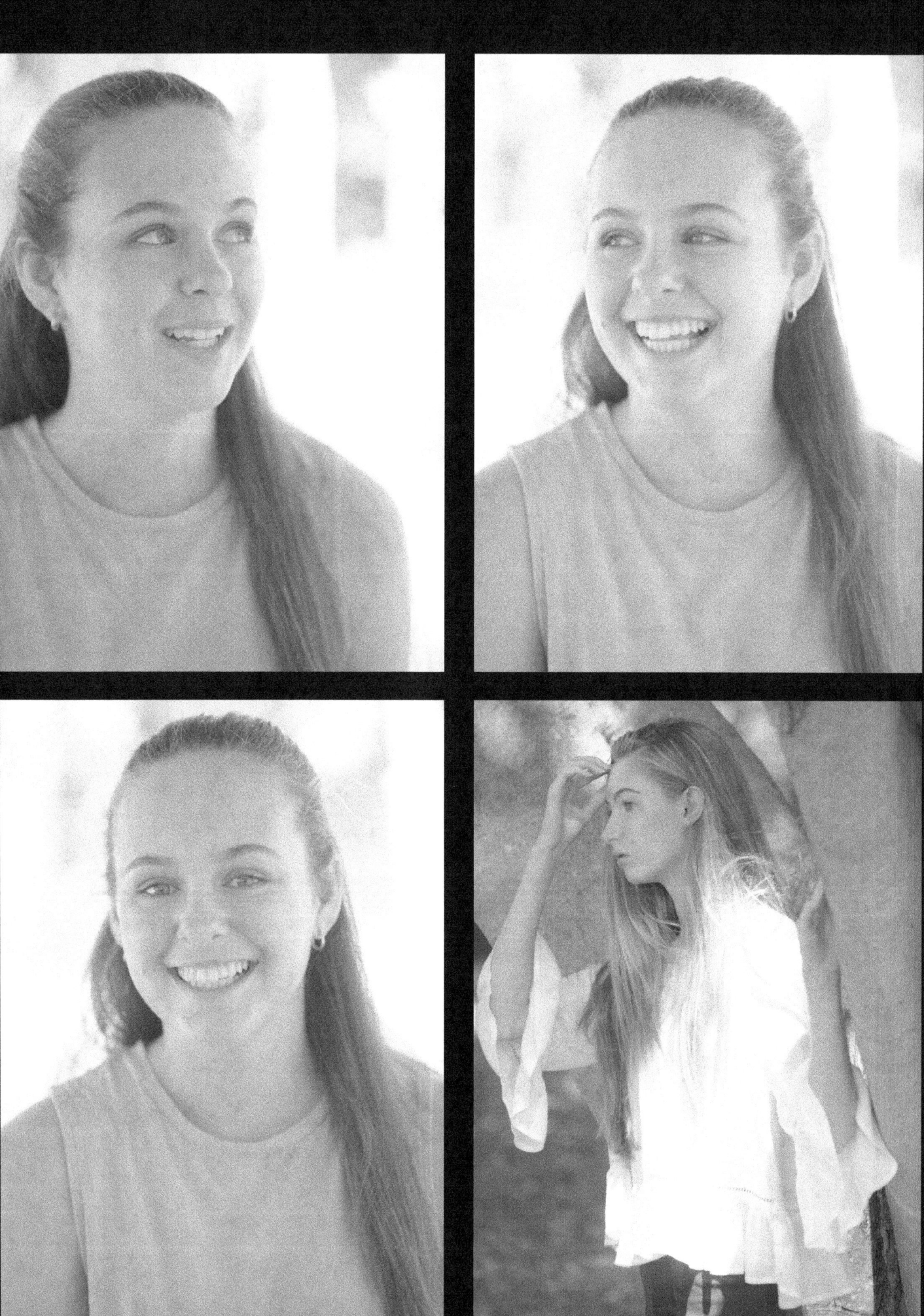

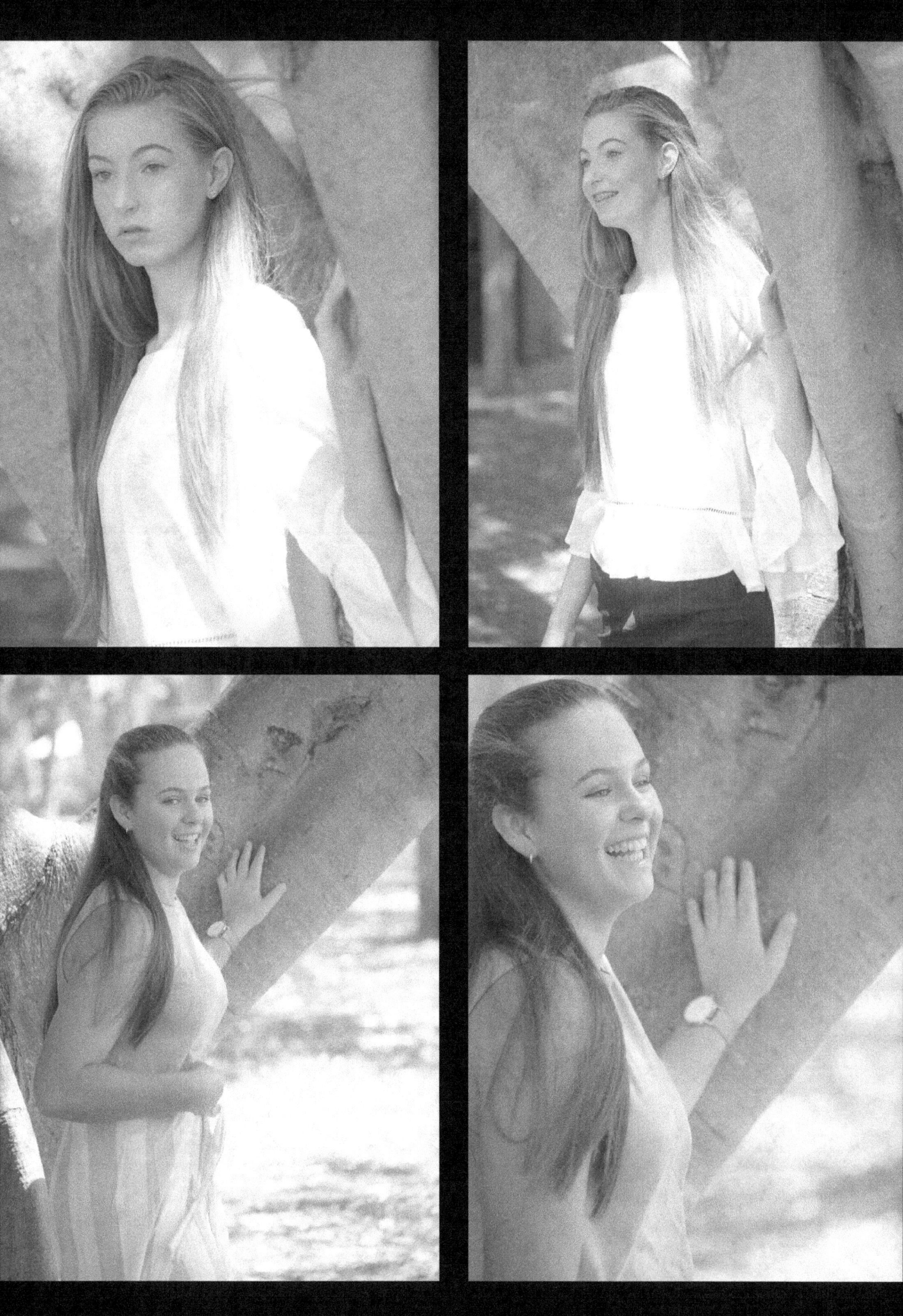

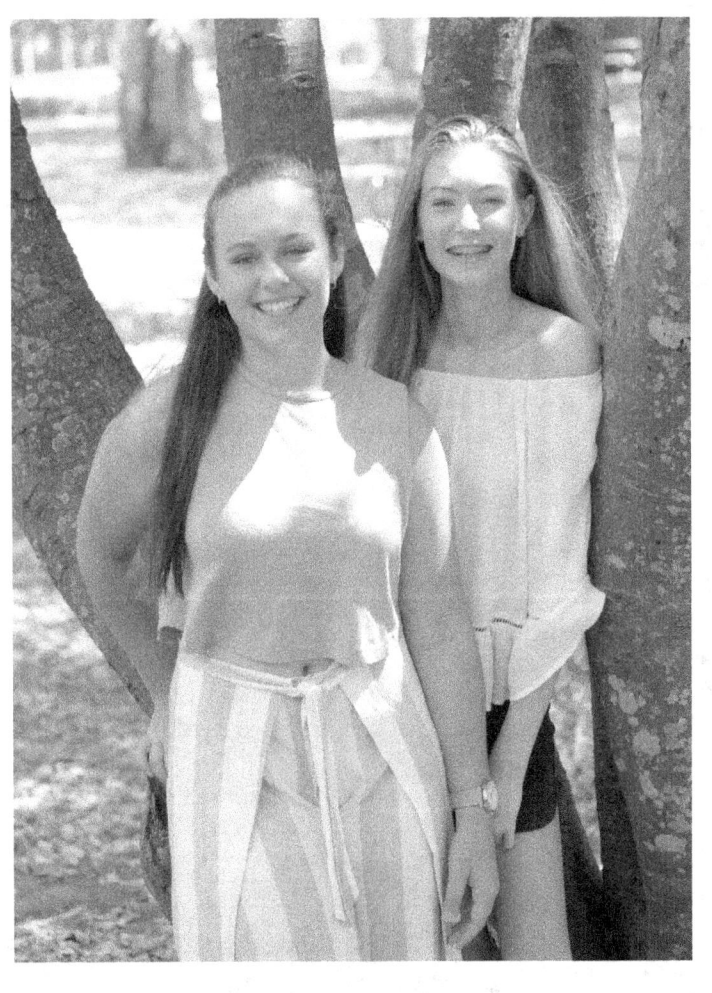
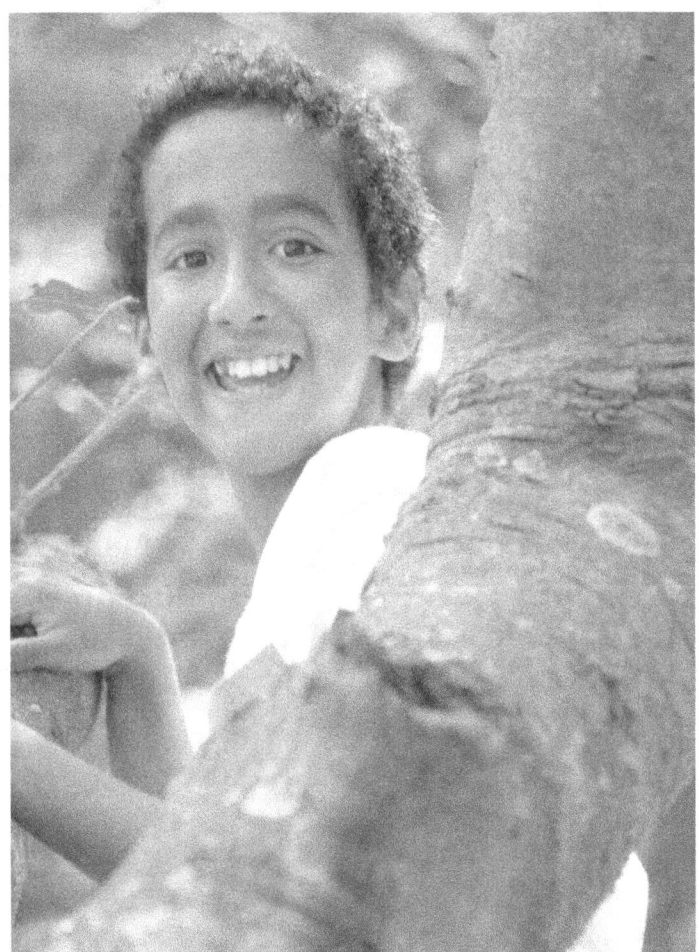
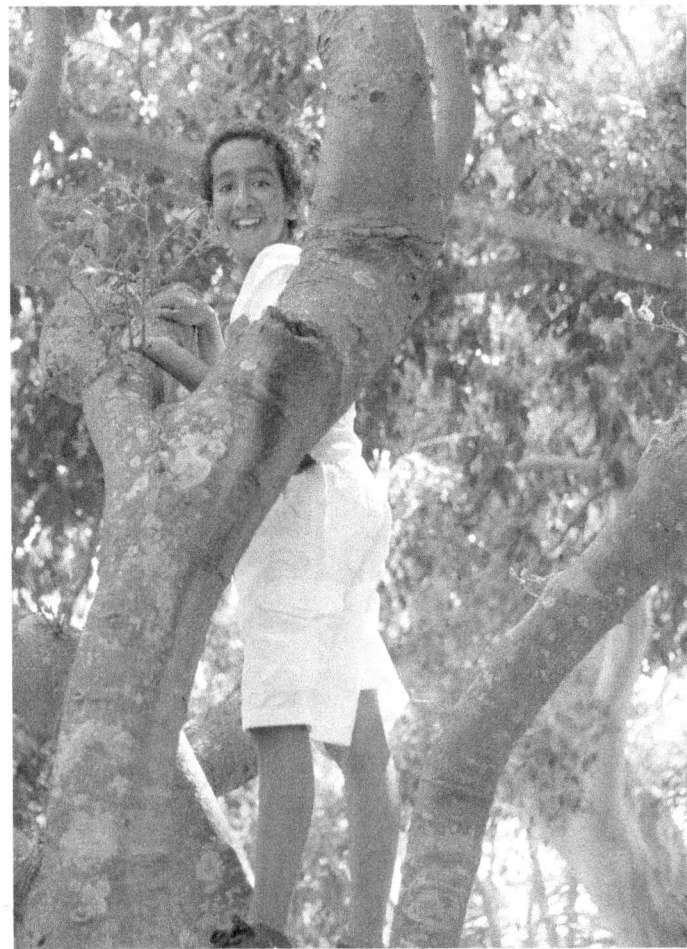
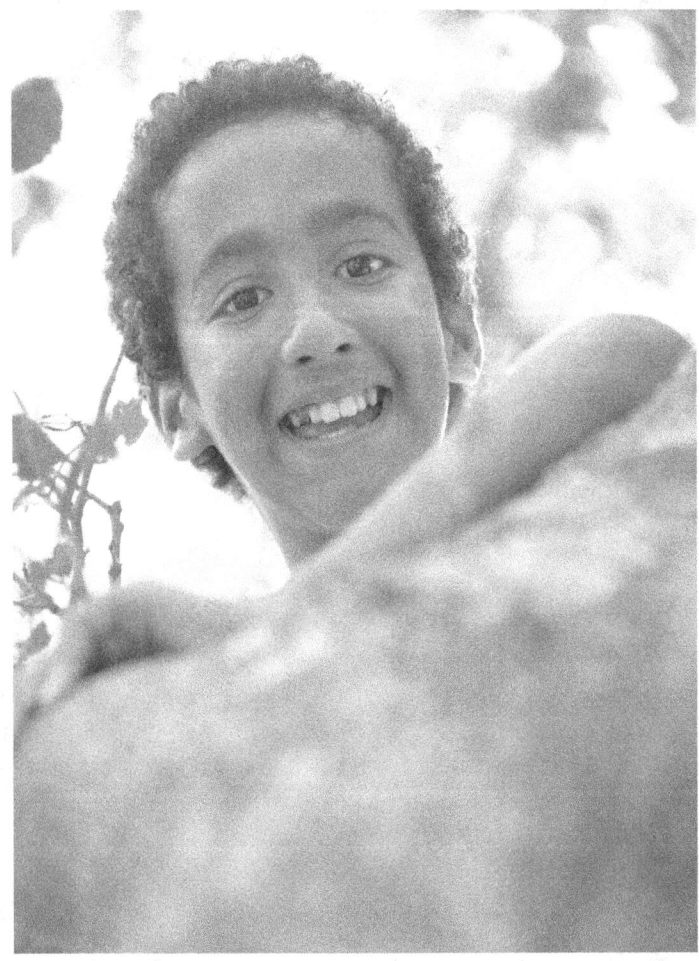

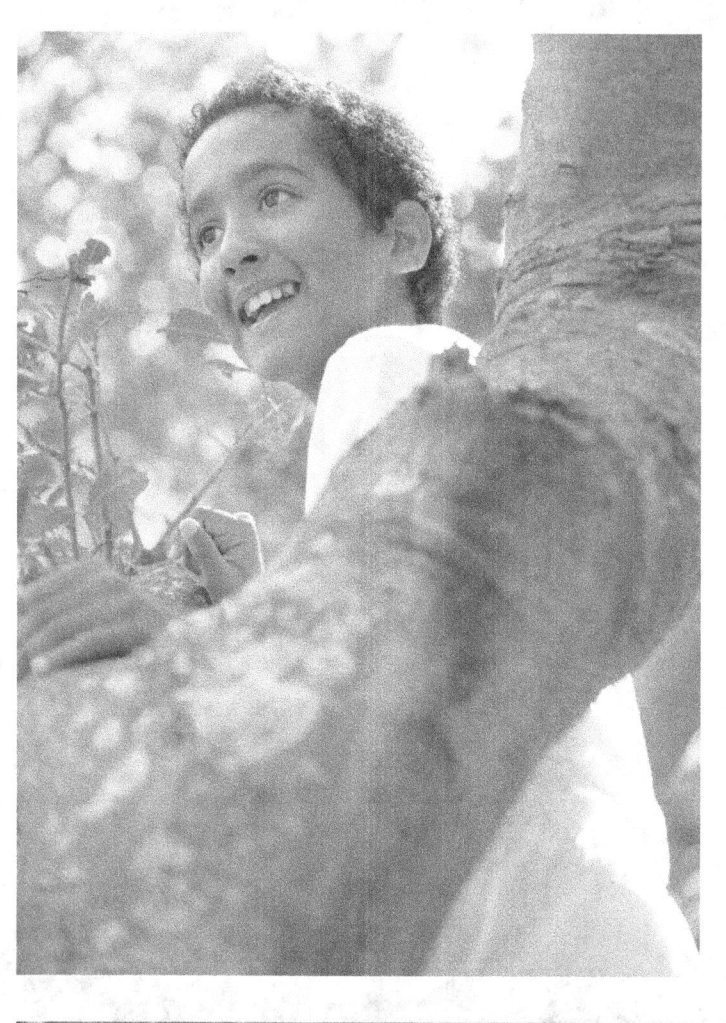
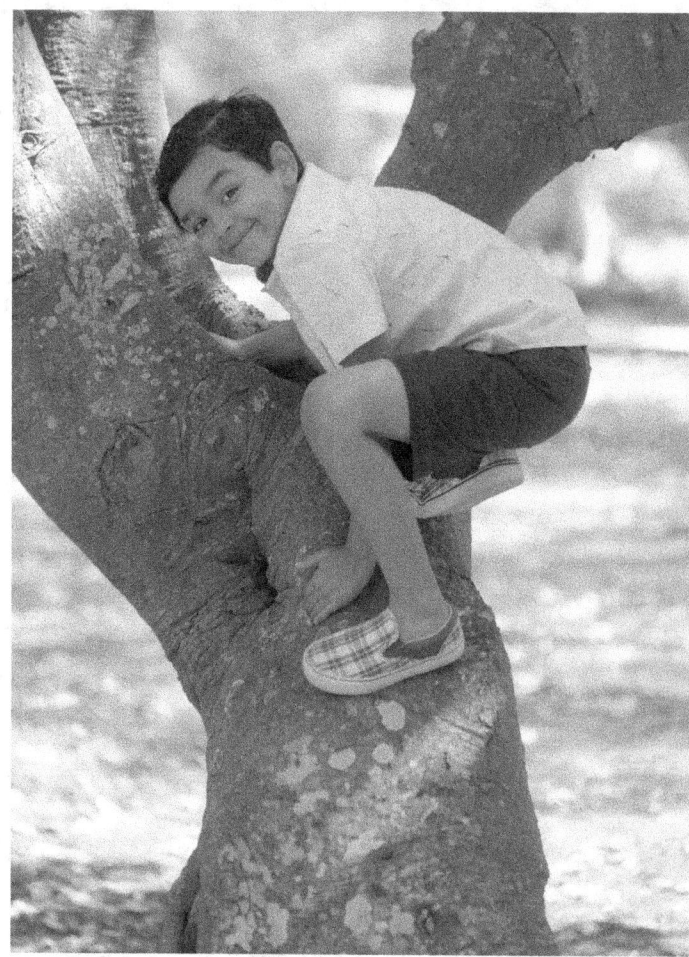
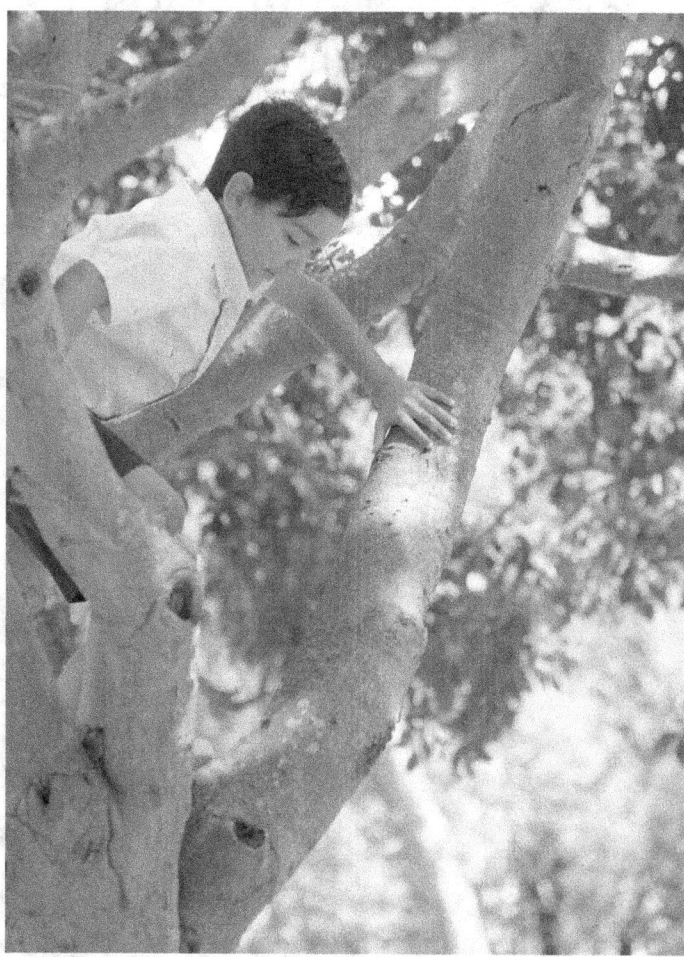
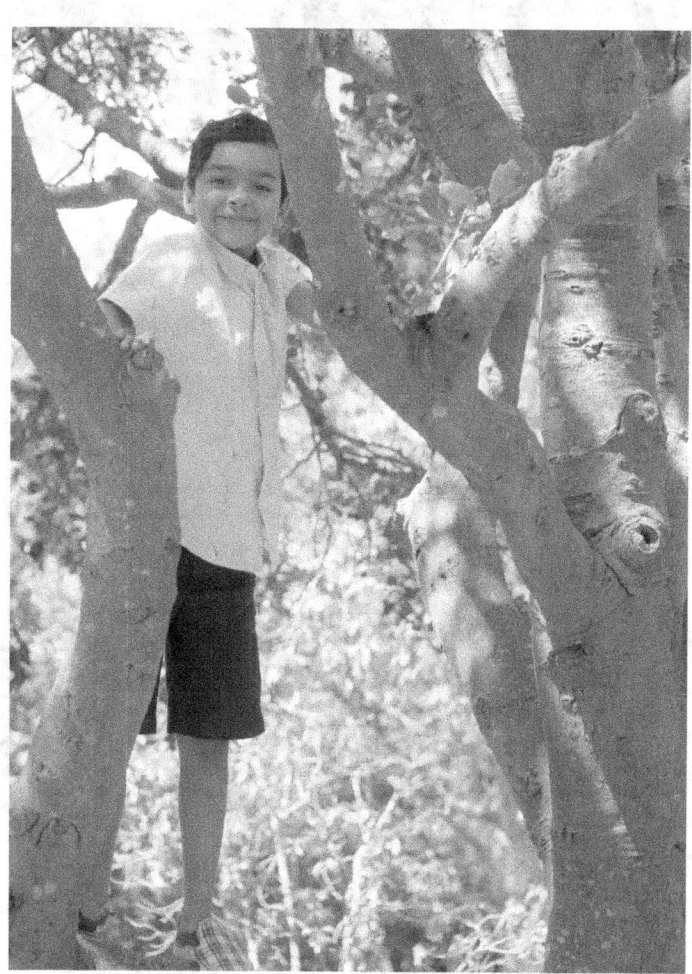

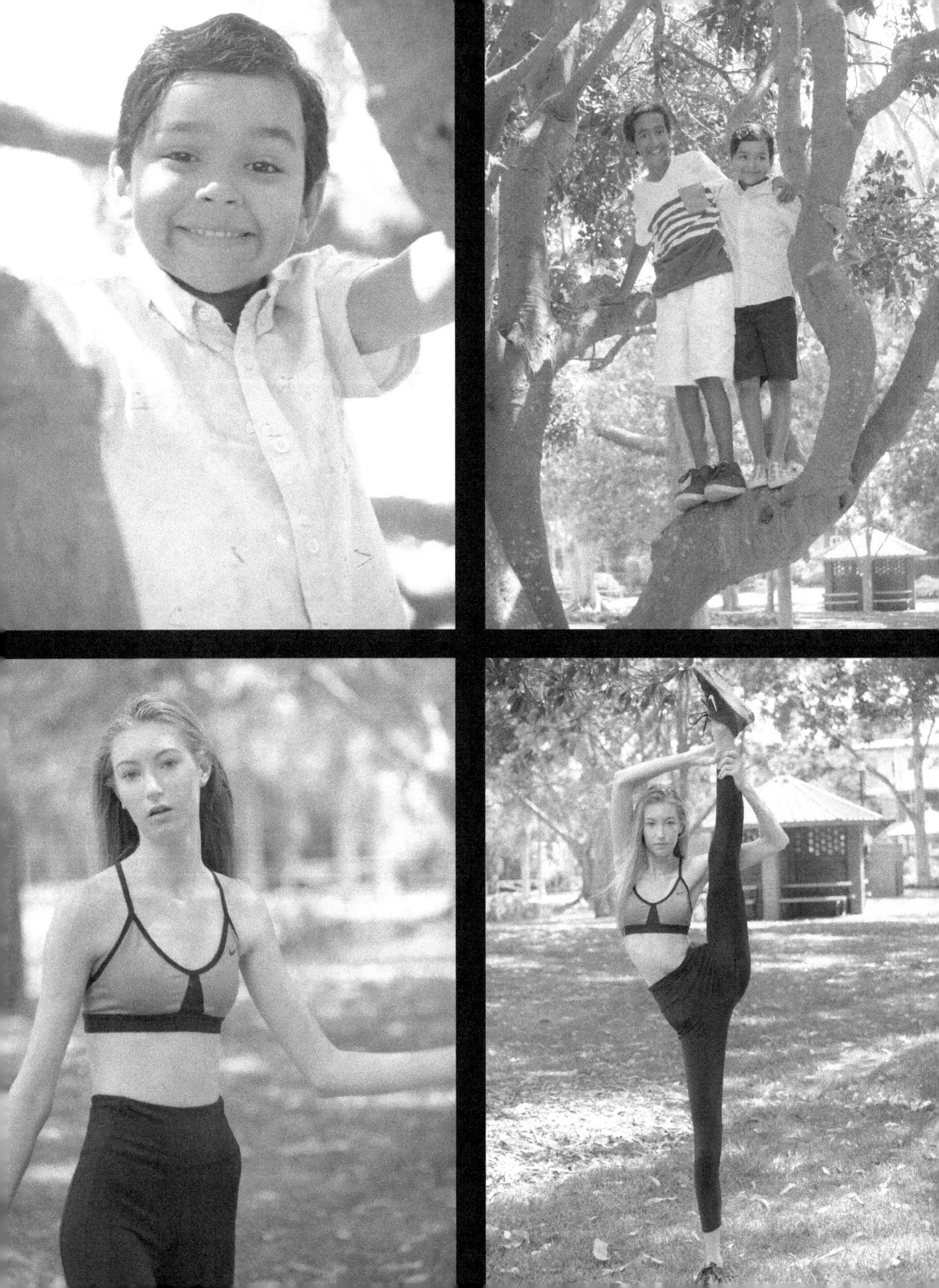

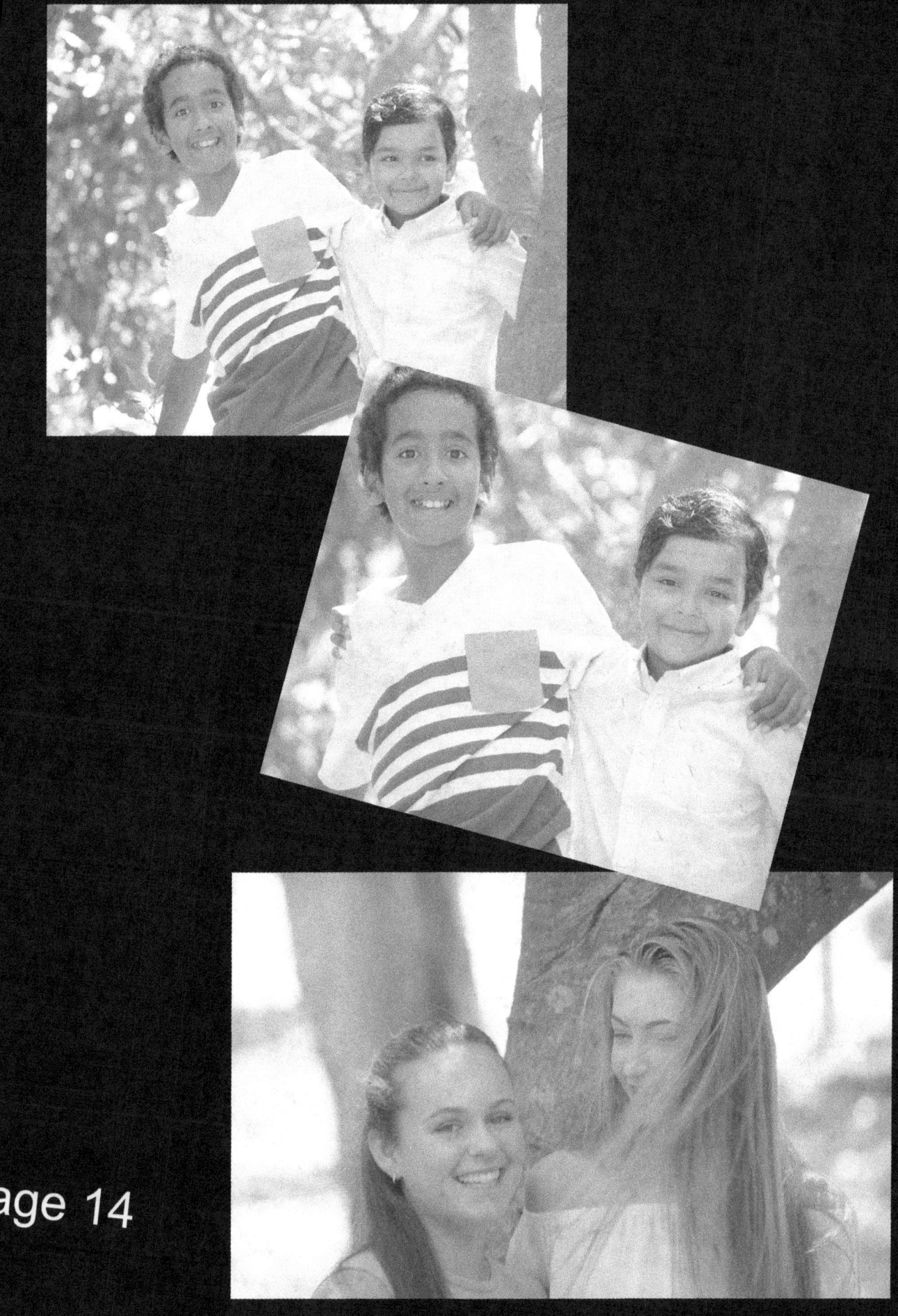

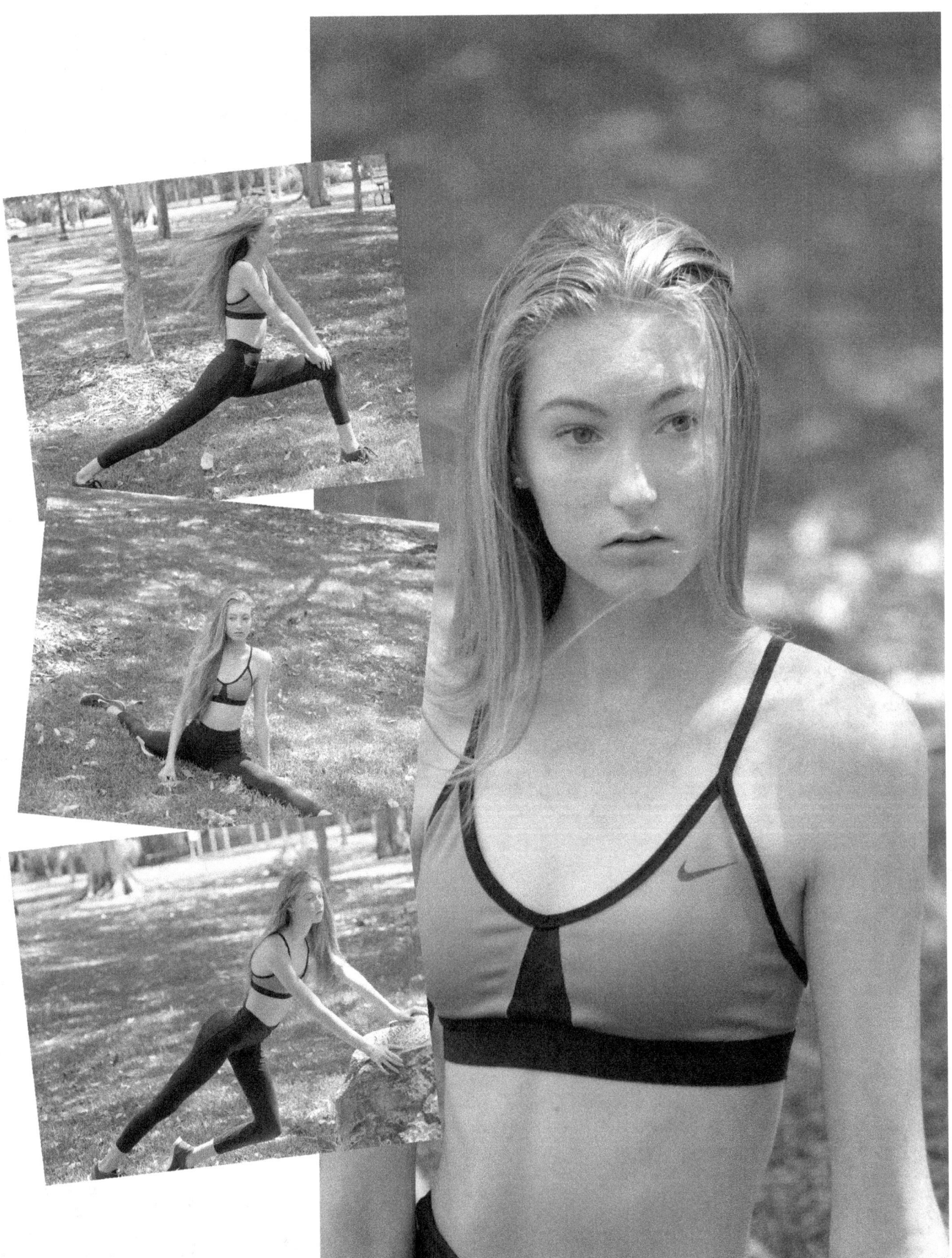

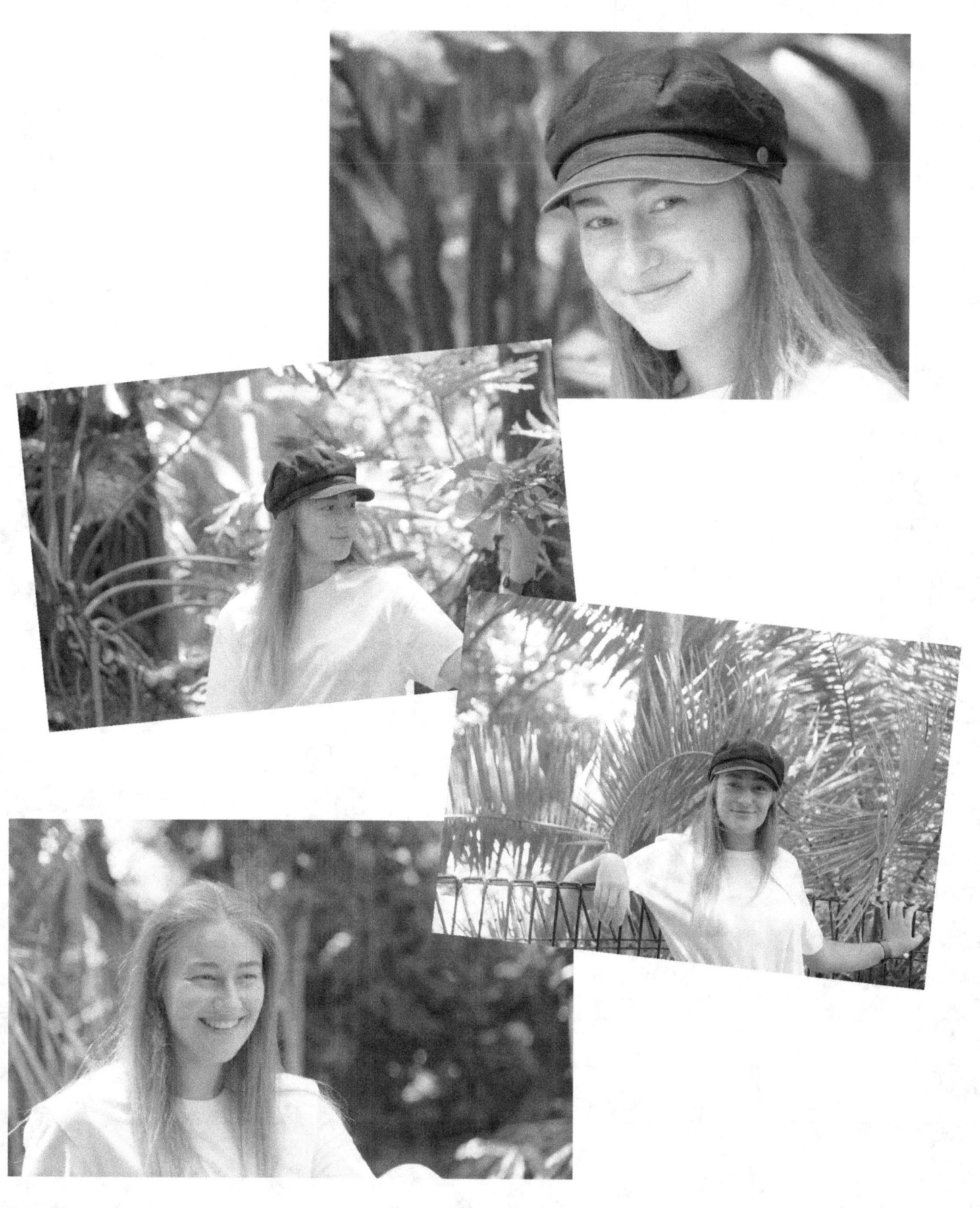

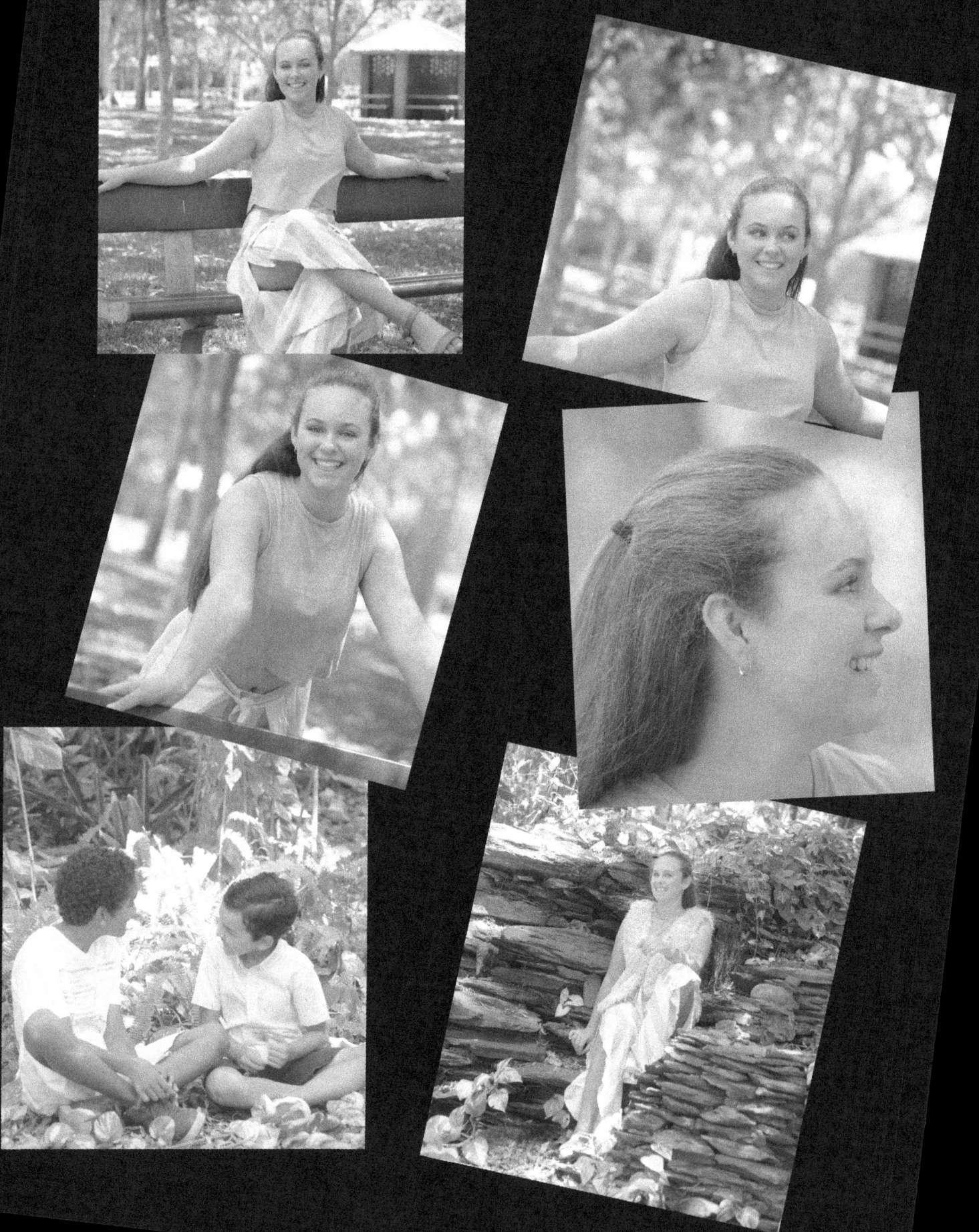

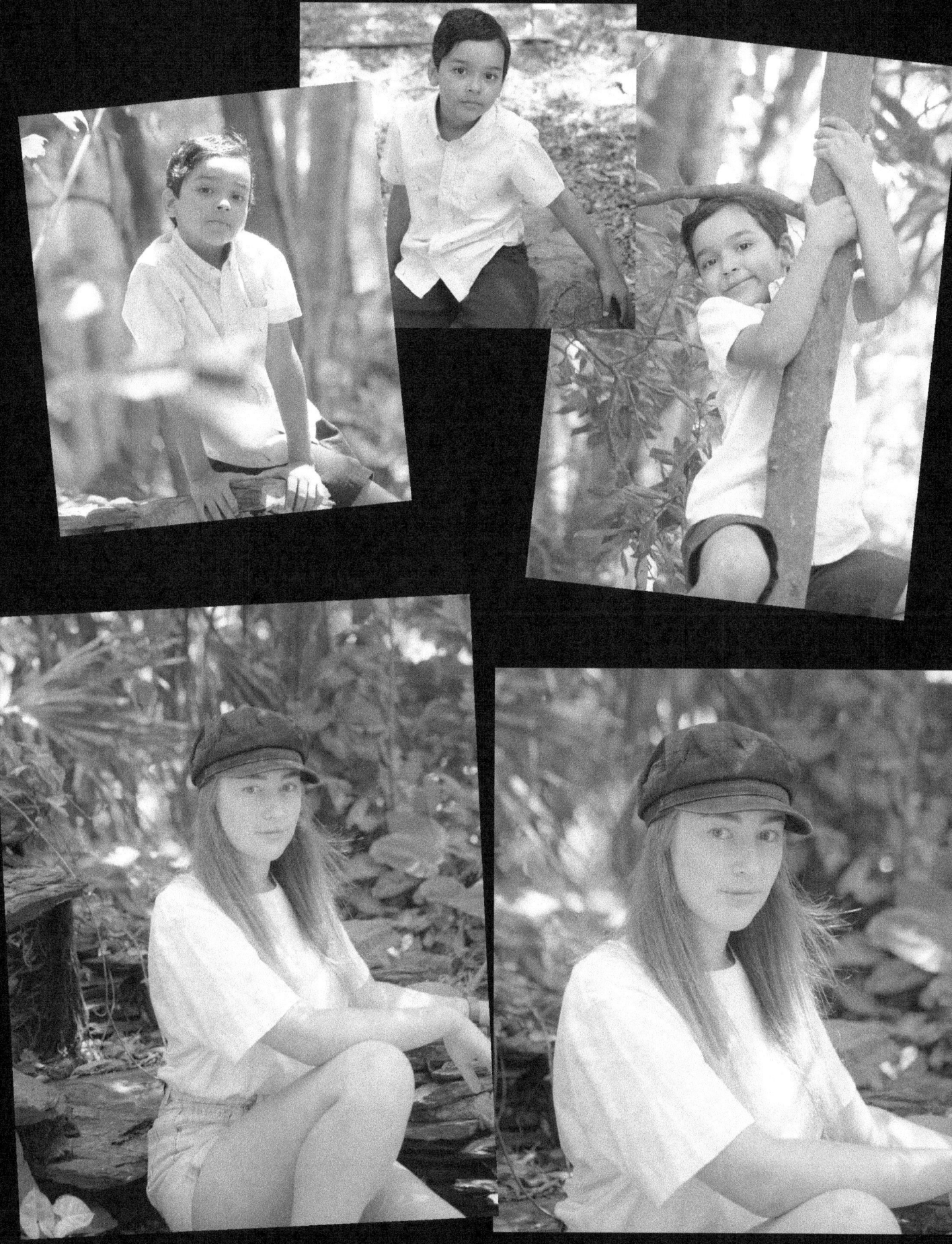

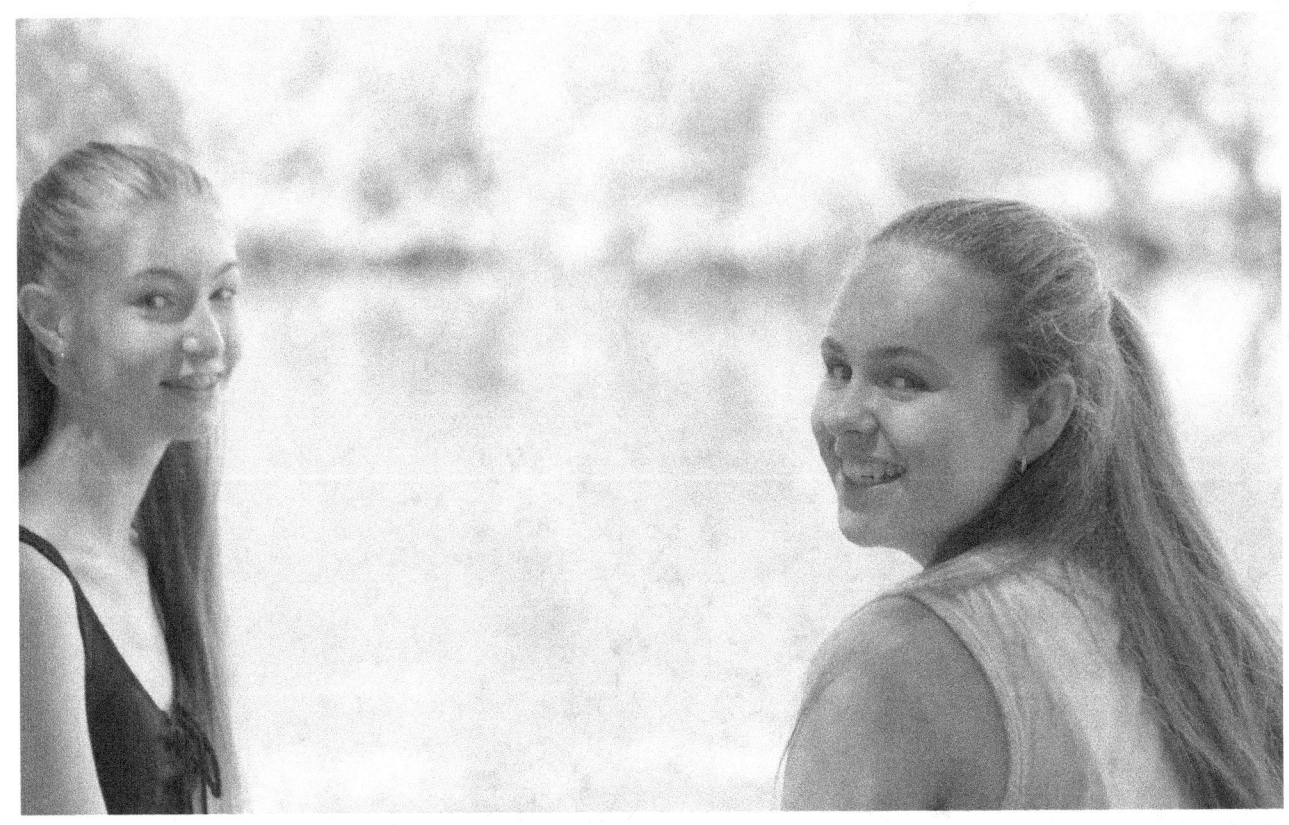

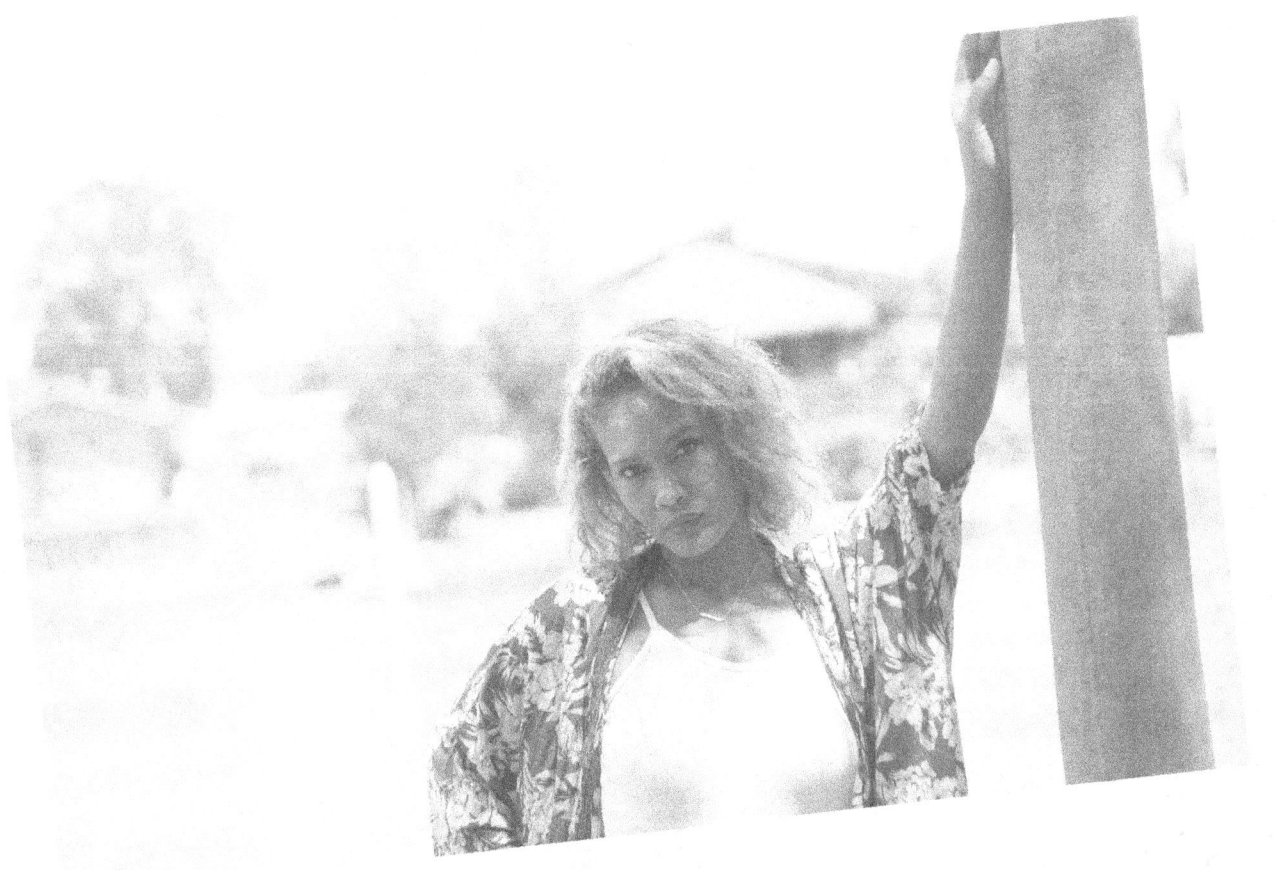

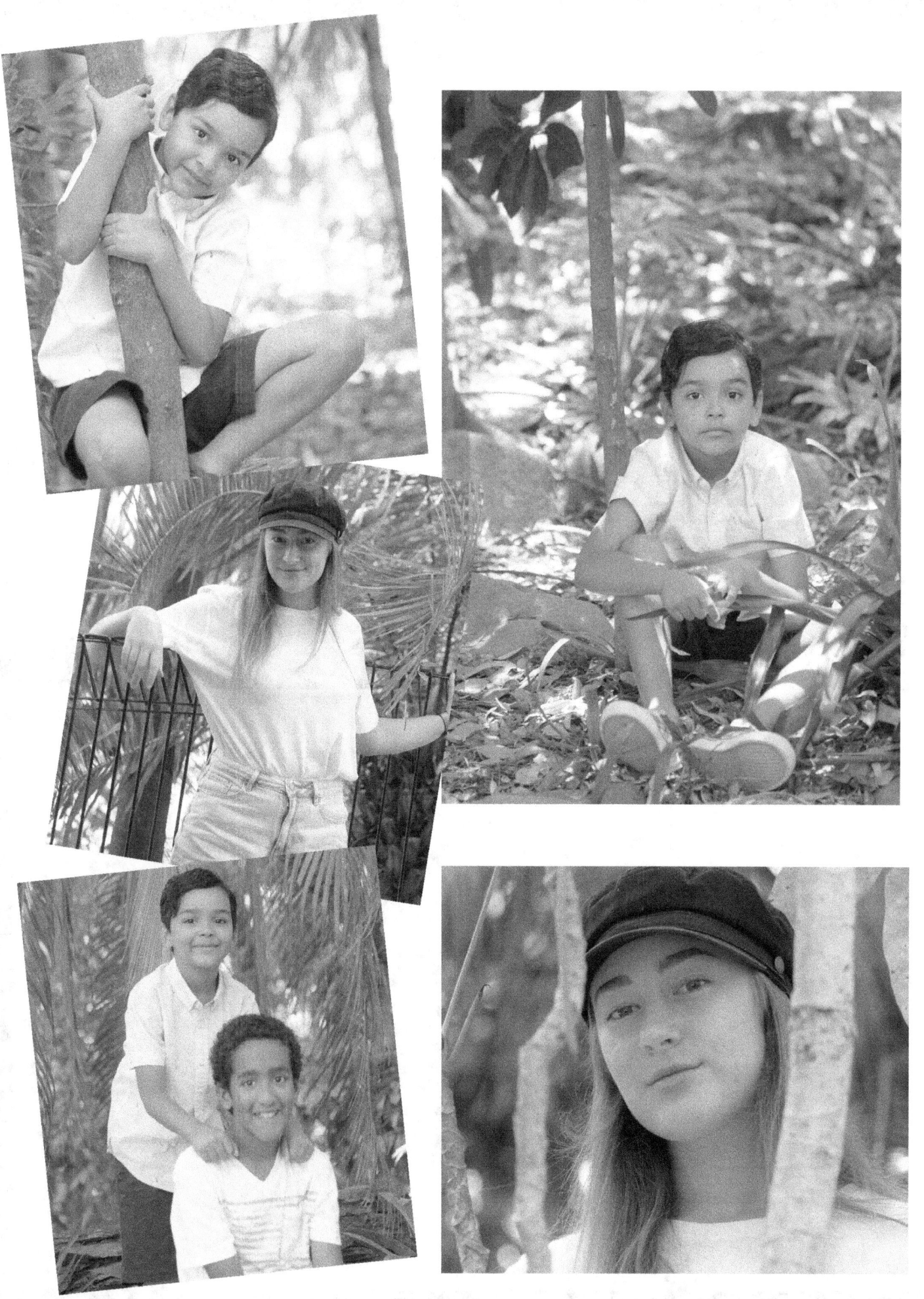

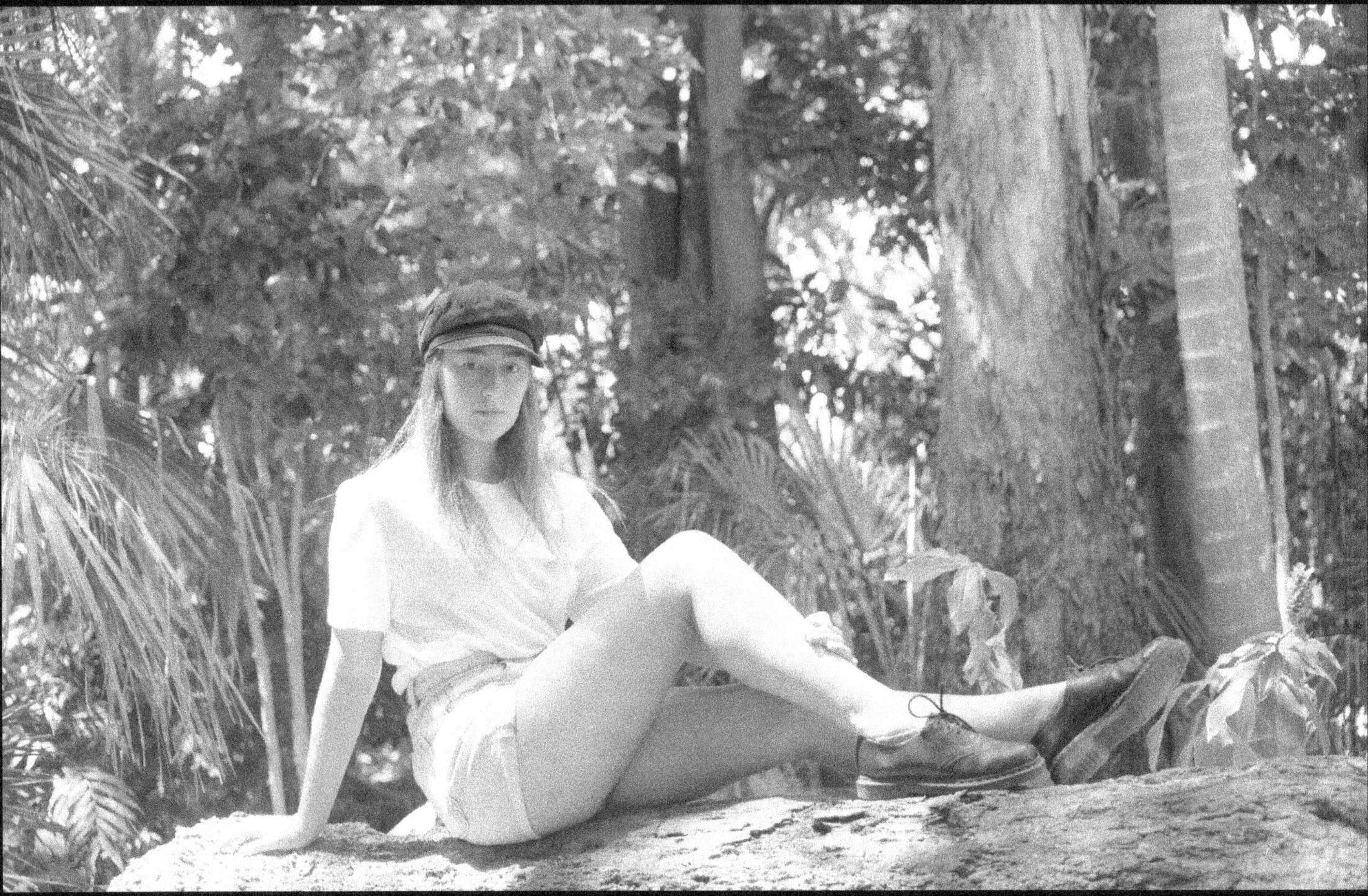

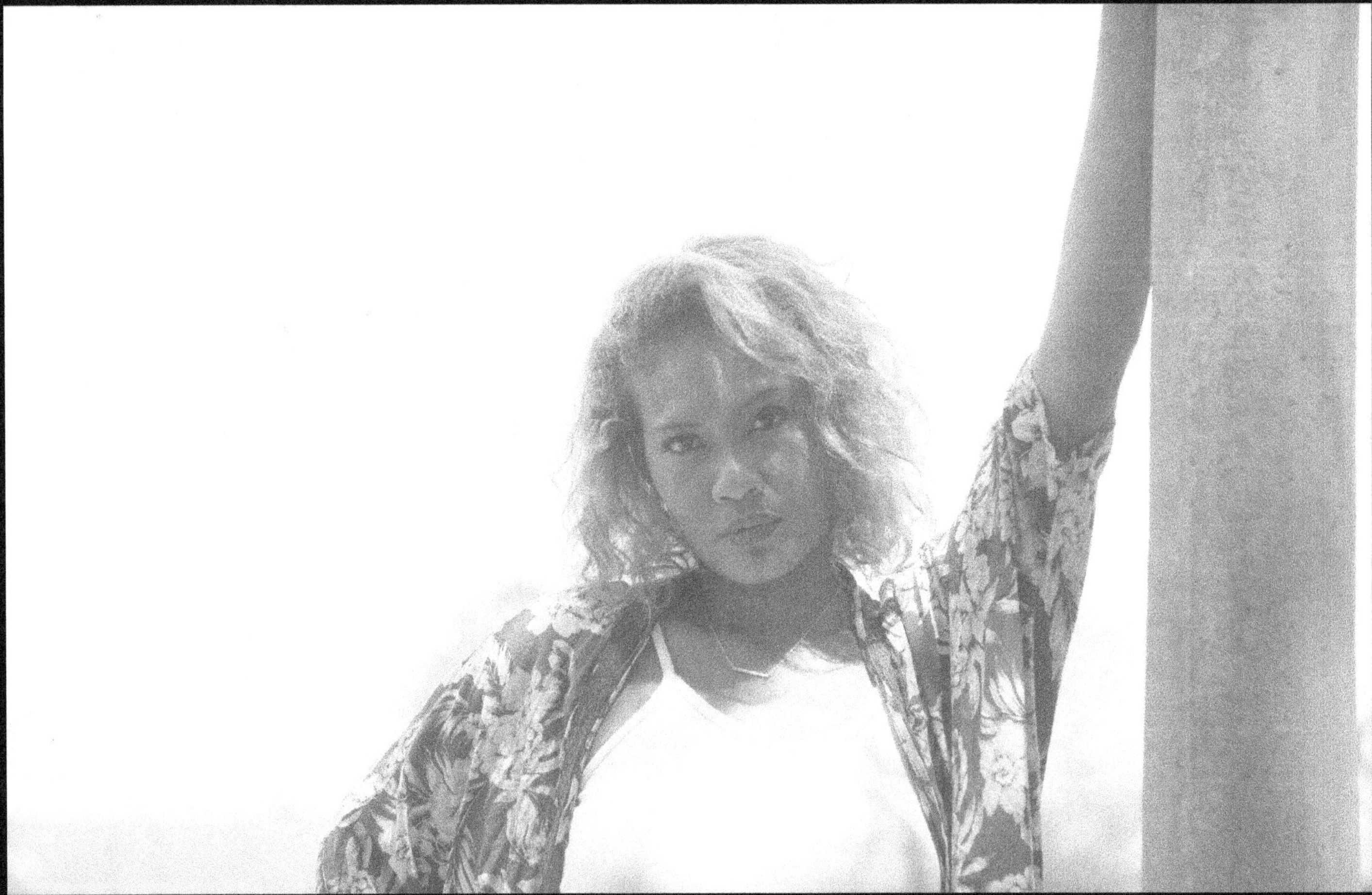

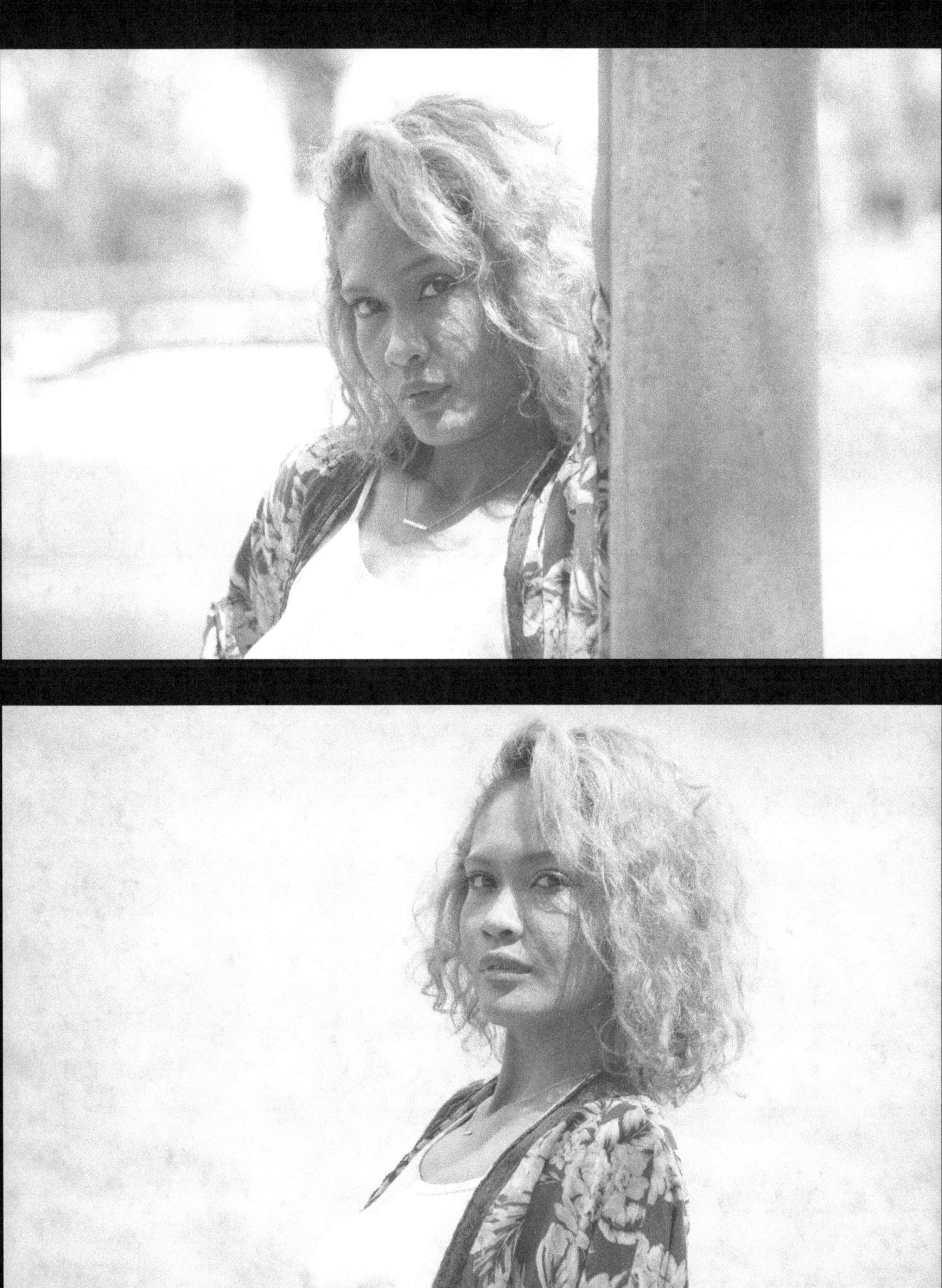

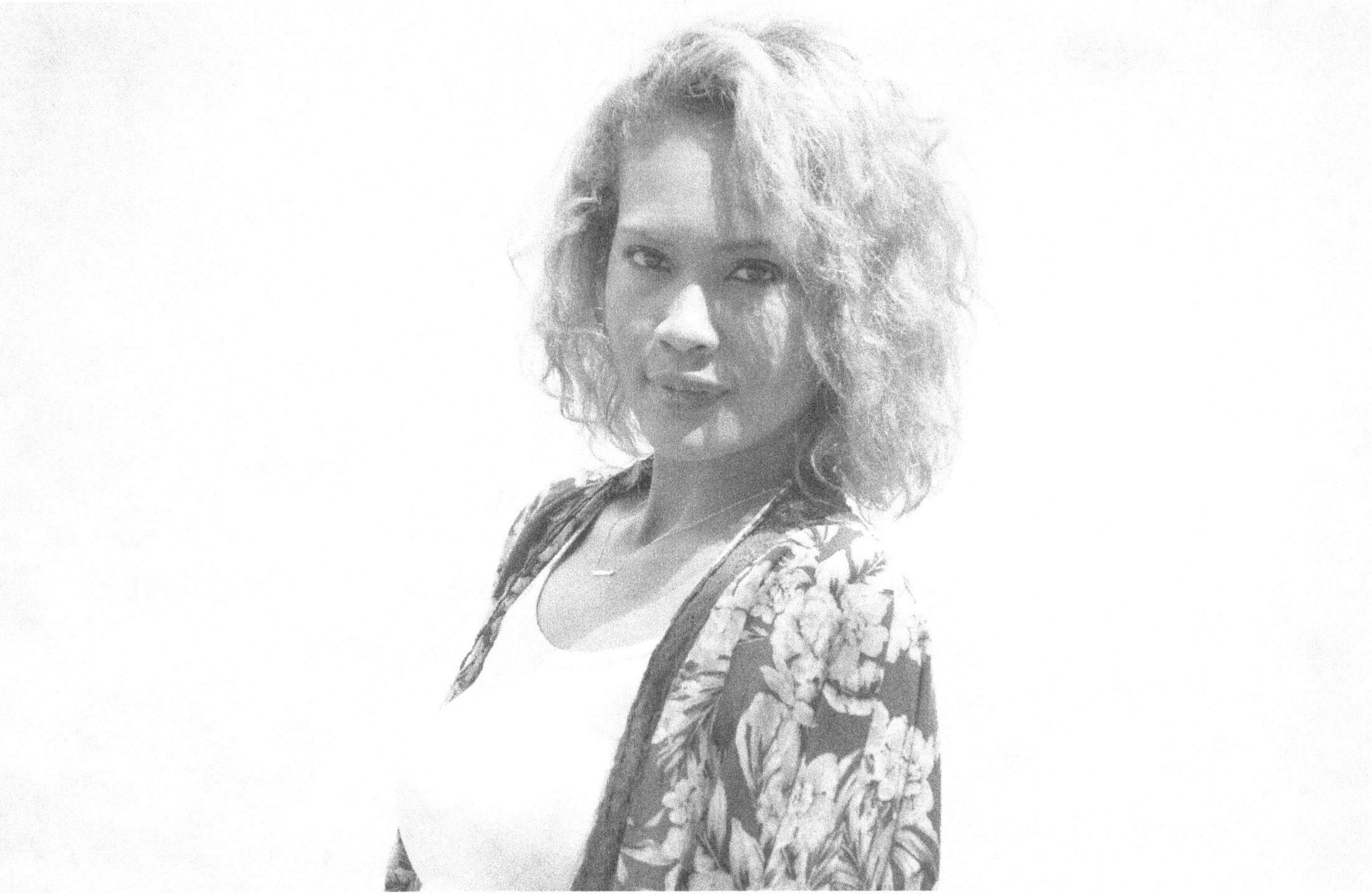

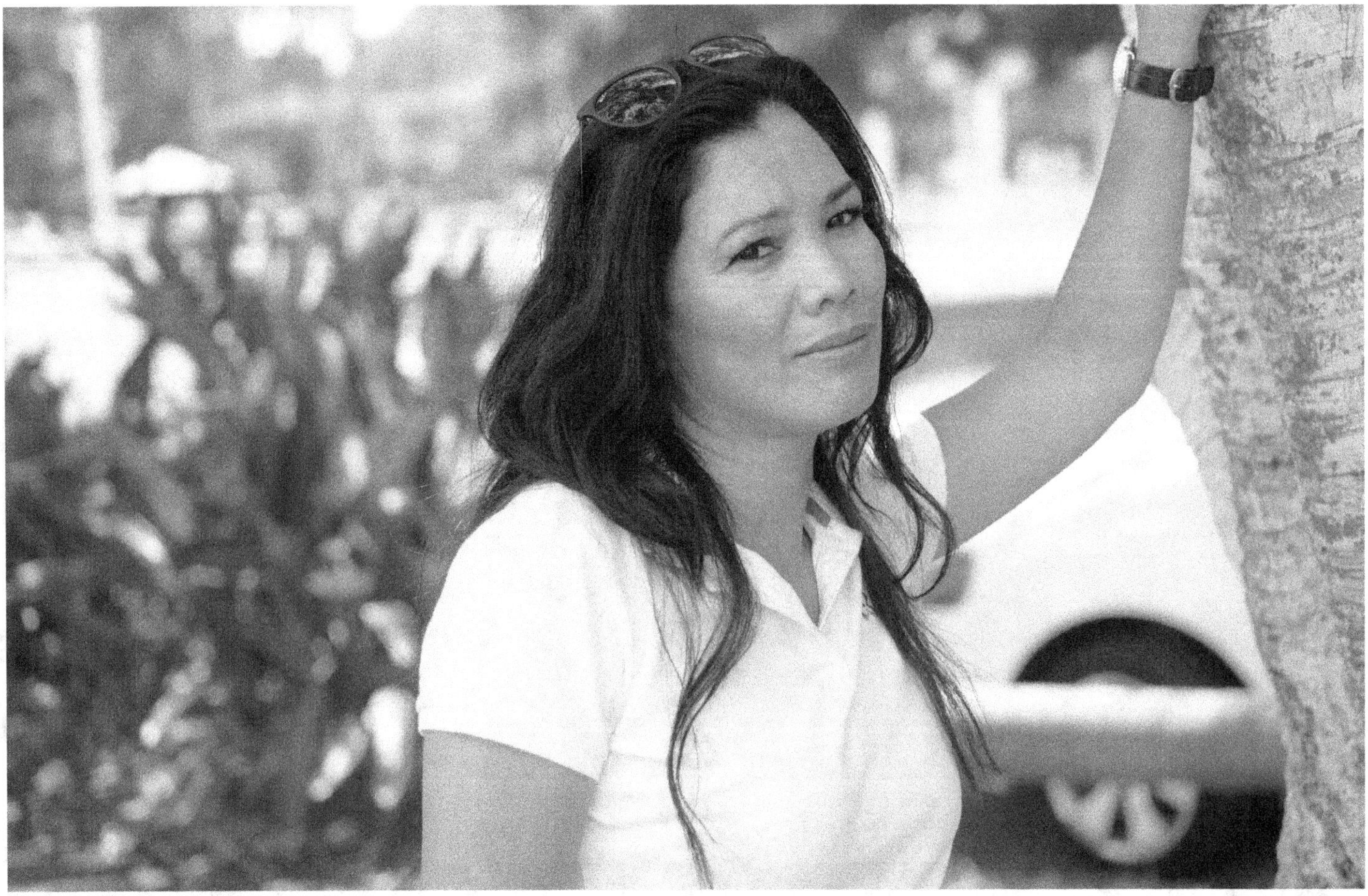

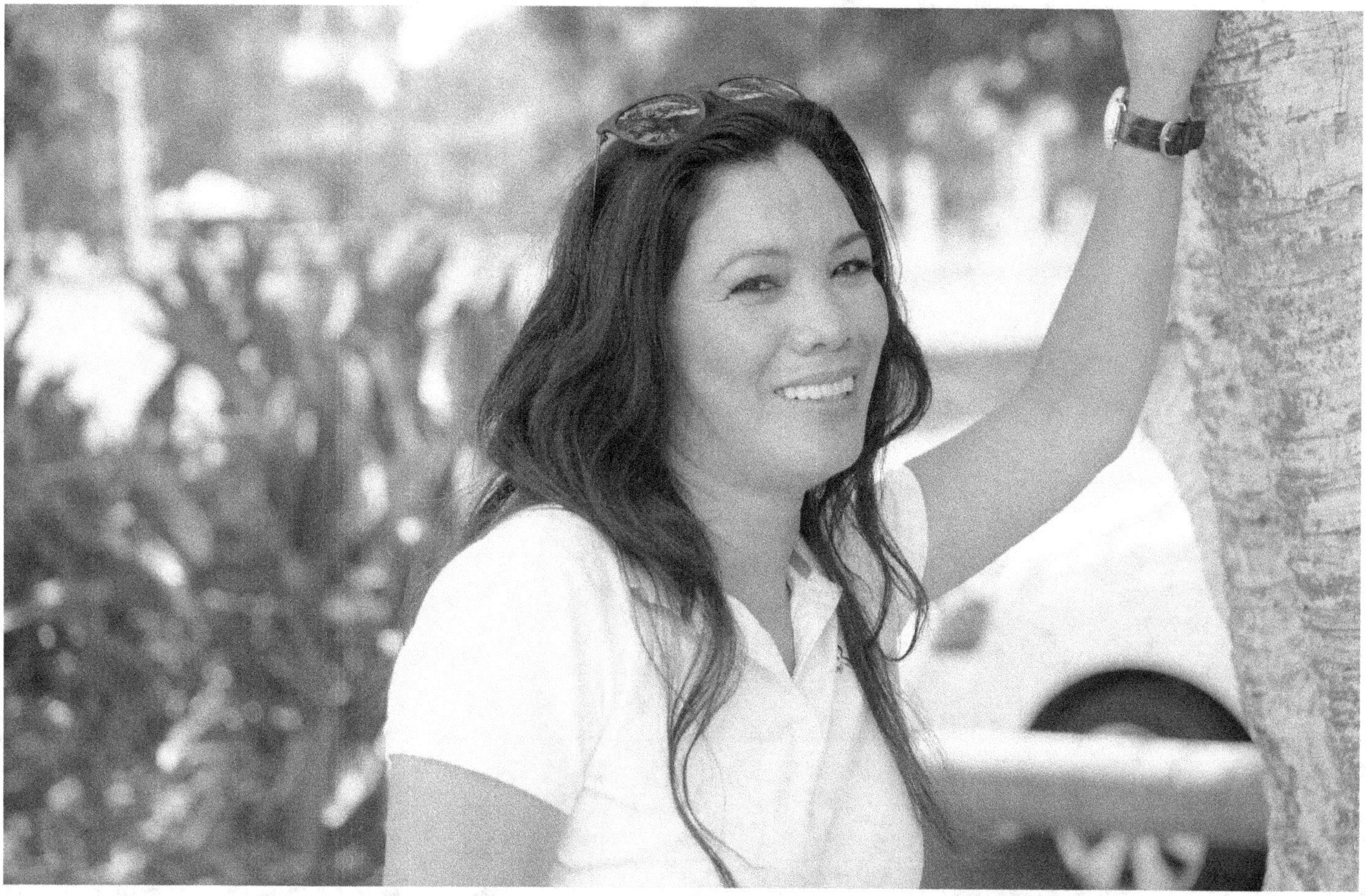

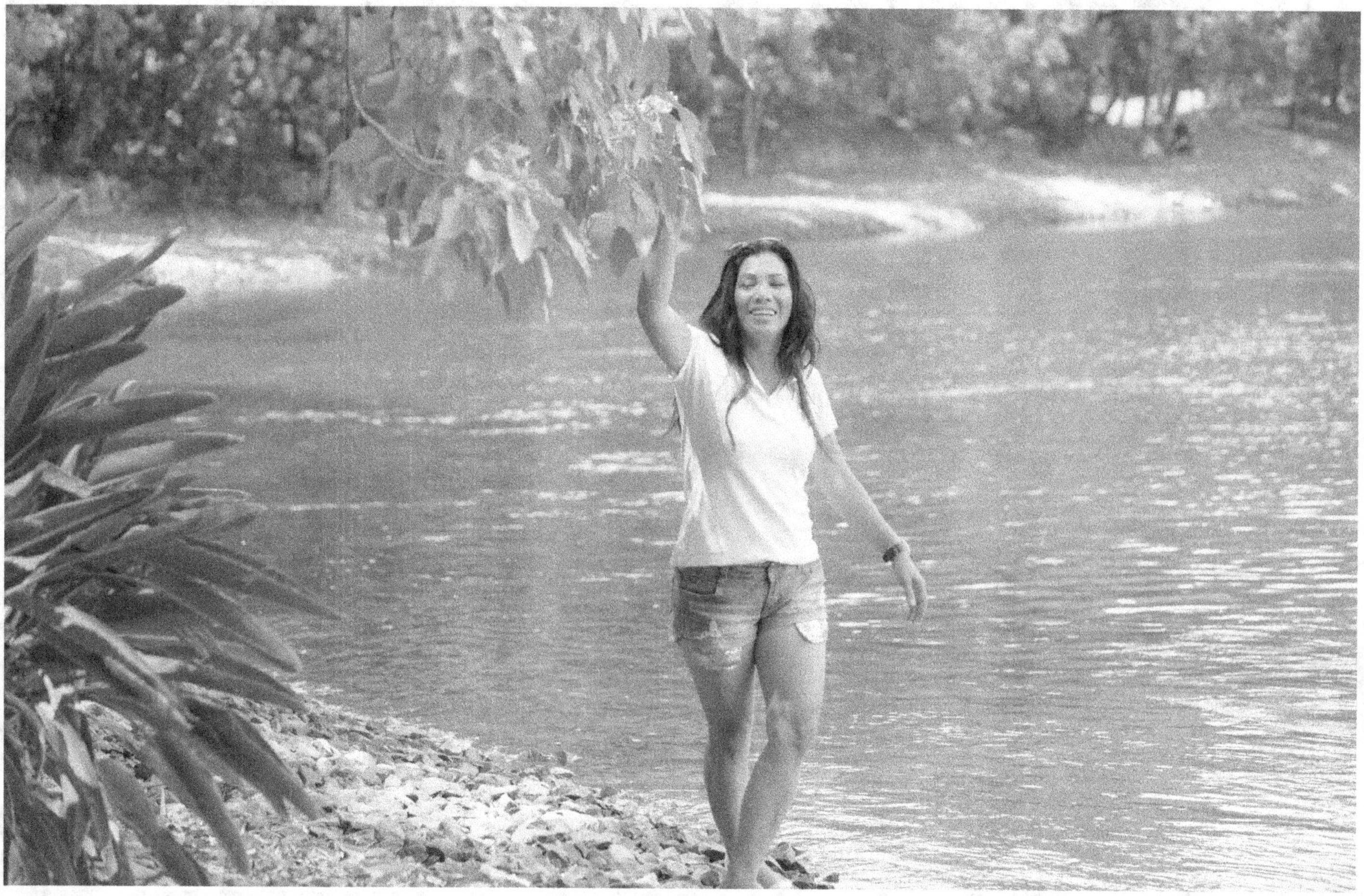

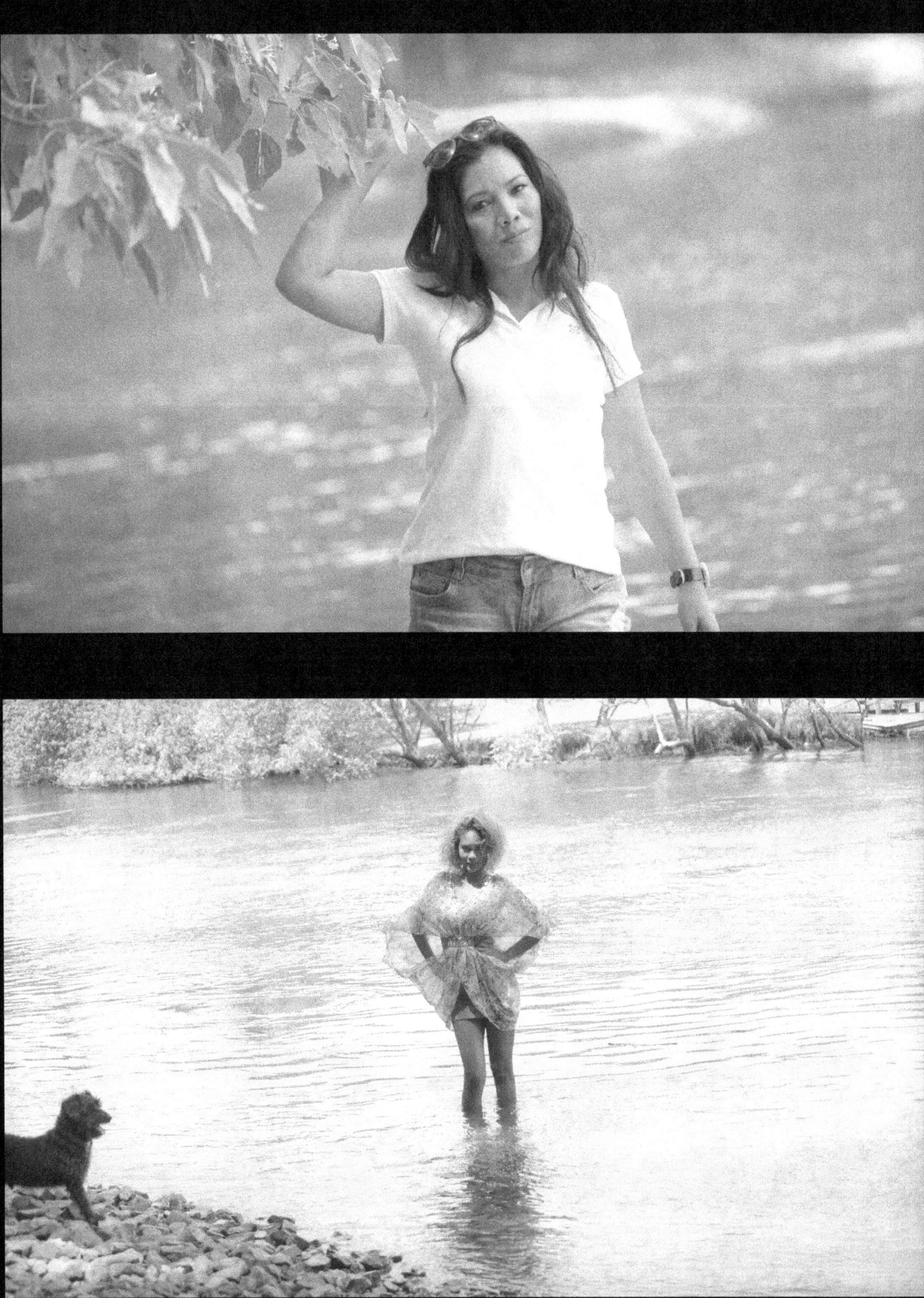

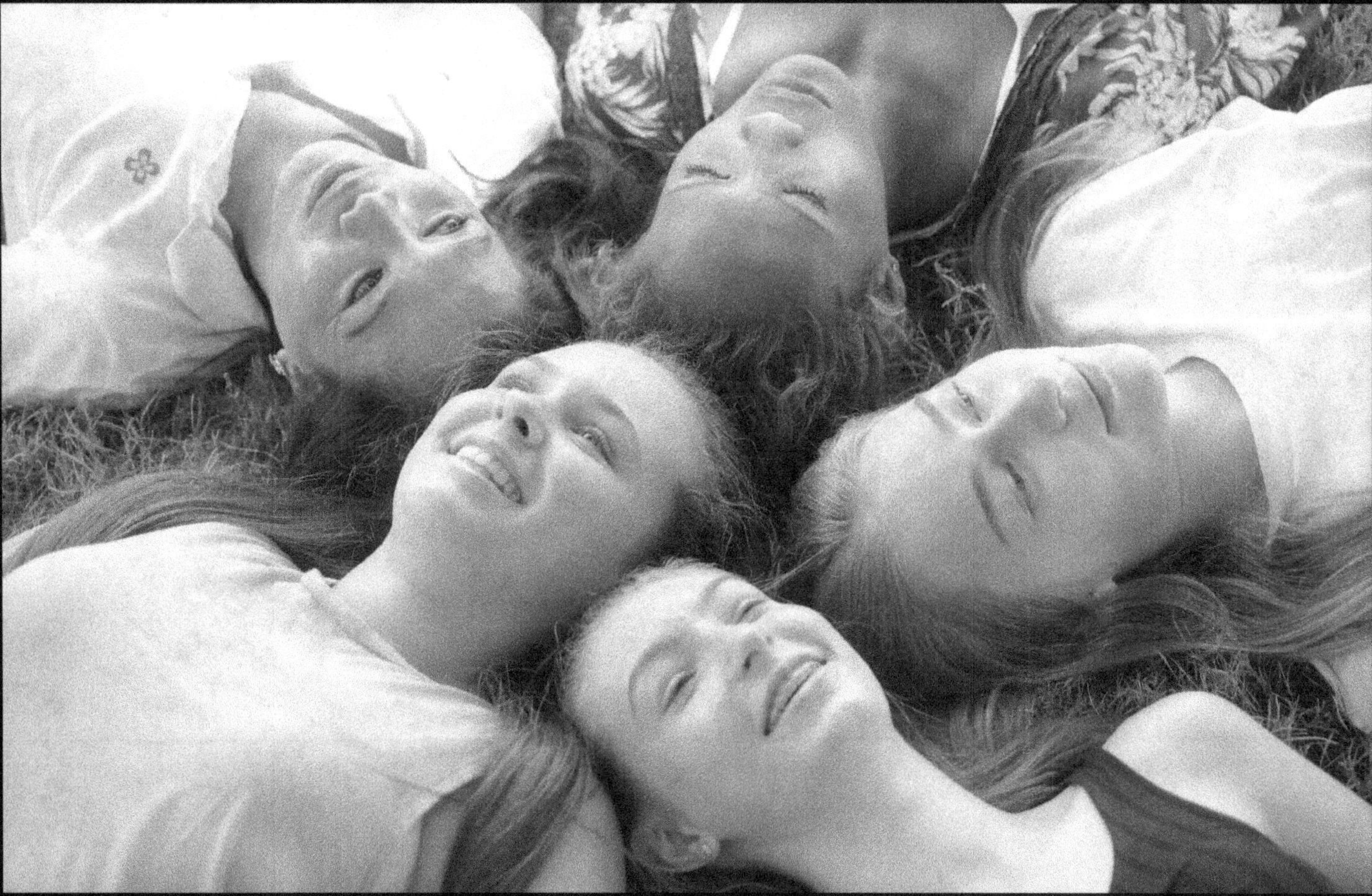

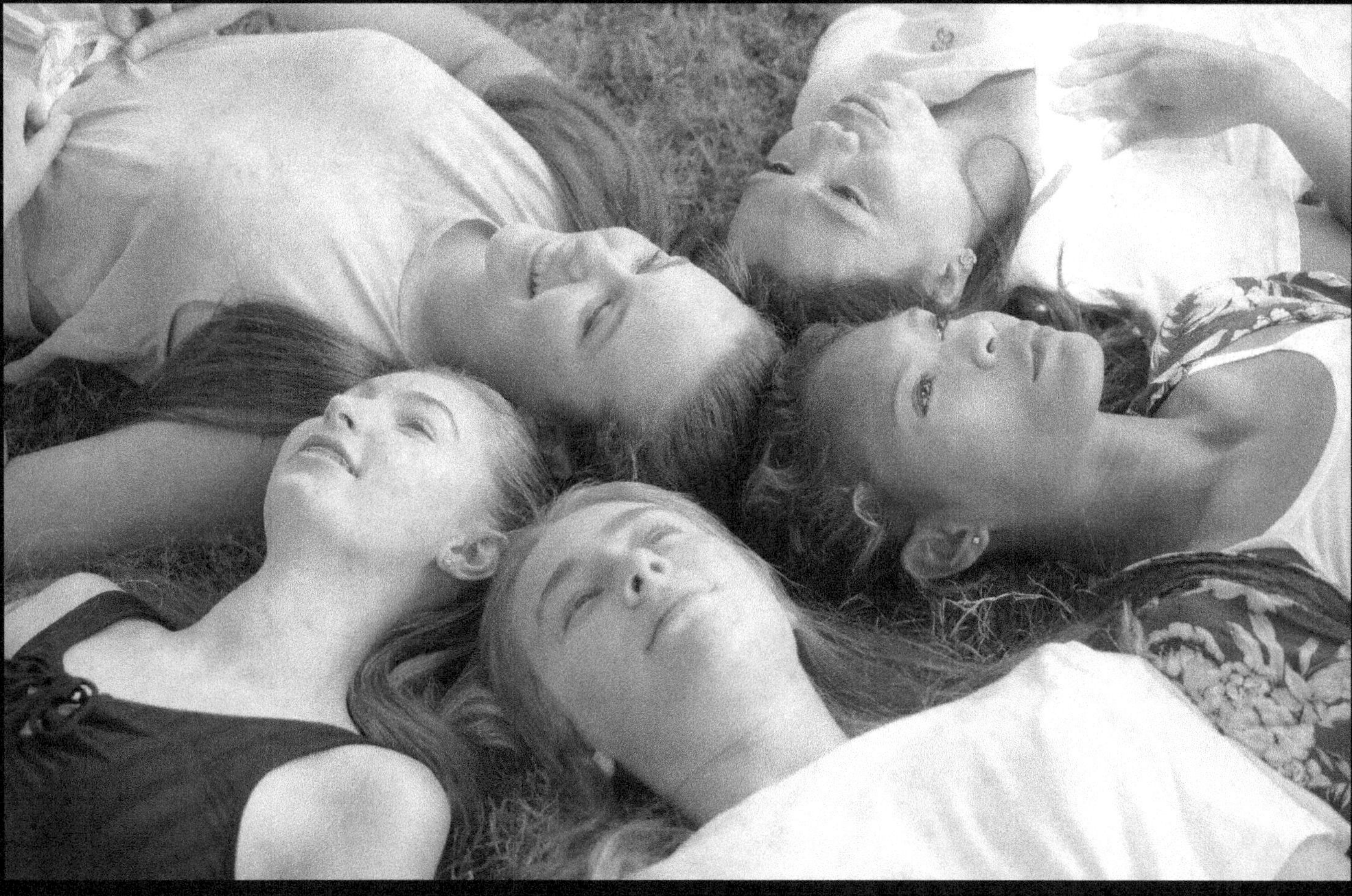

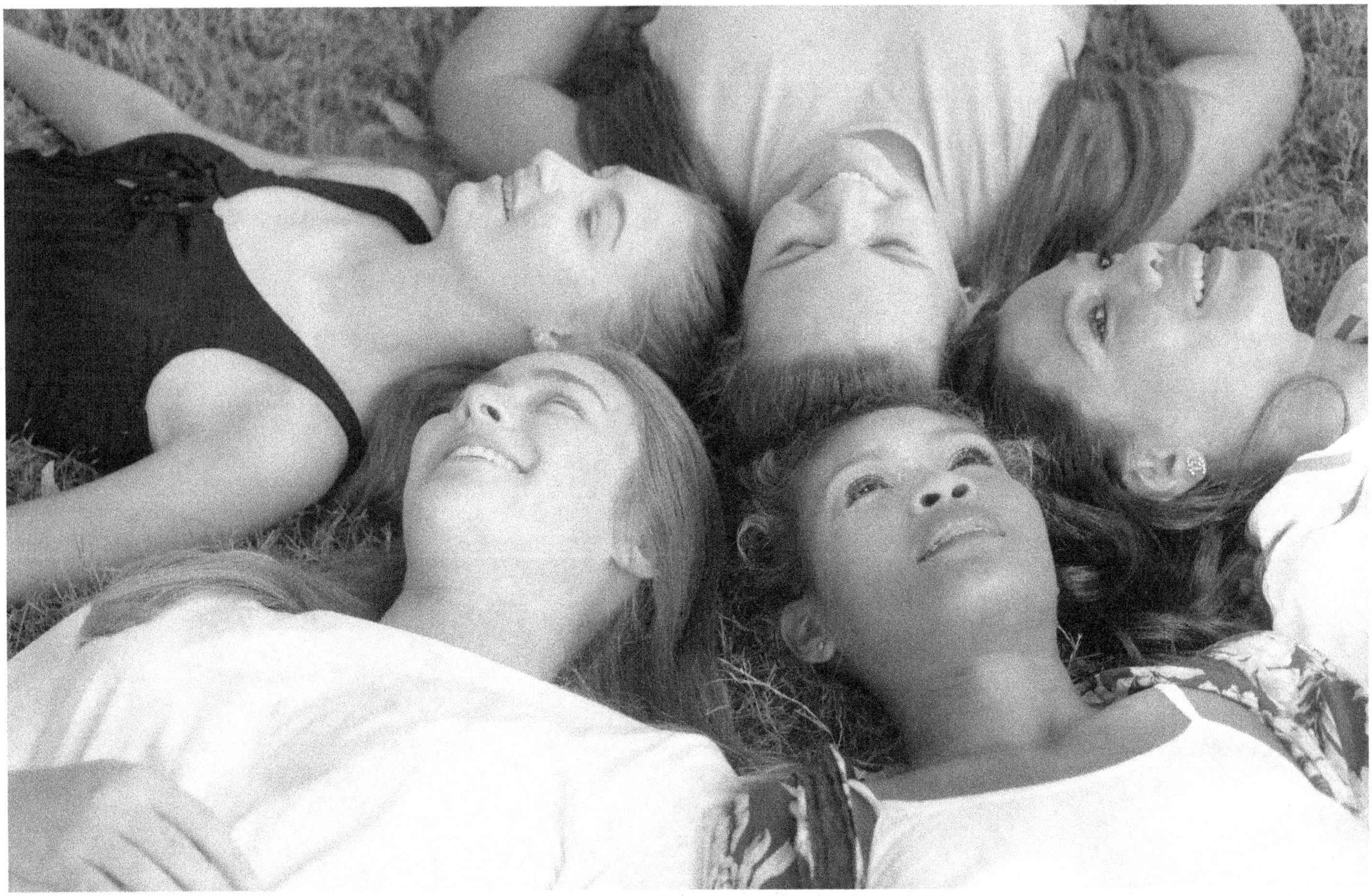

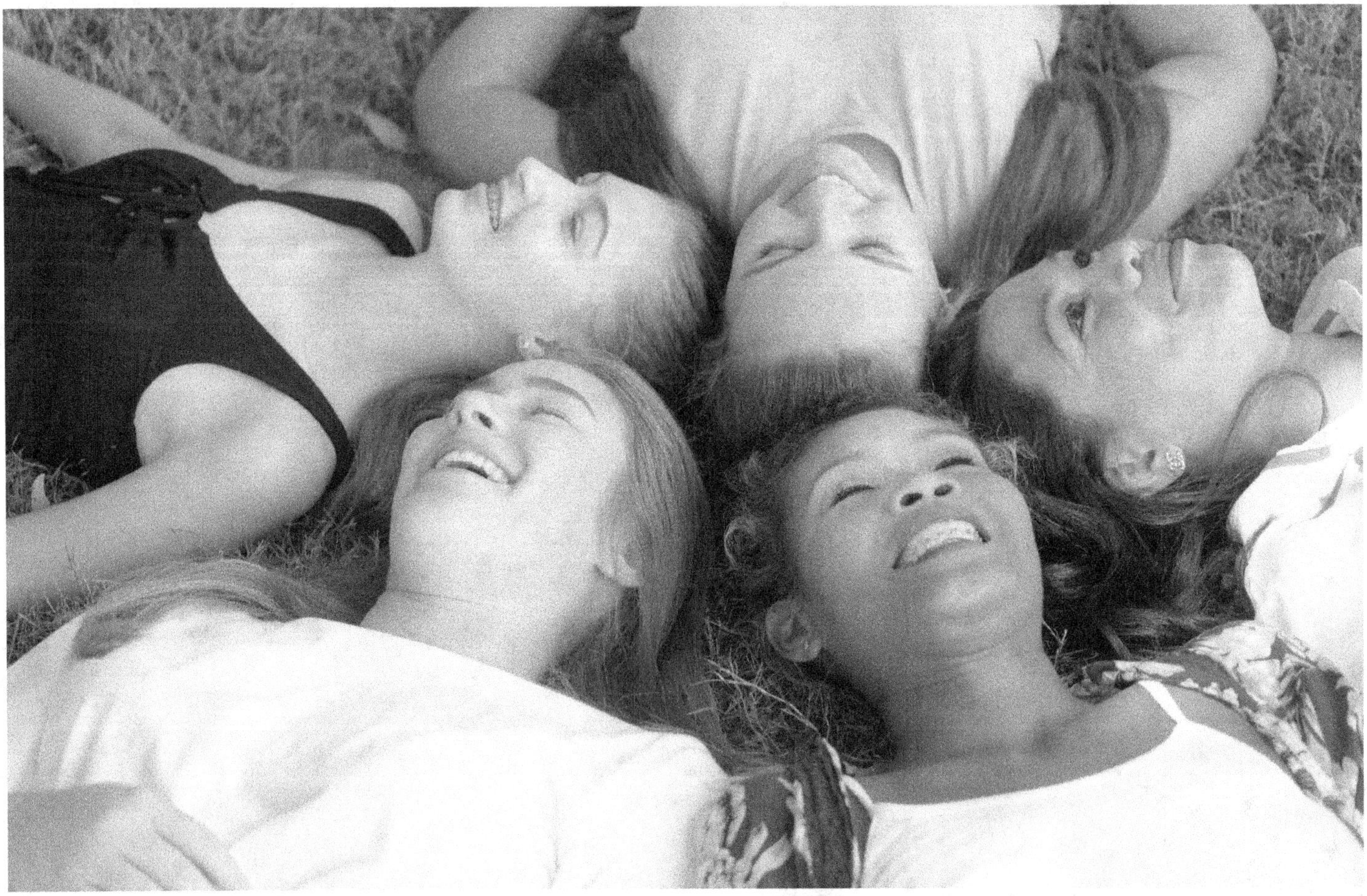

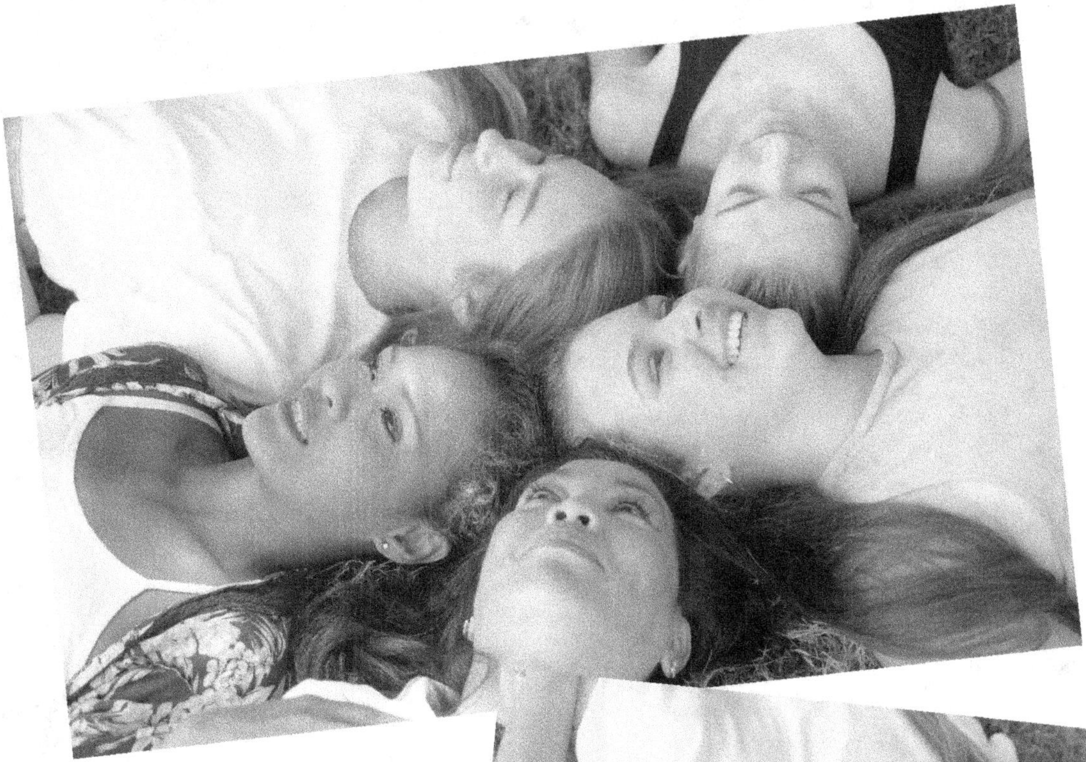

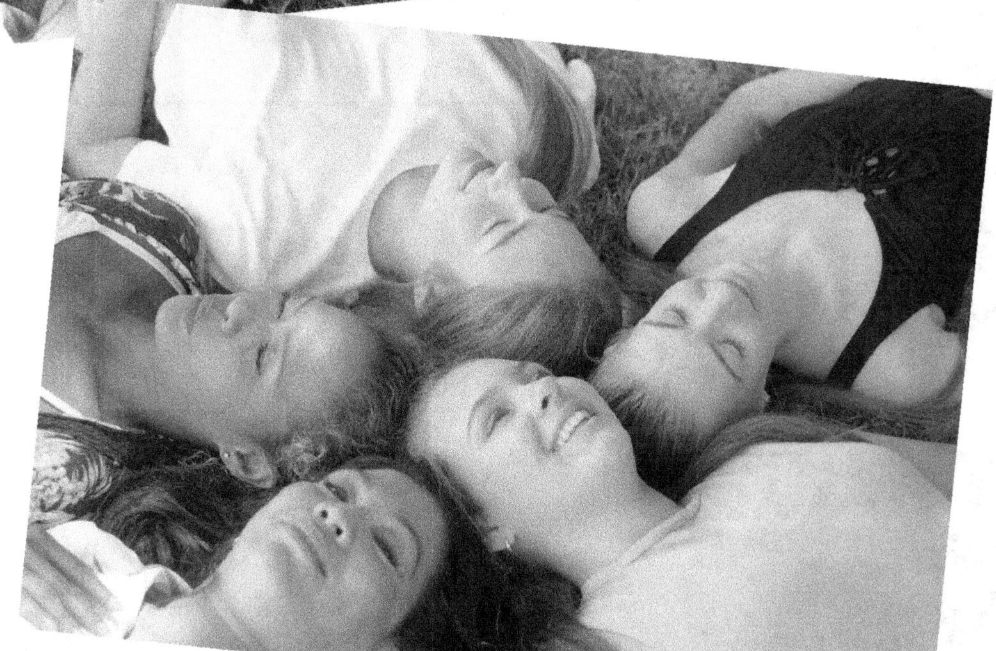

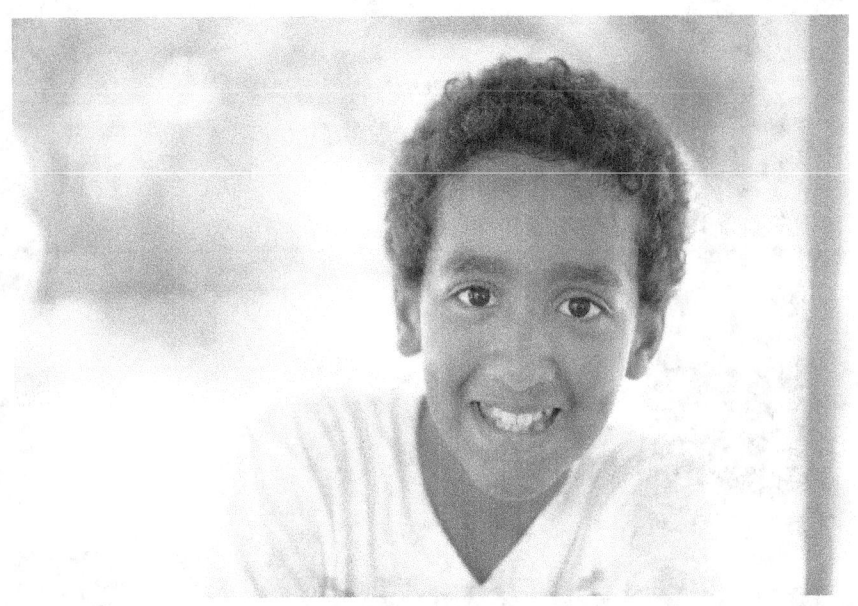

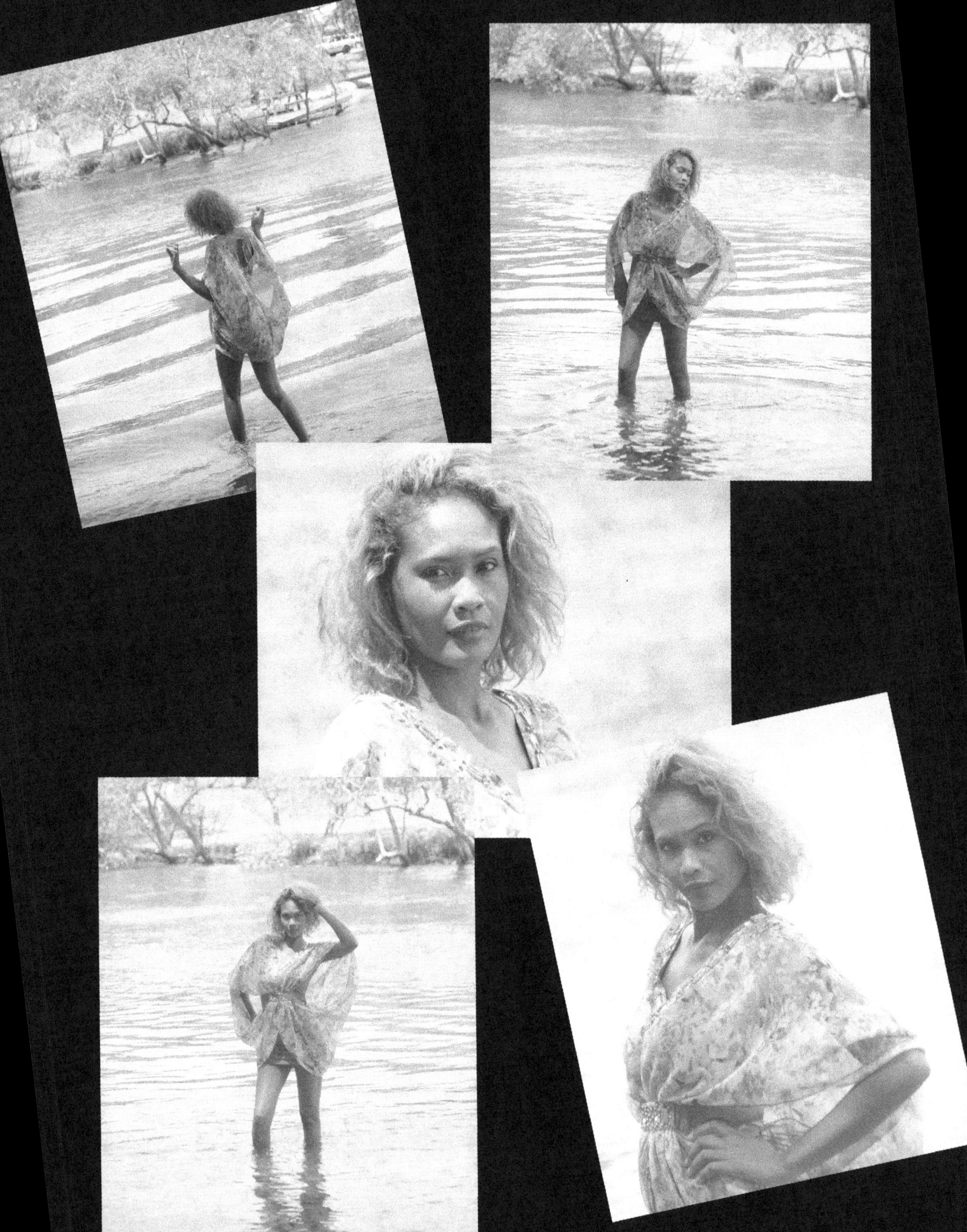

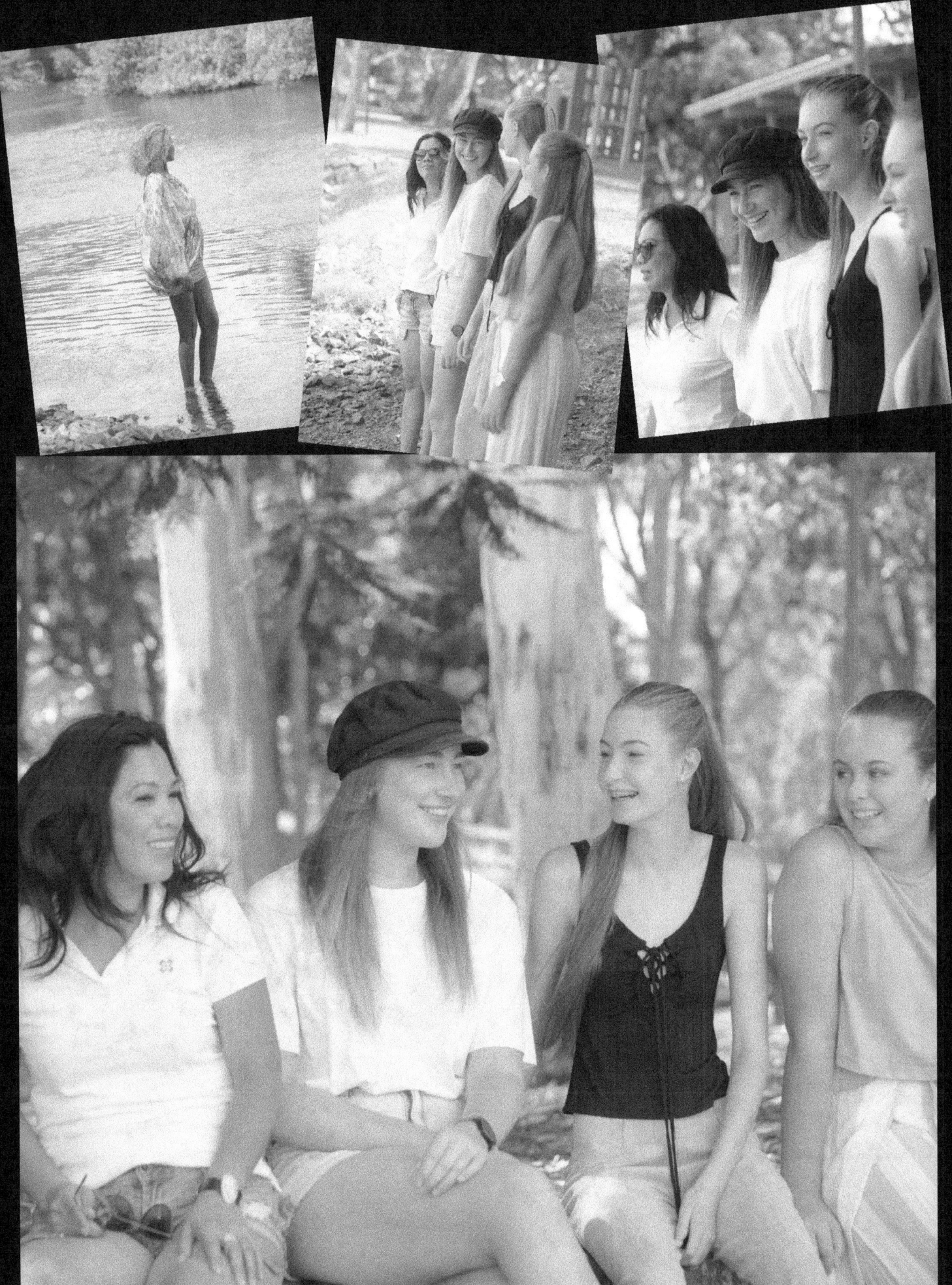

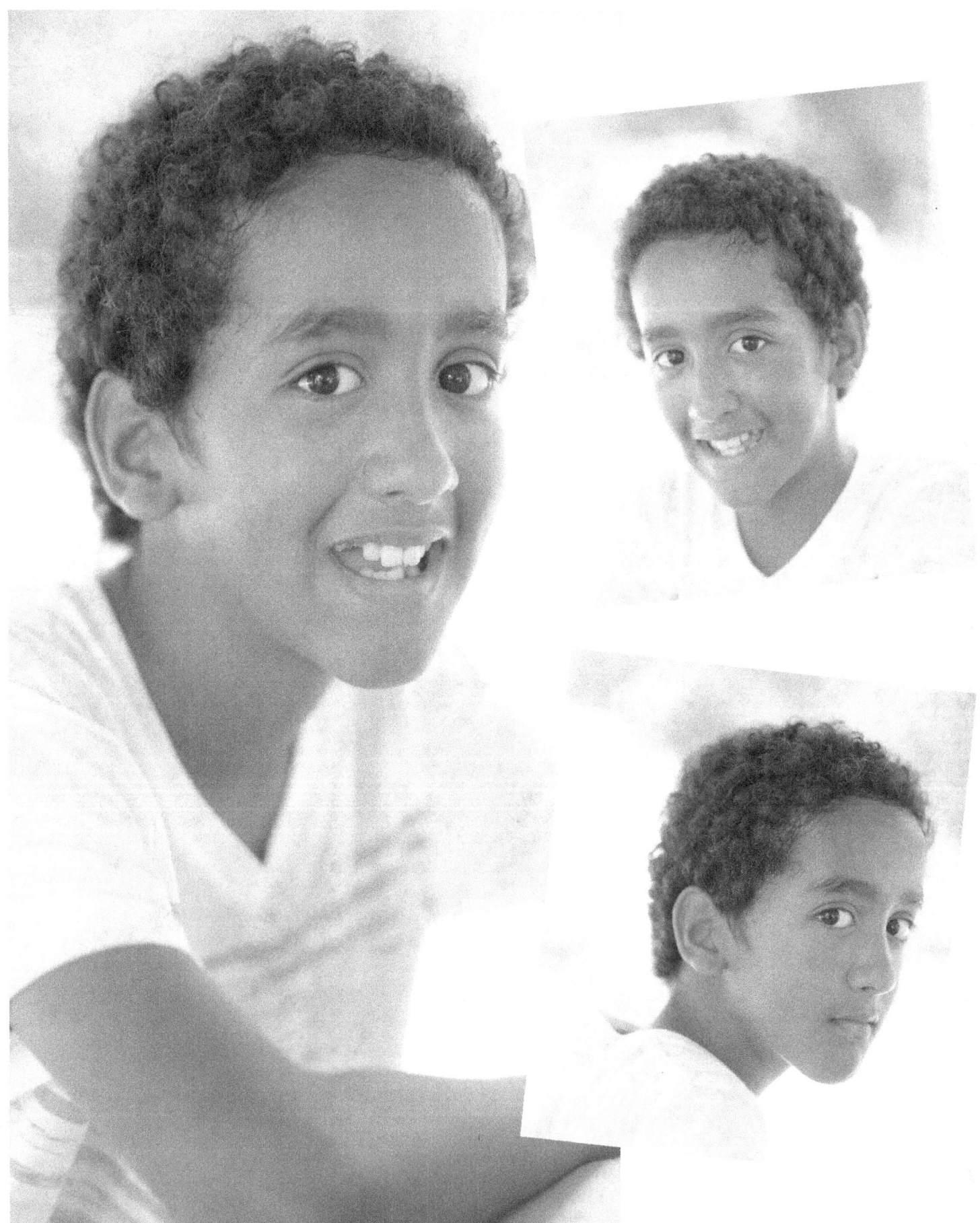

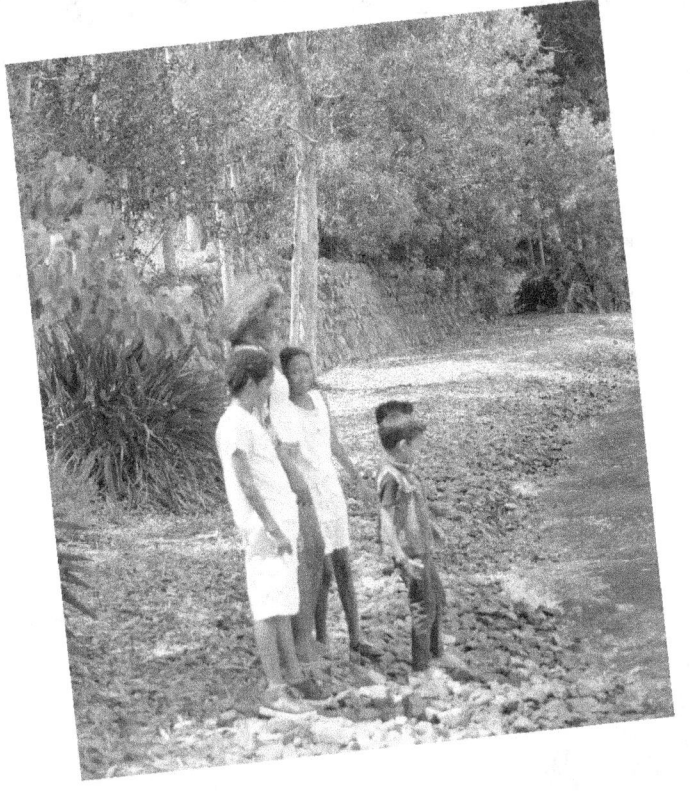

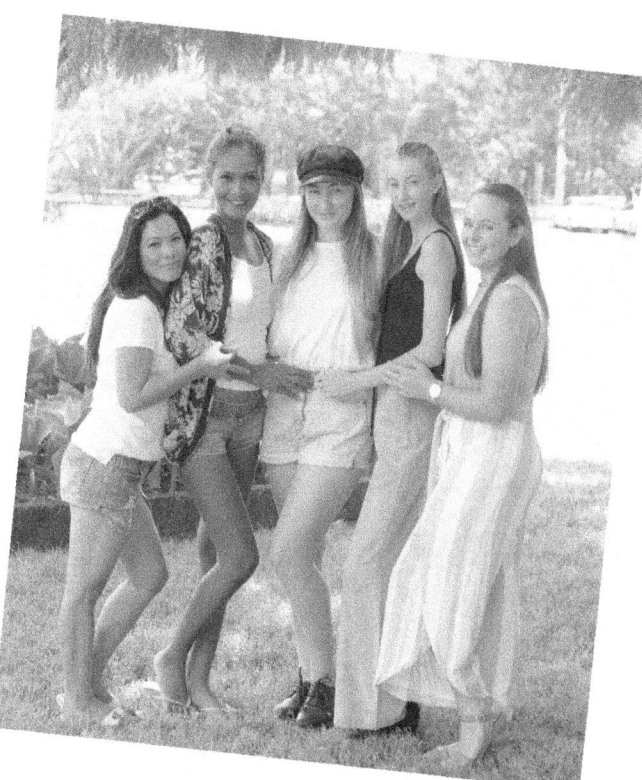

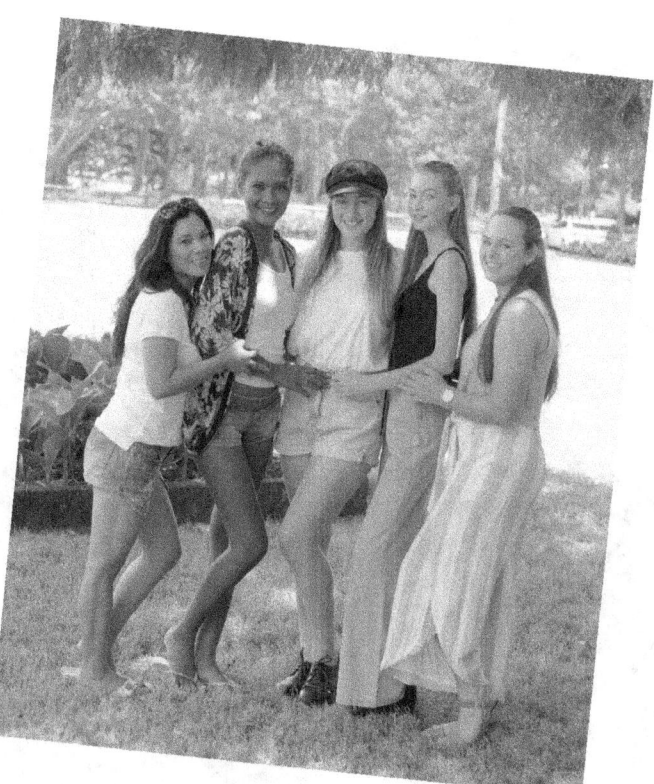

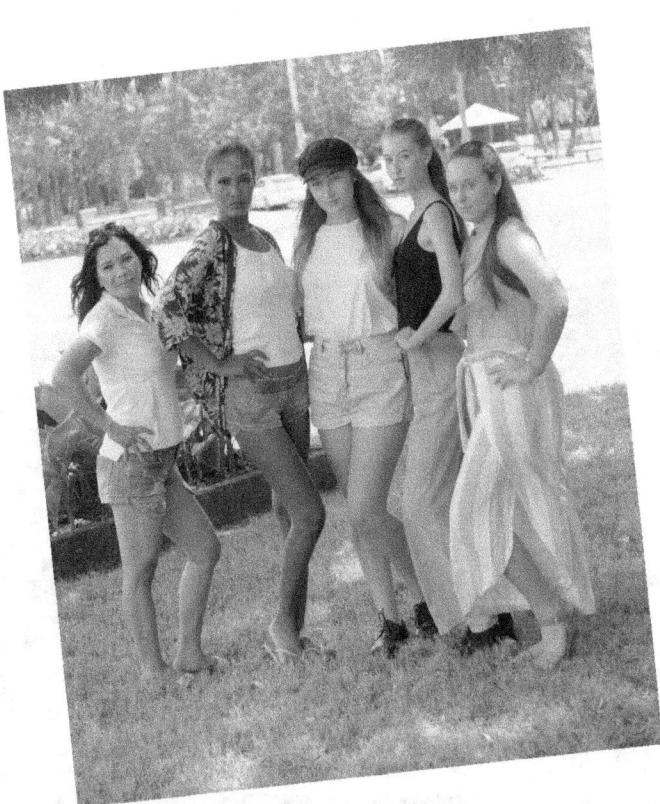

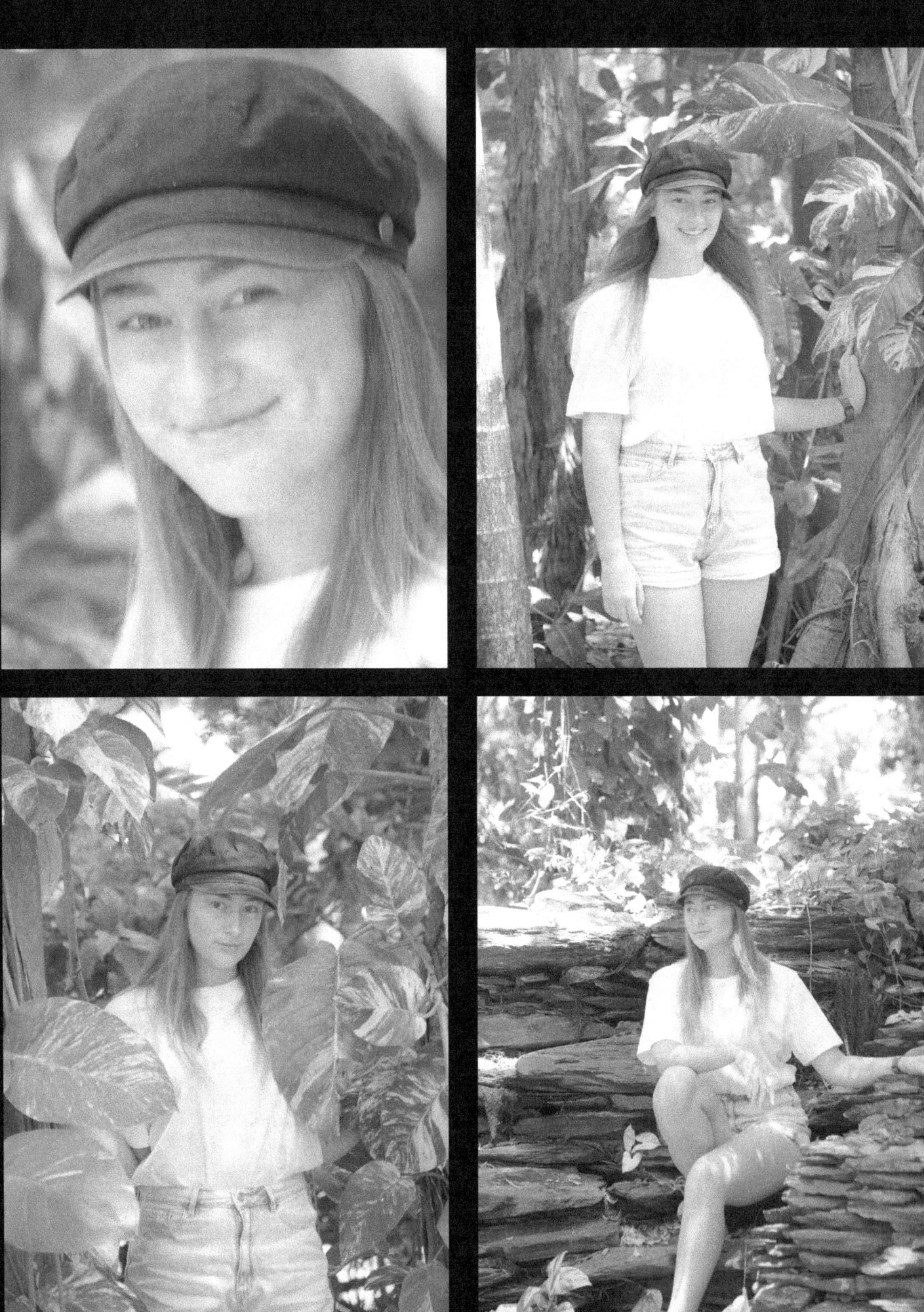

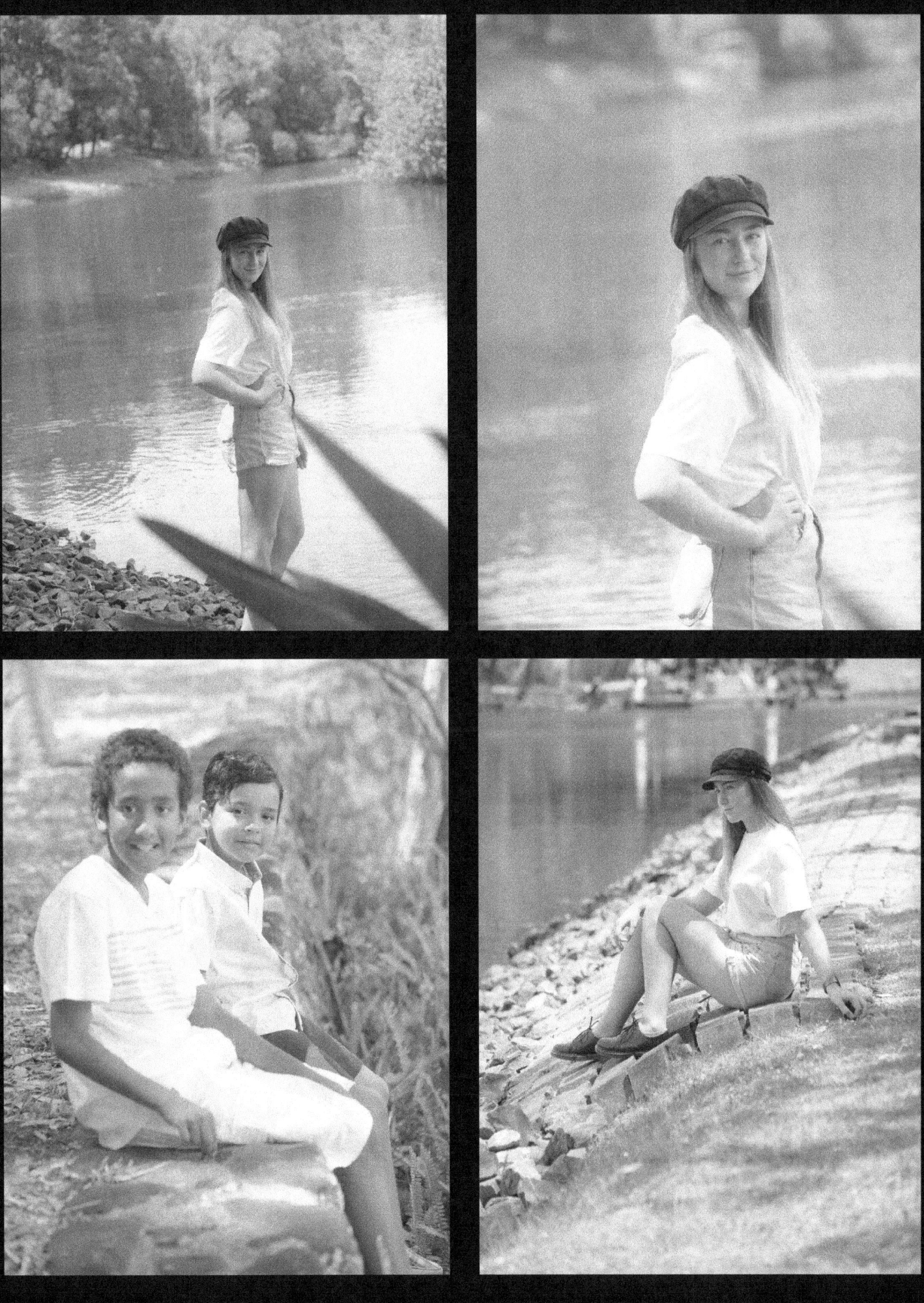

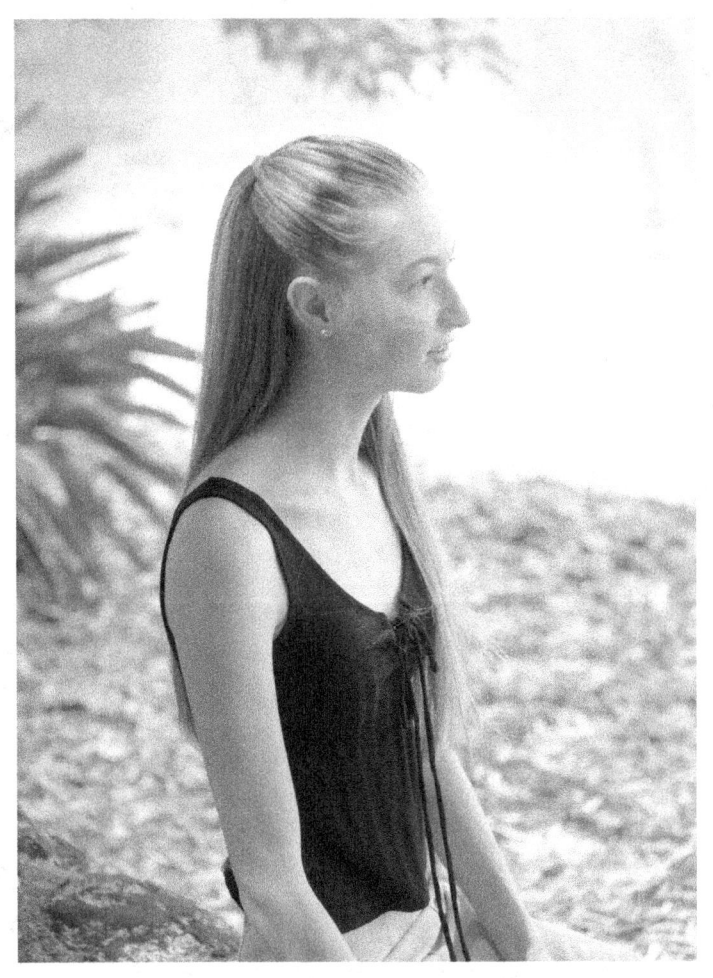
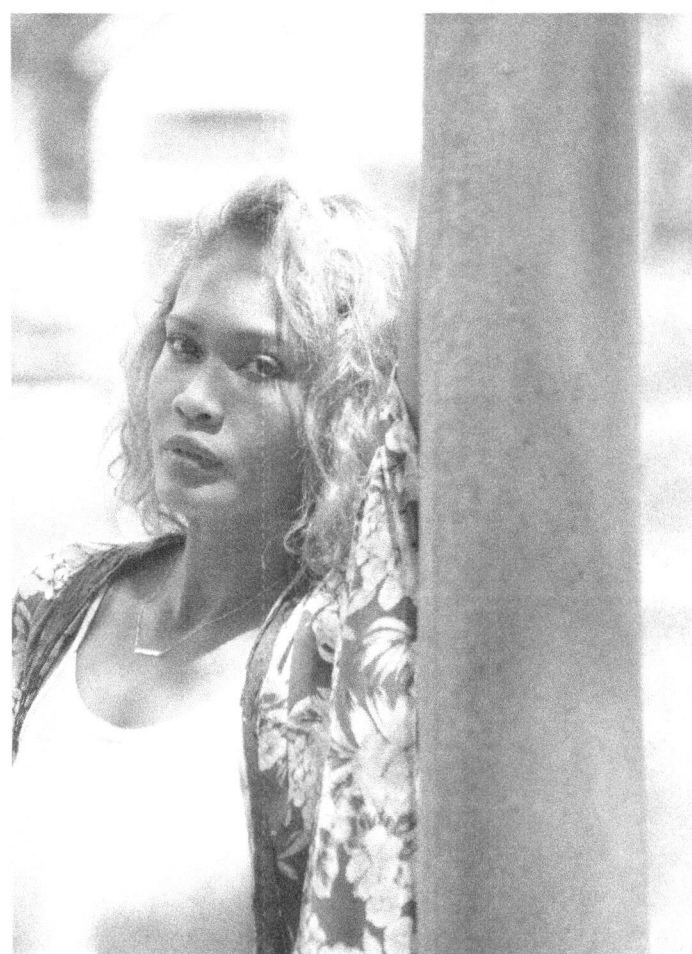
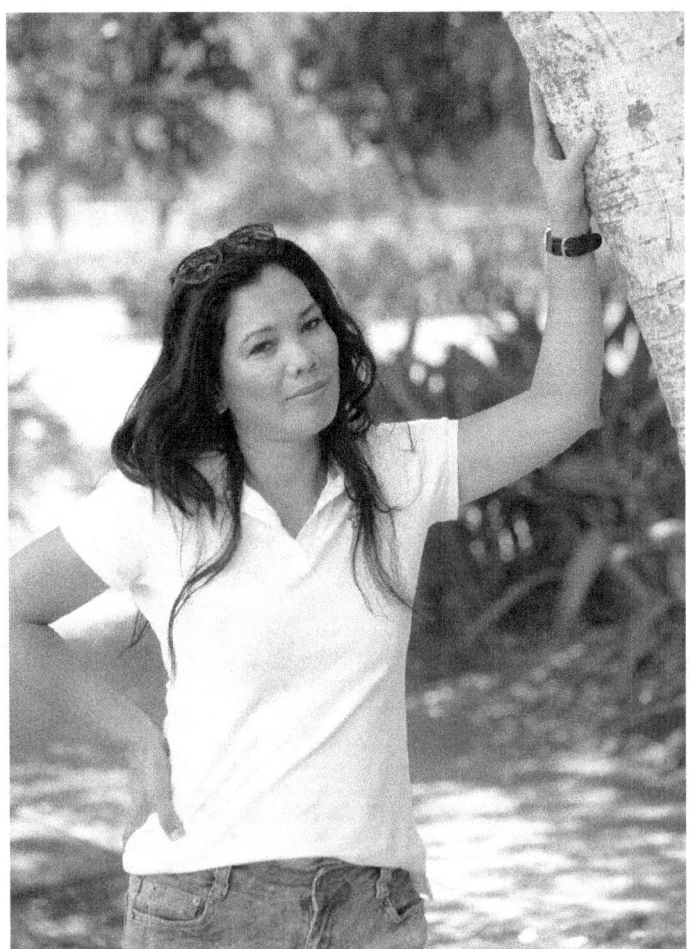
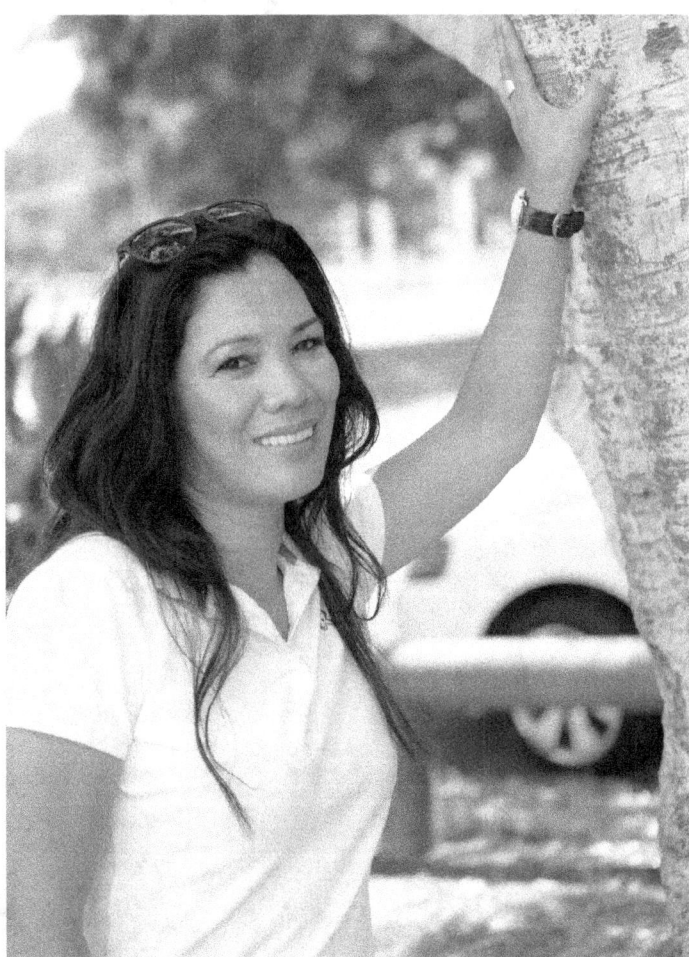

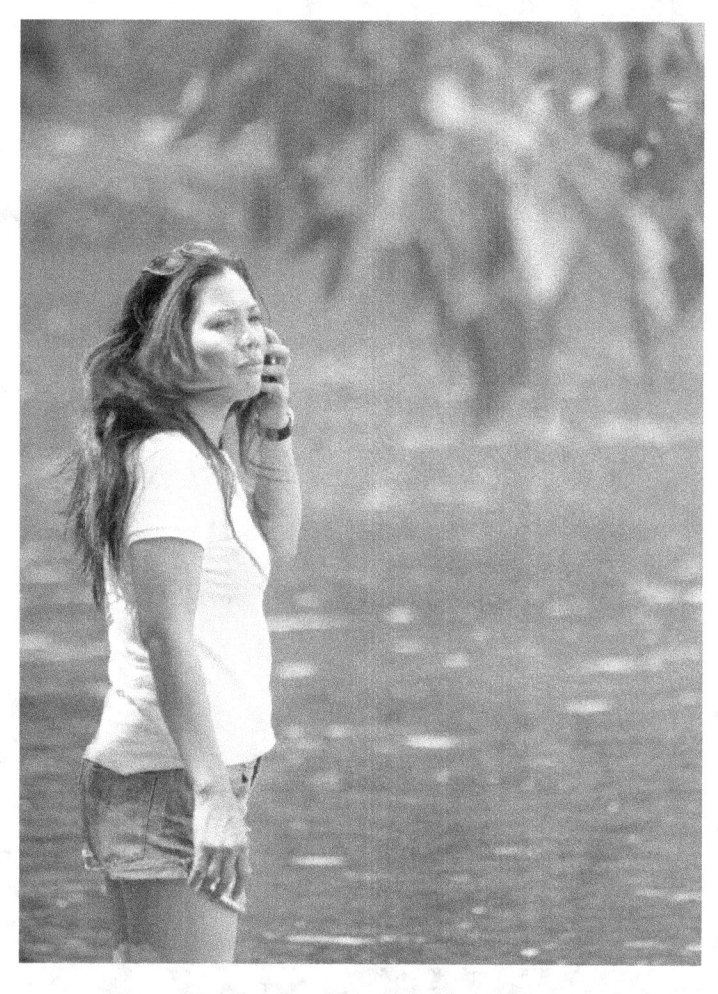
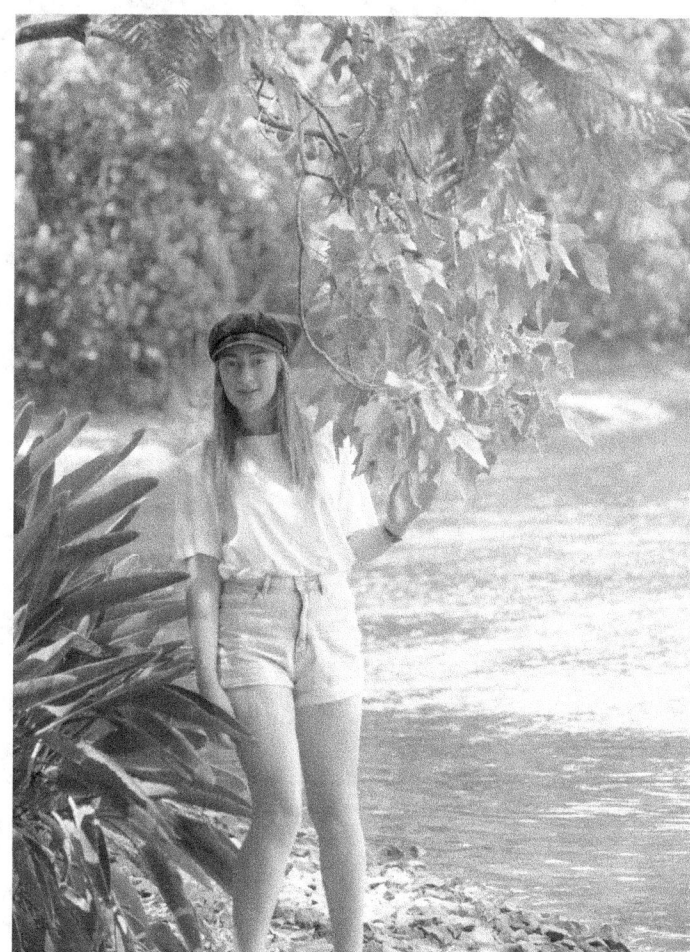
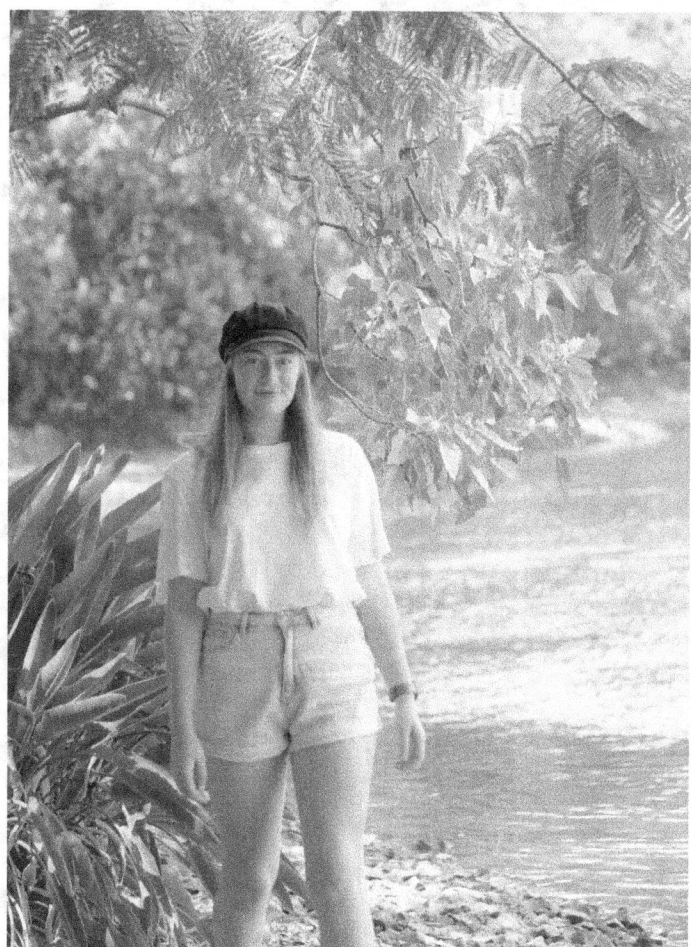
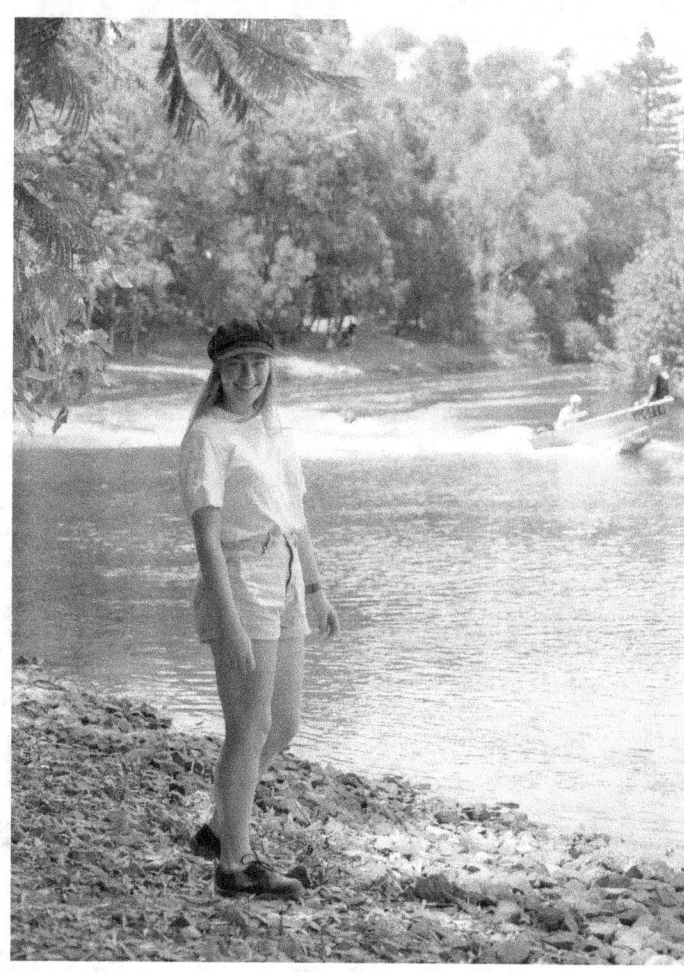

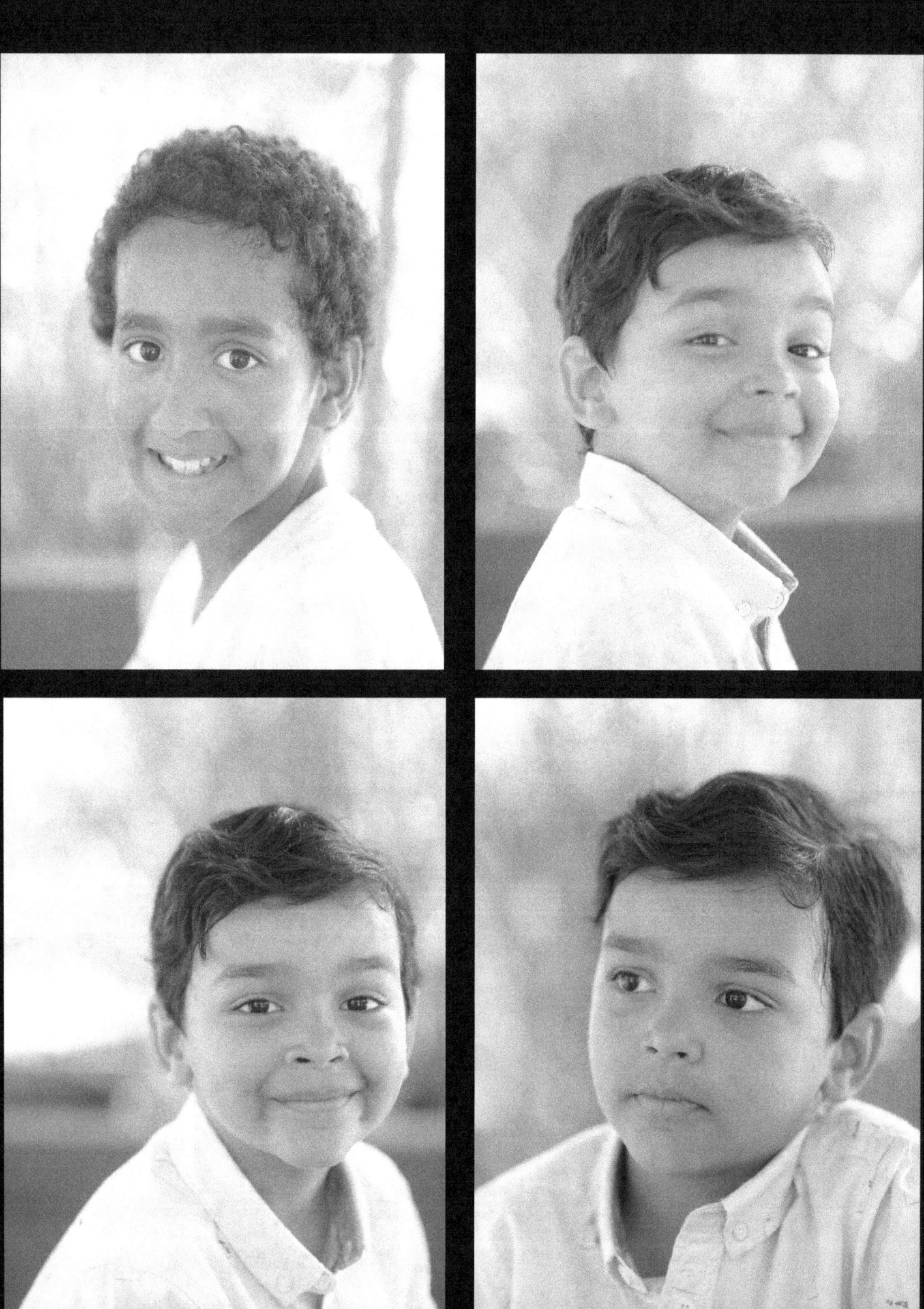

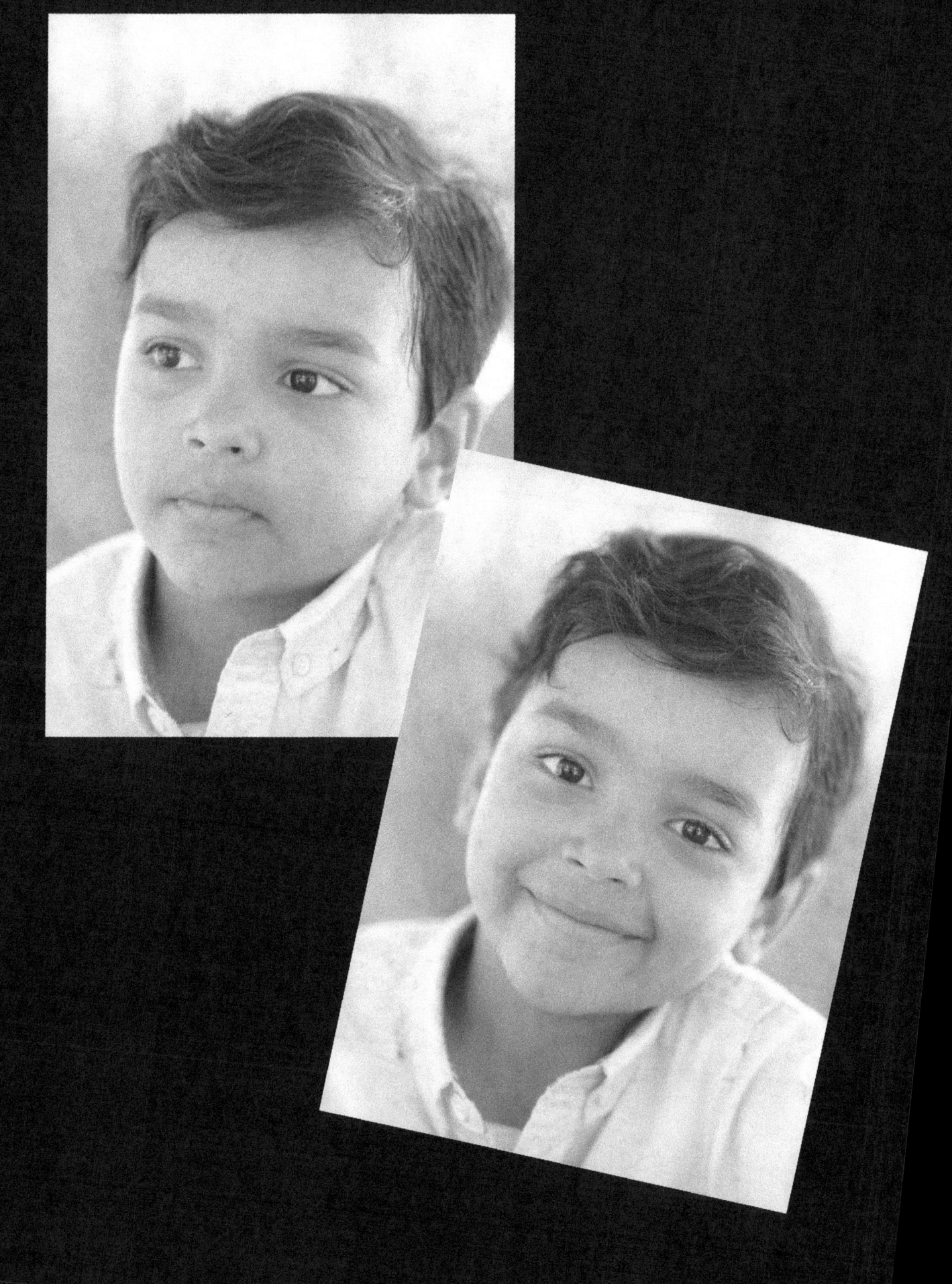

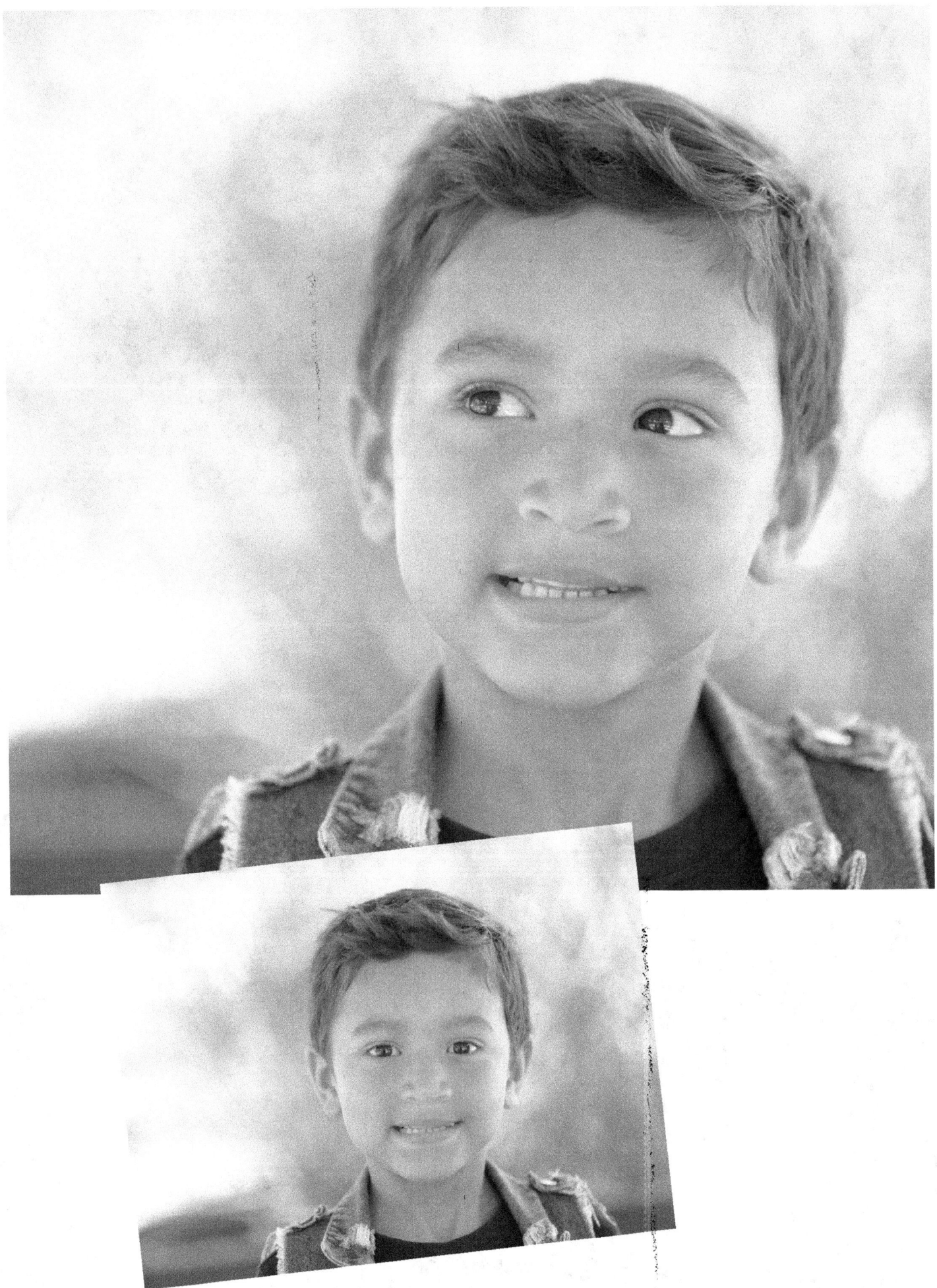

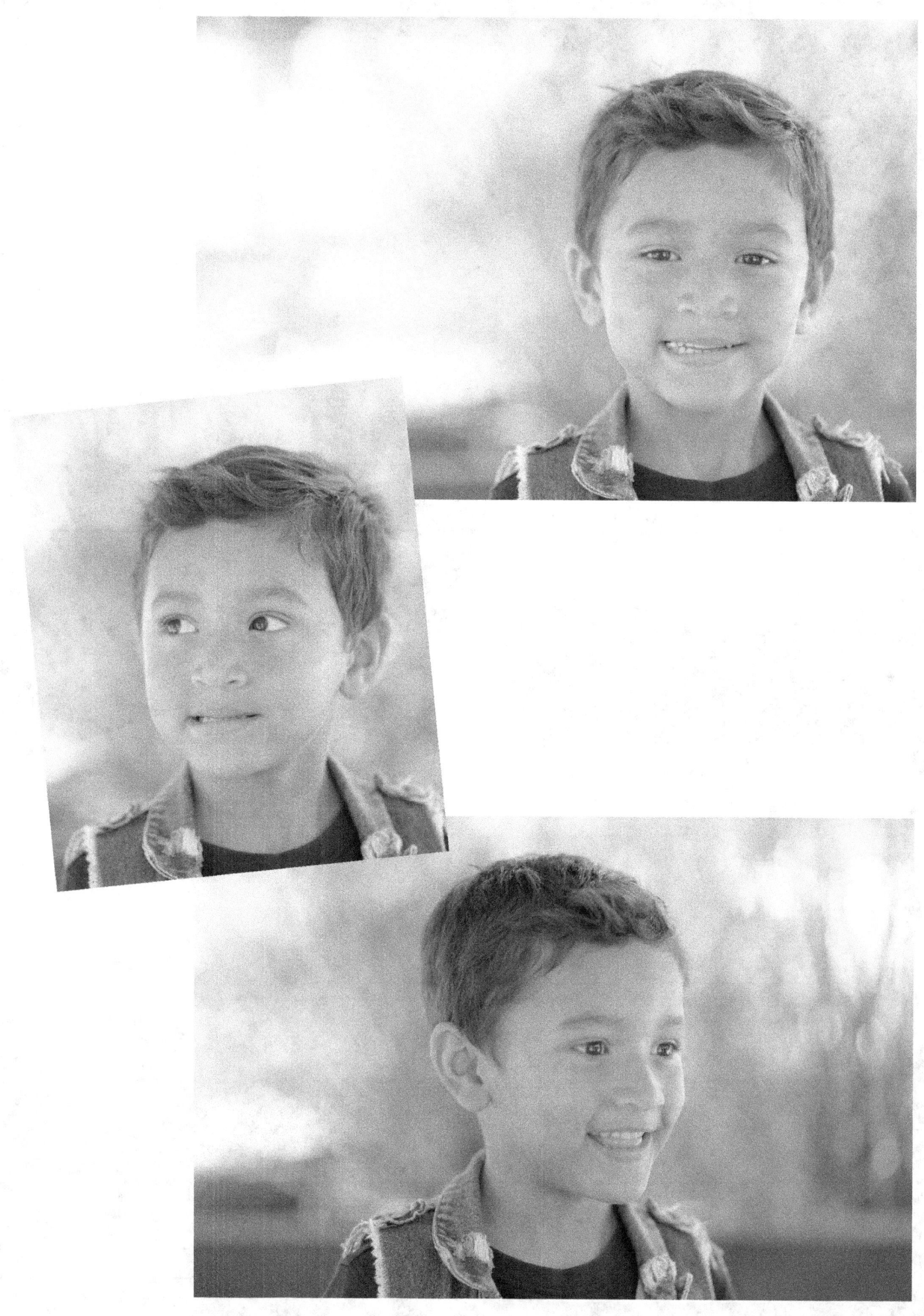

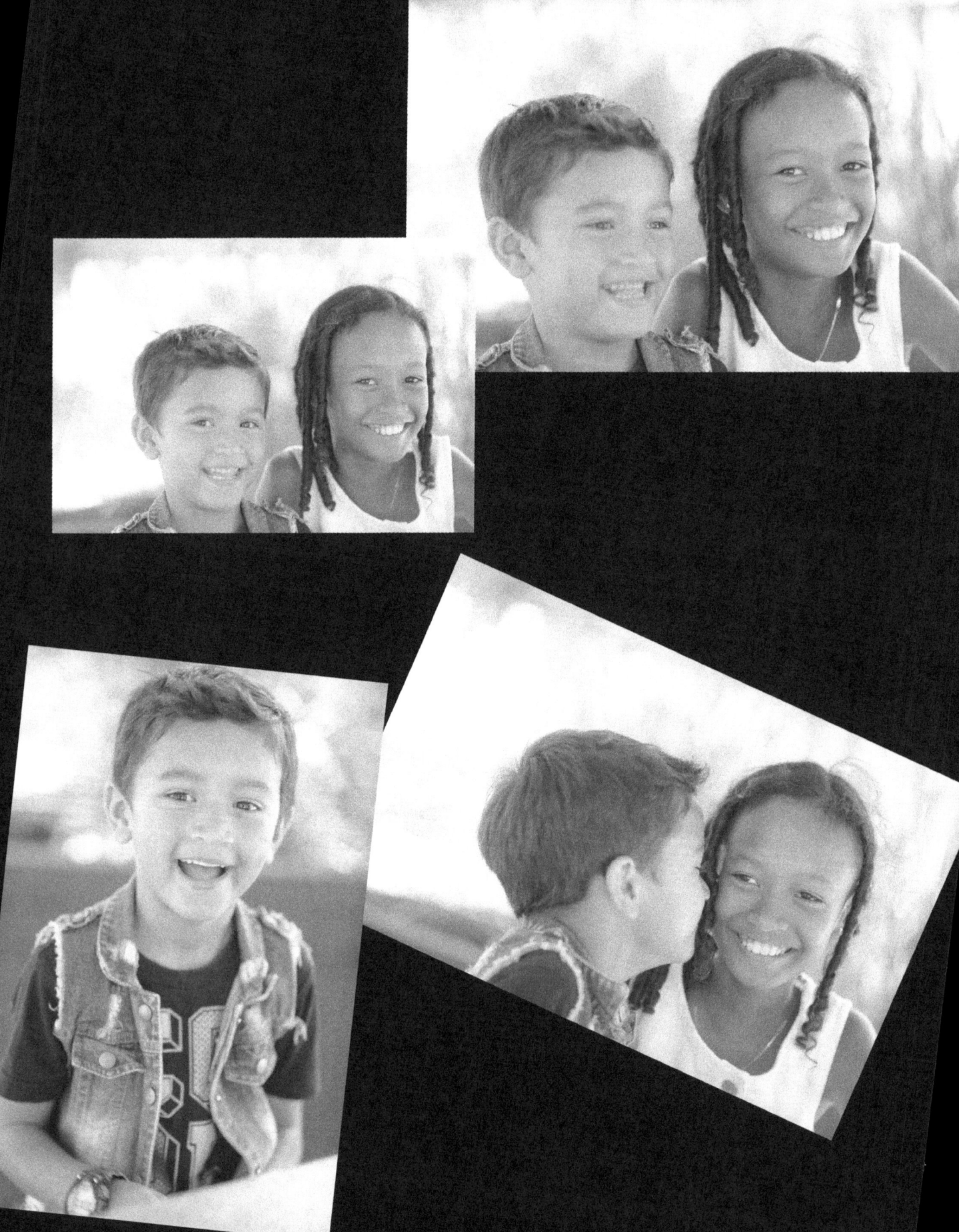

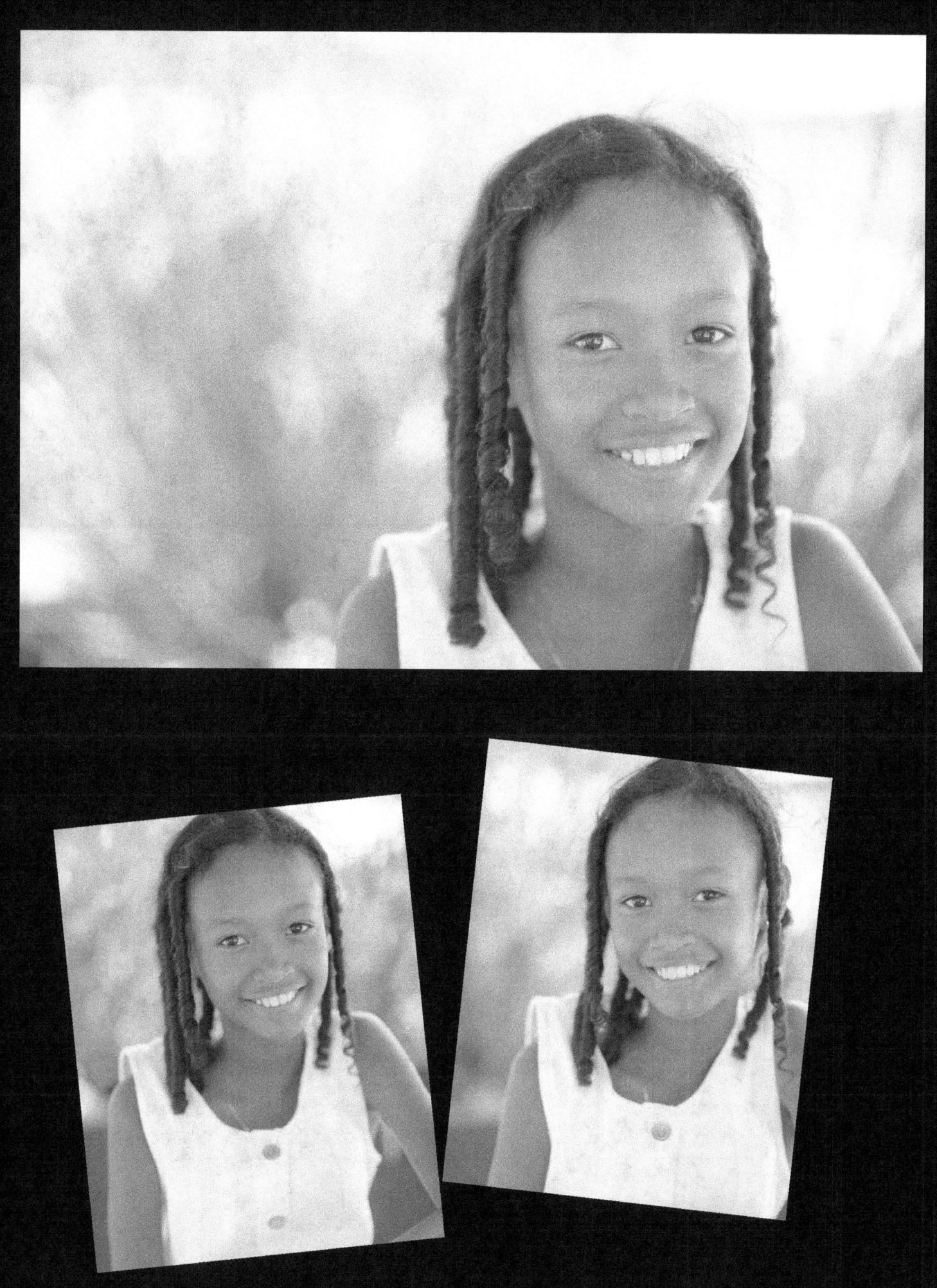

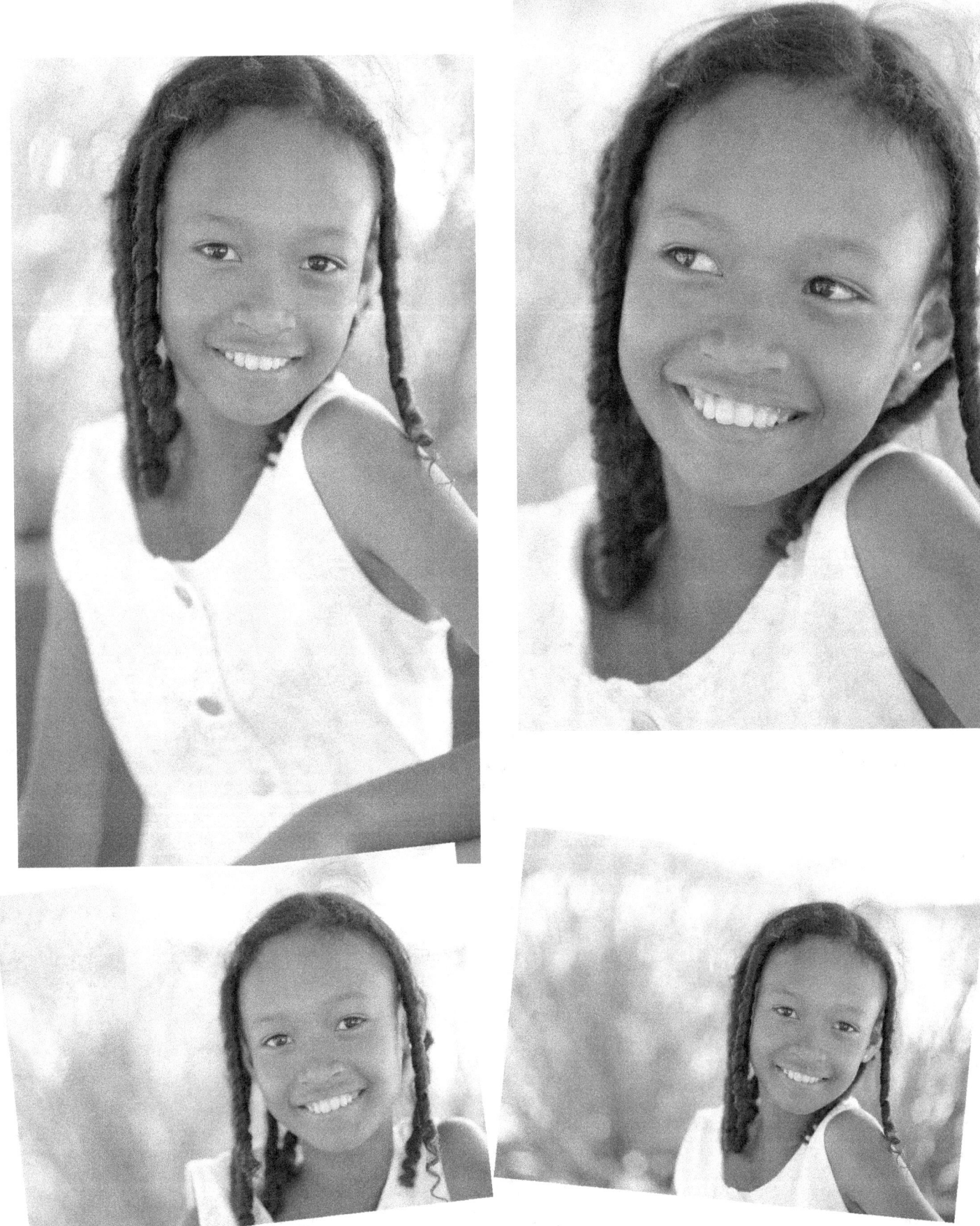

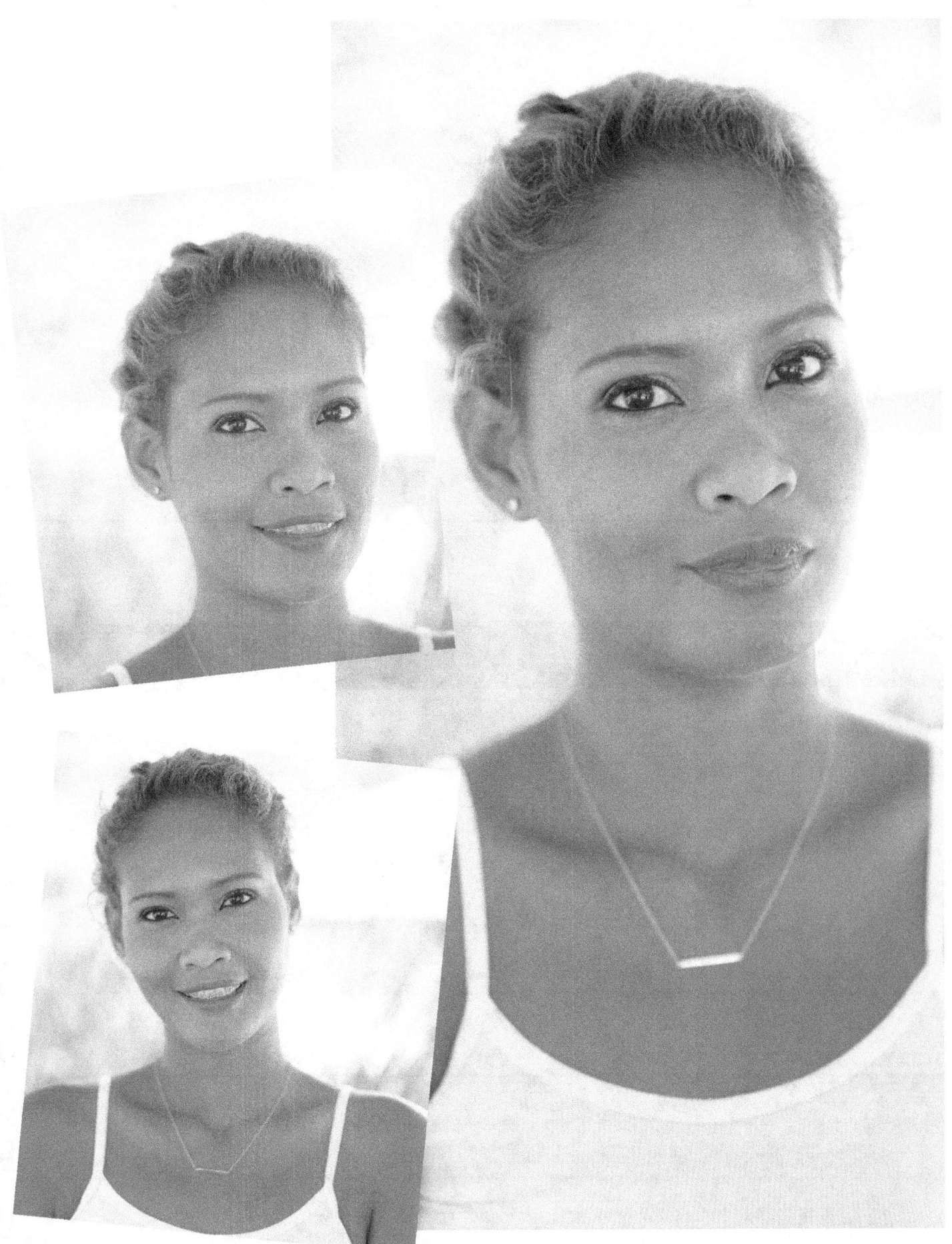

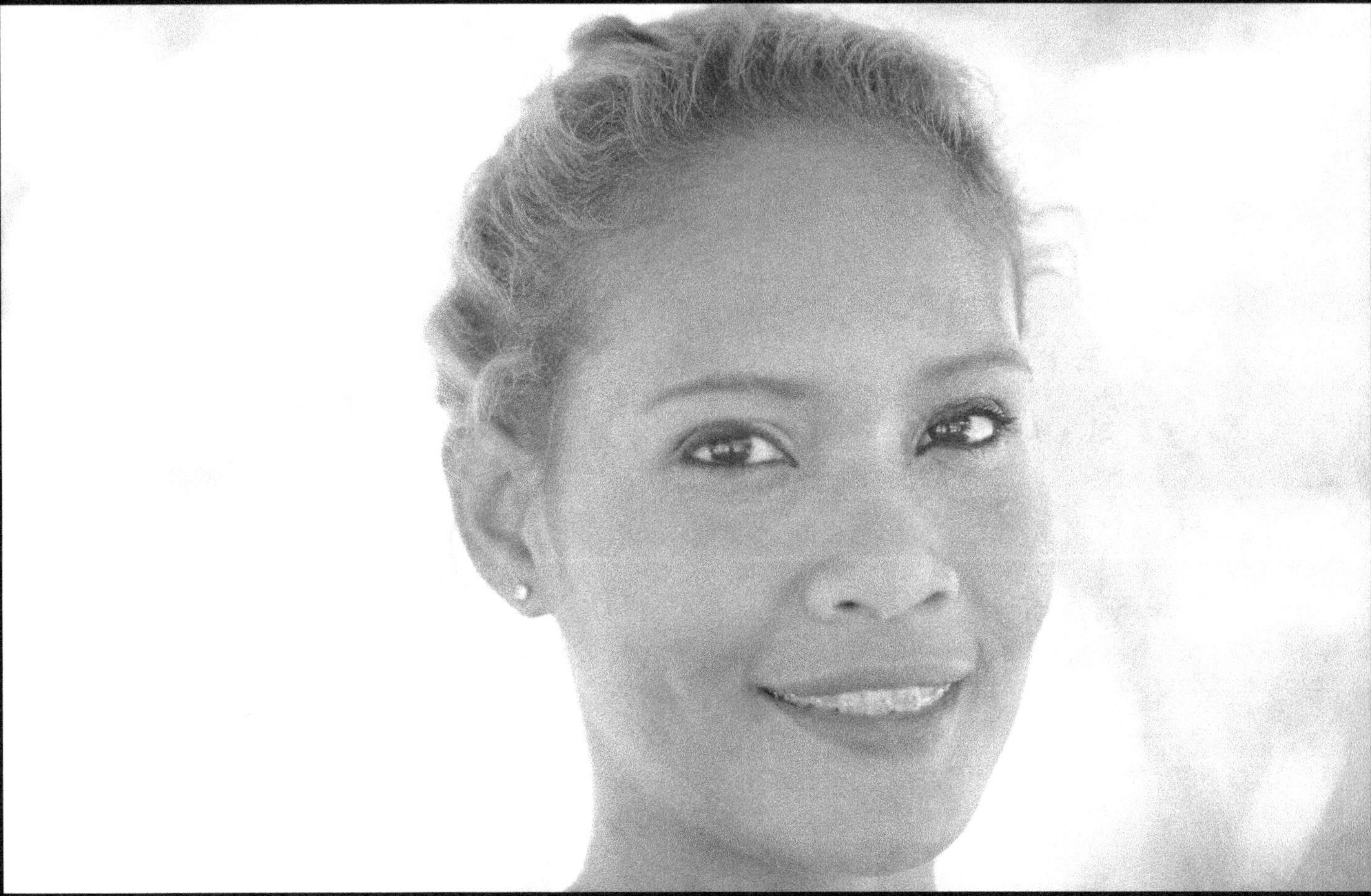

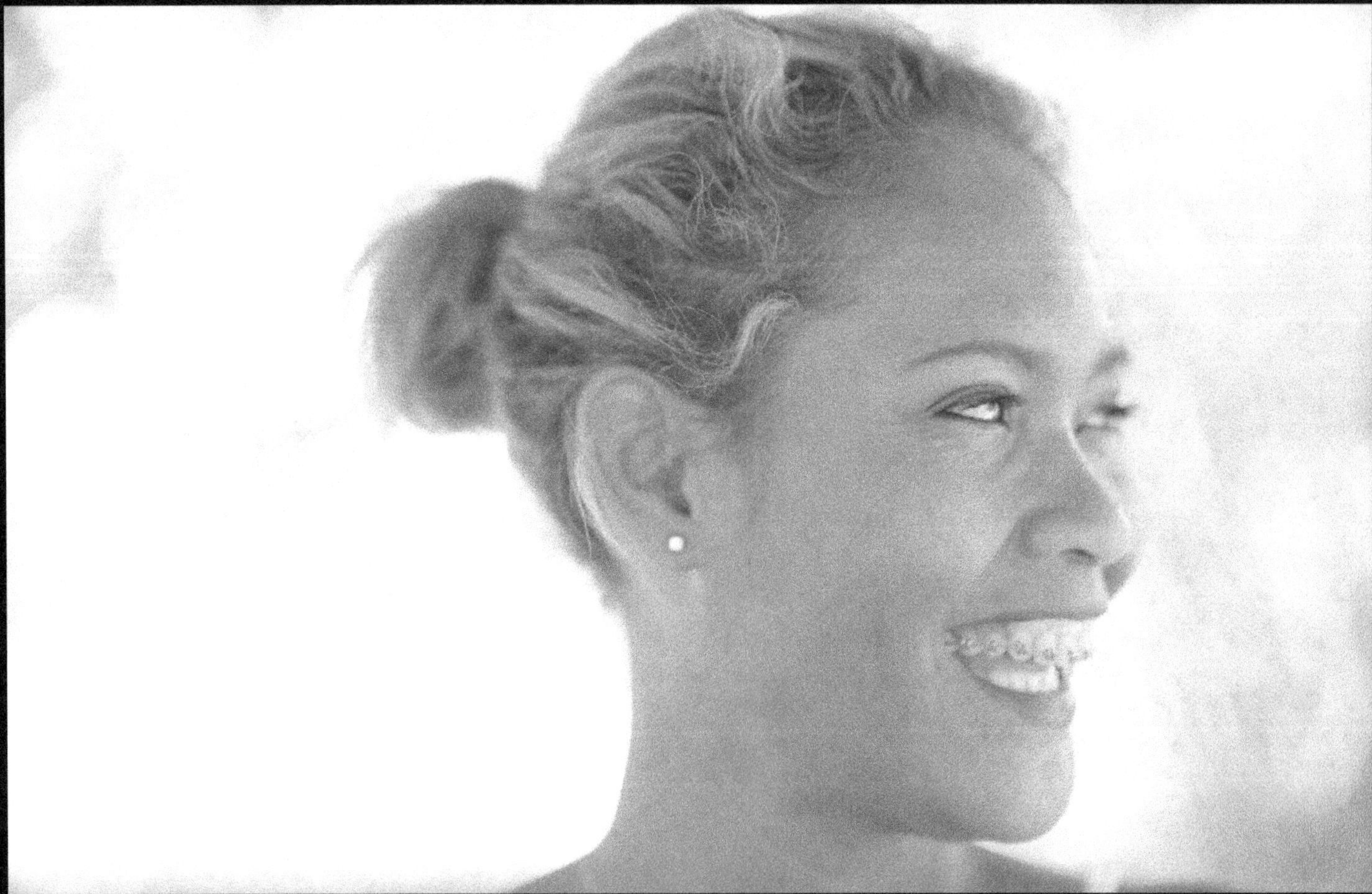

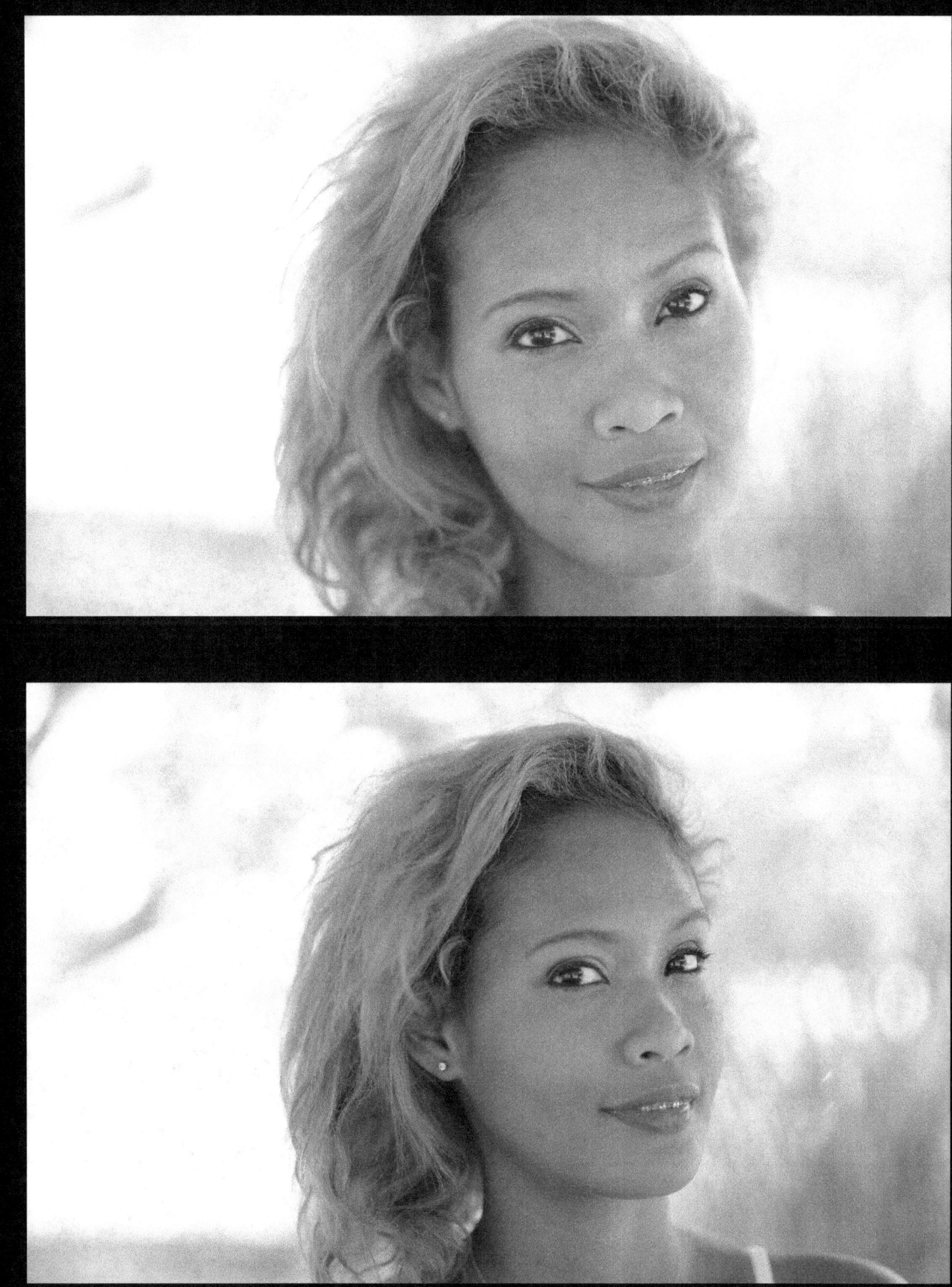

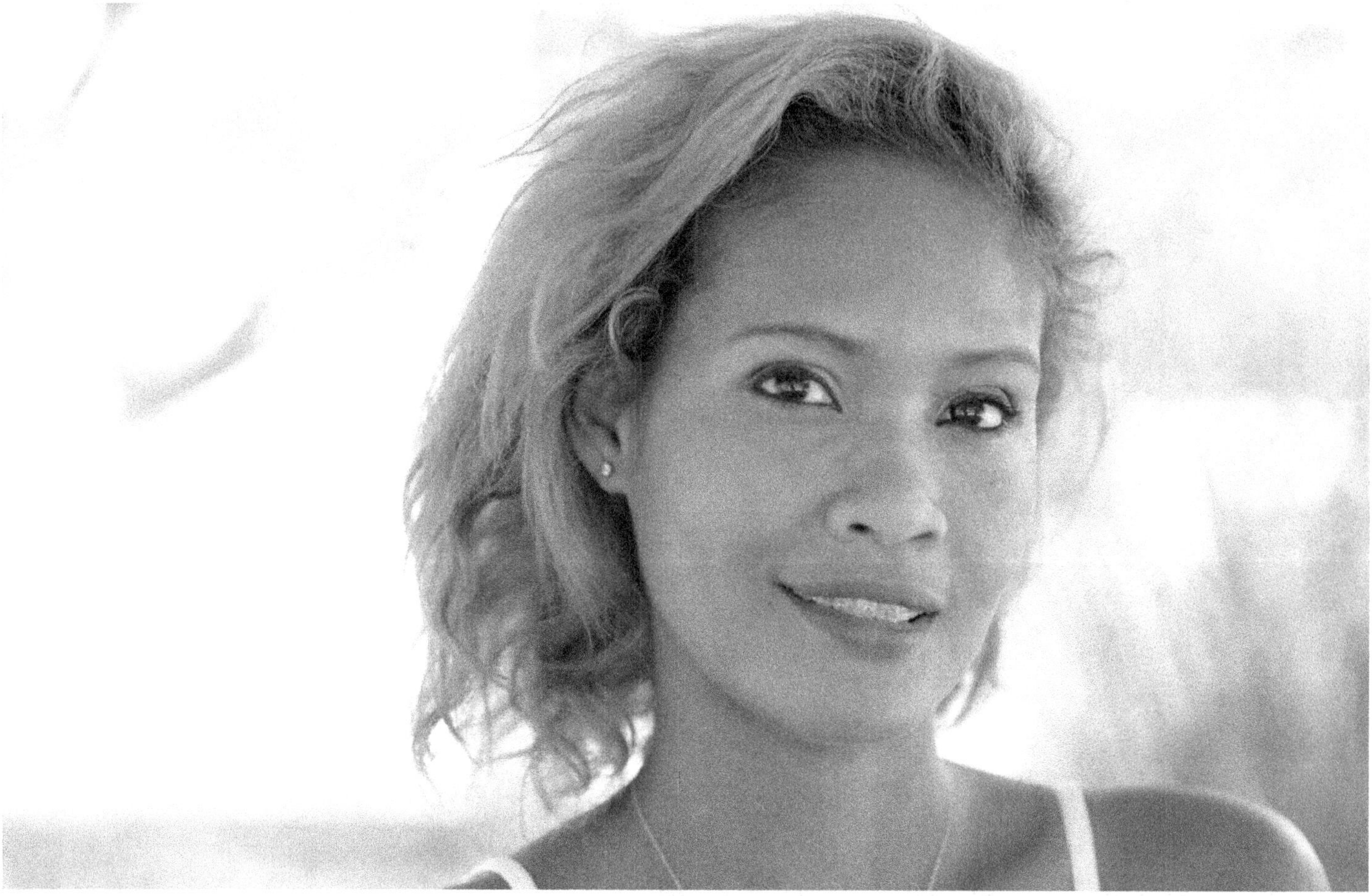

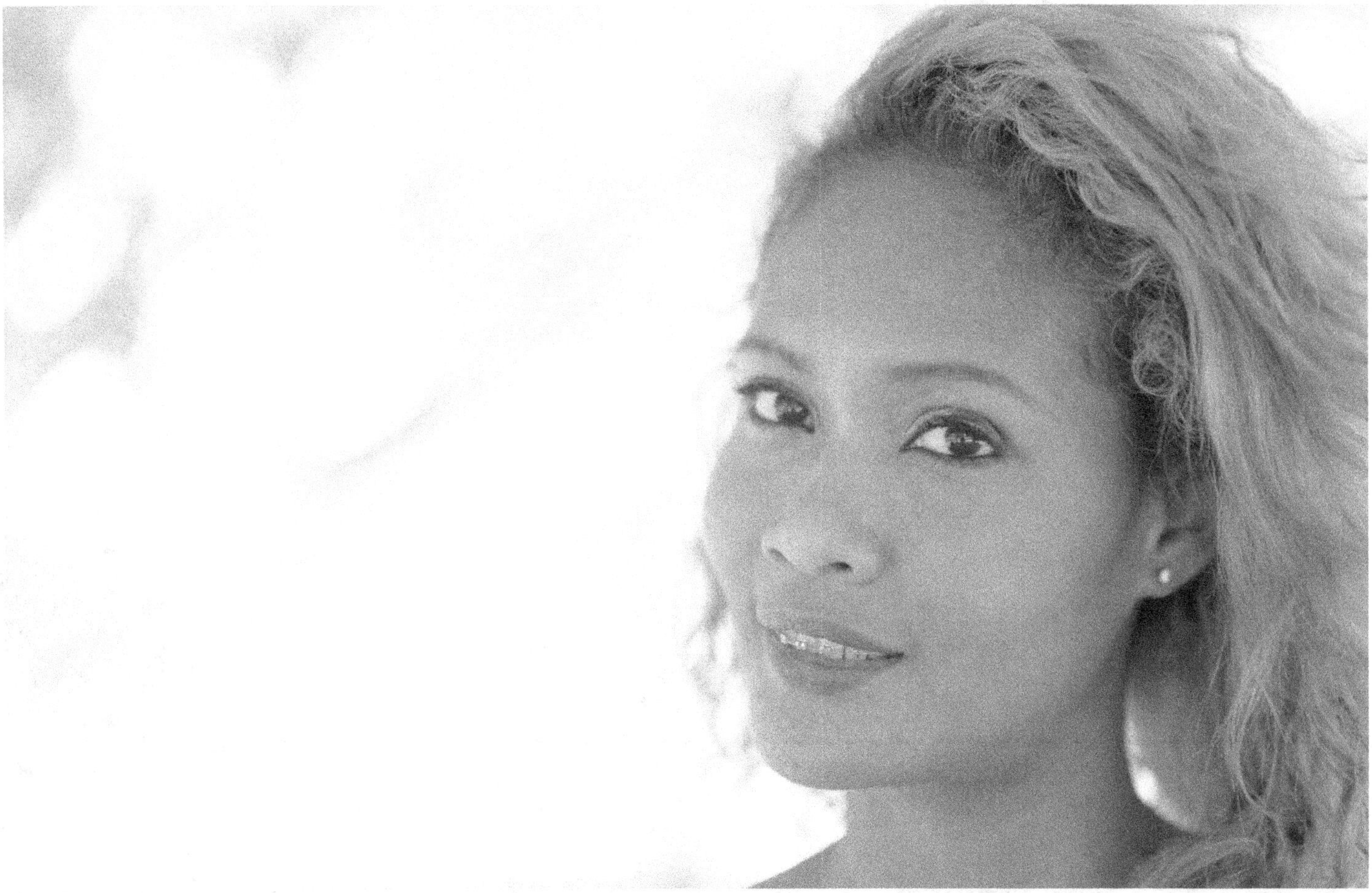

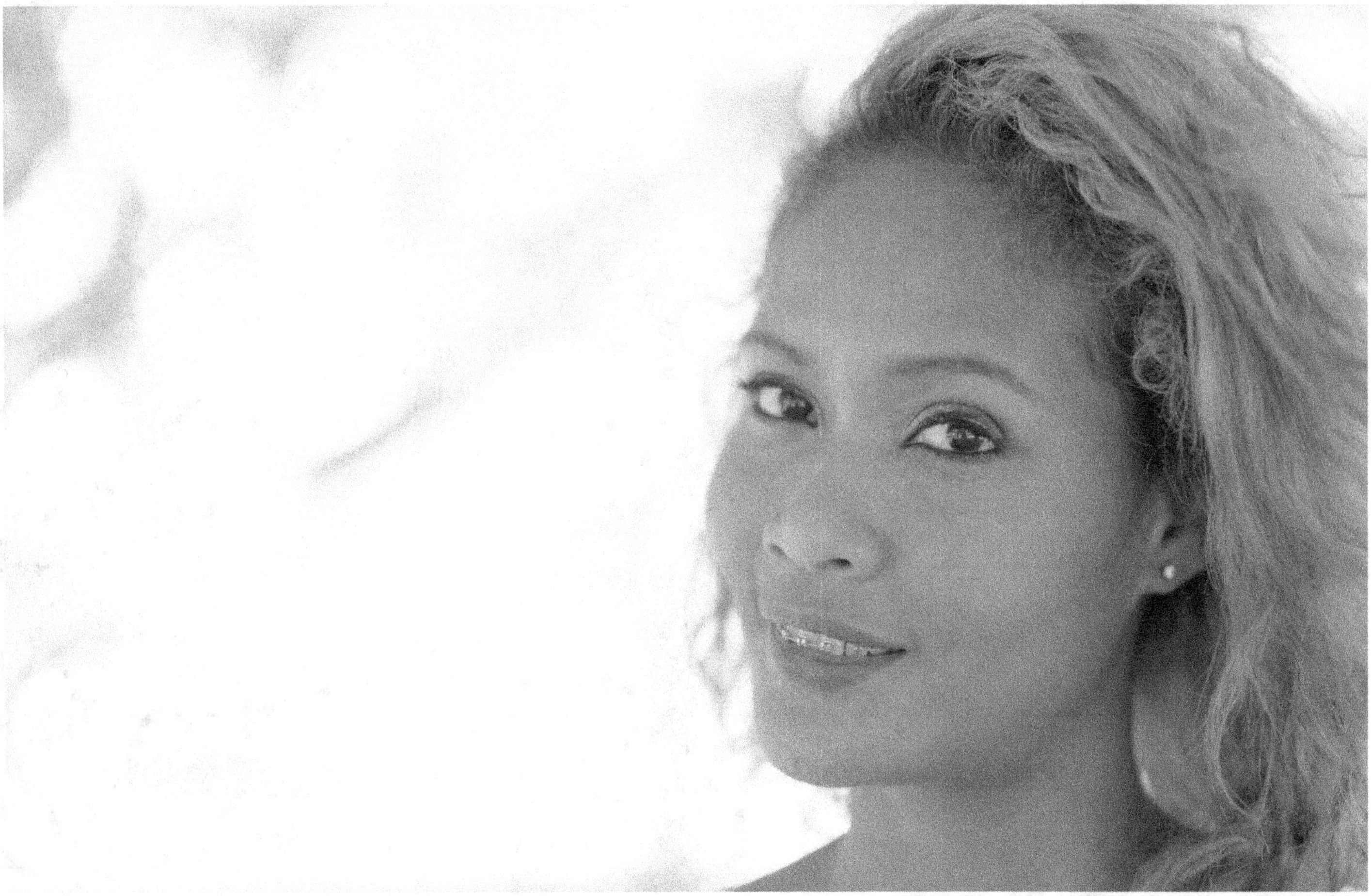

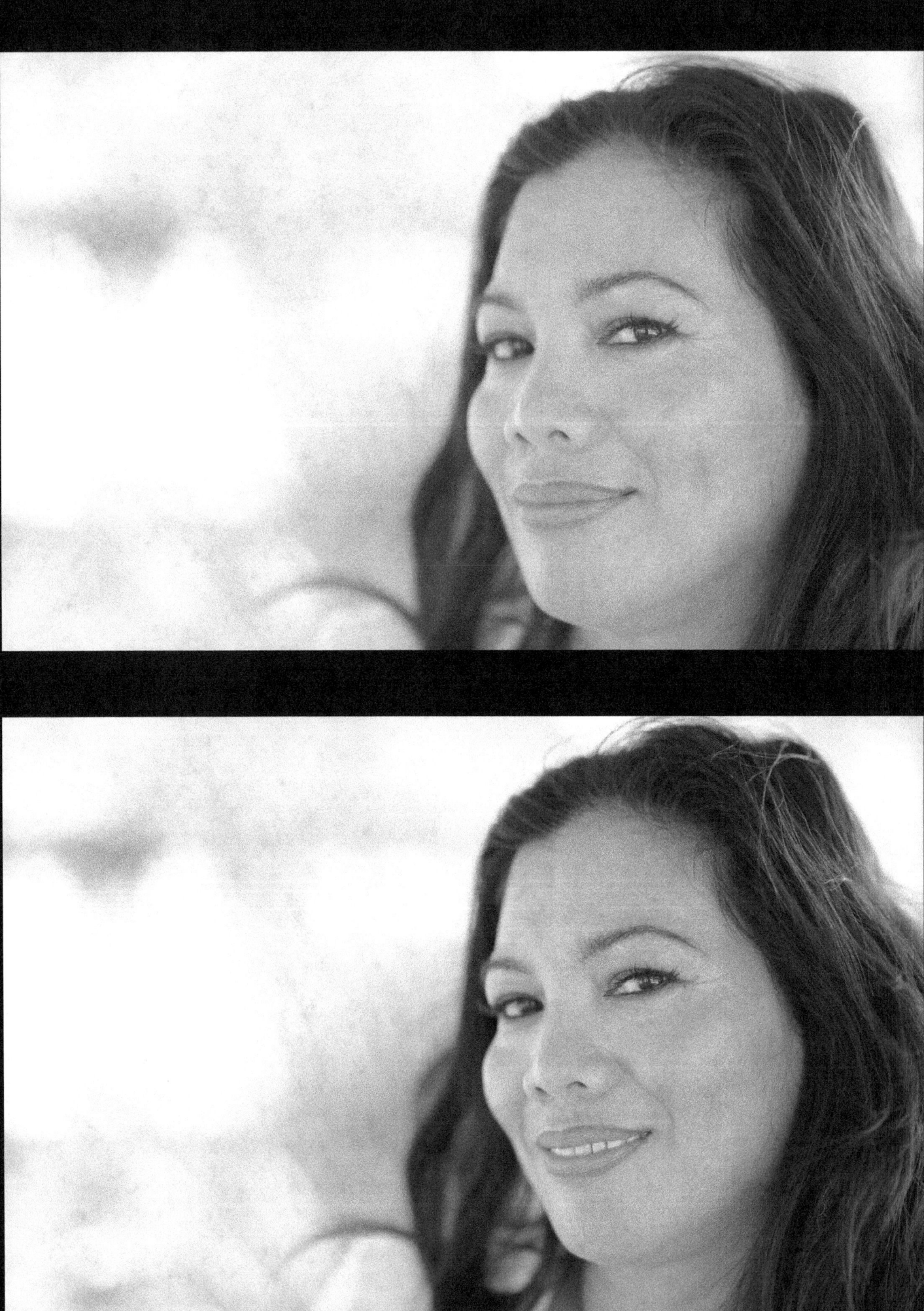

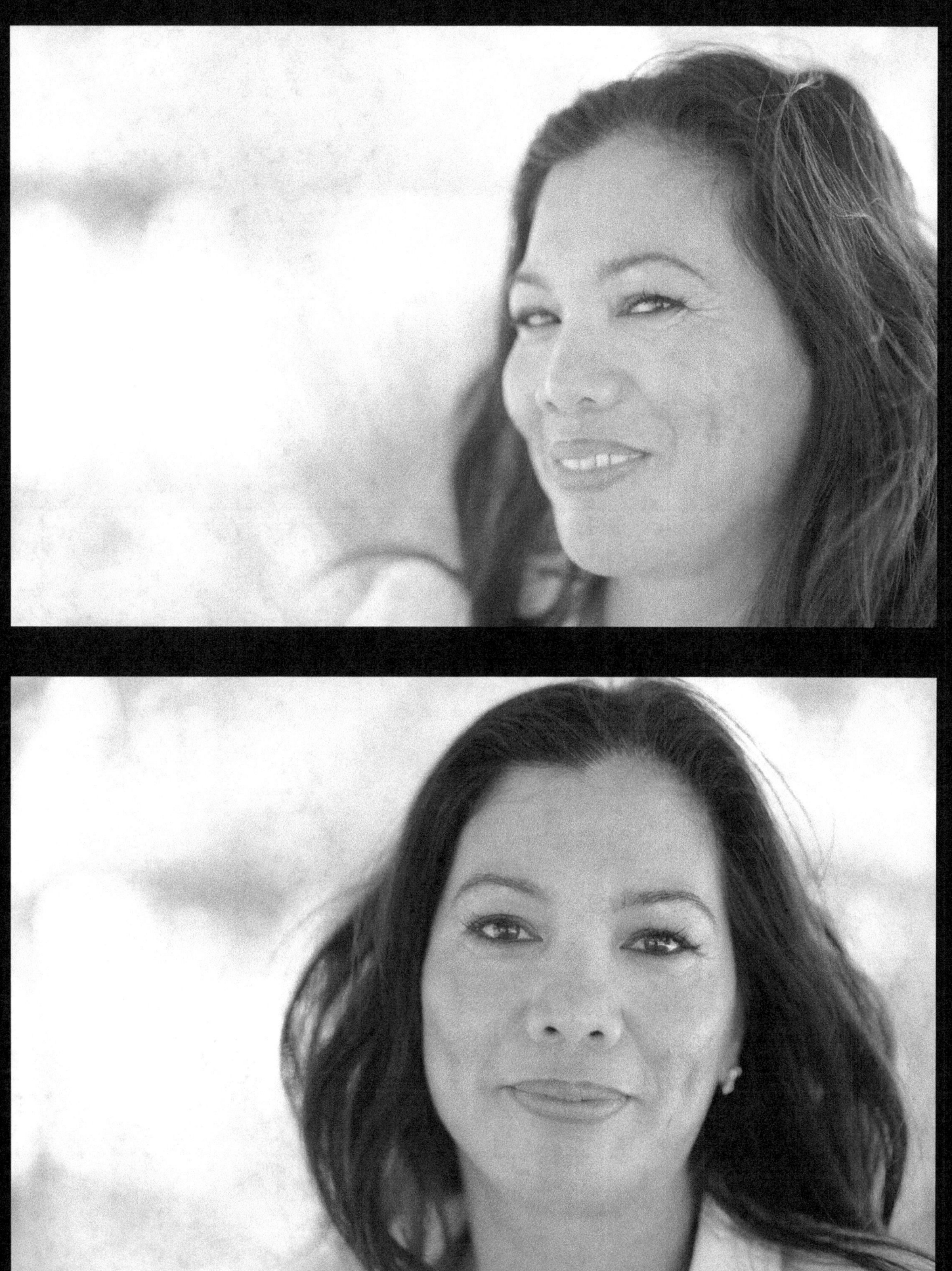

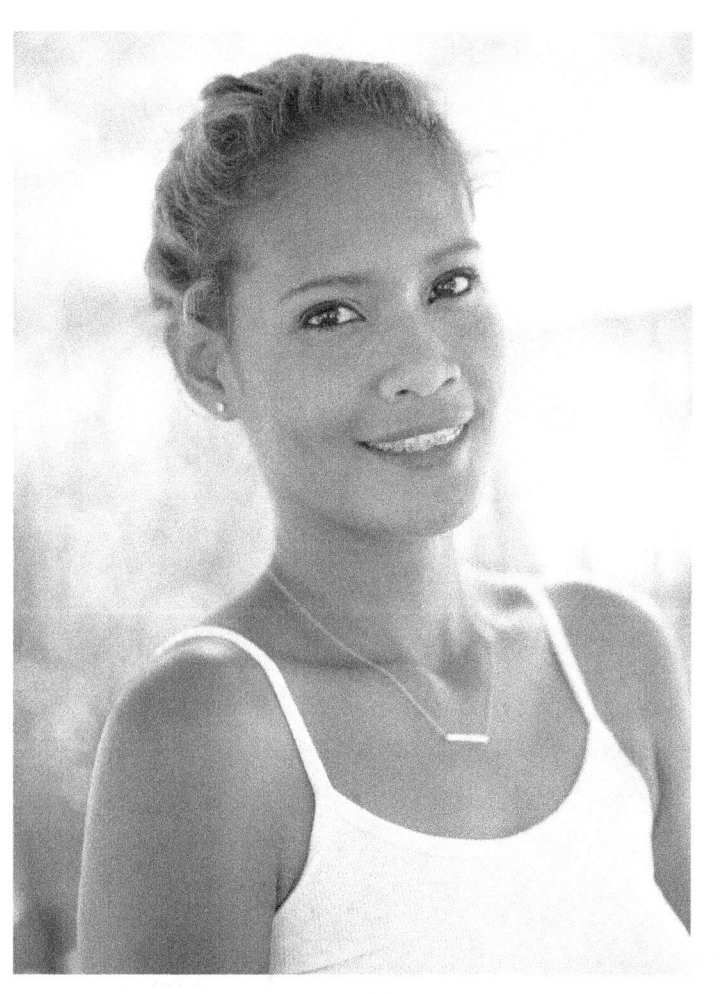

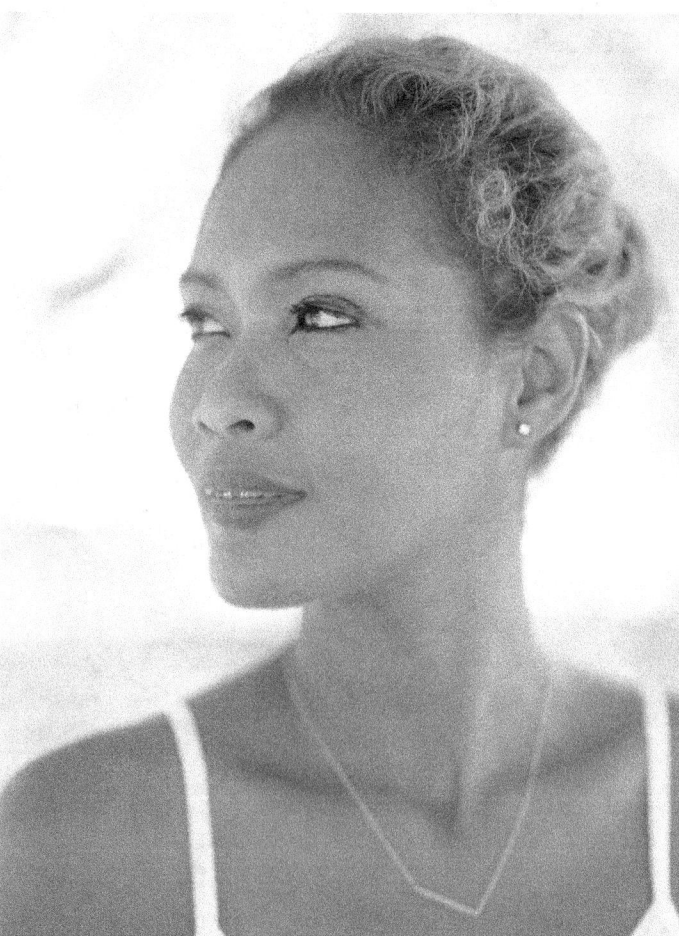

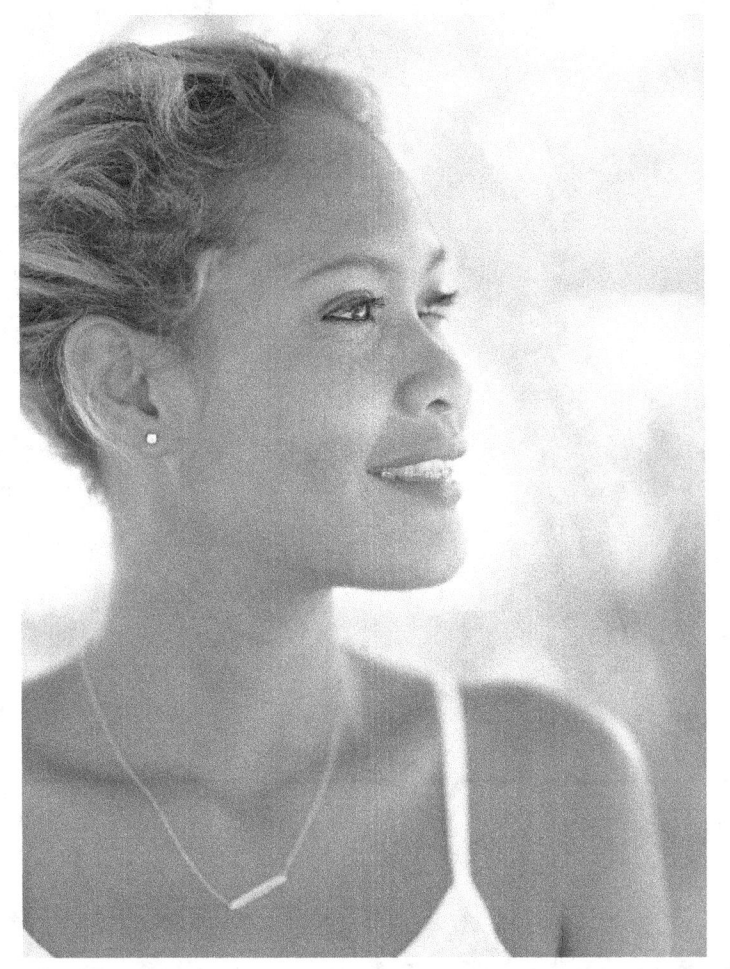
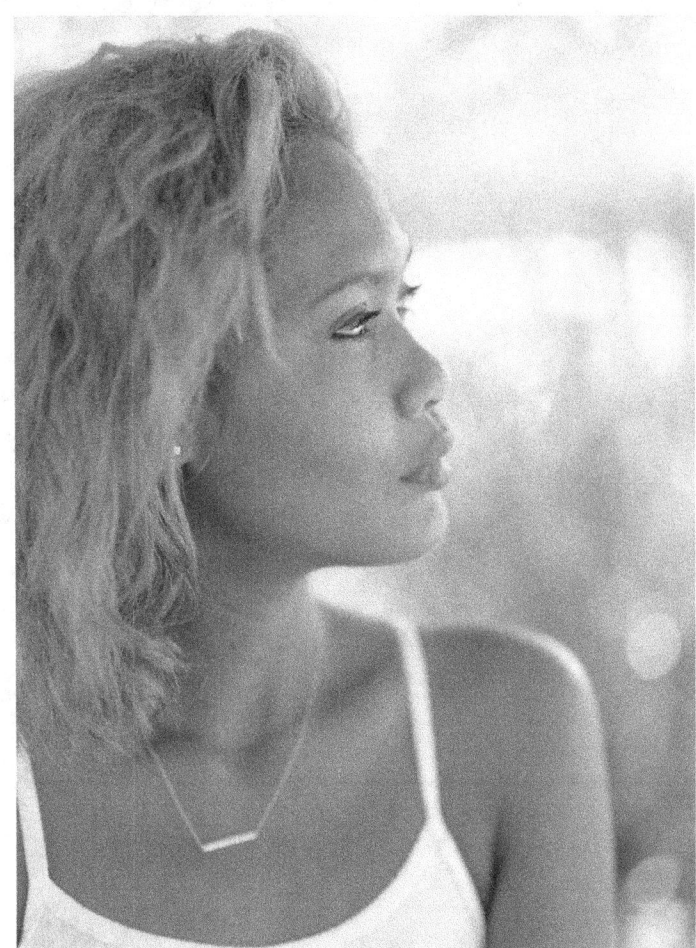
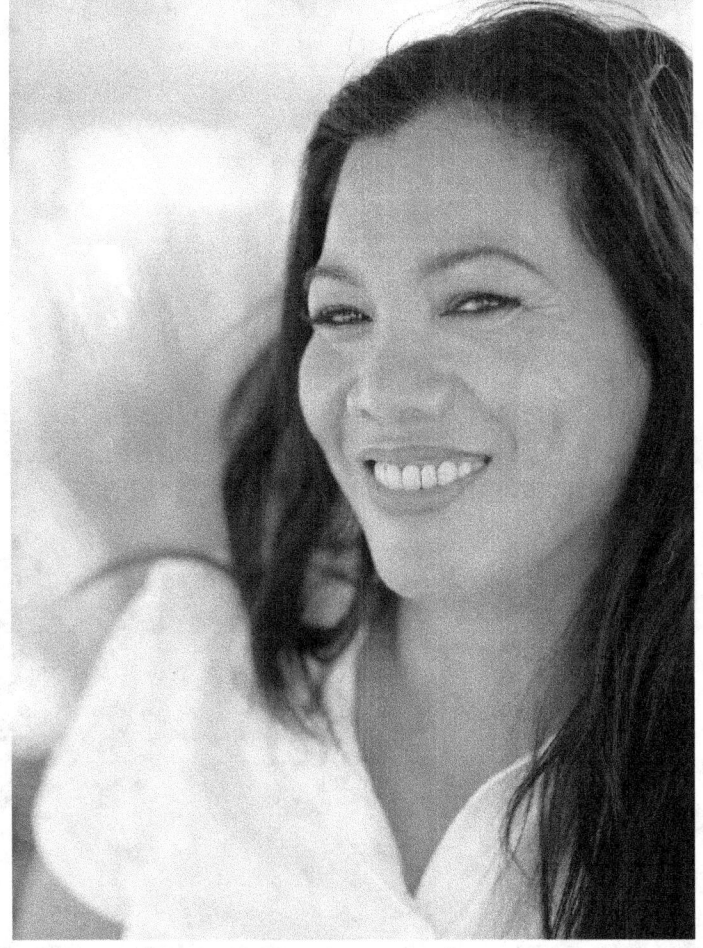
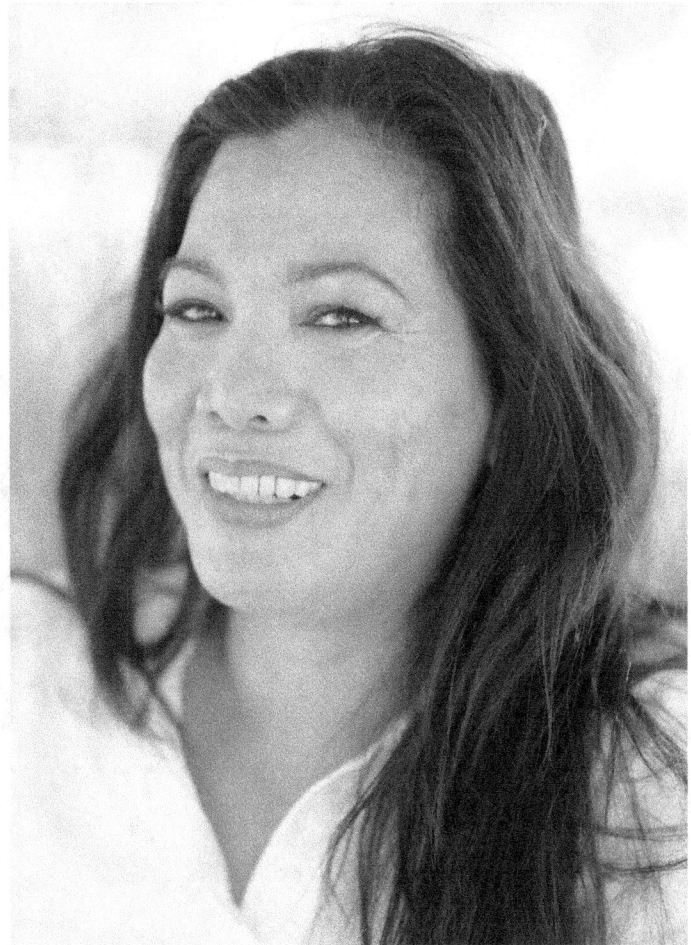

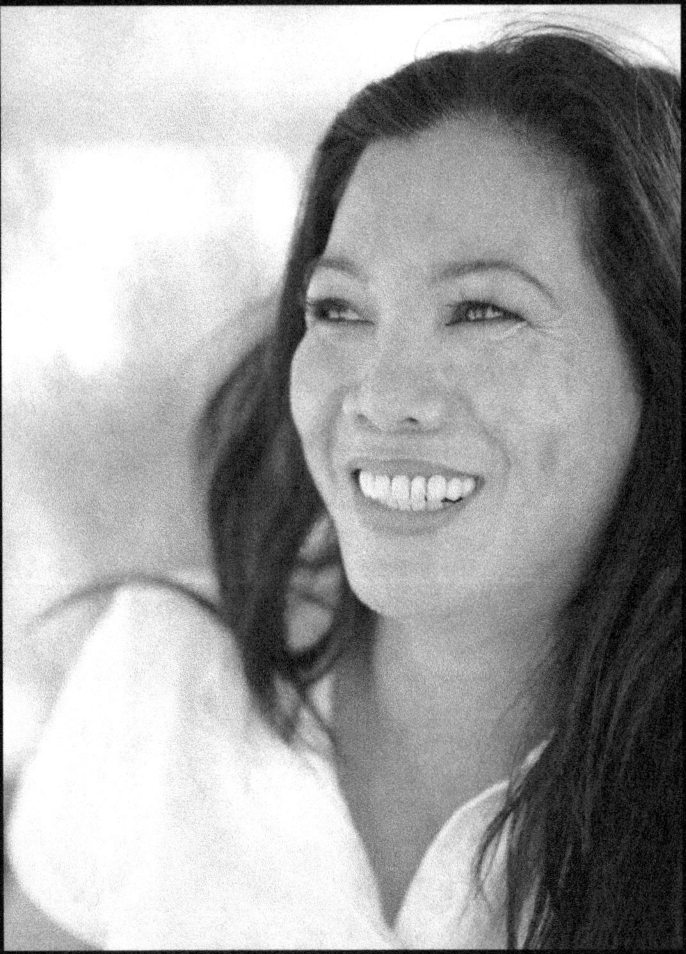

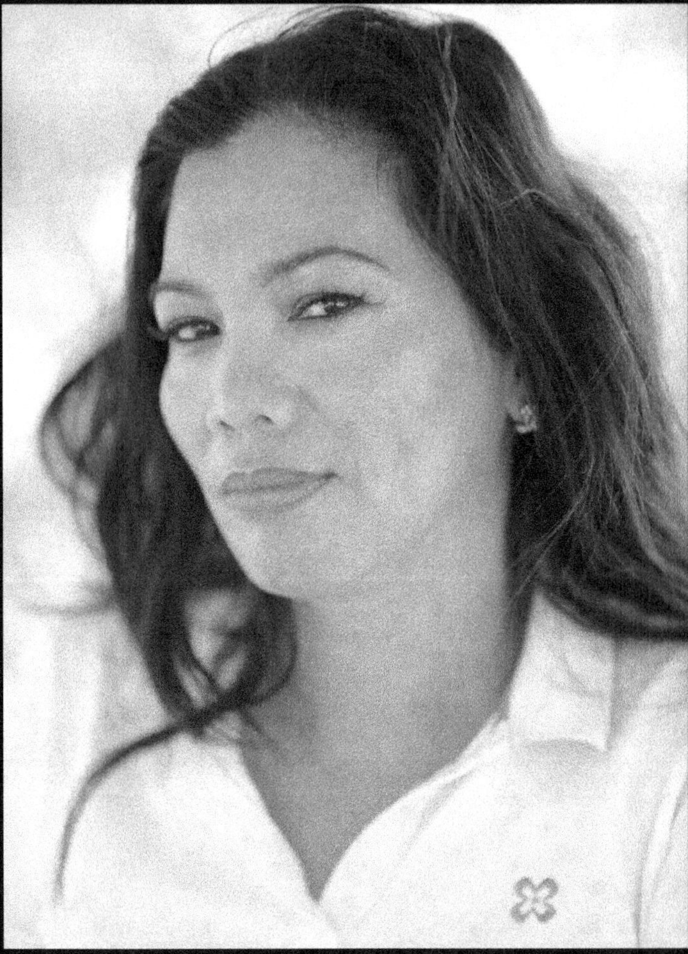

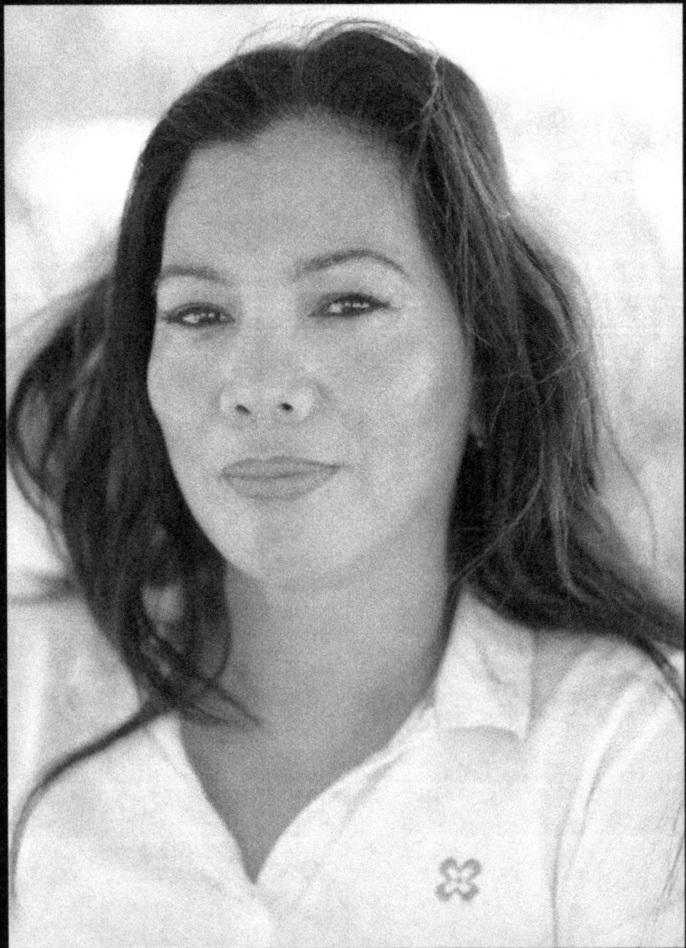

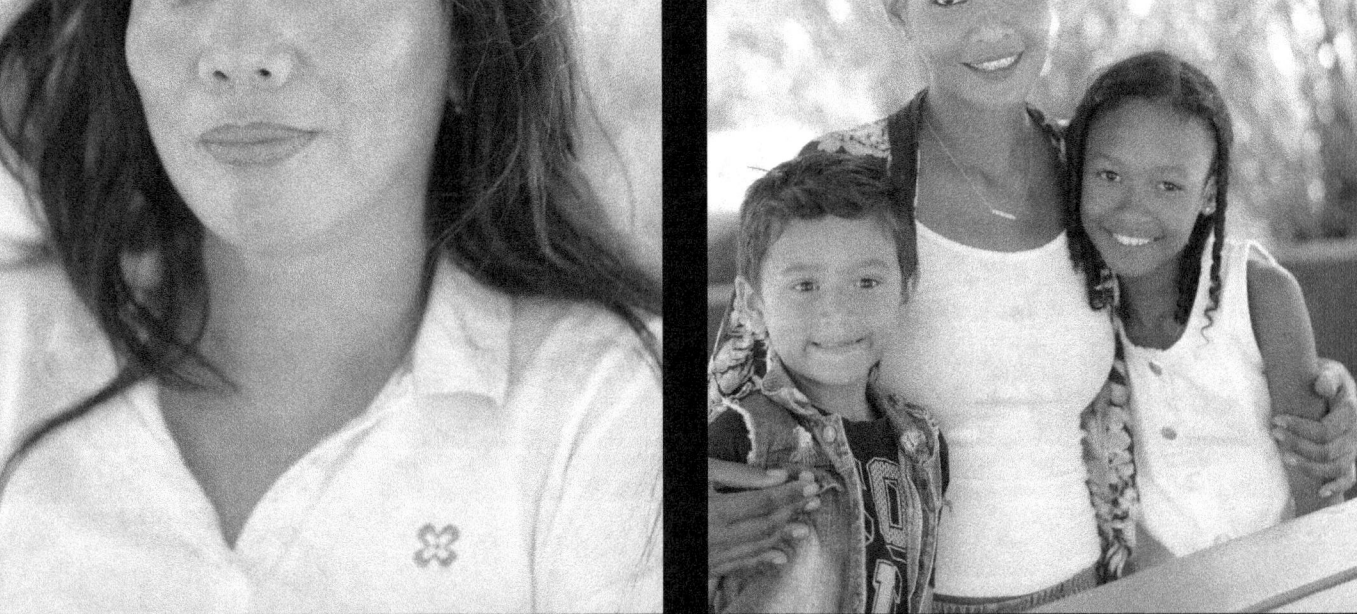

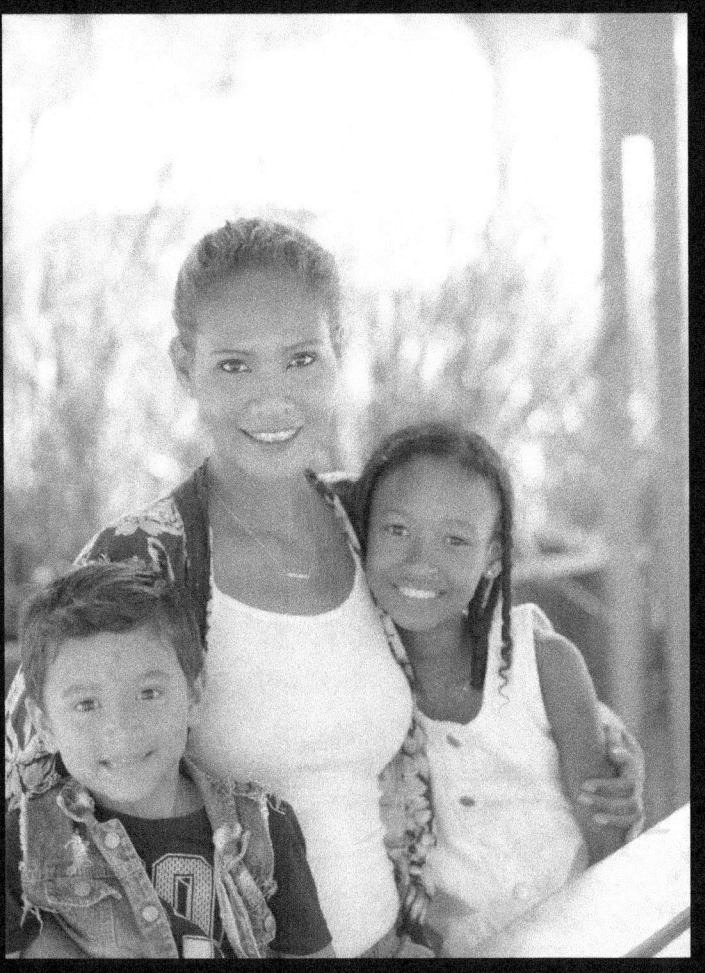
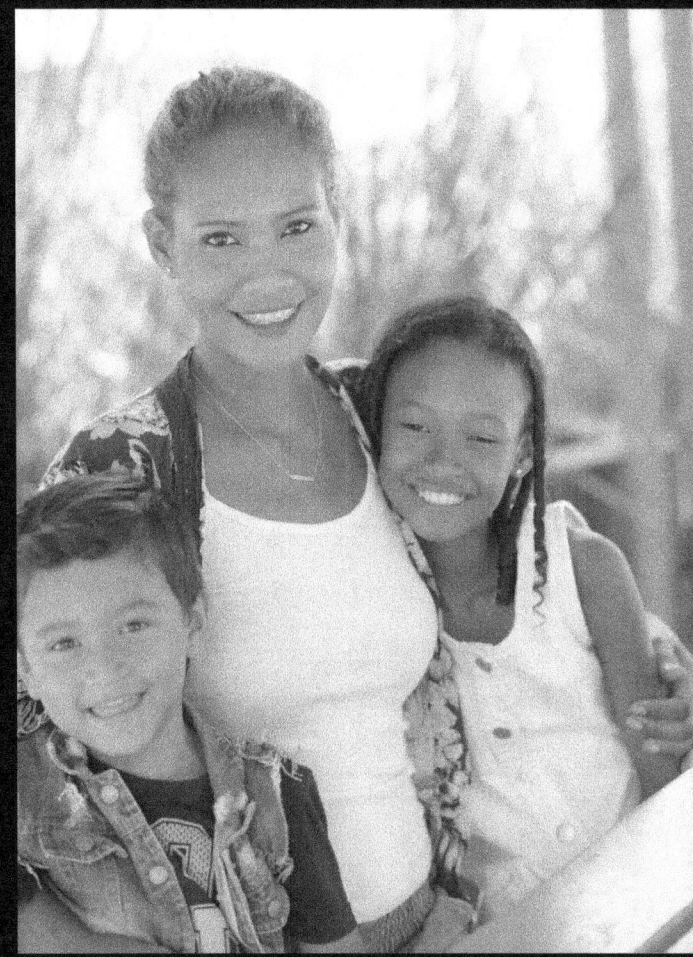

page 54

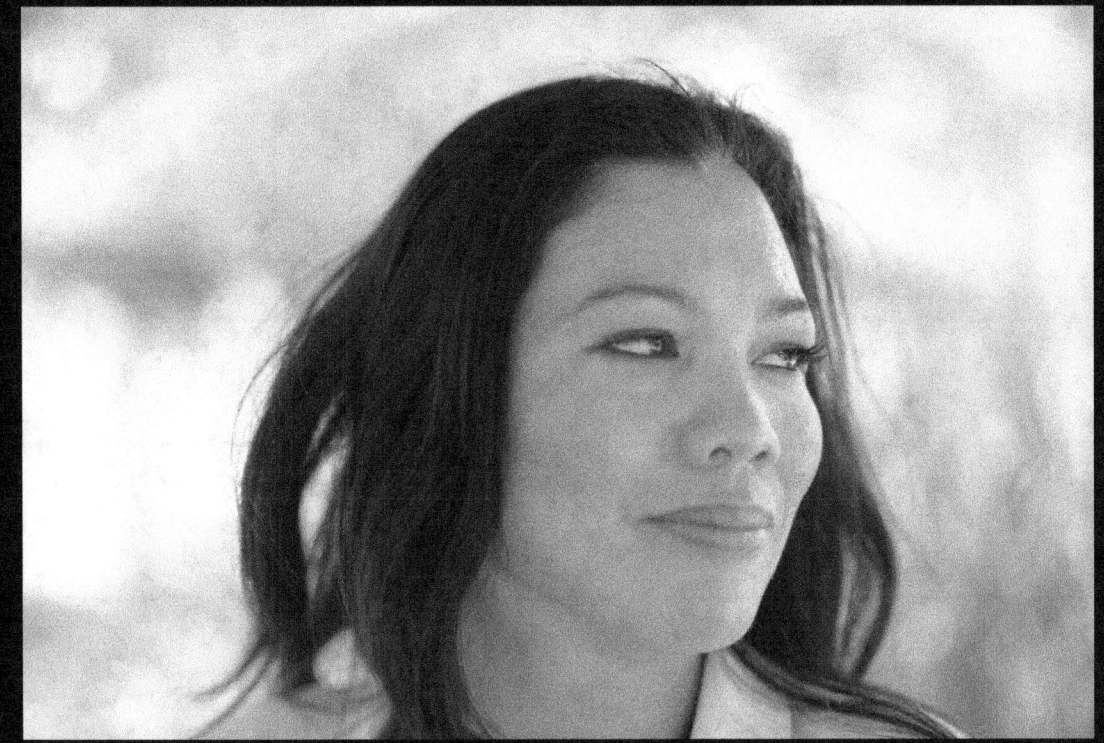

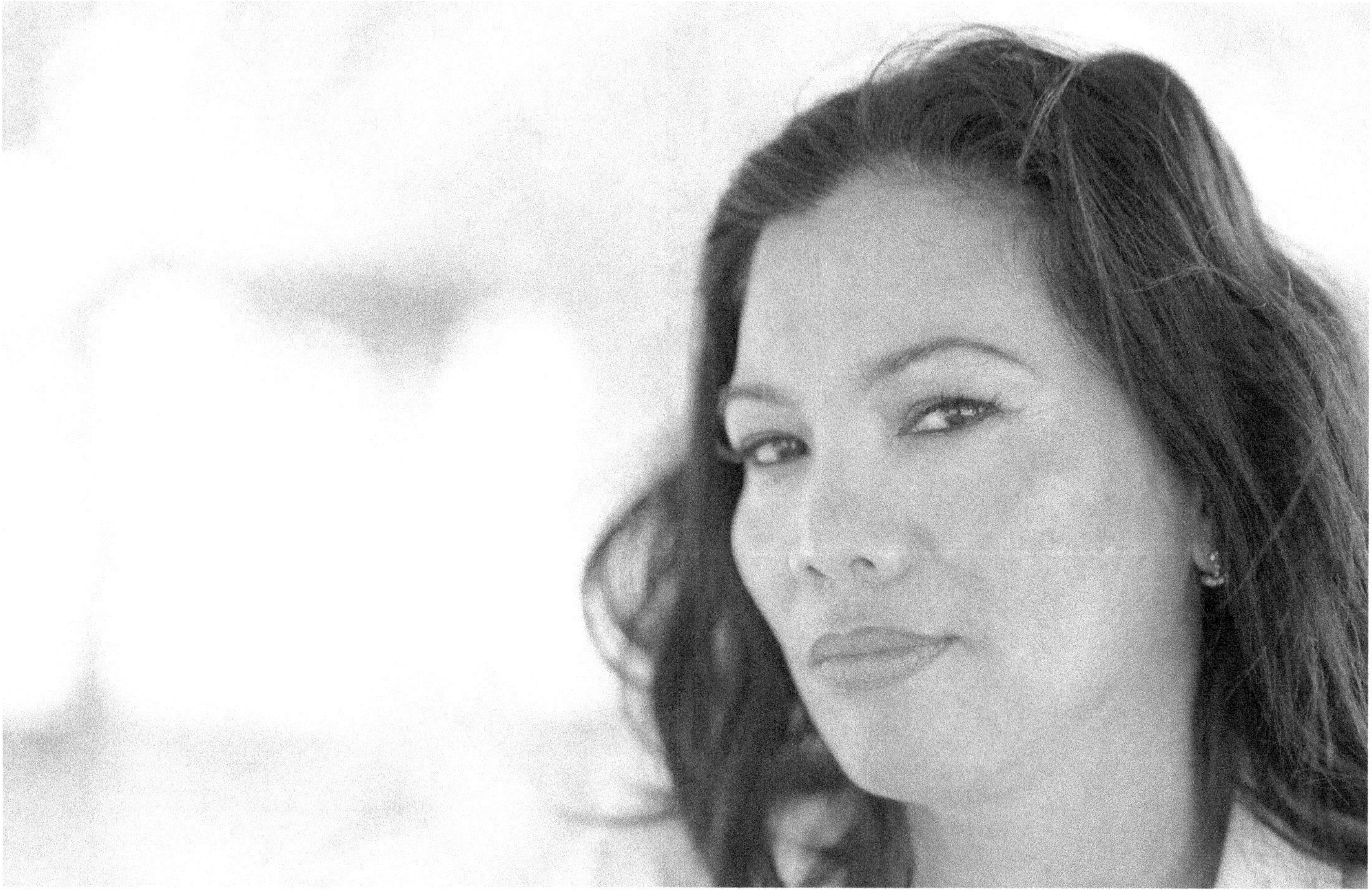

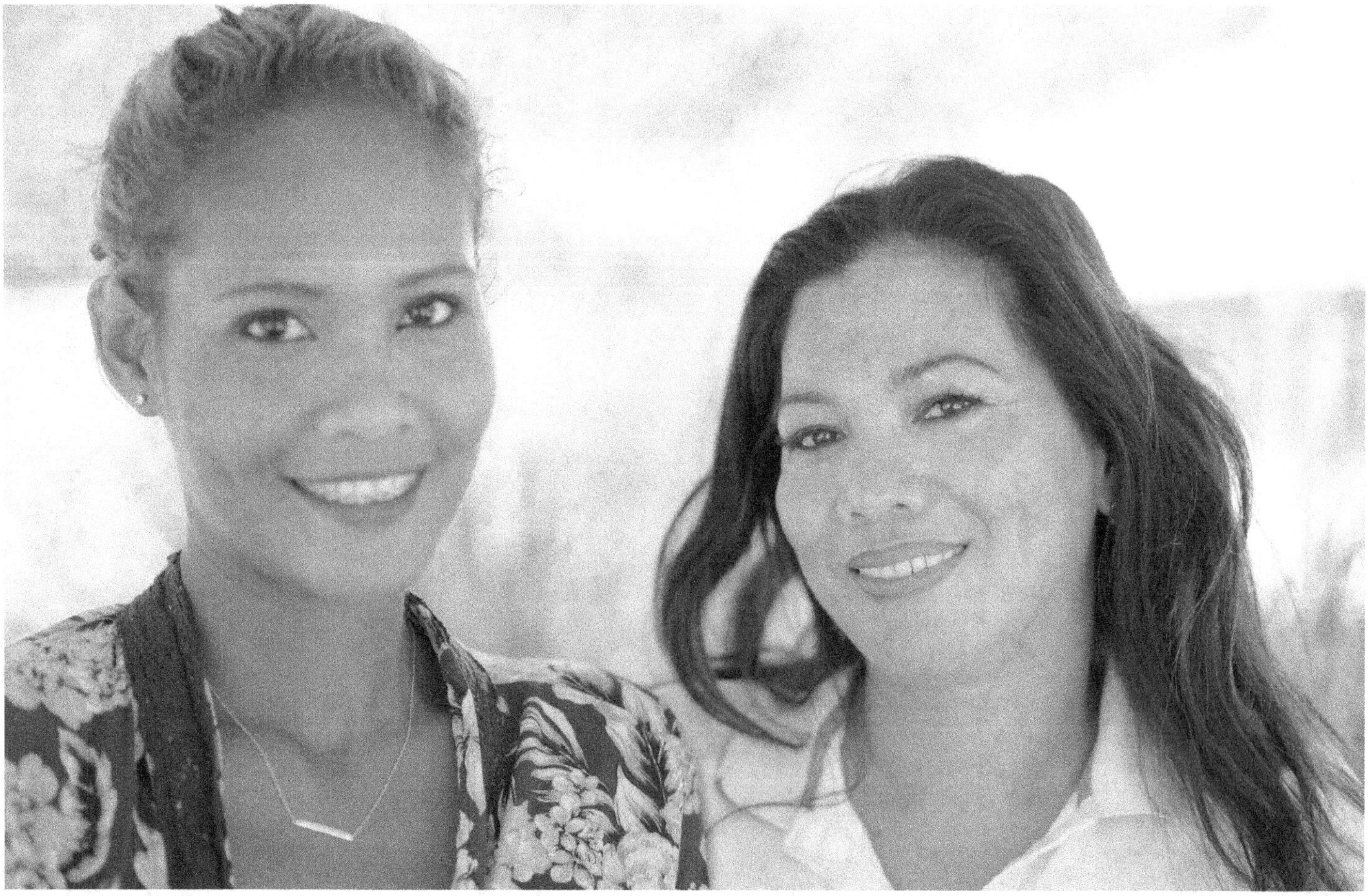

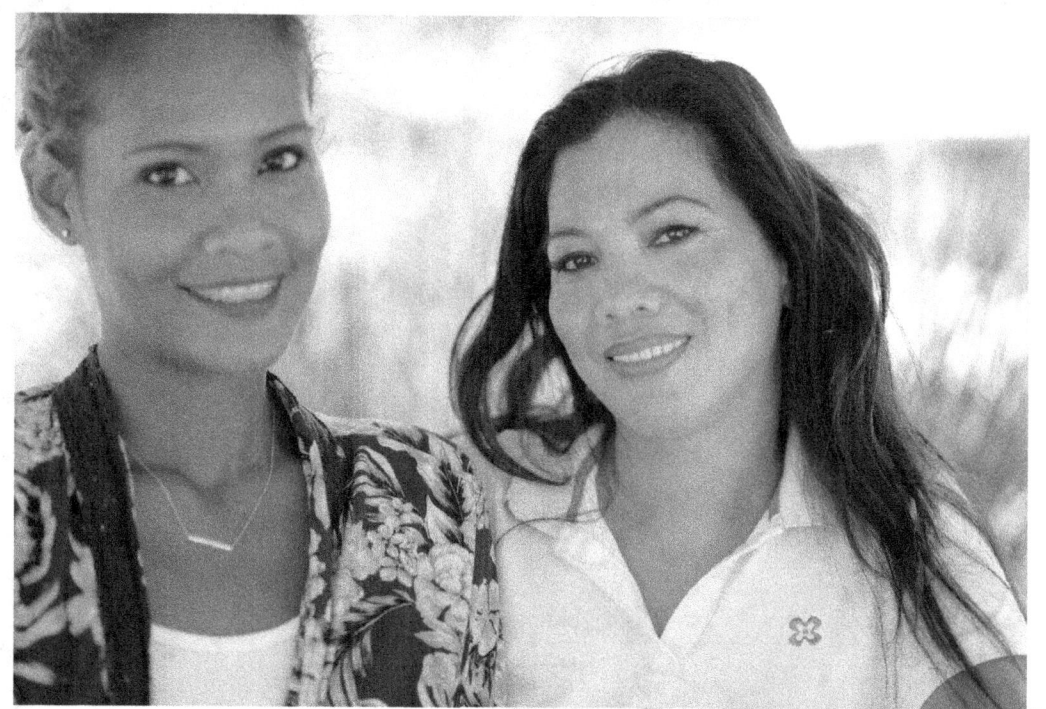

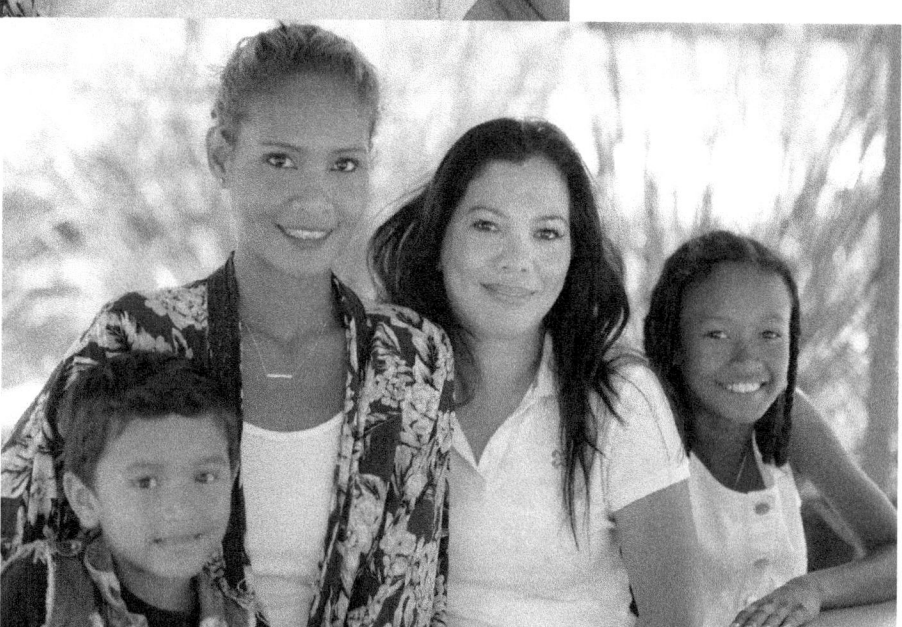

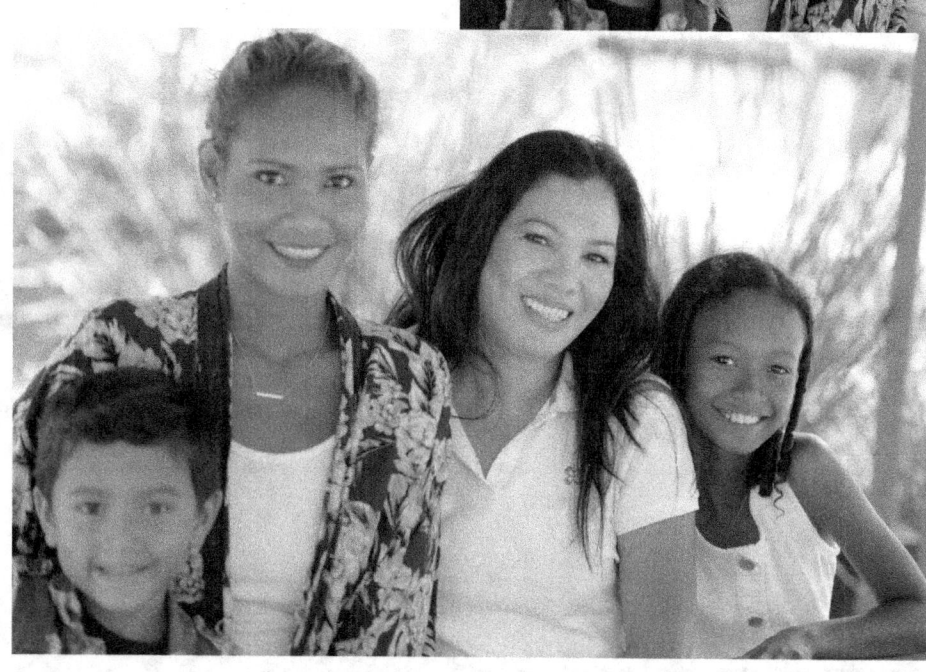

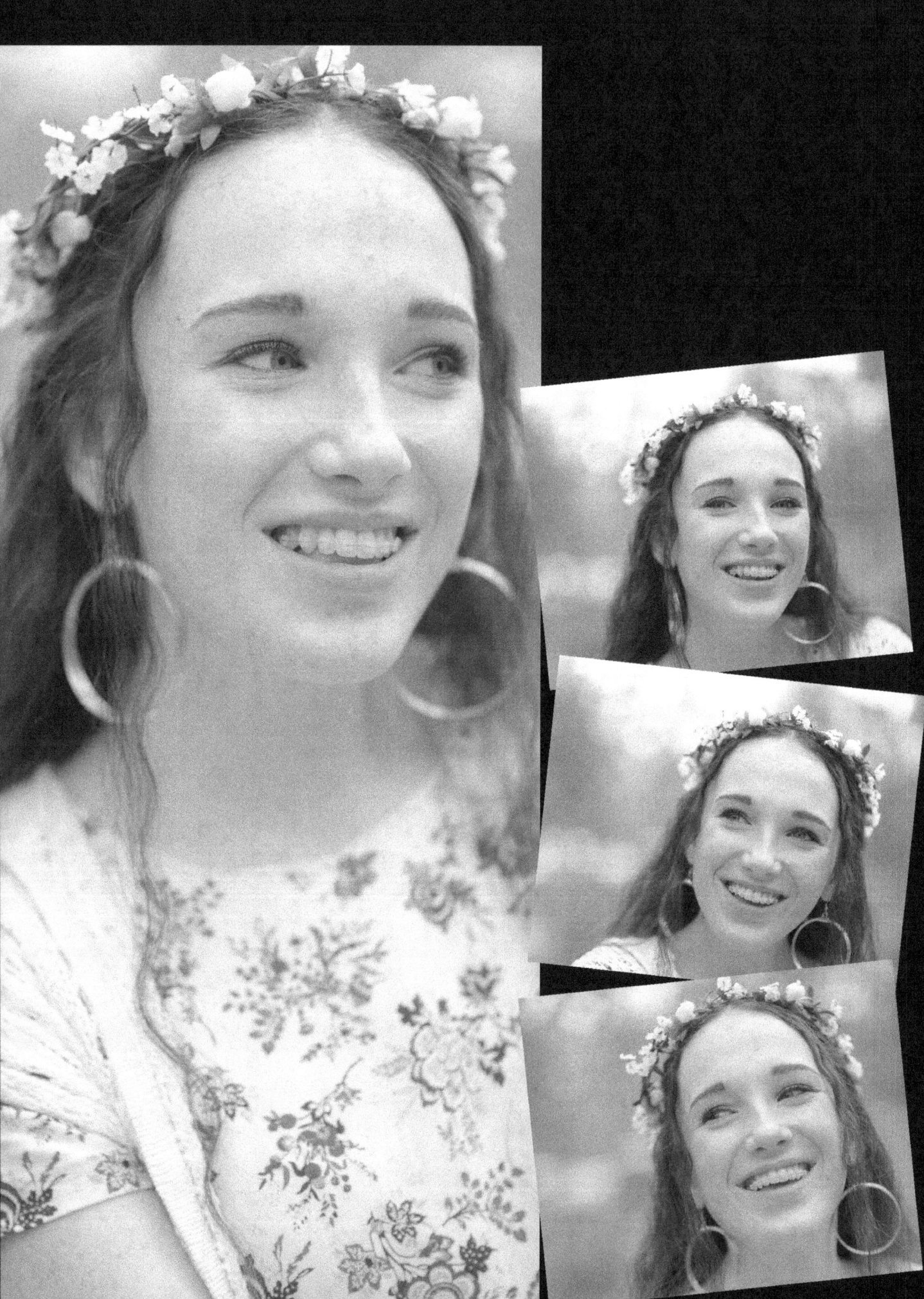

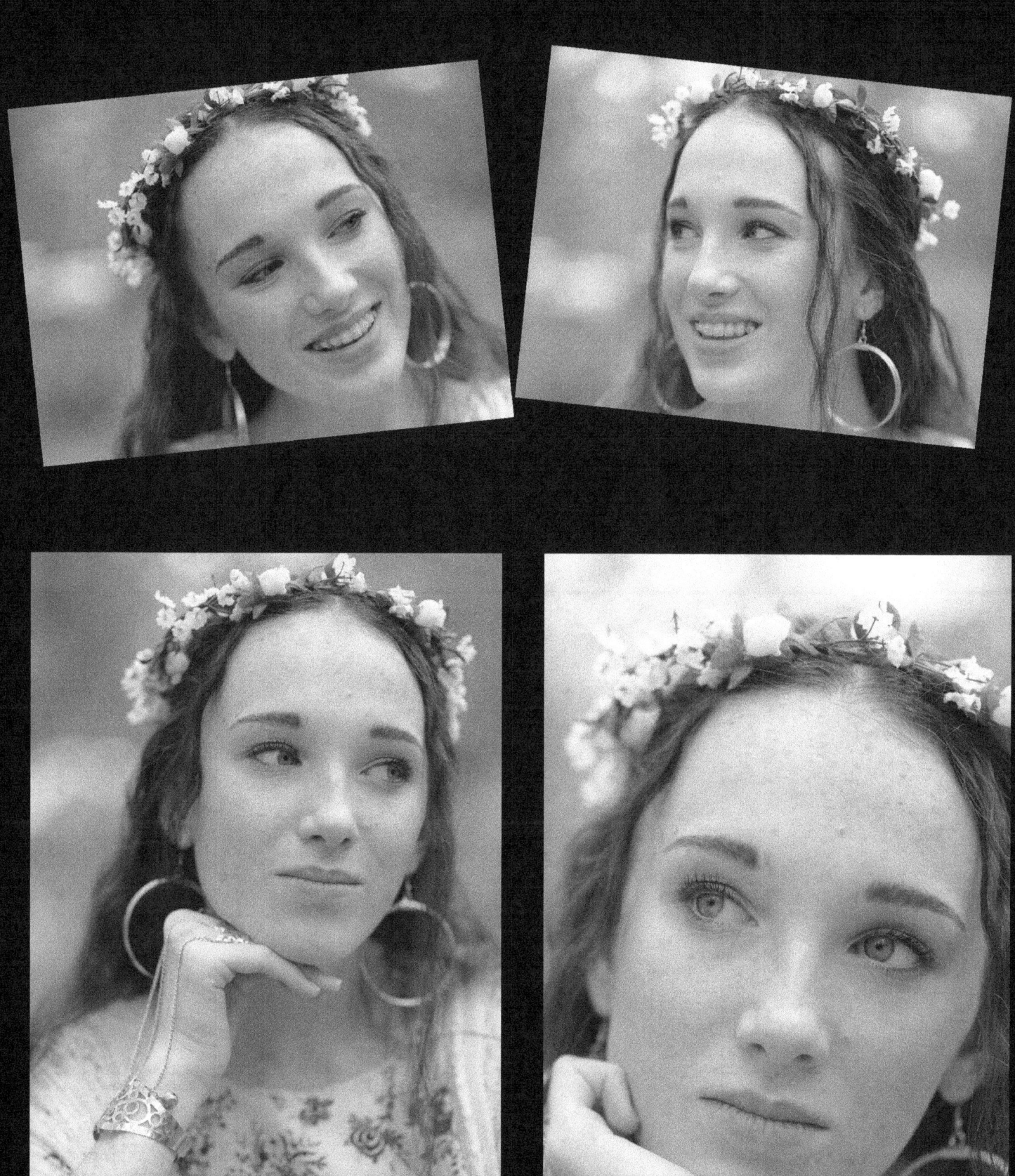

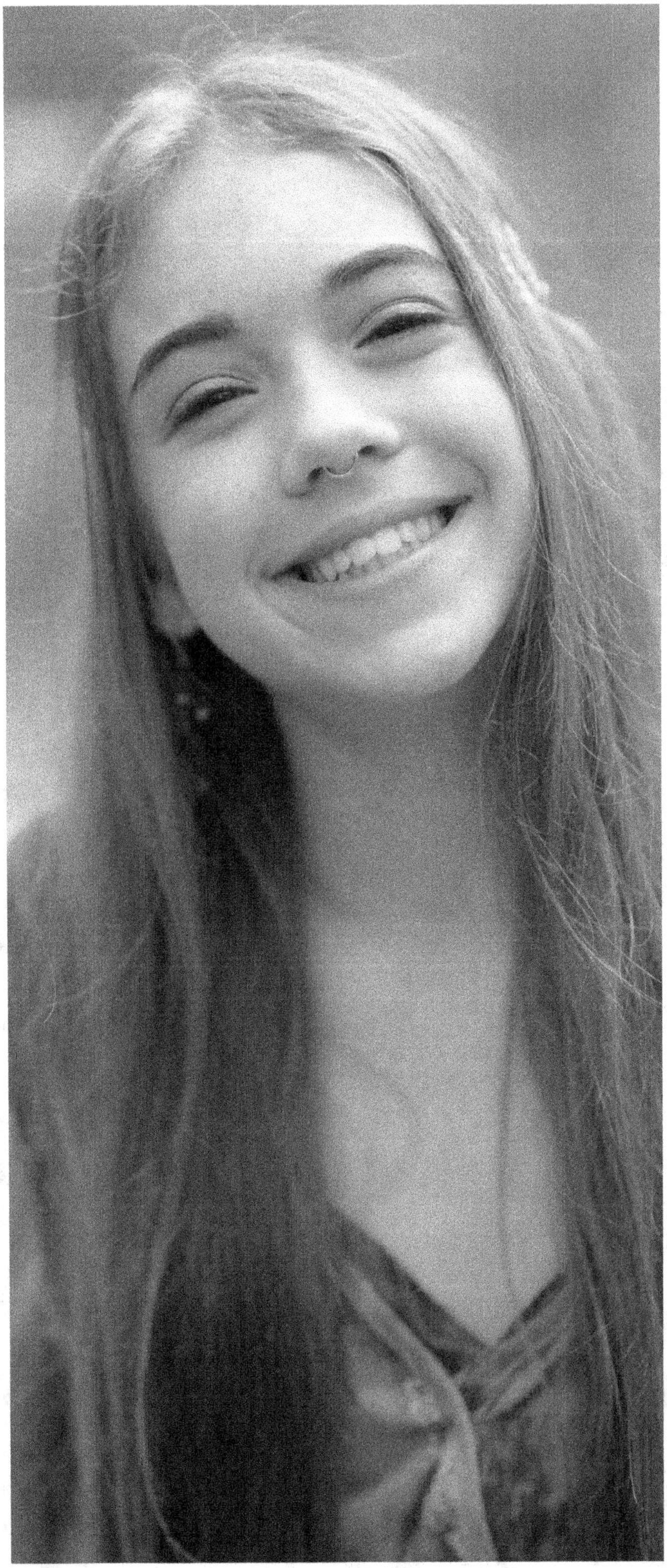

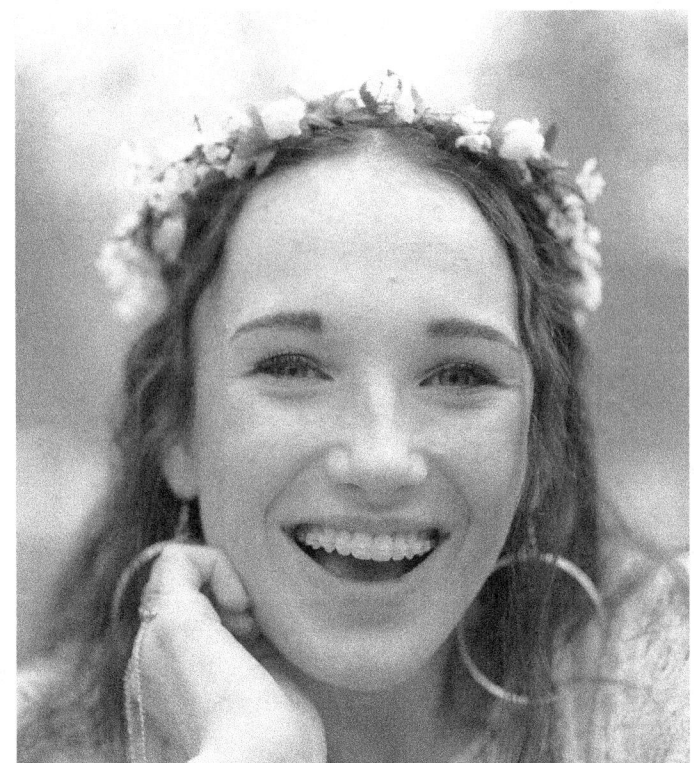
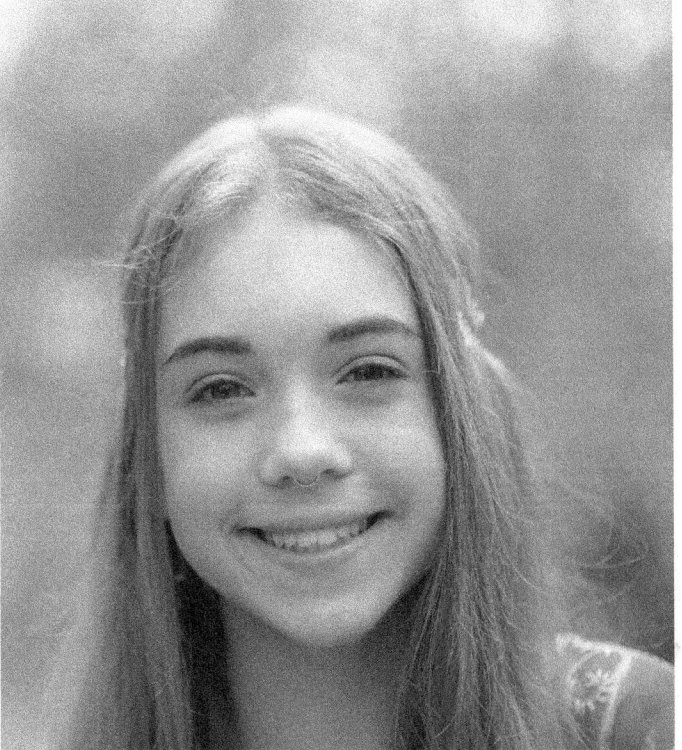

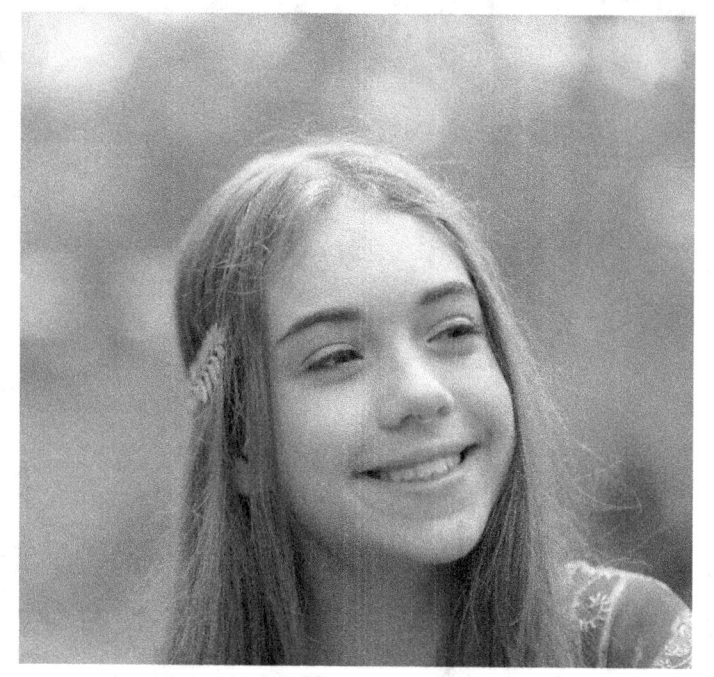

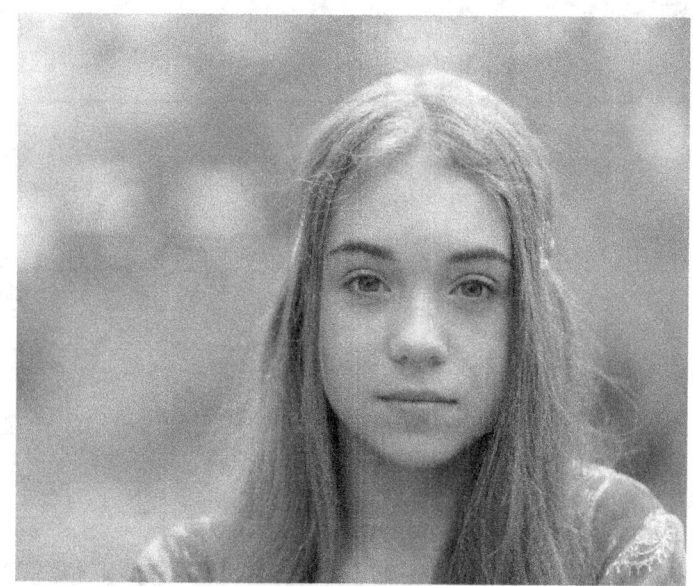

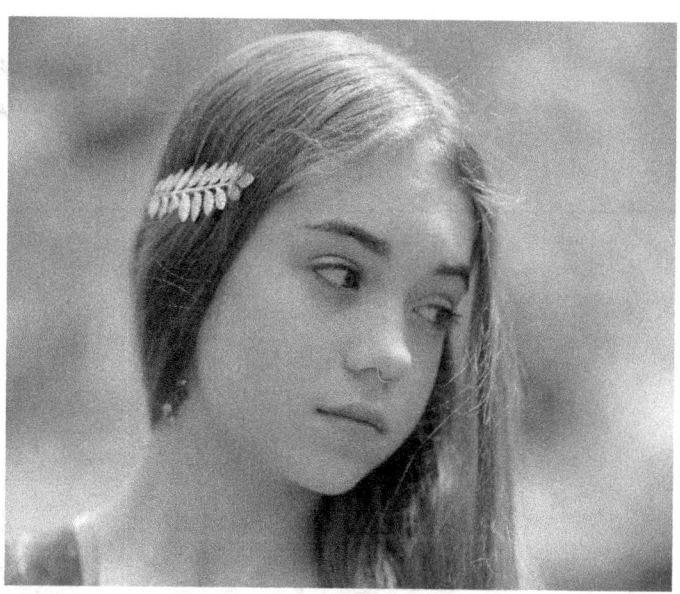

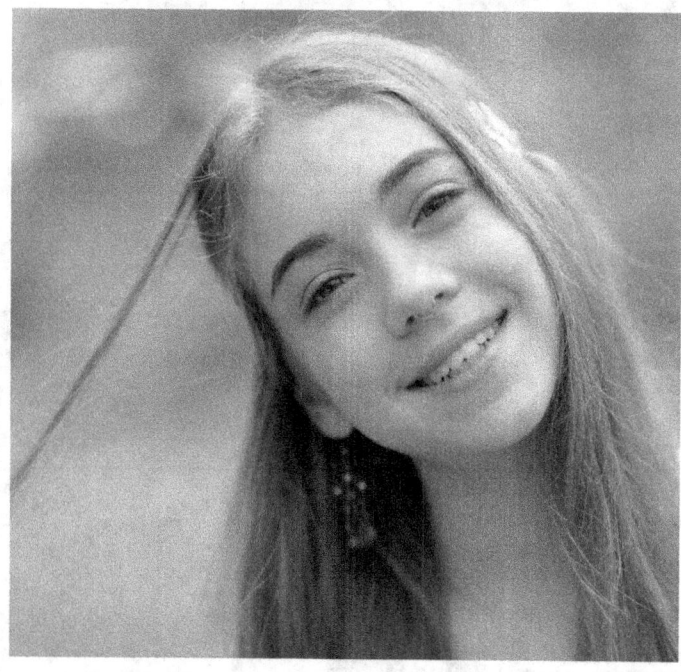

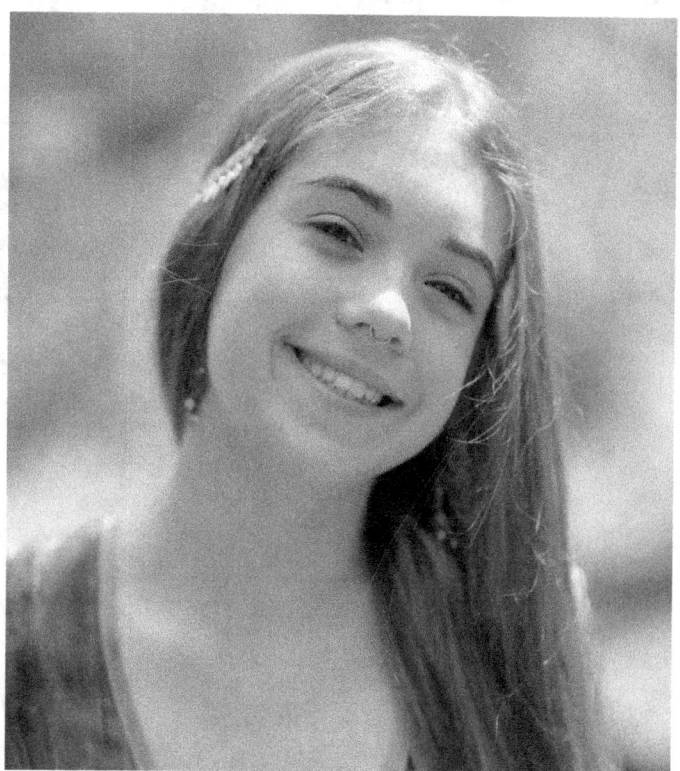

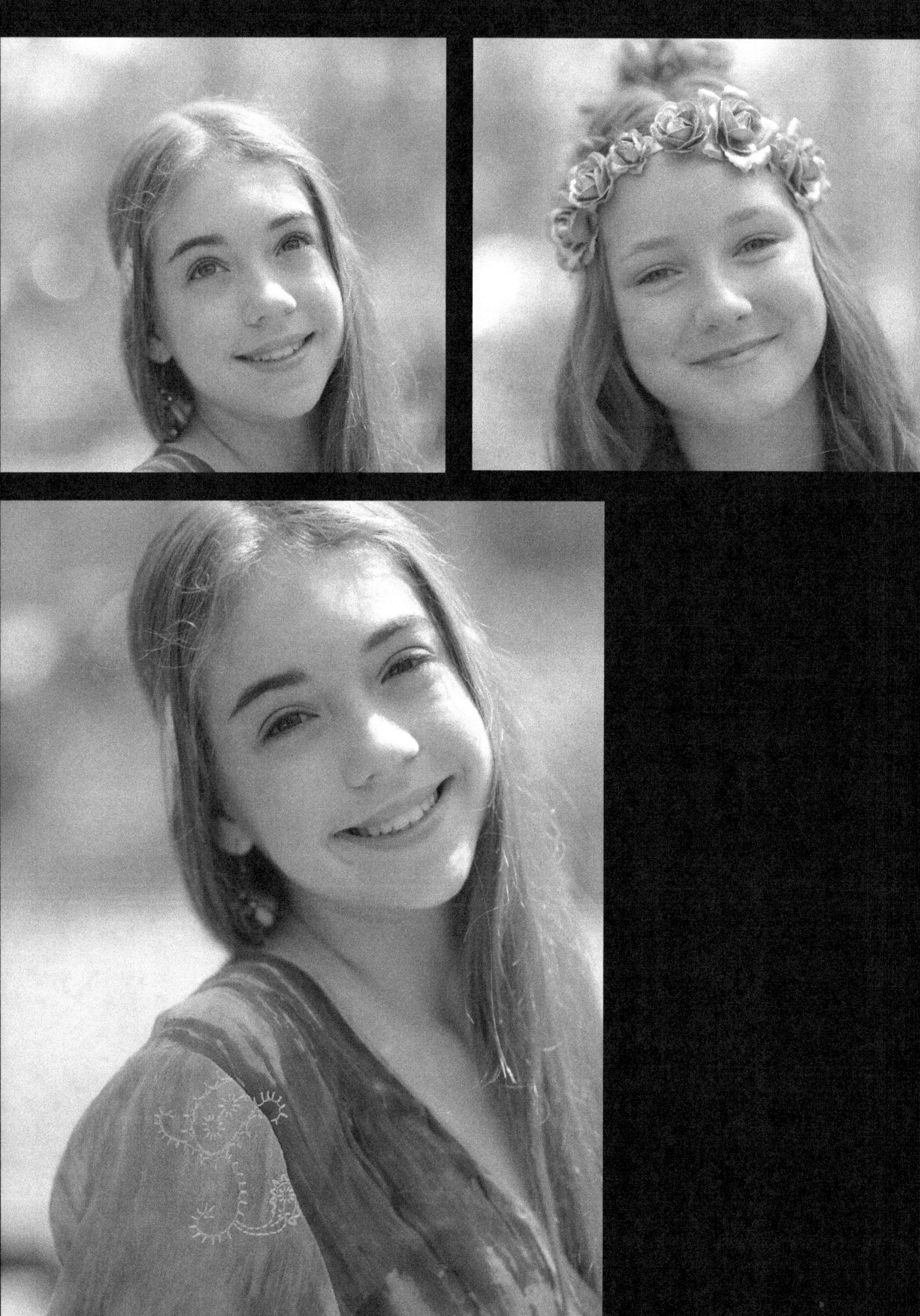

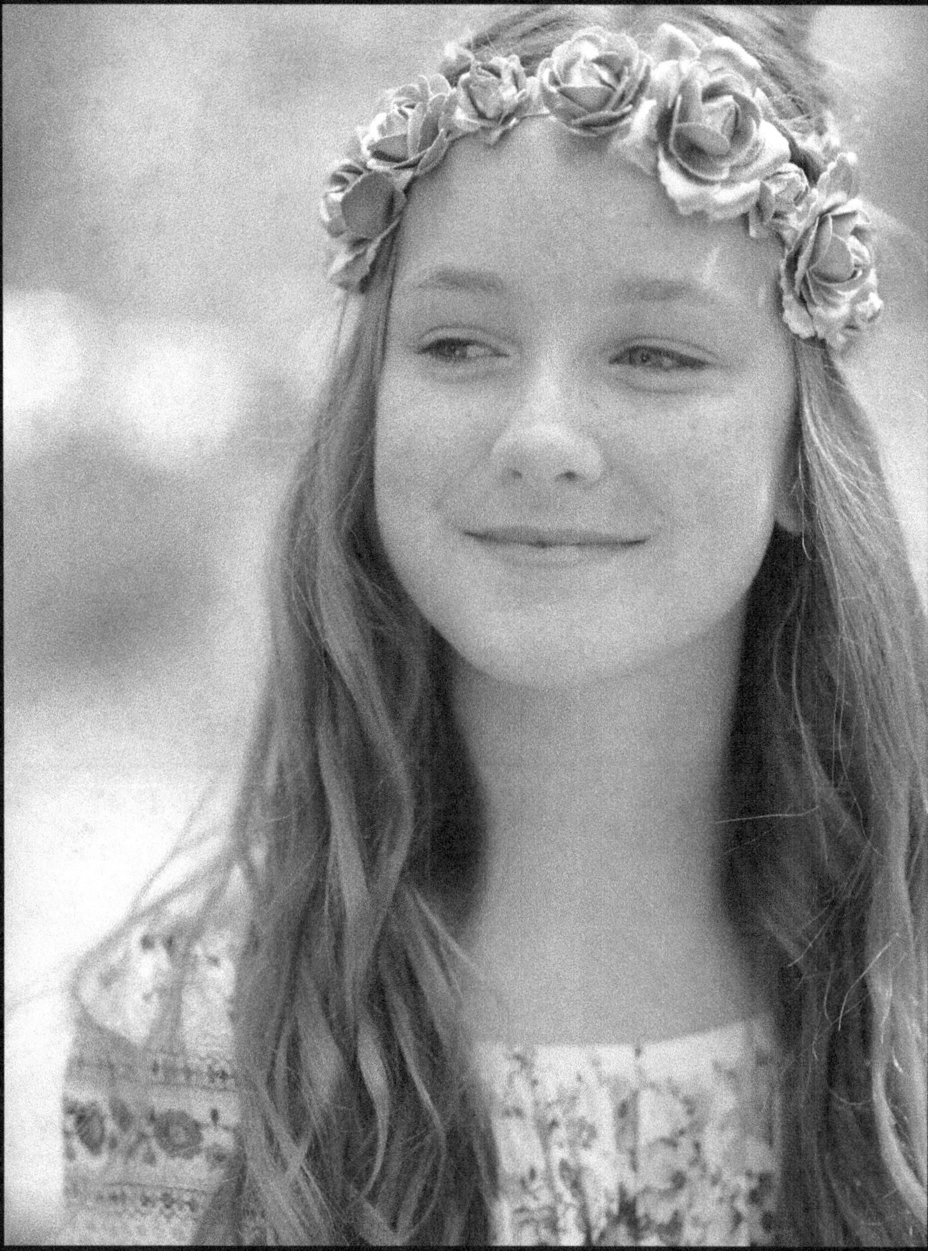

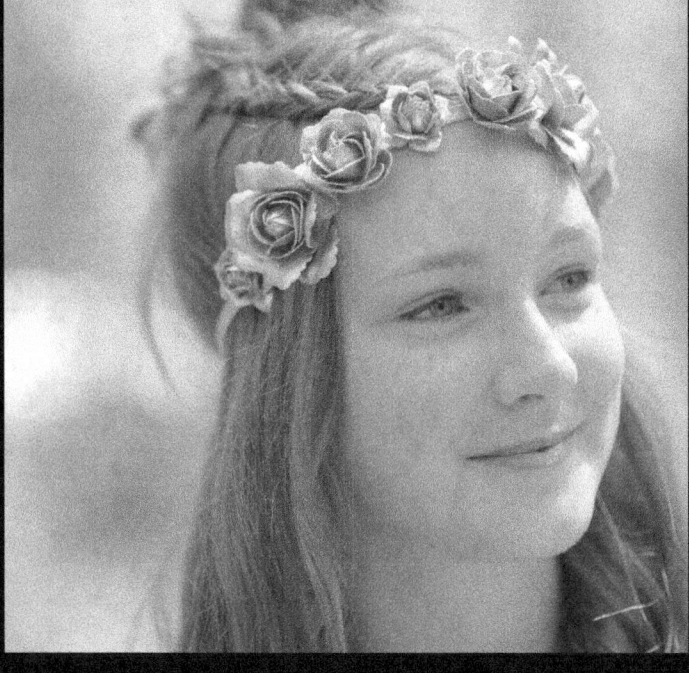

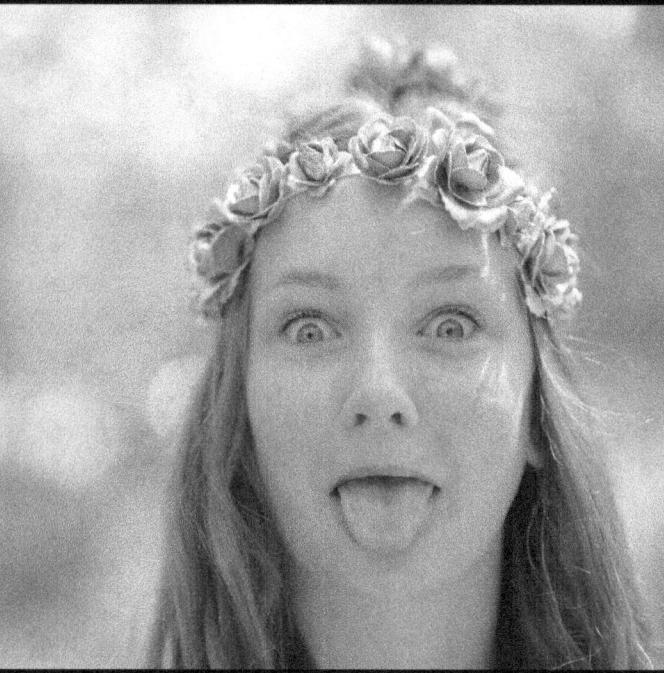

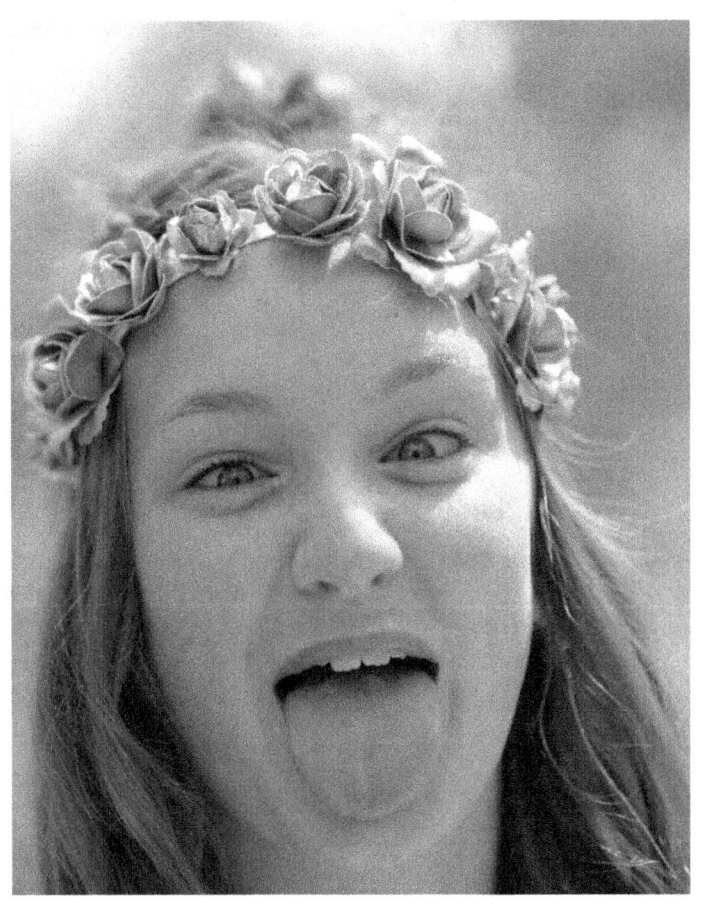
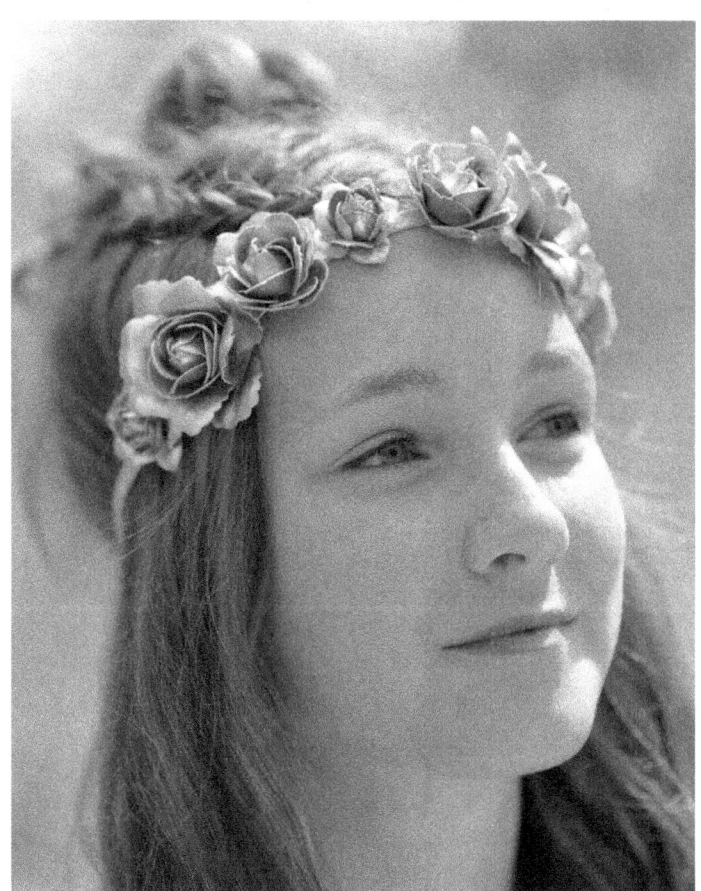
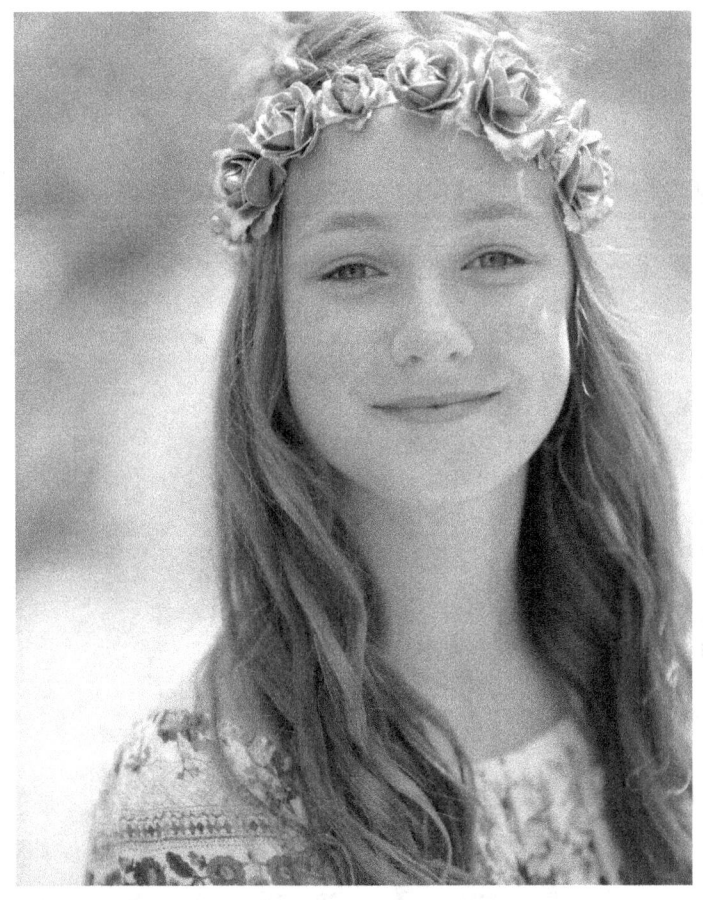
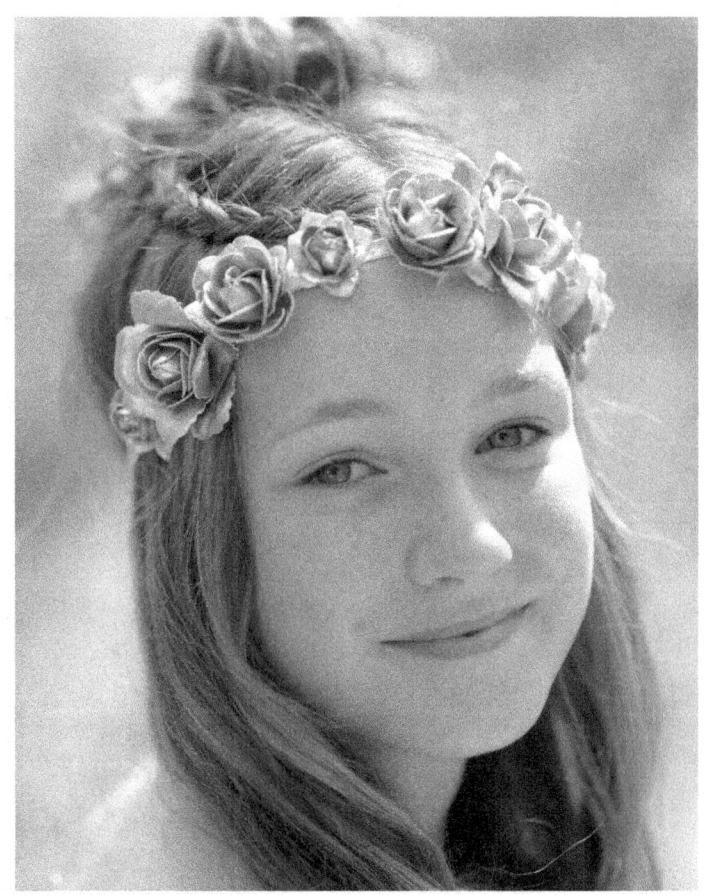

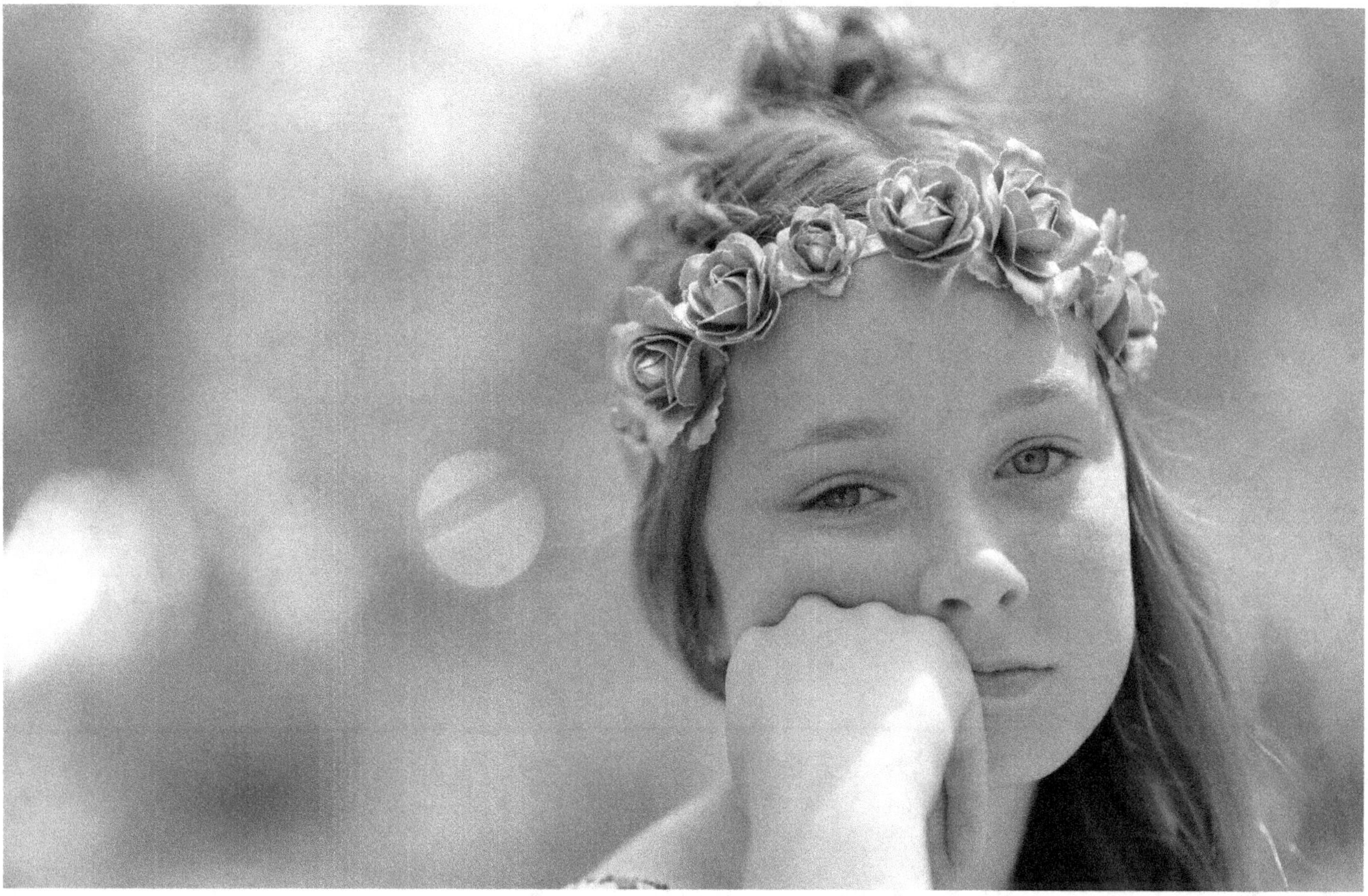

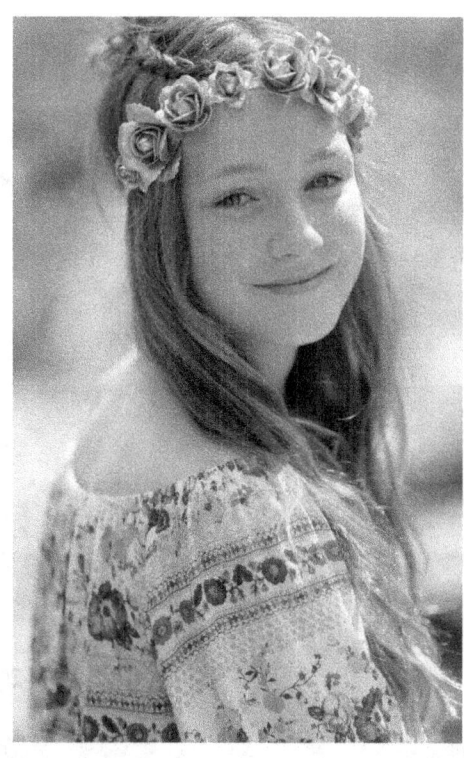
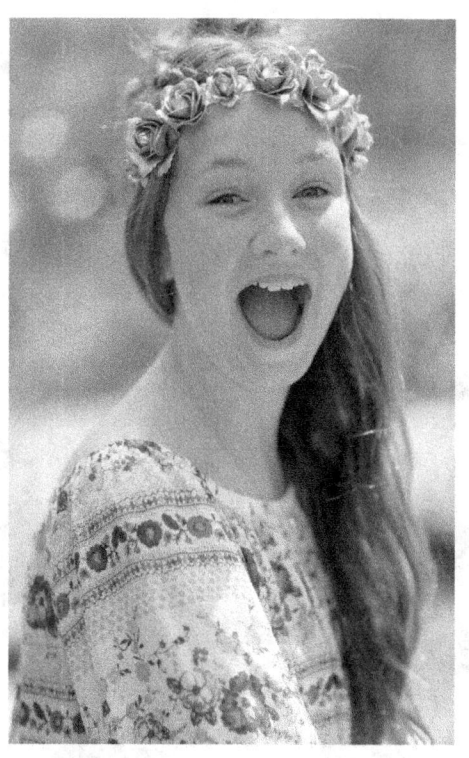

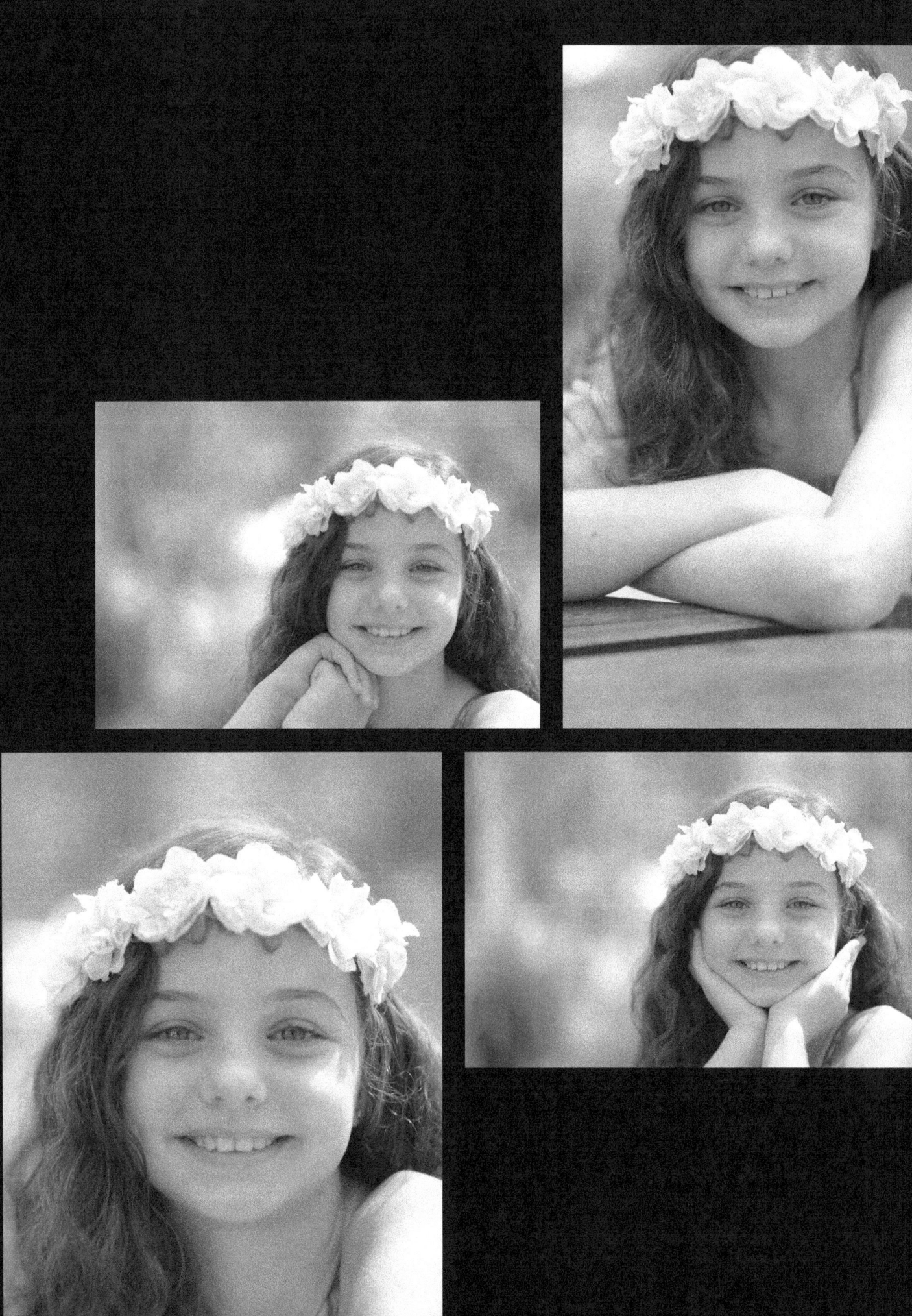

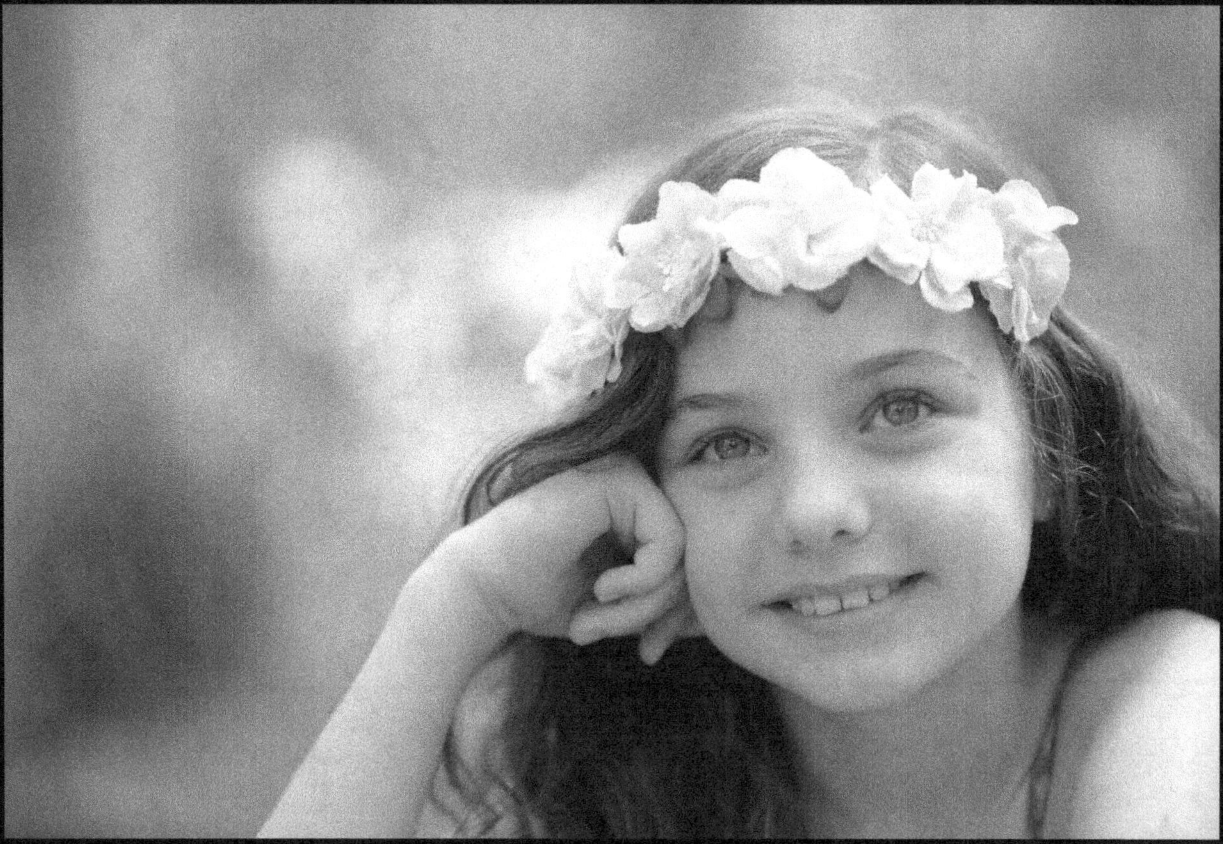

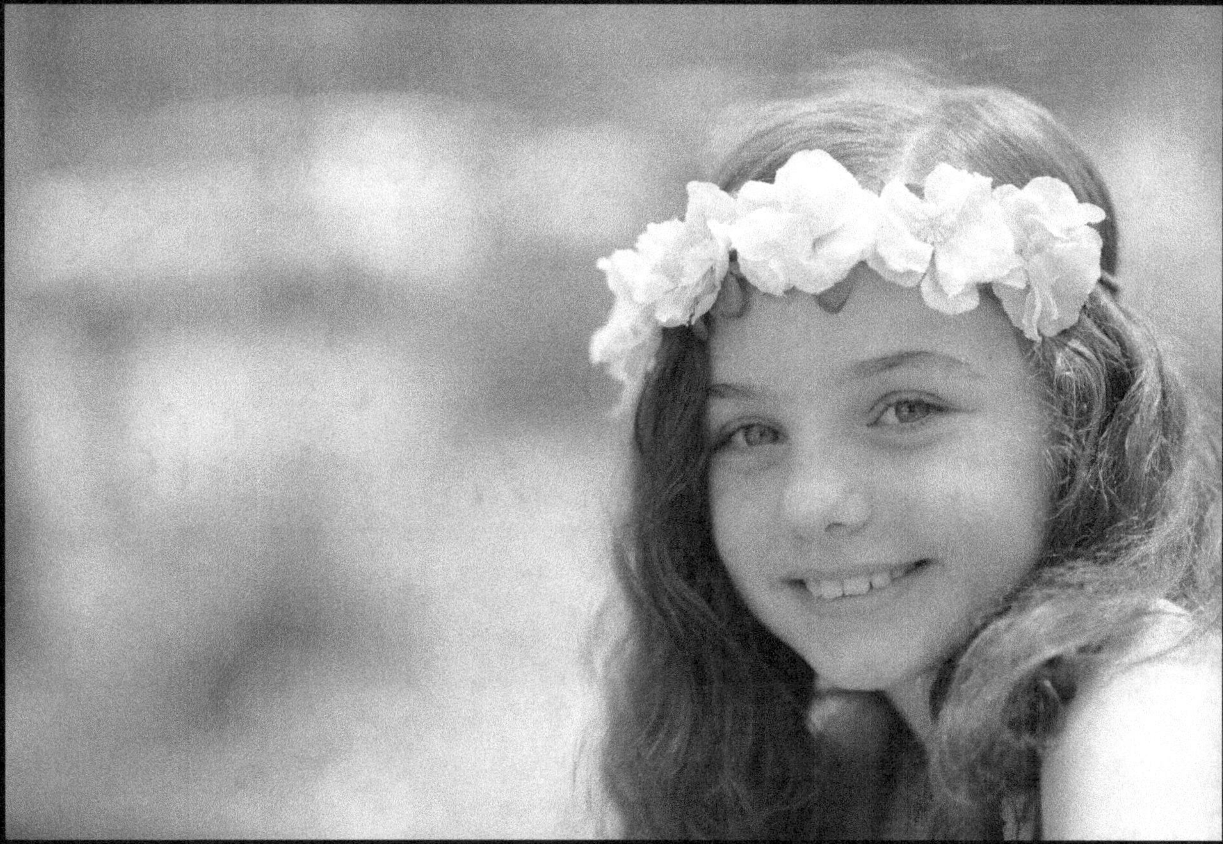

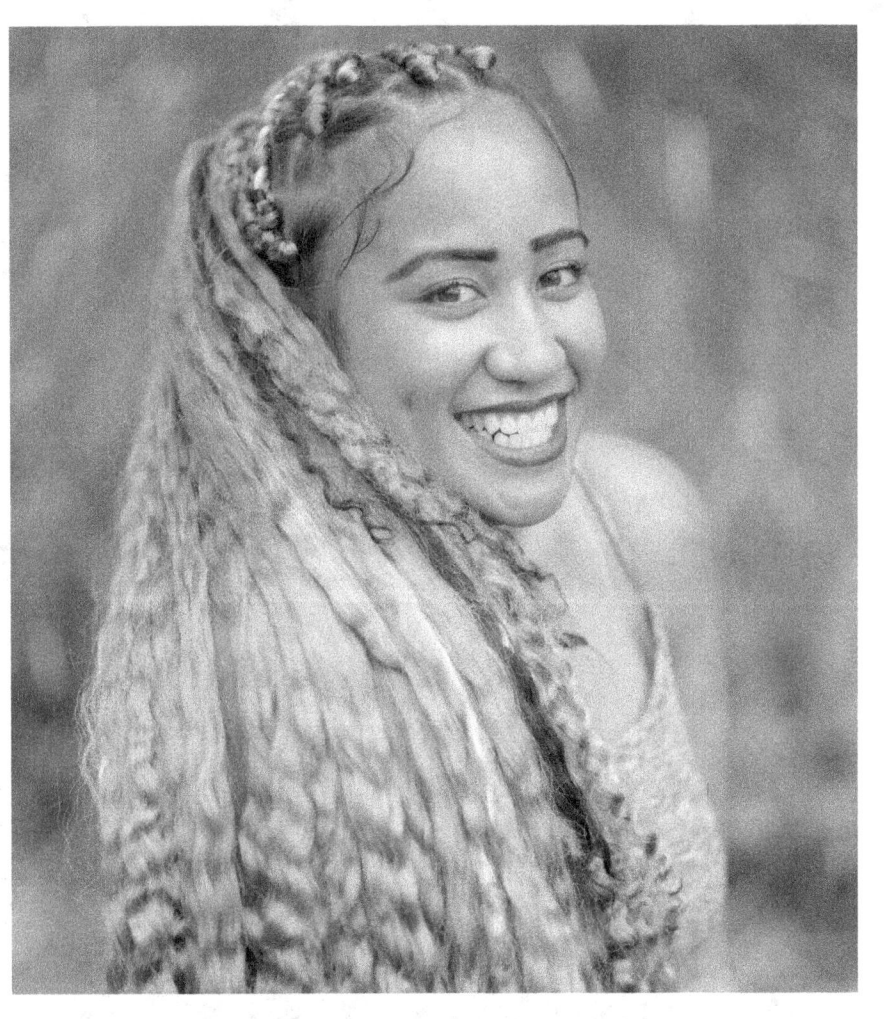
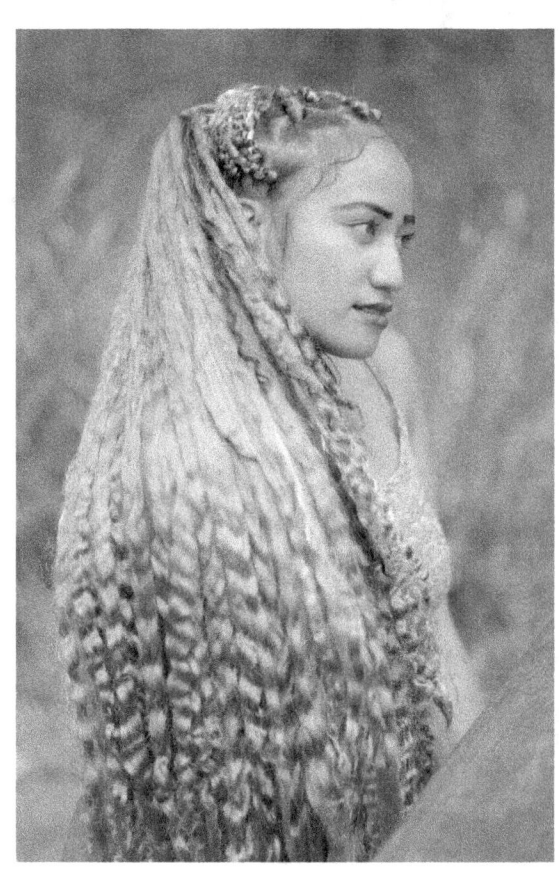
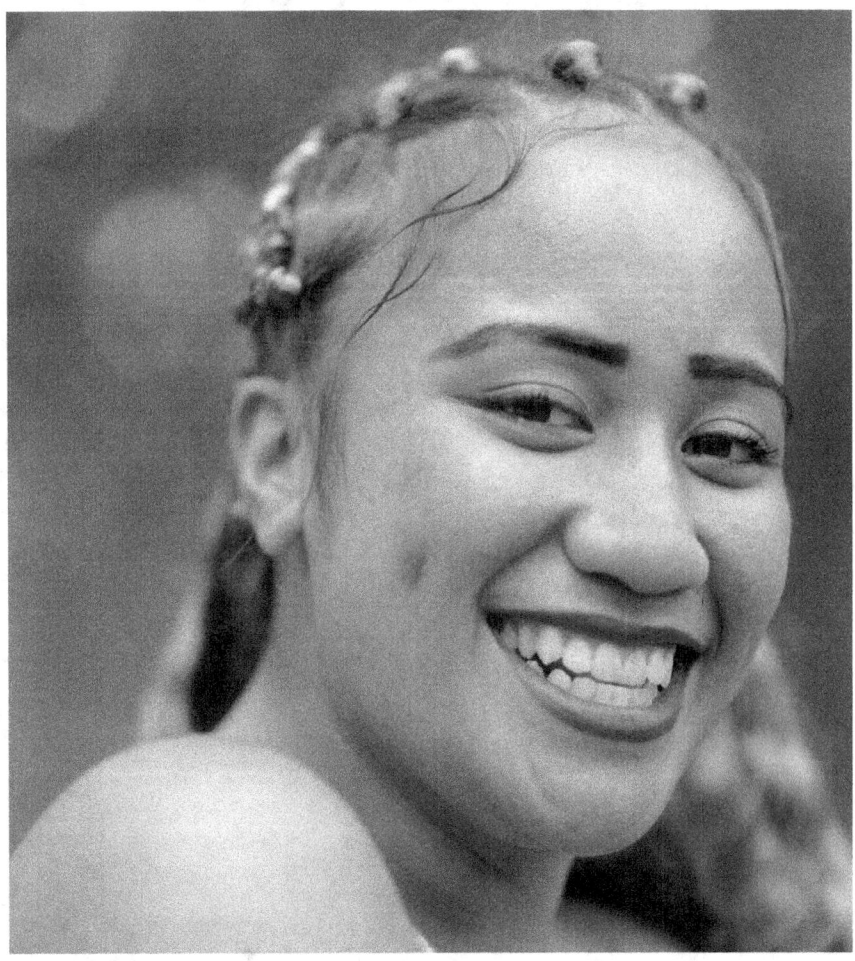
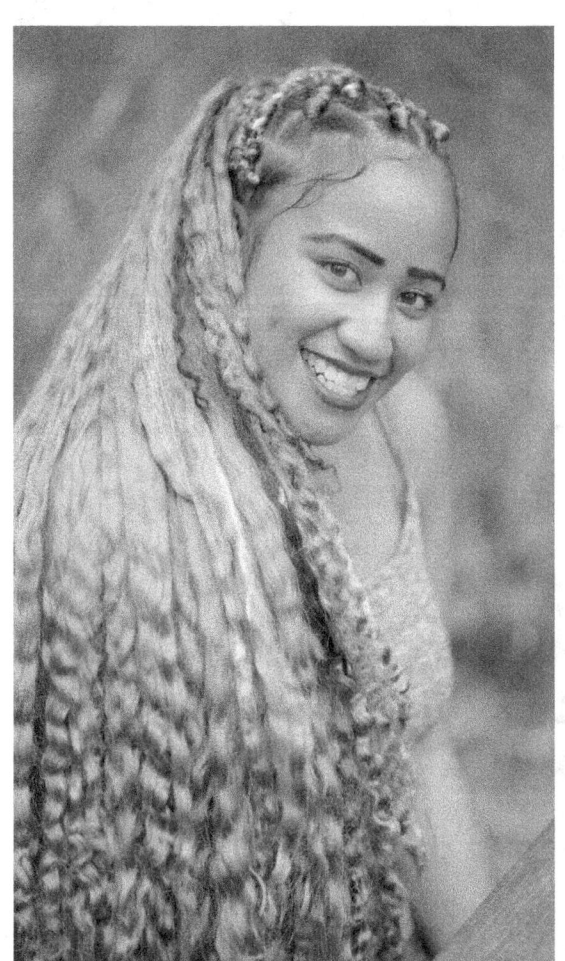

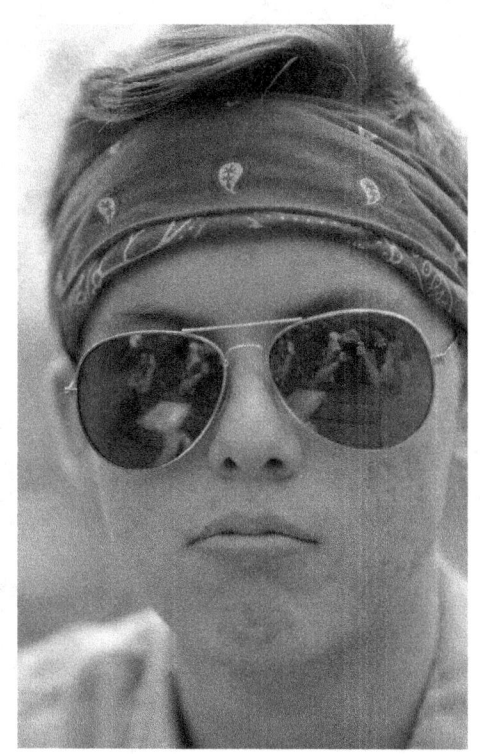
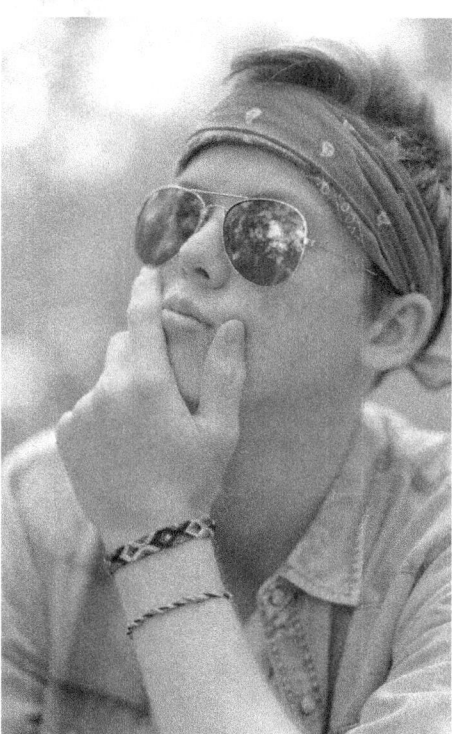
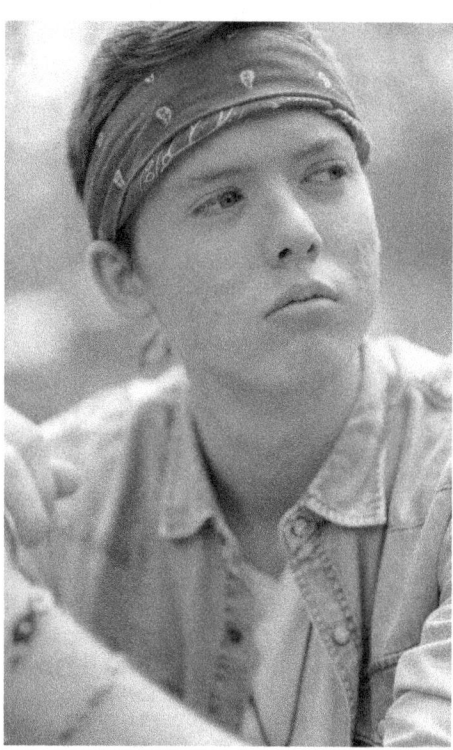

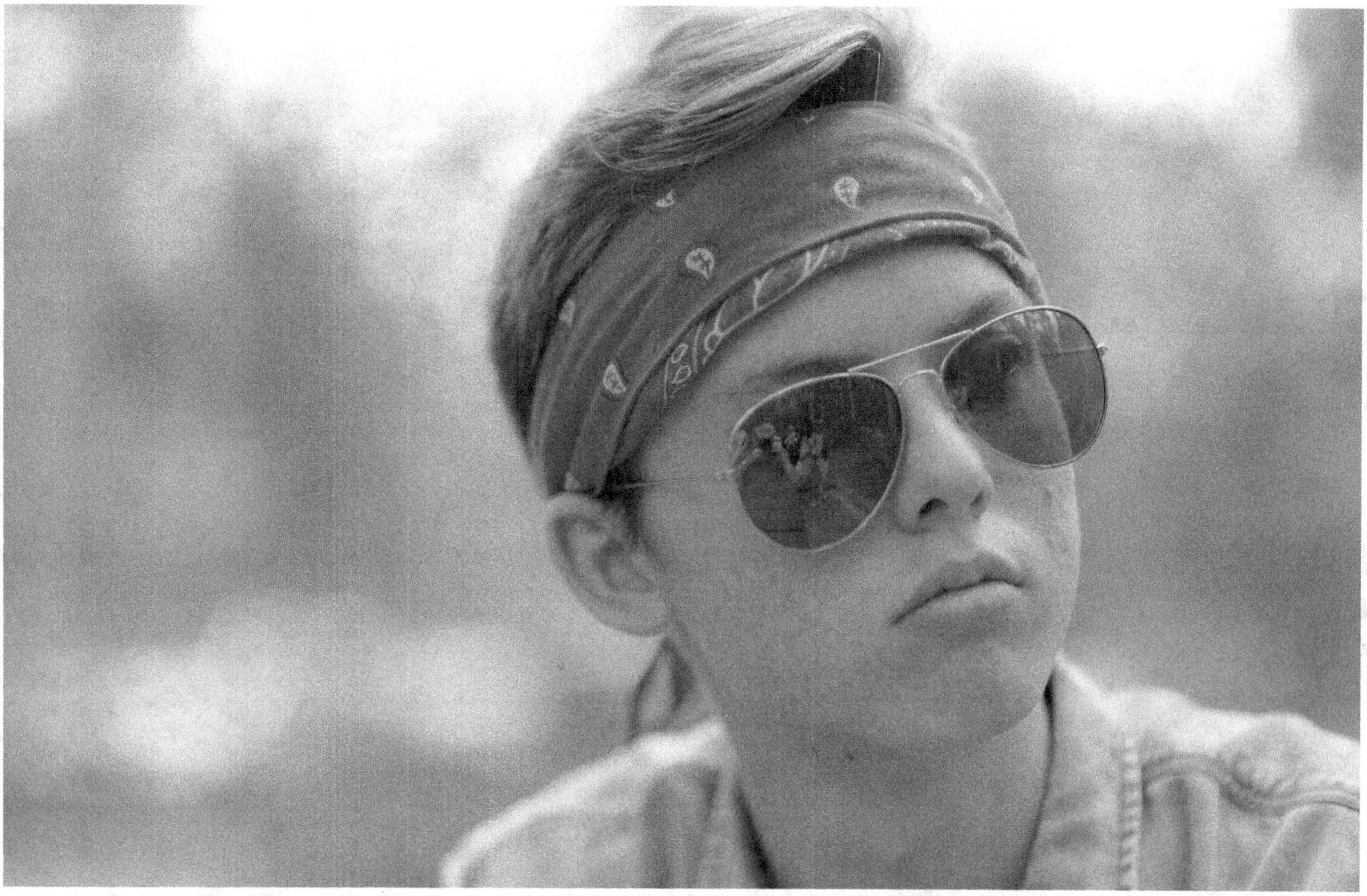

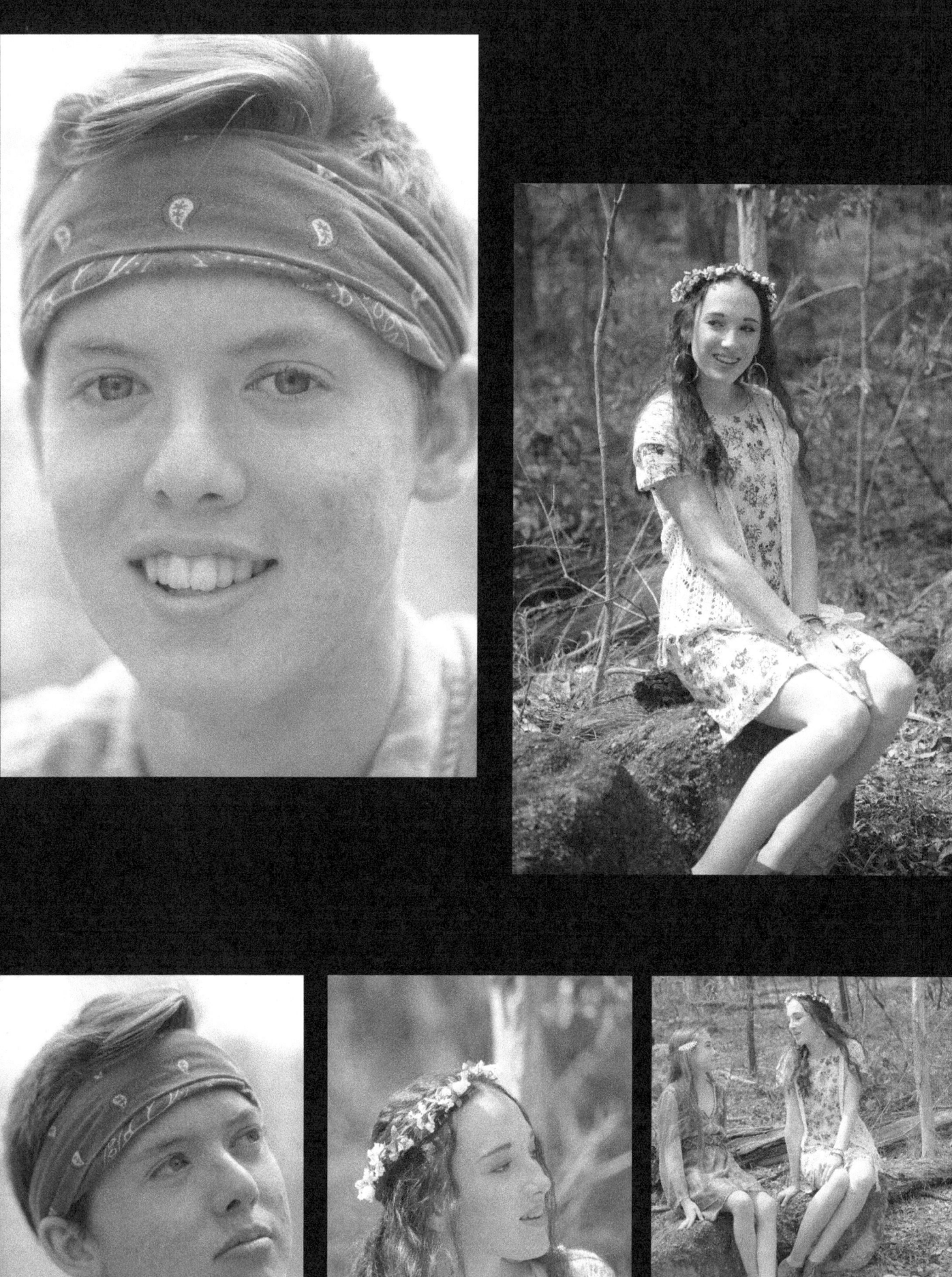

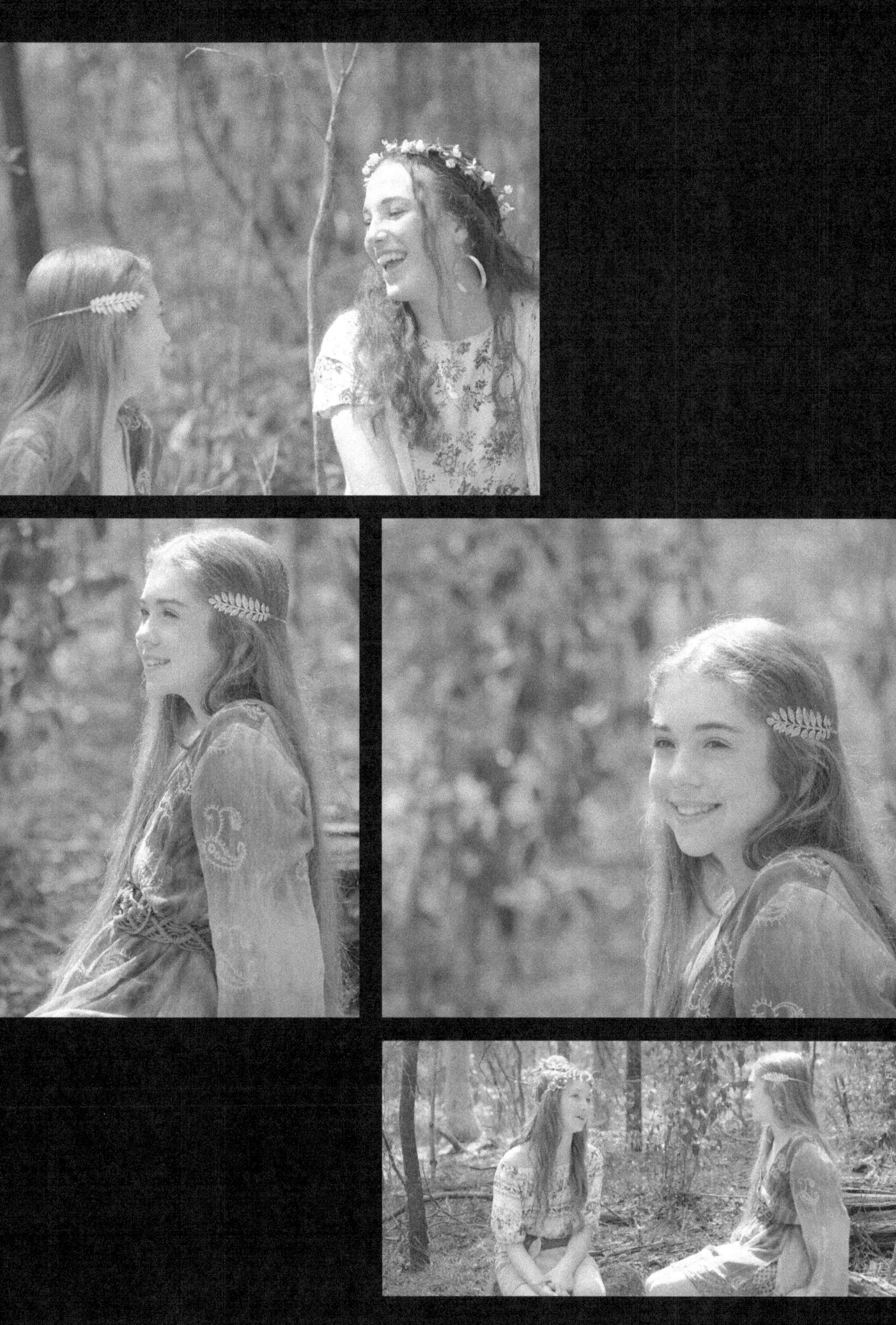

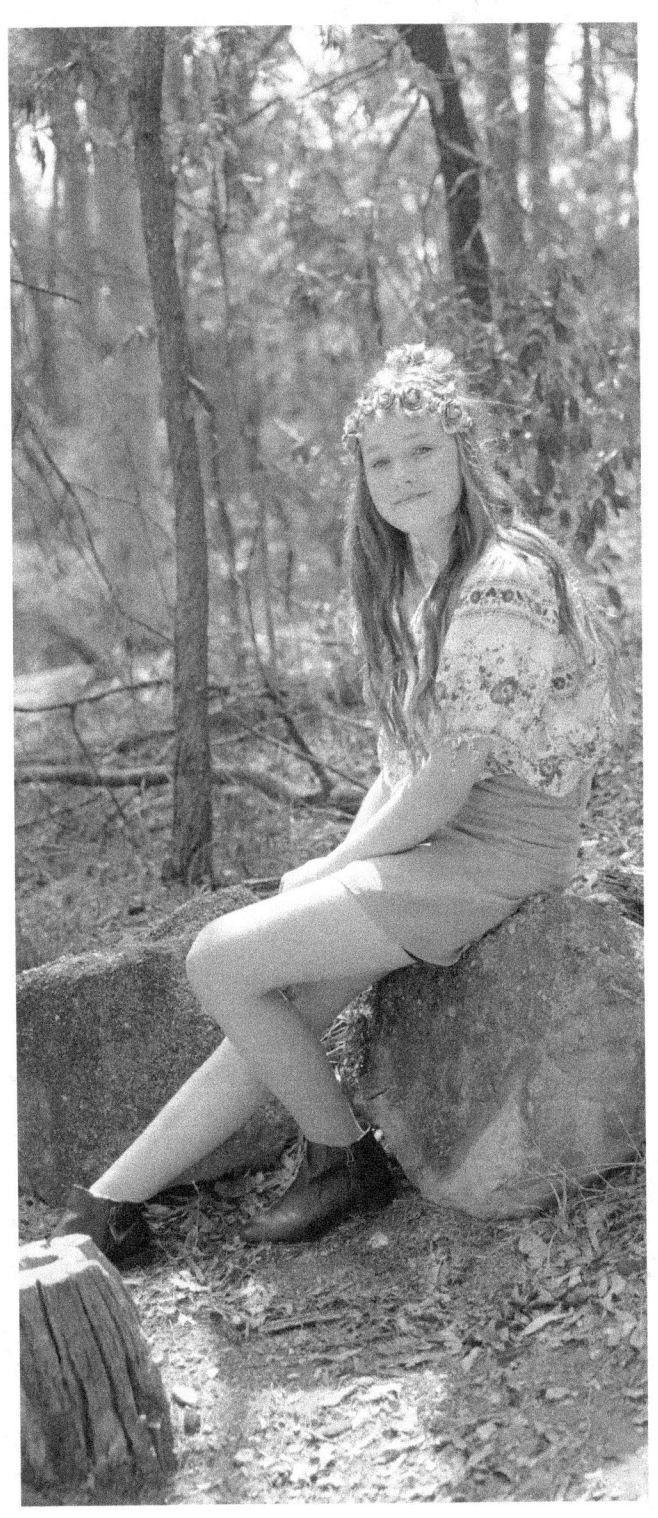
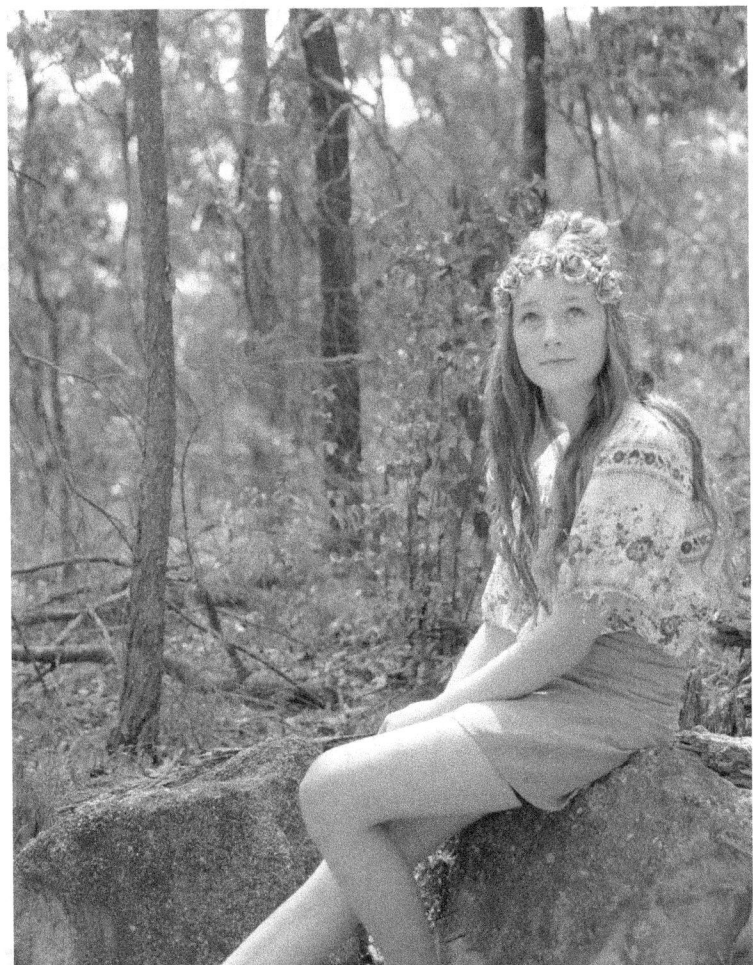
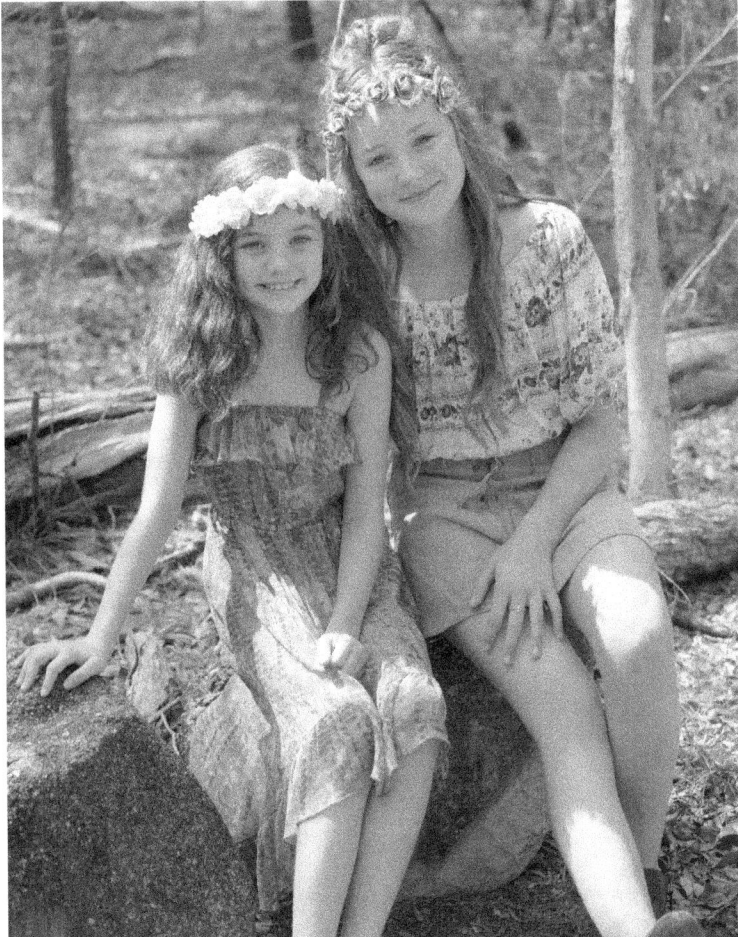

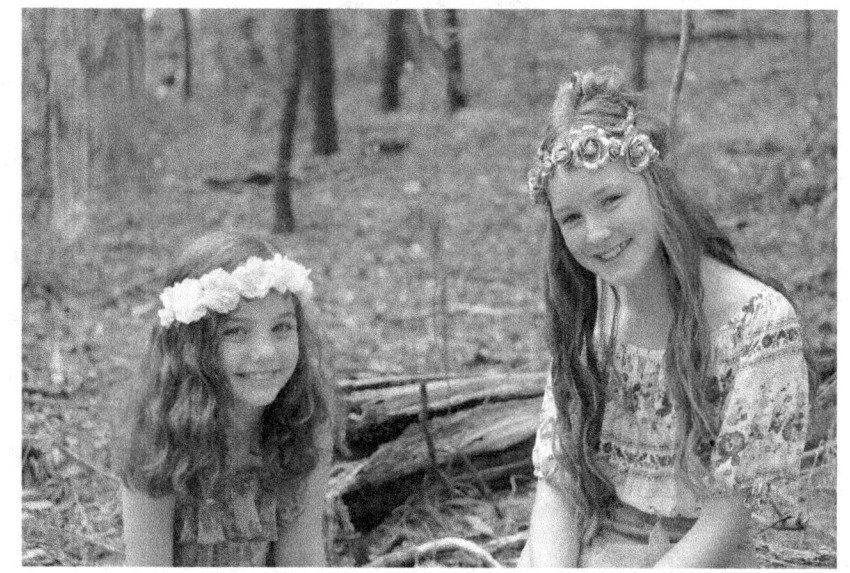

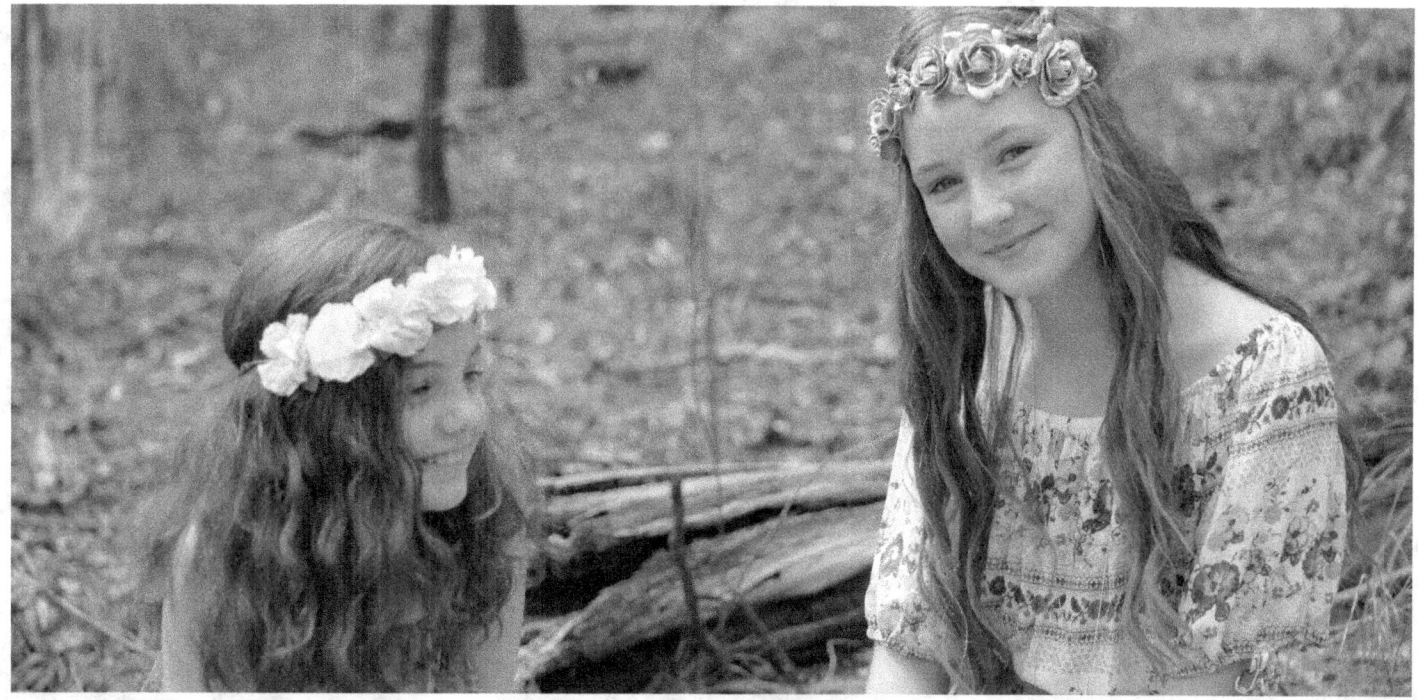

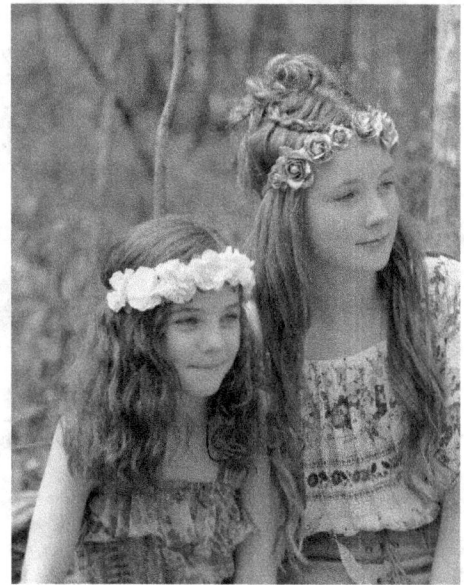

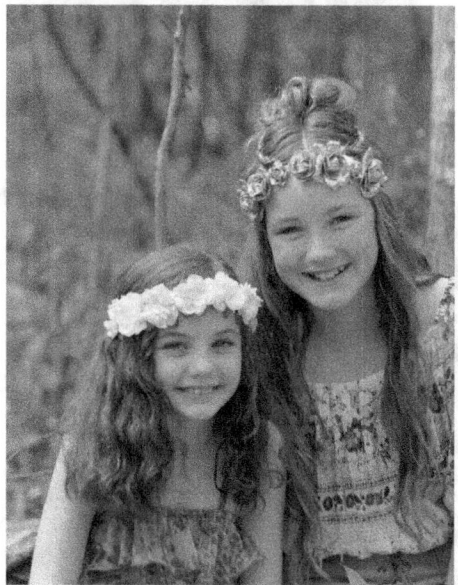

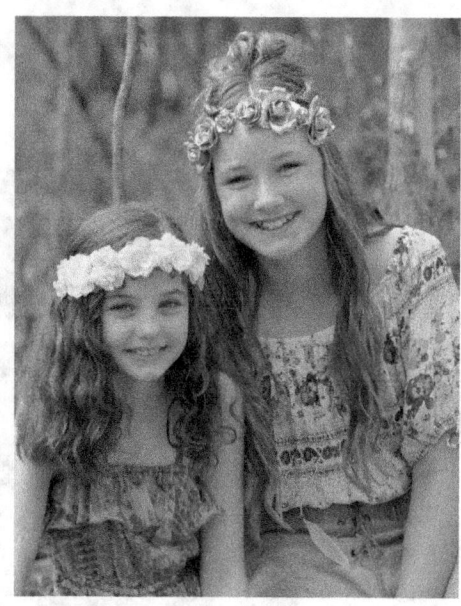

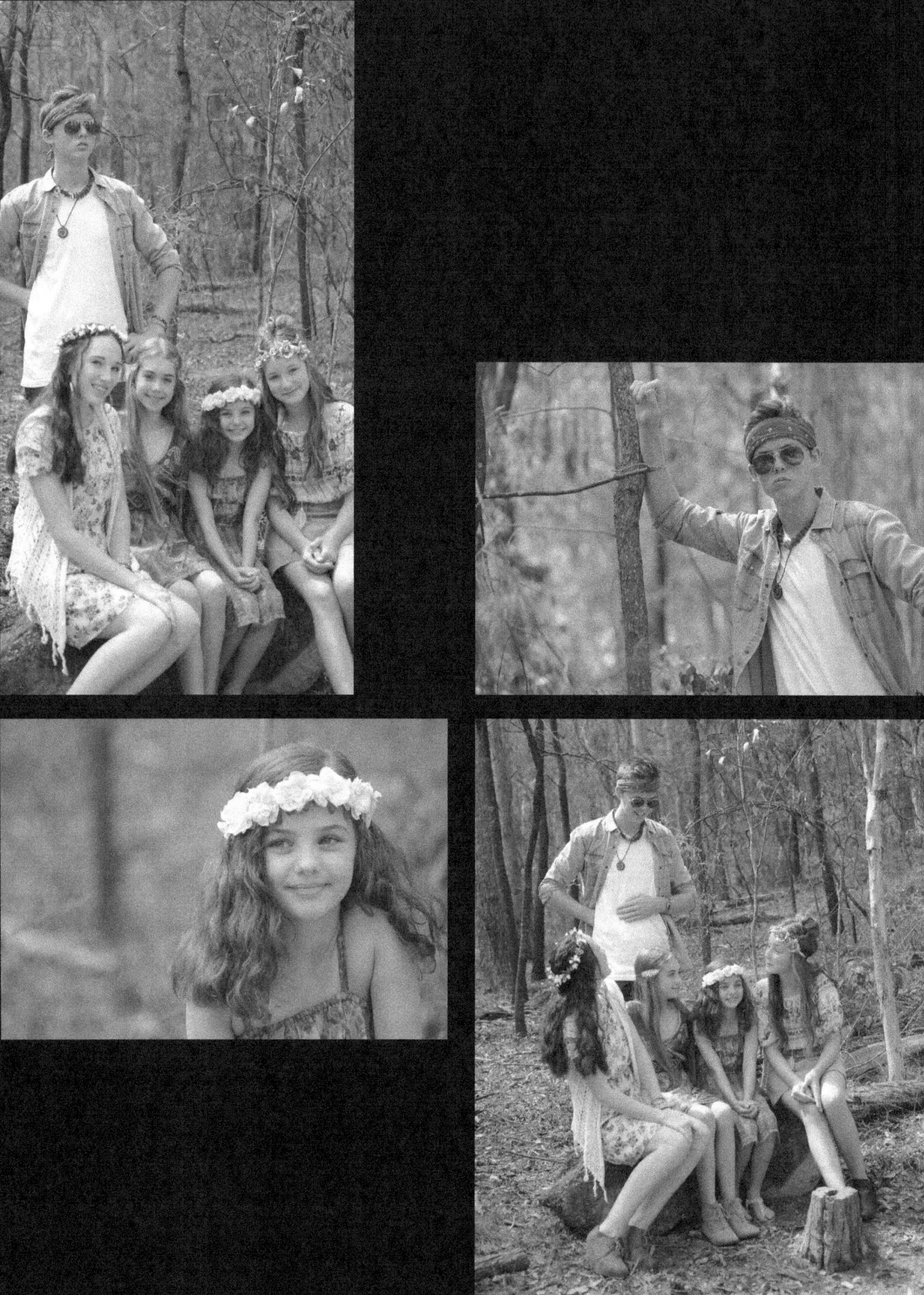

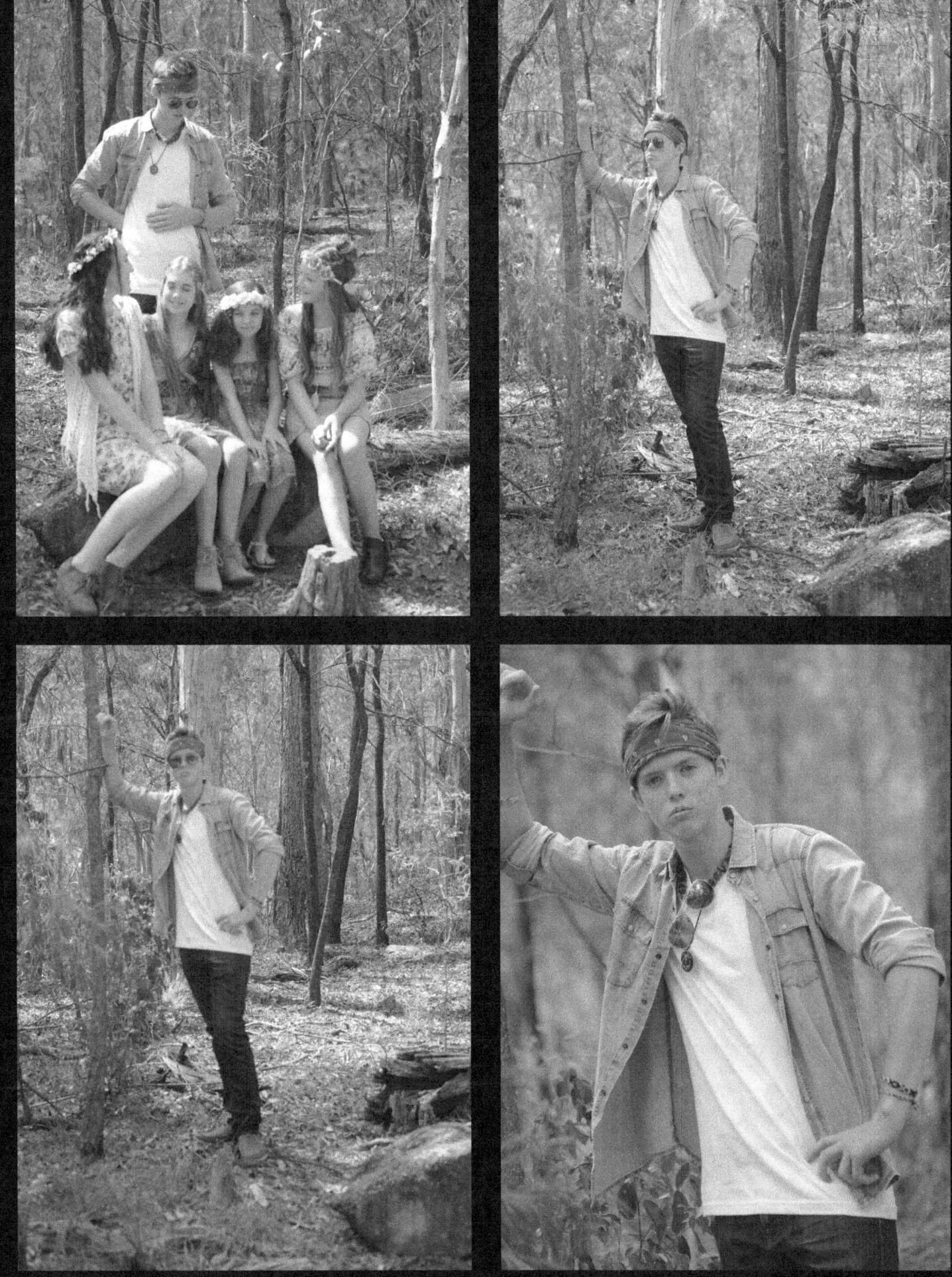

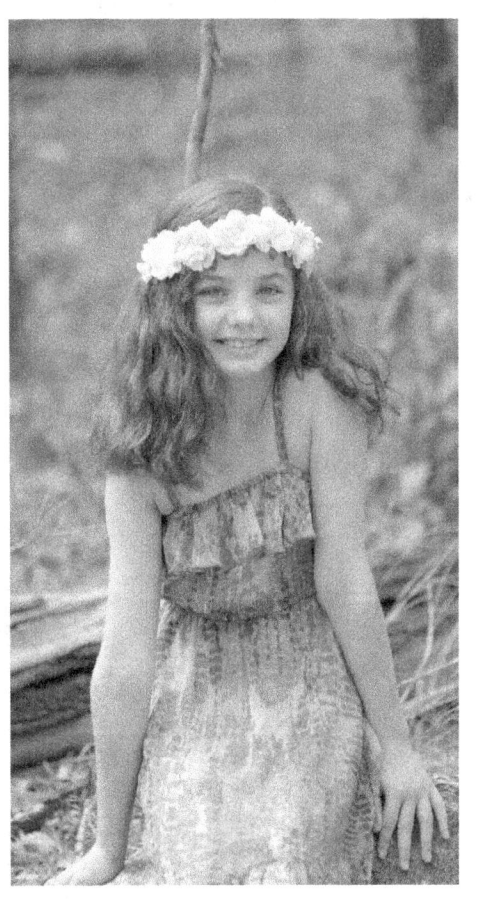
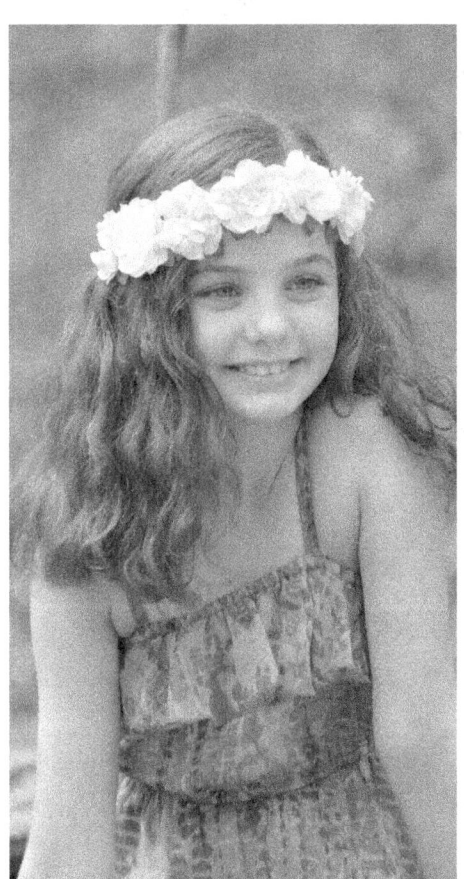
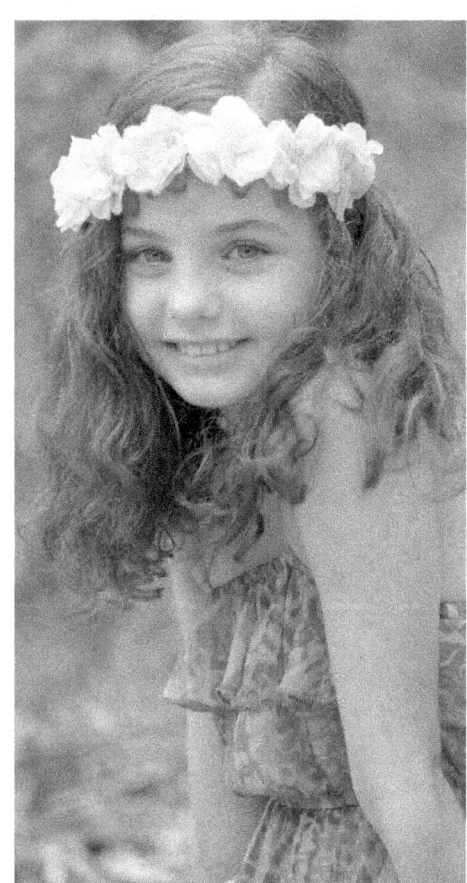

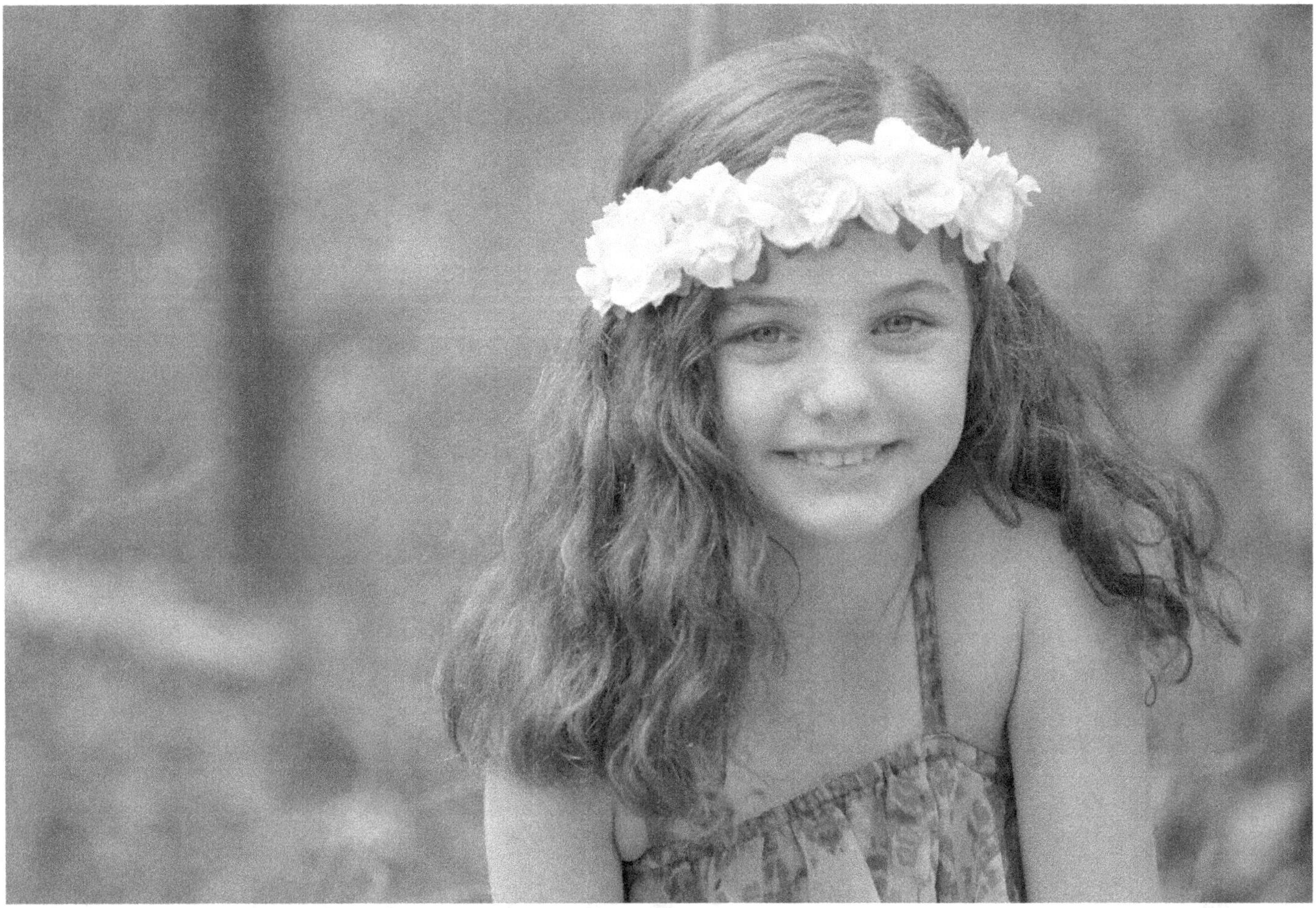

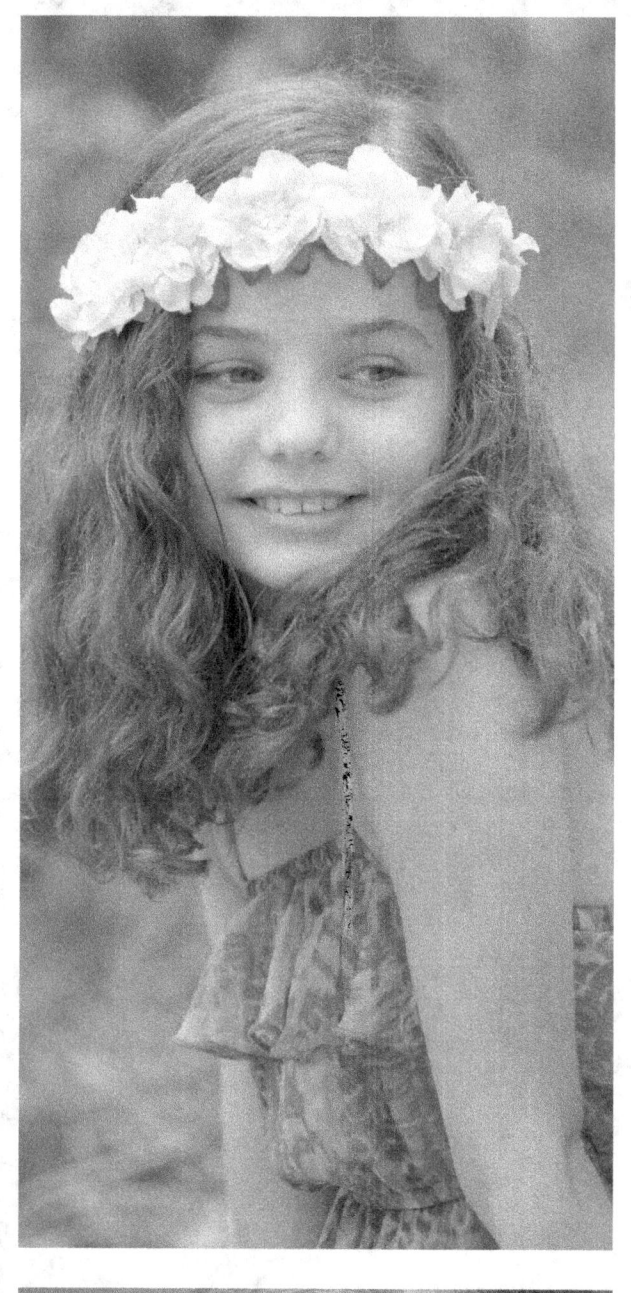
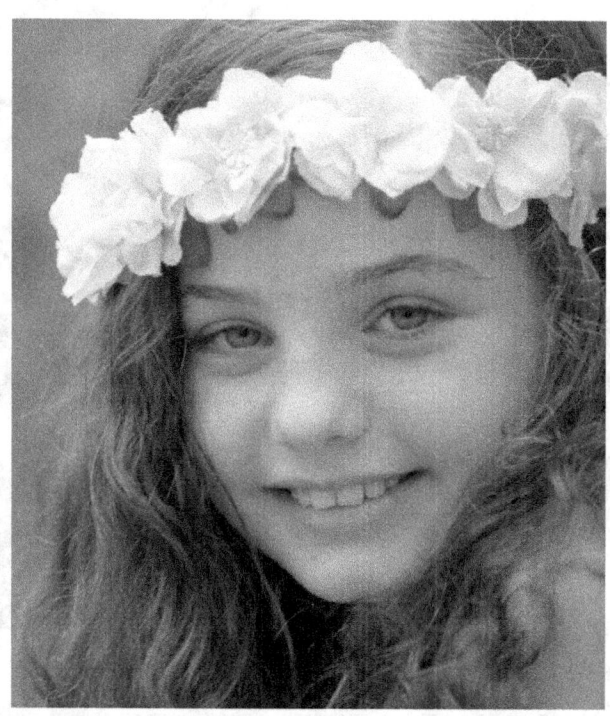

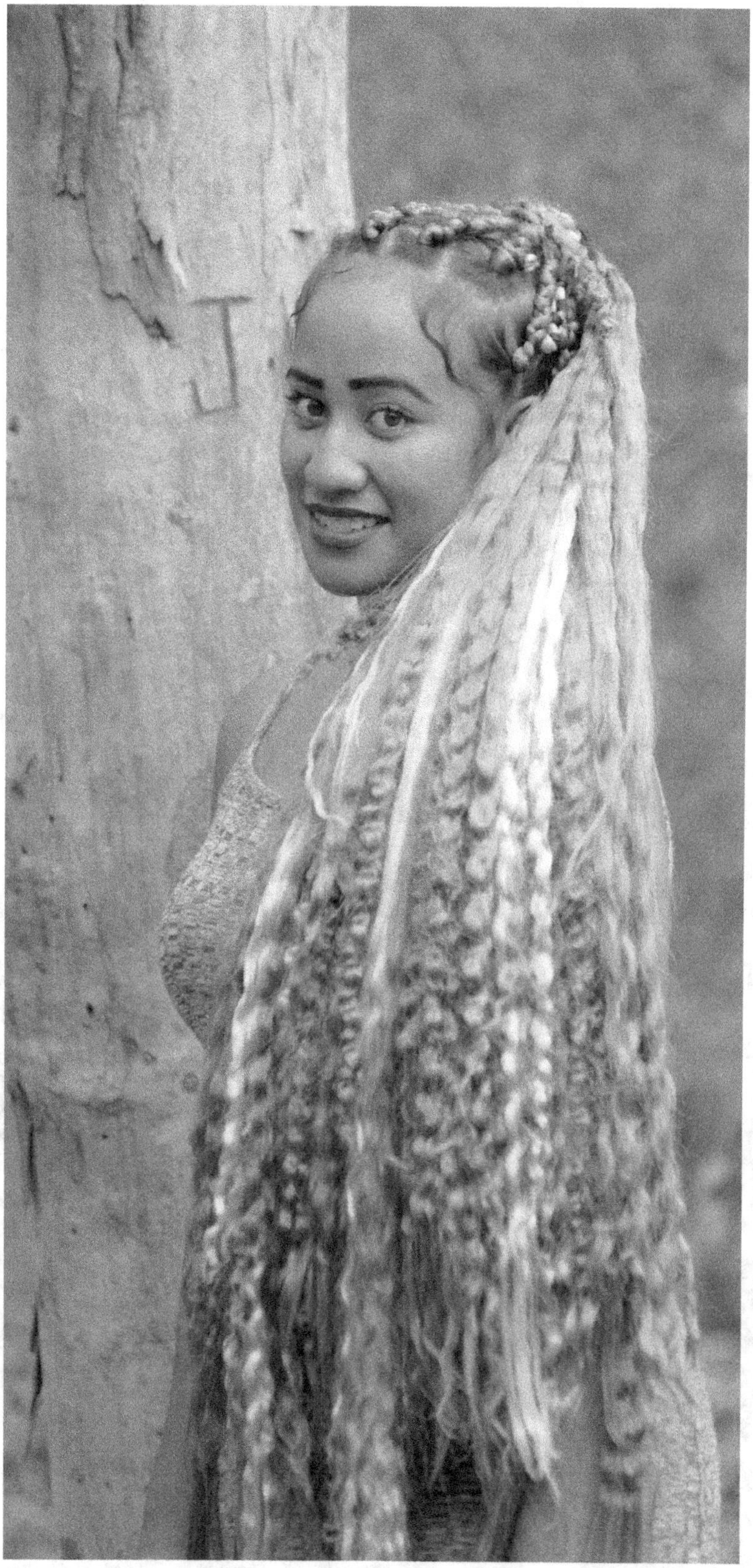

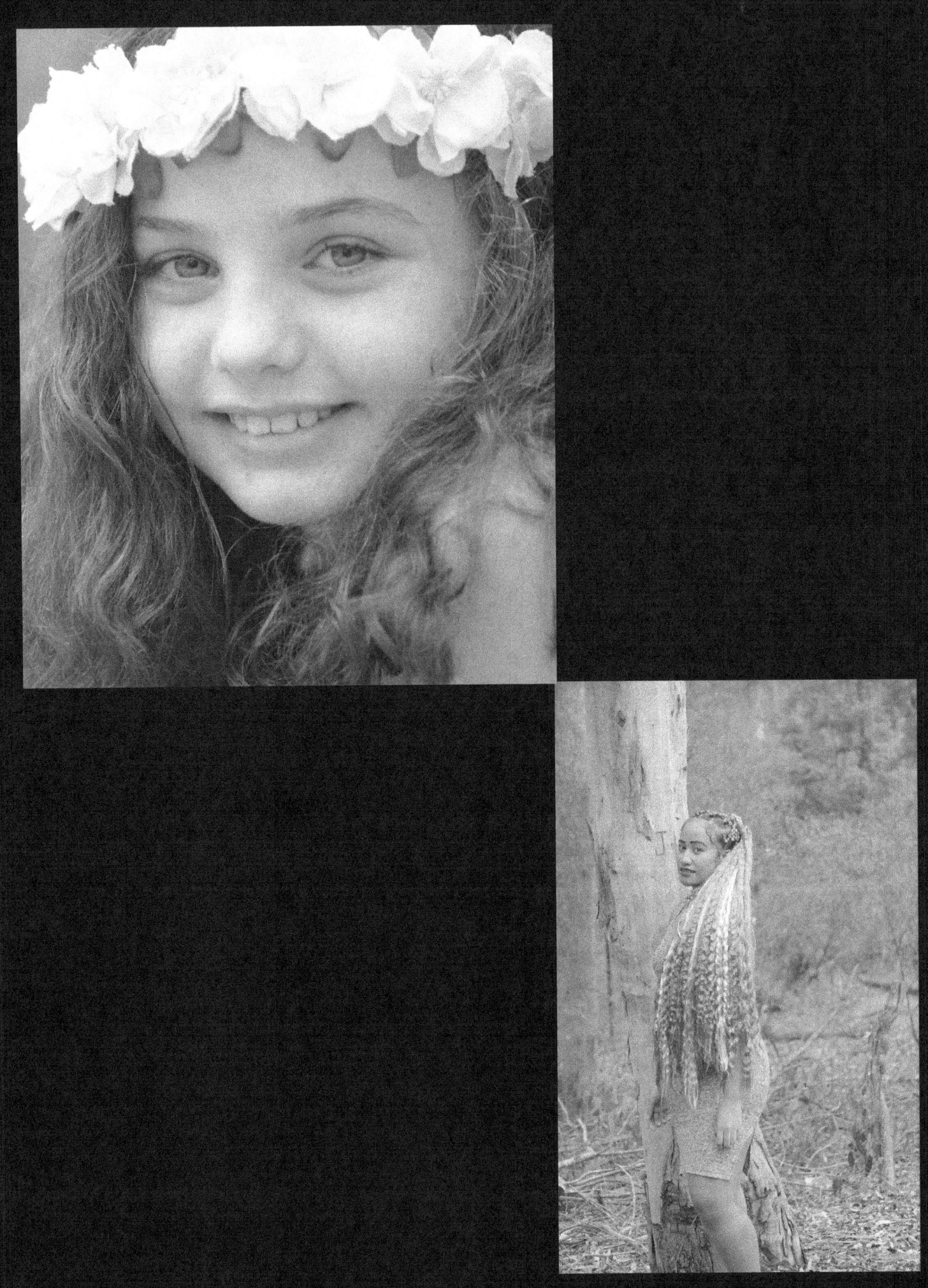

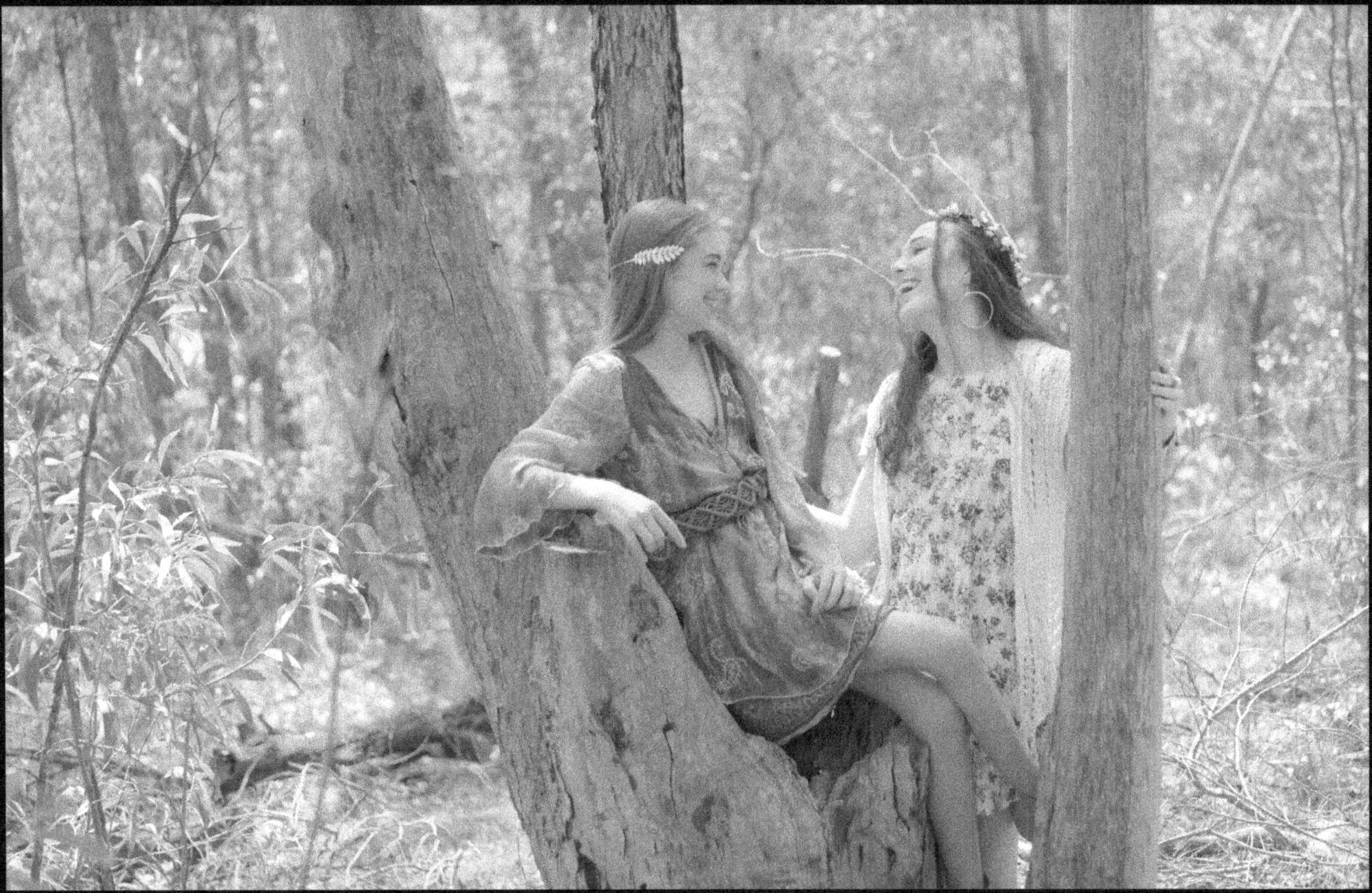

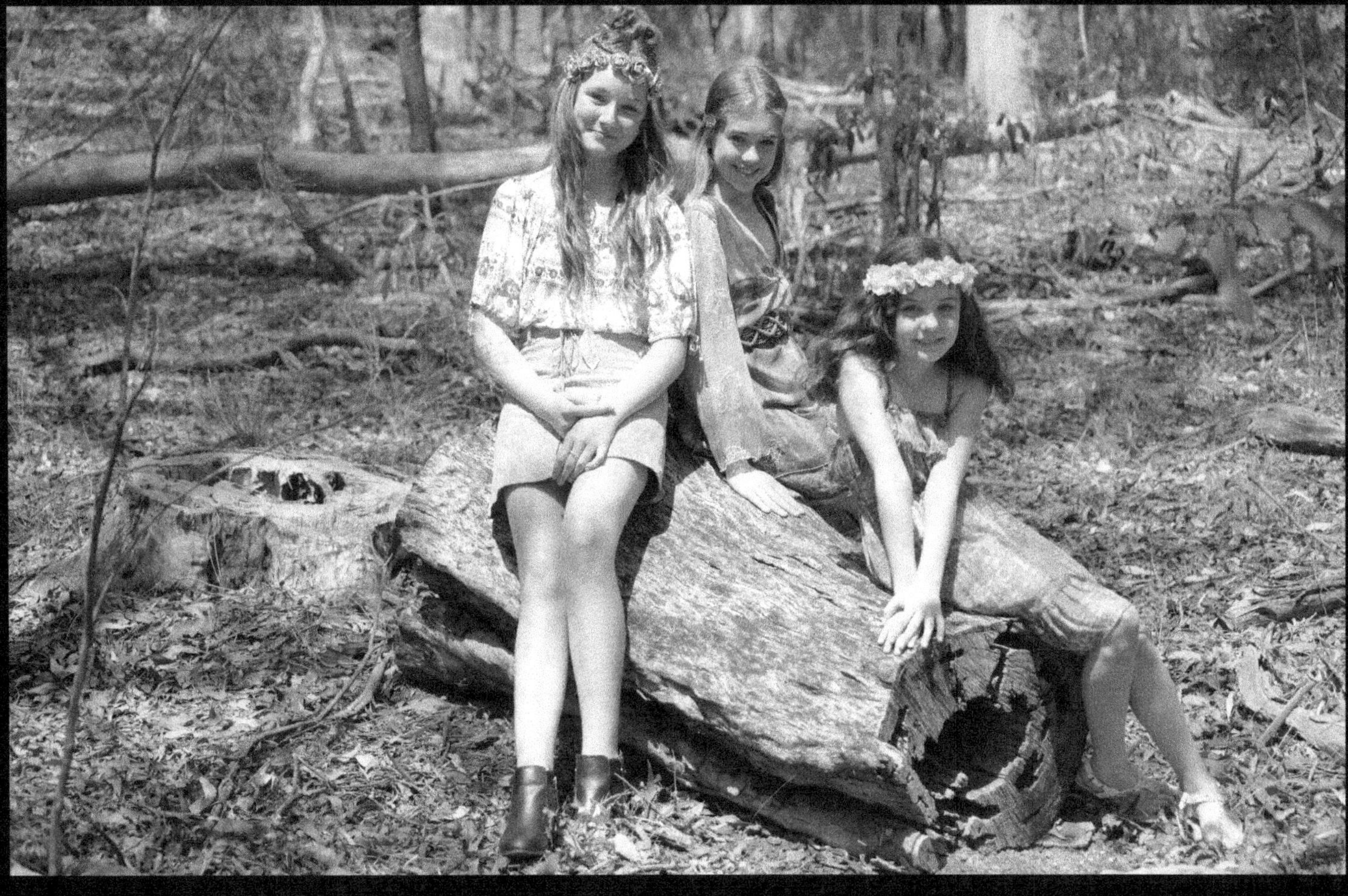

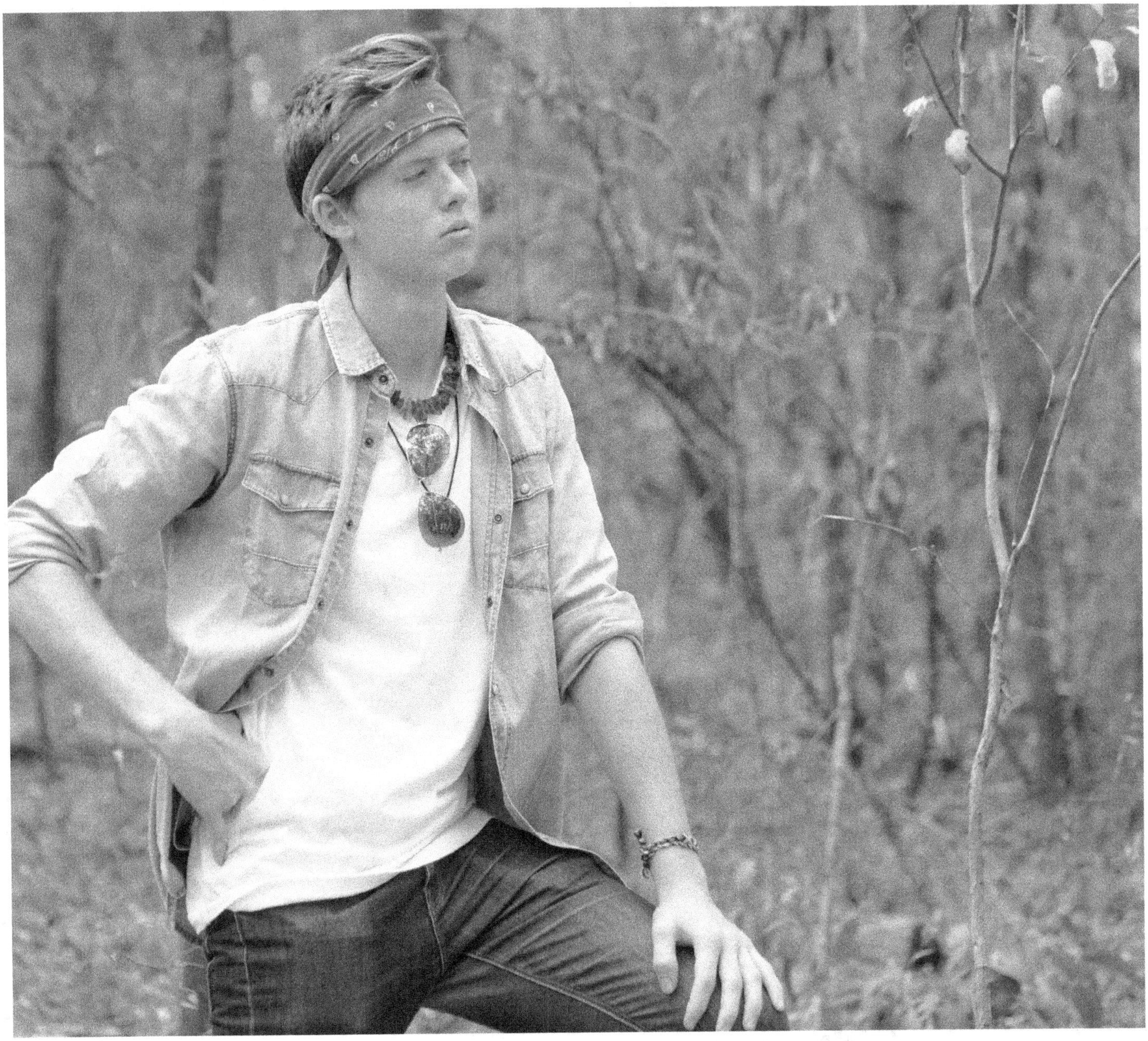

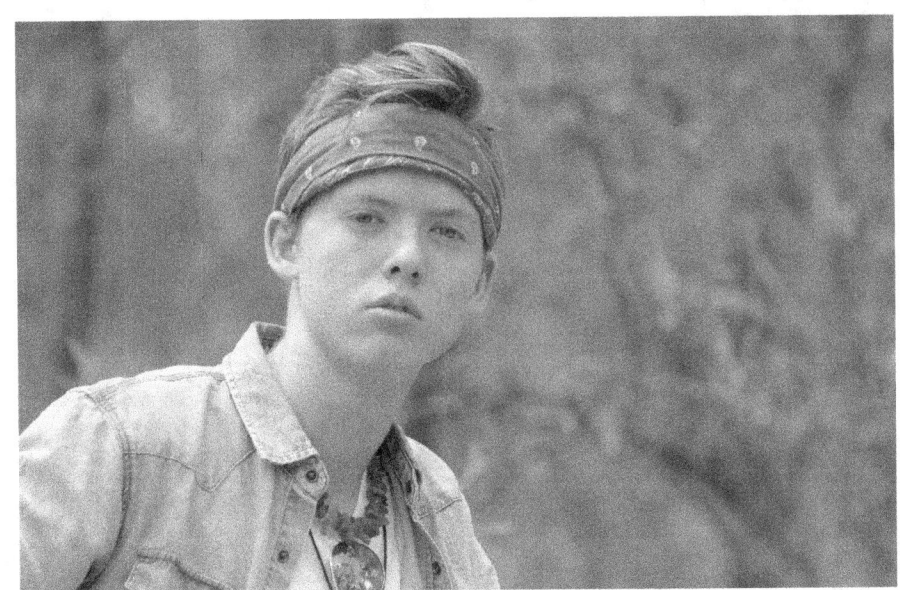

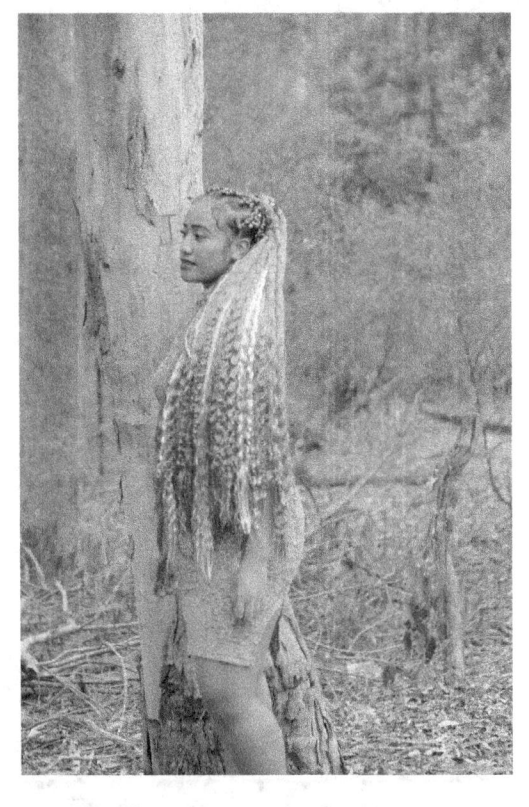

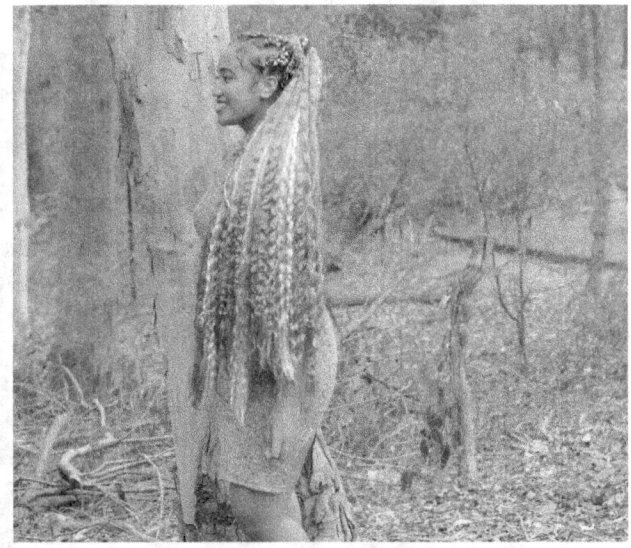

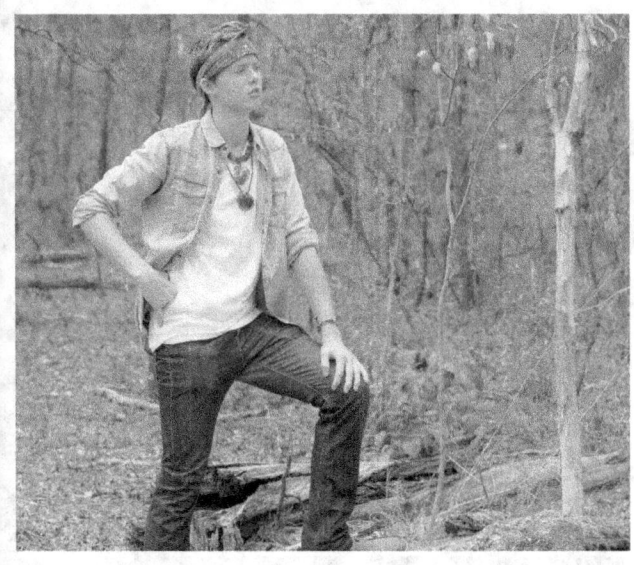

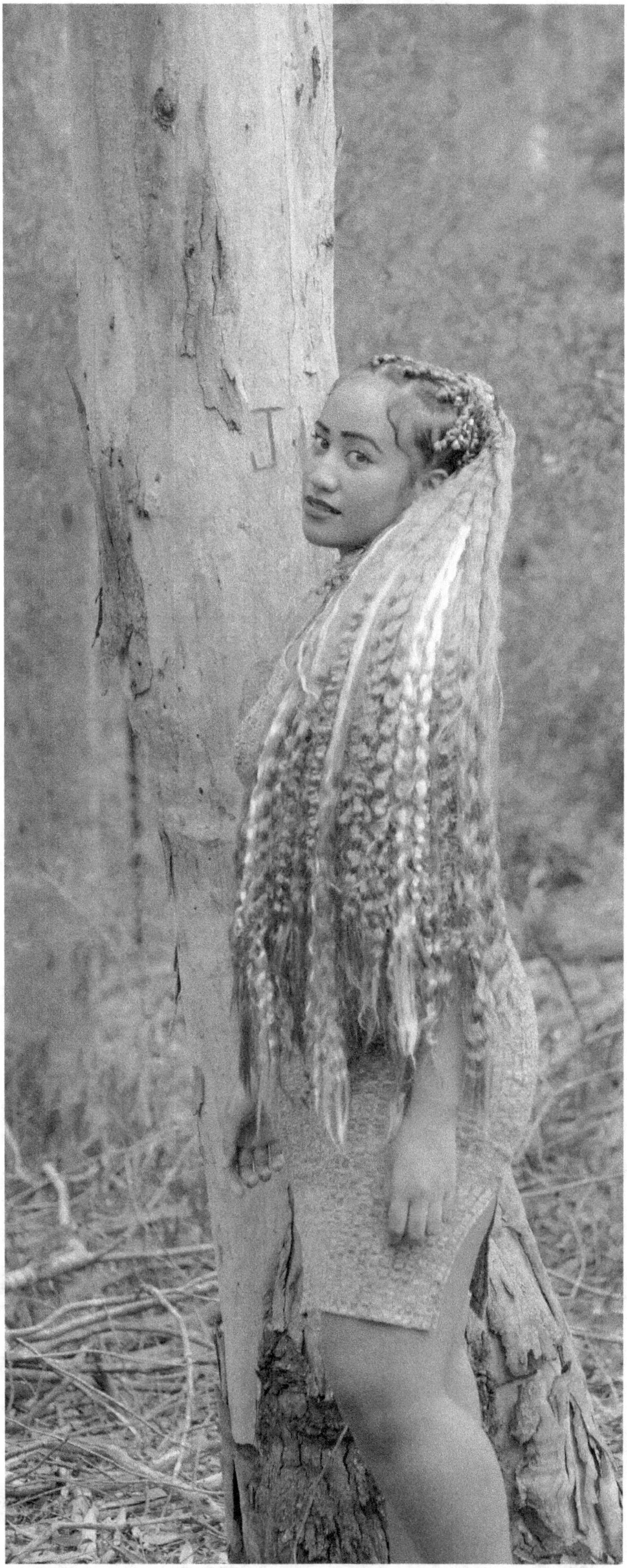

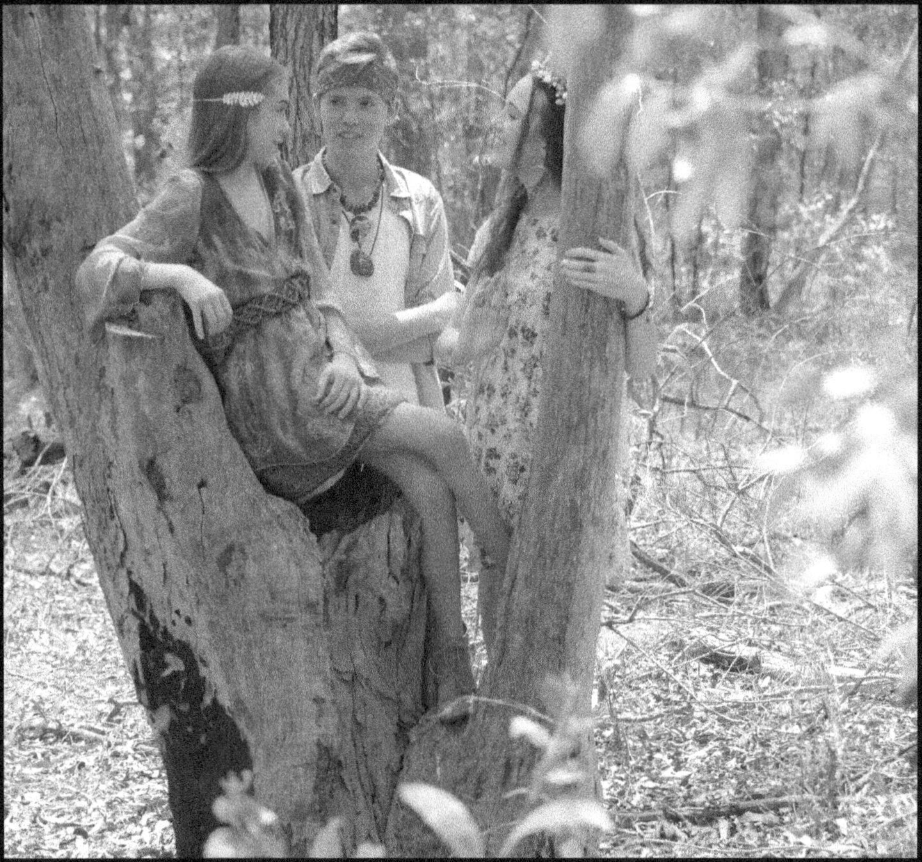

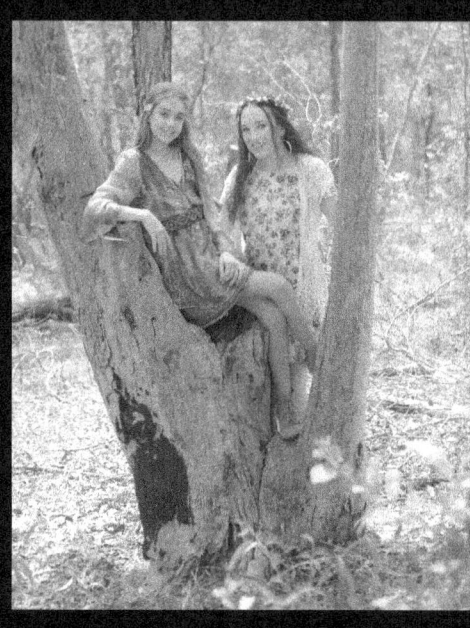

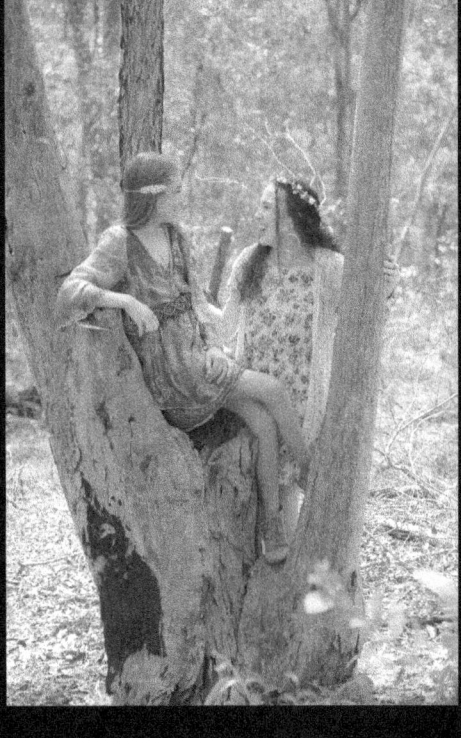

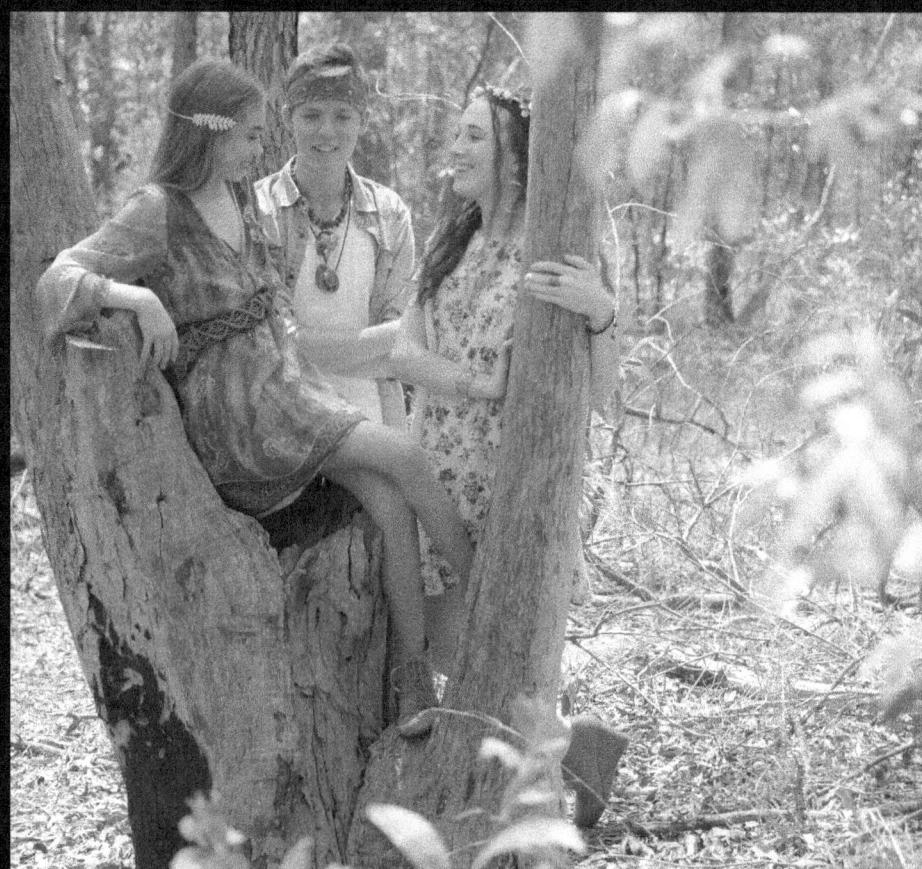

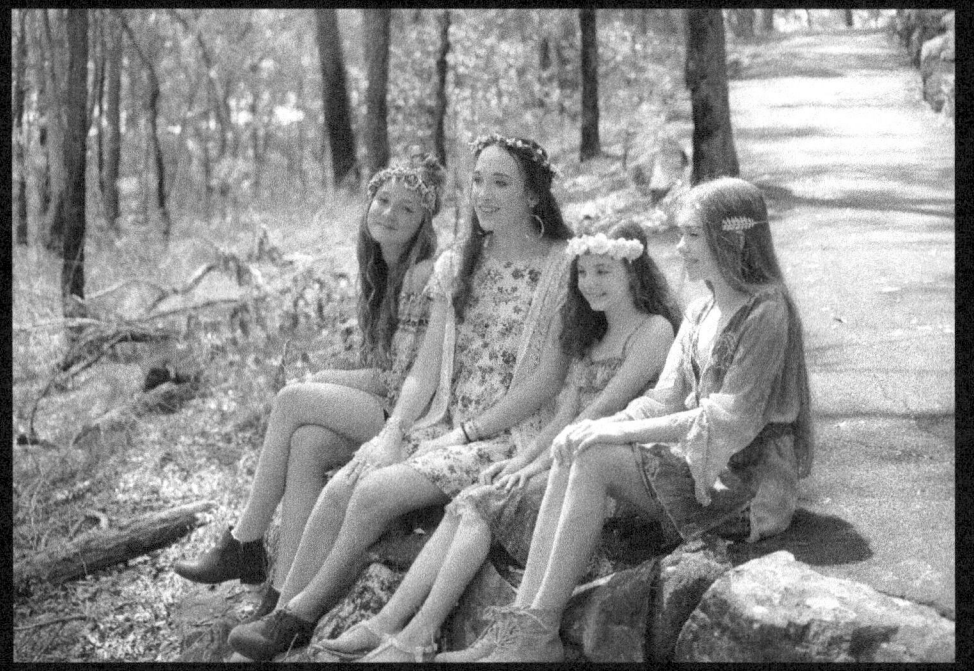

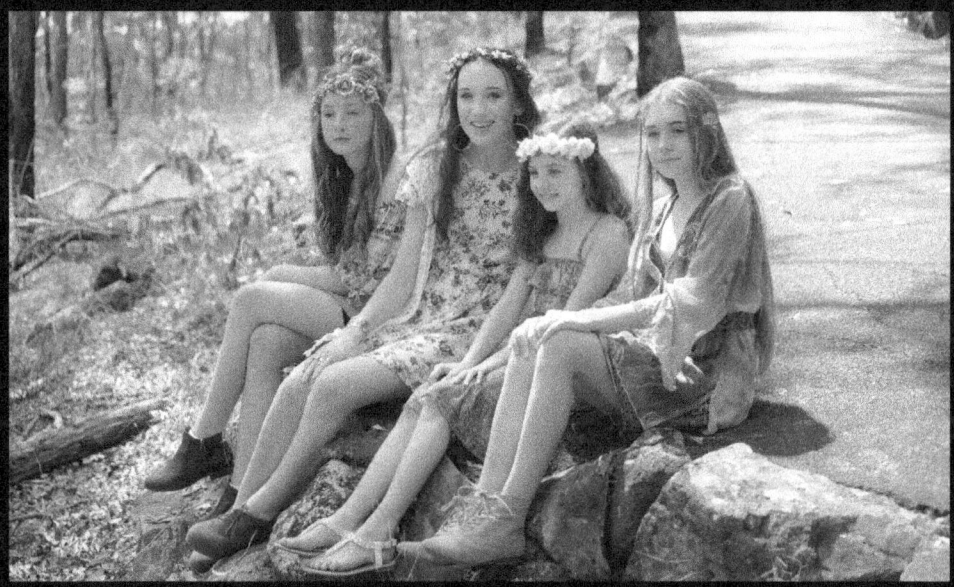

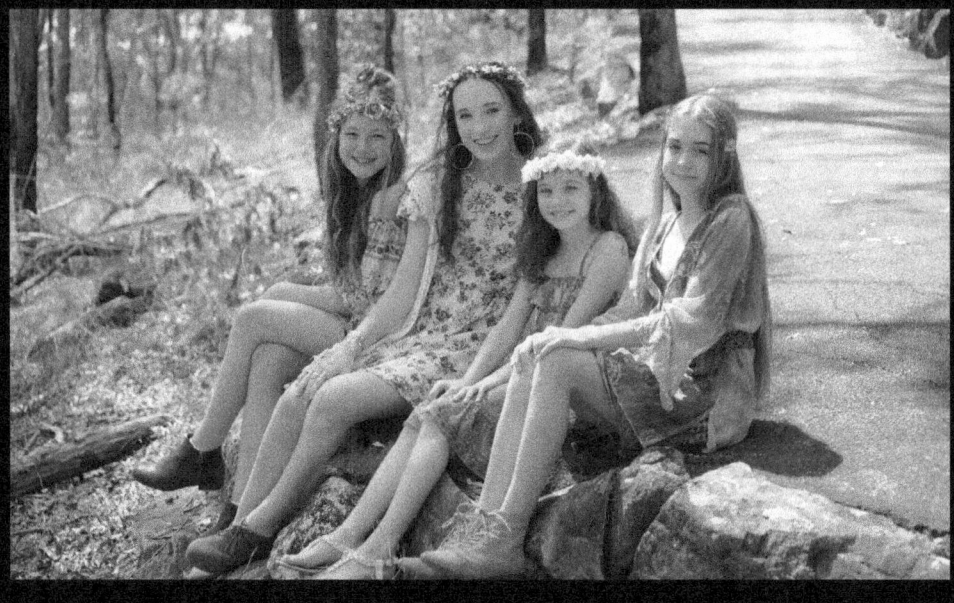

page 82

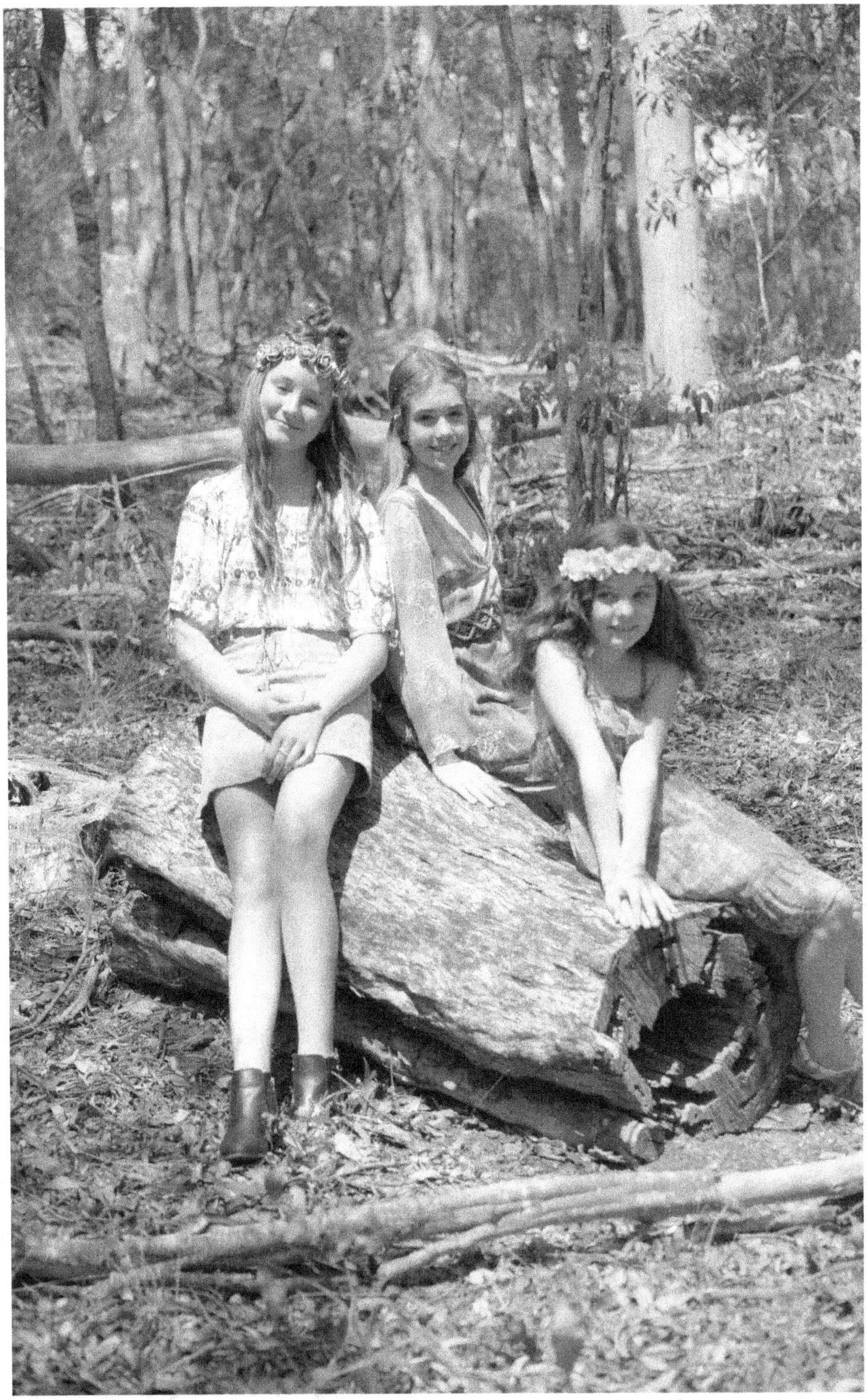

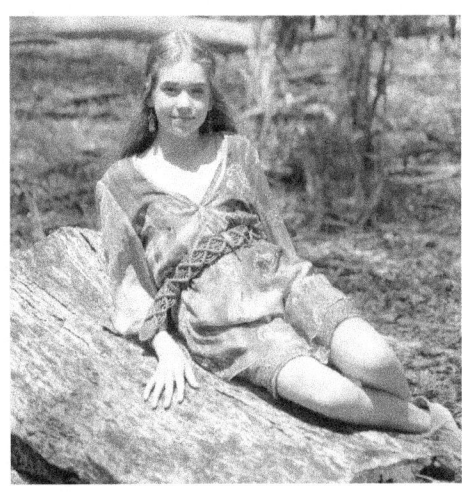

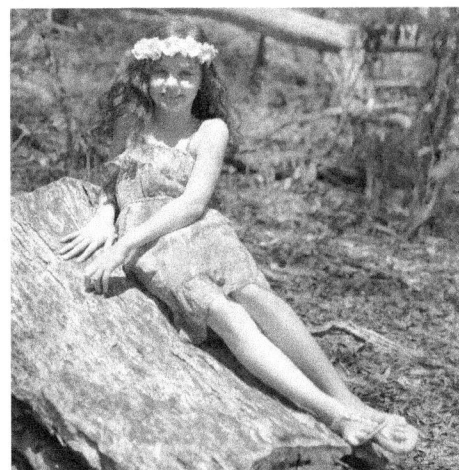

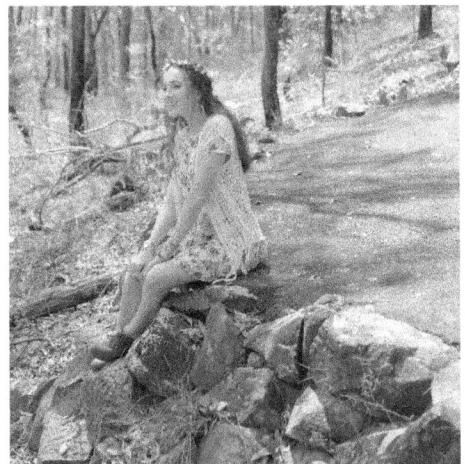

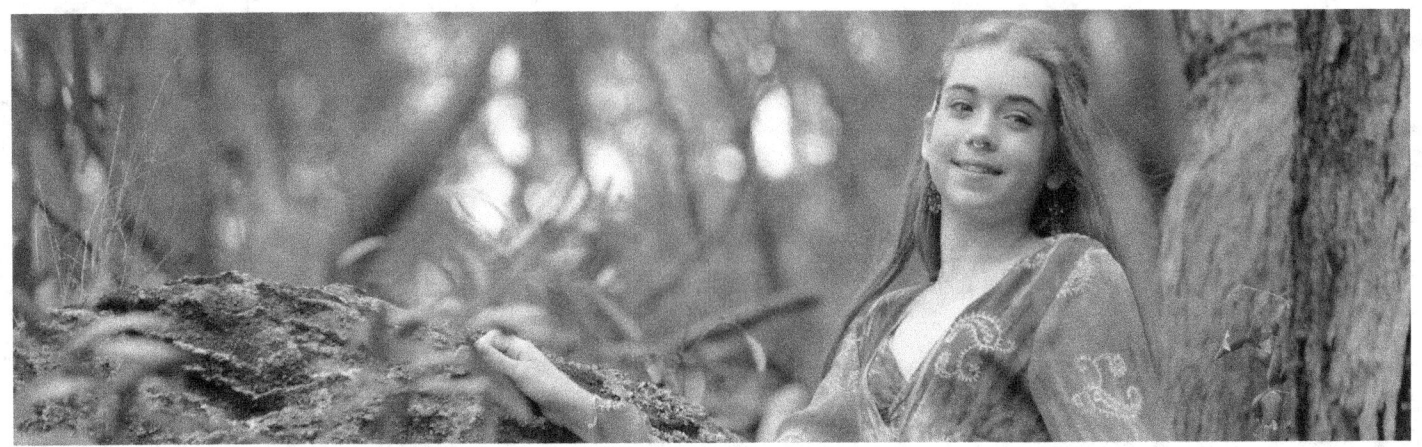

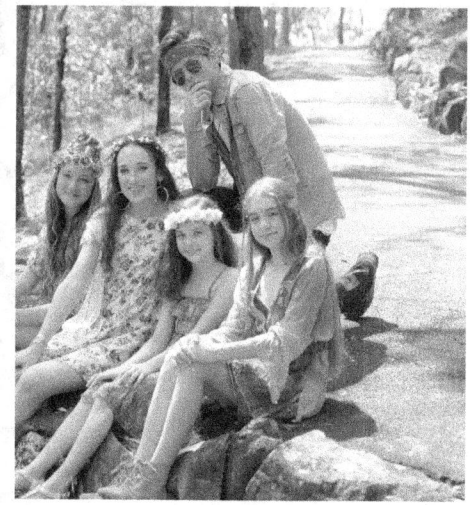
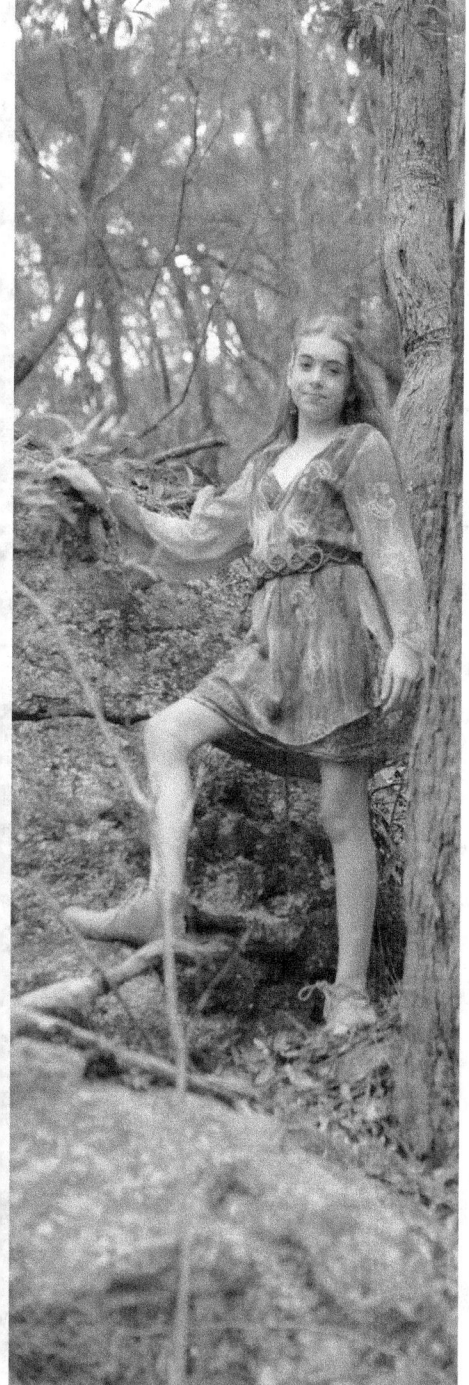
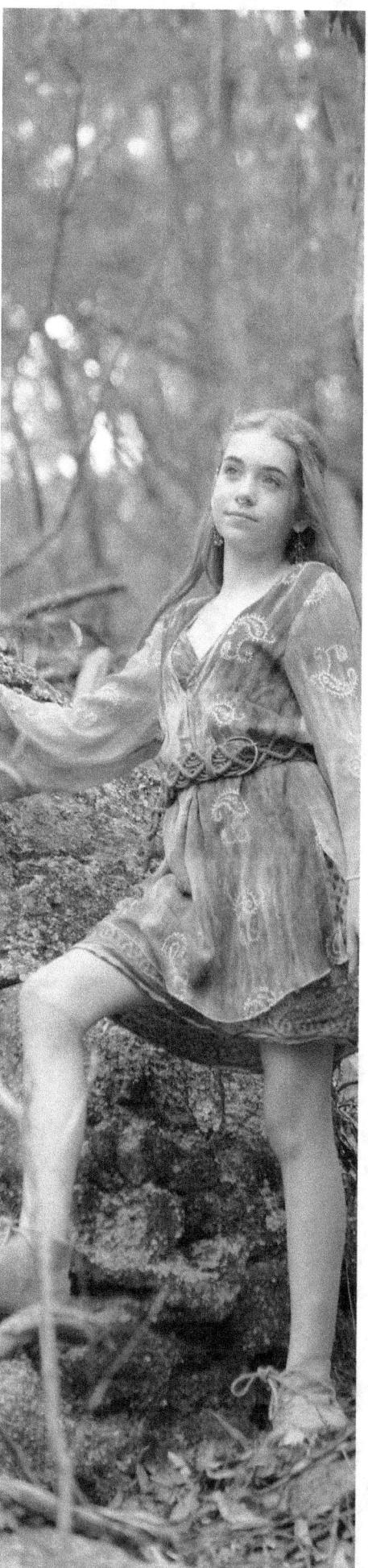
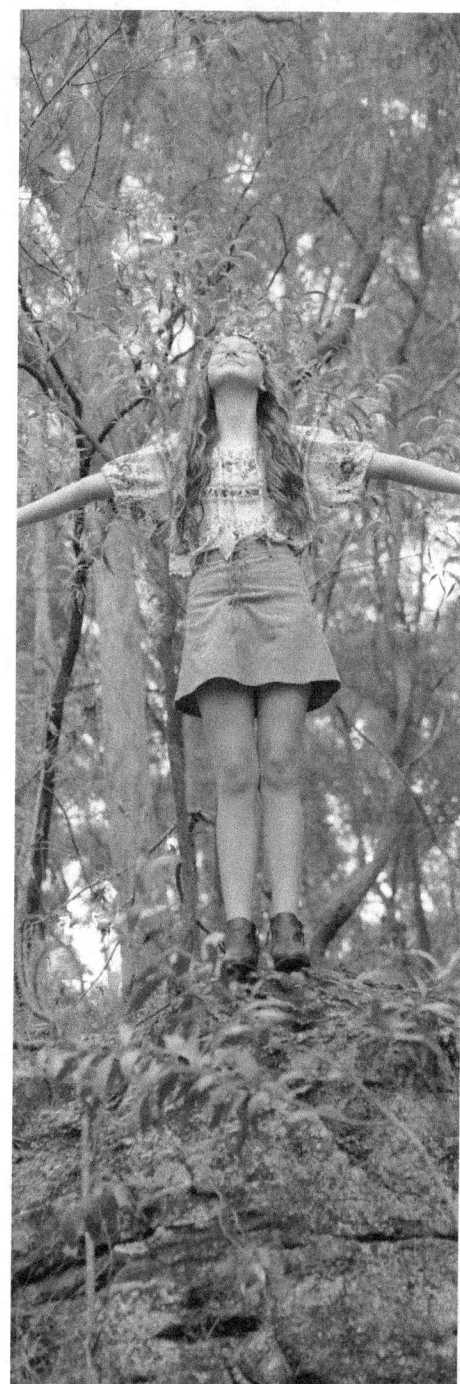
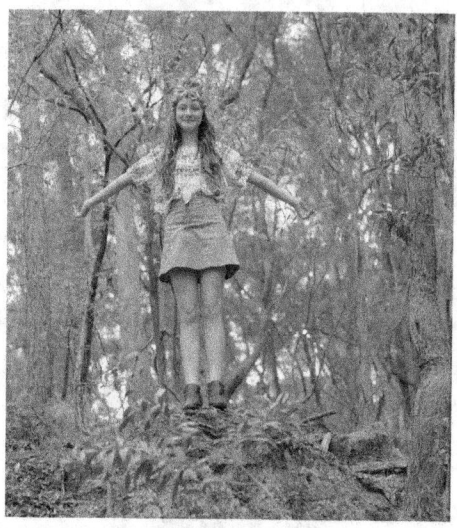

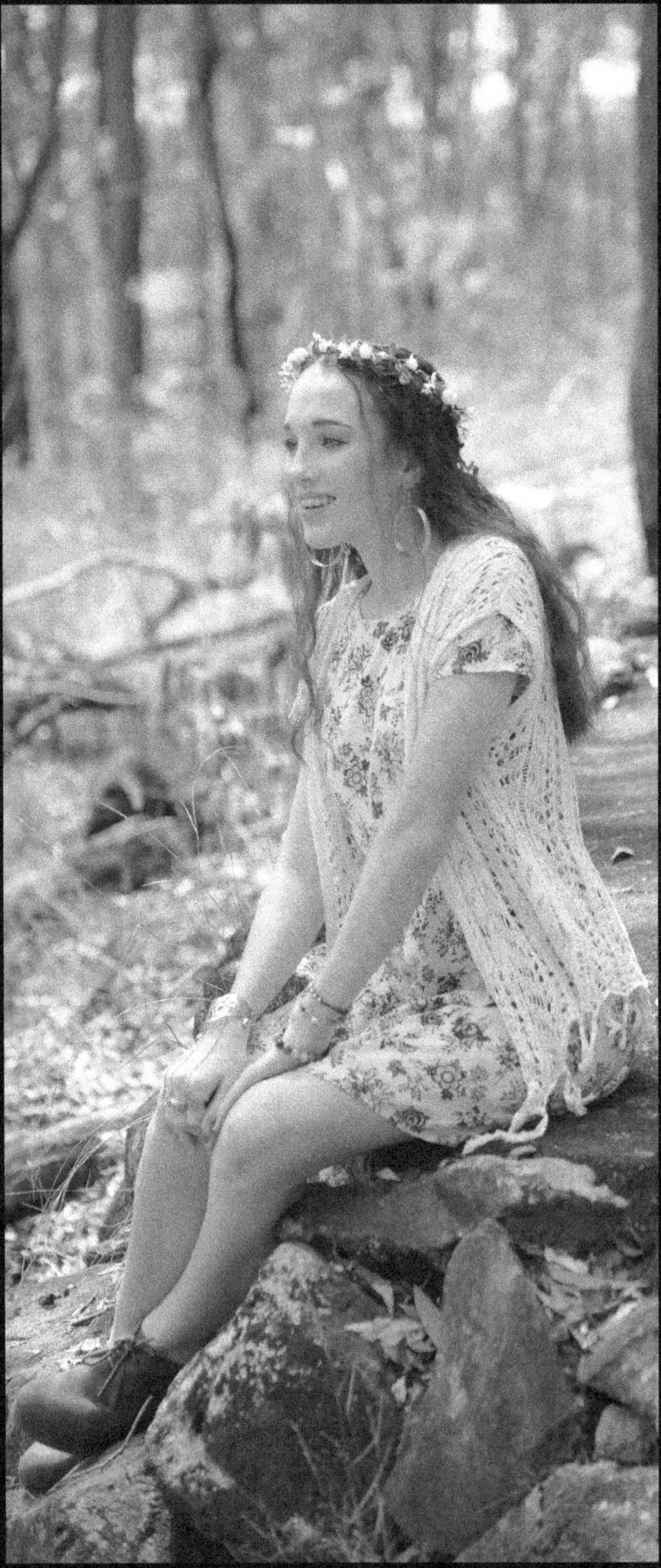

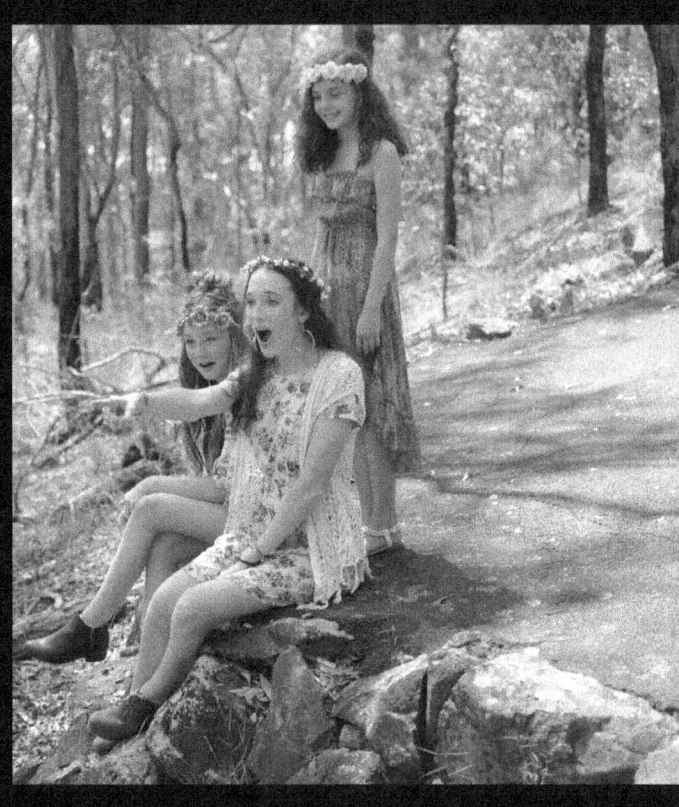

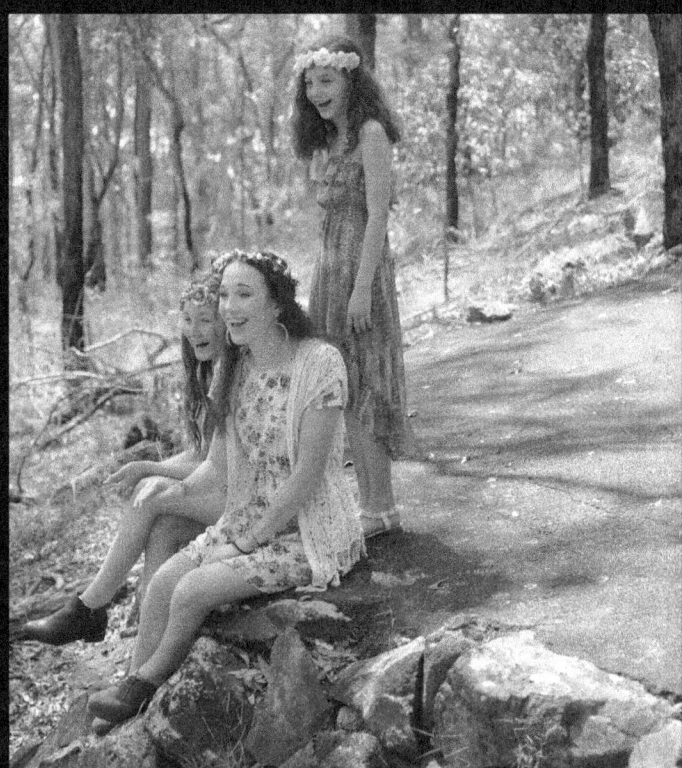

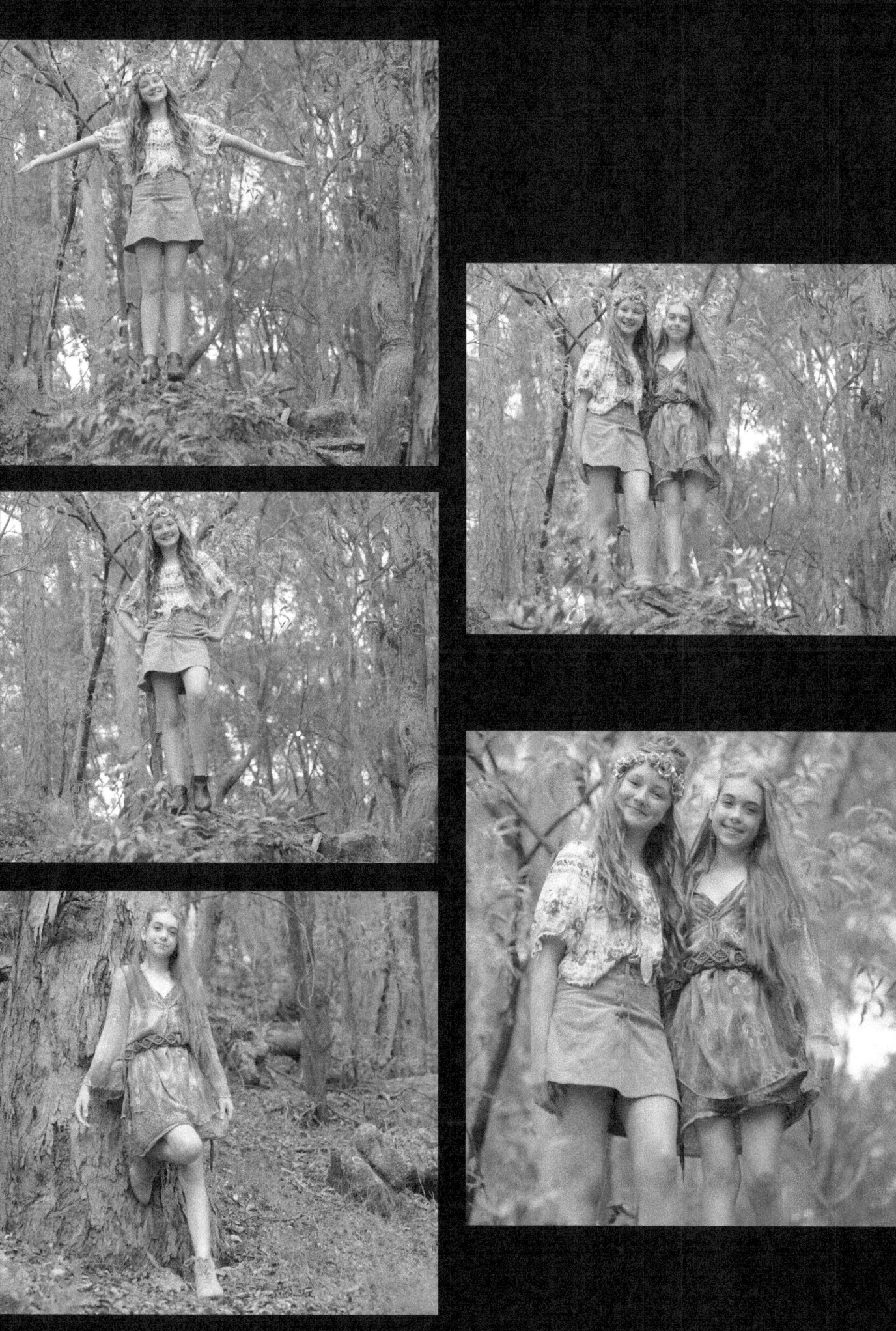

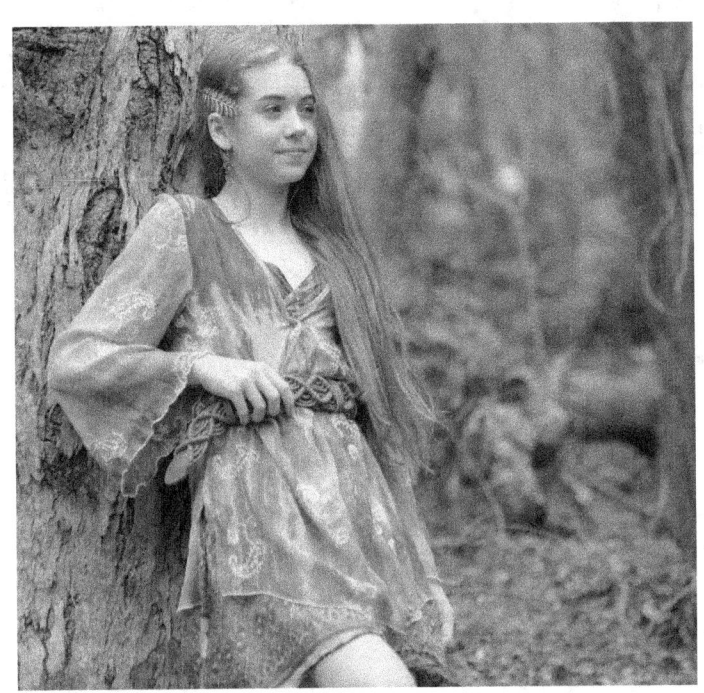
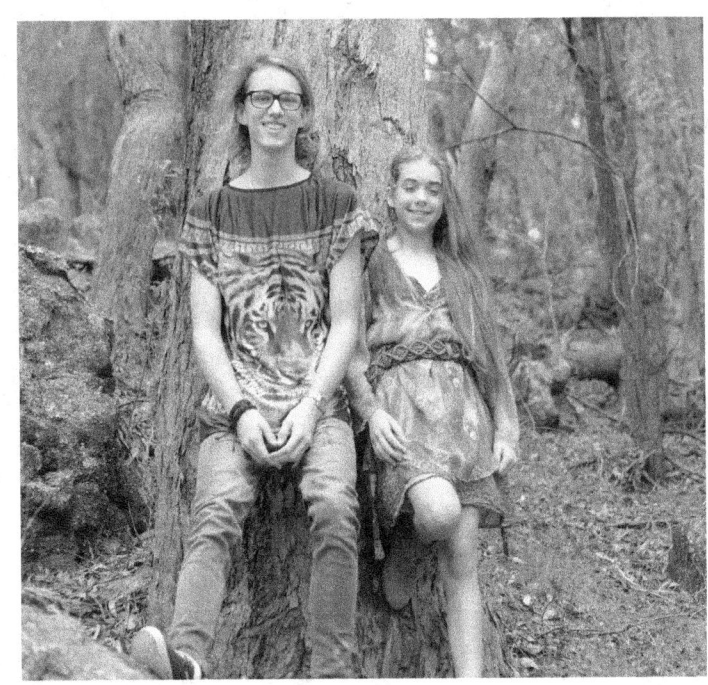

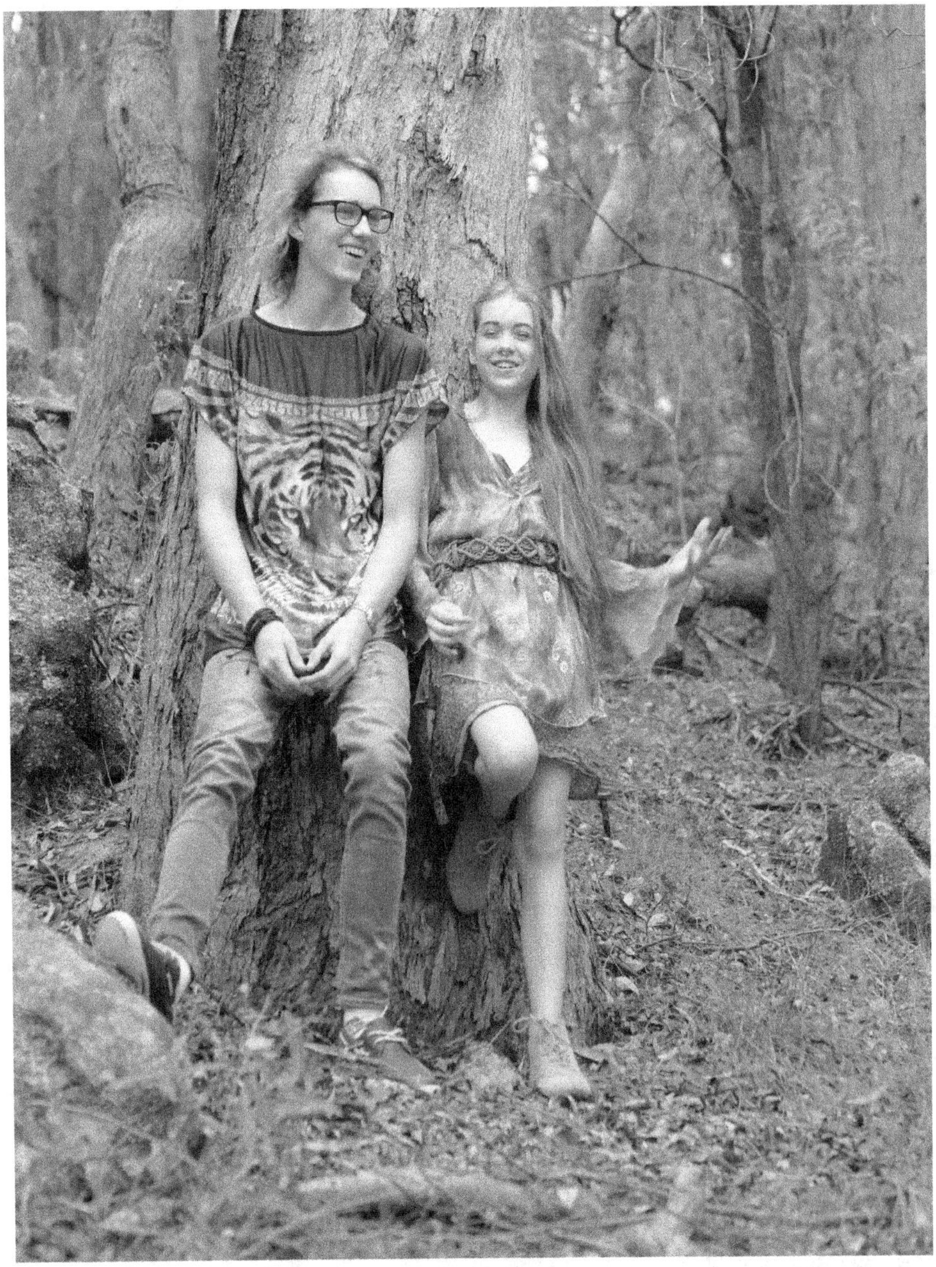

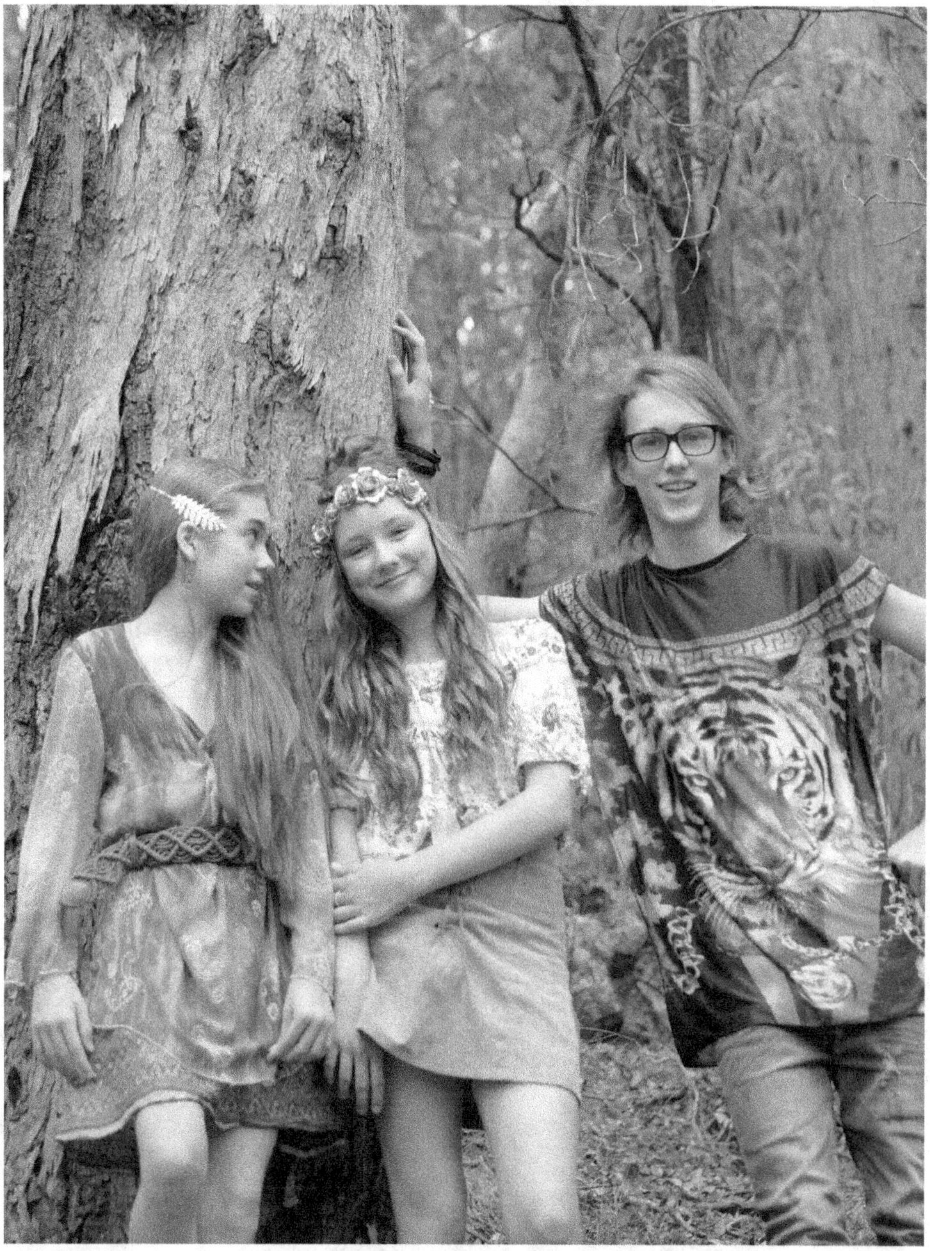

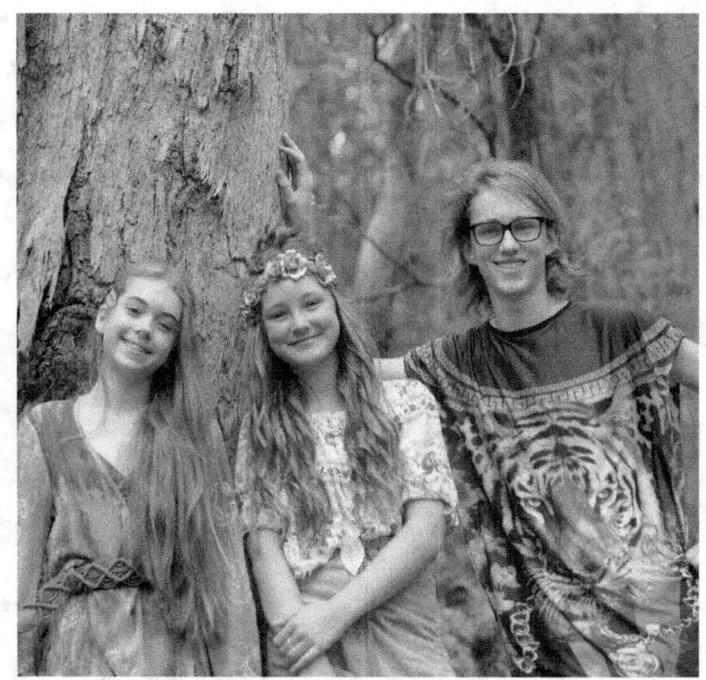
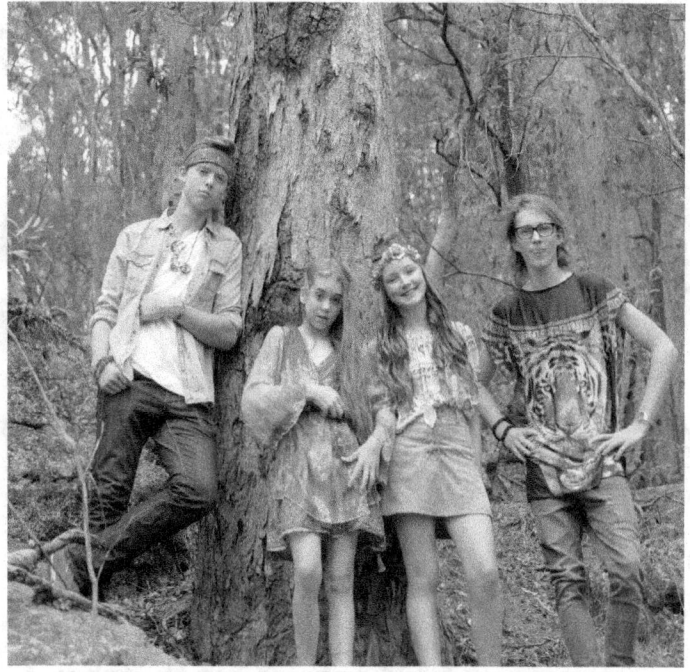

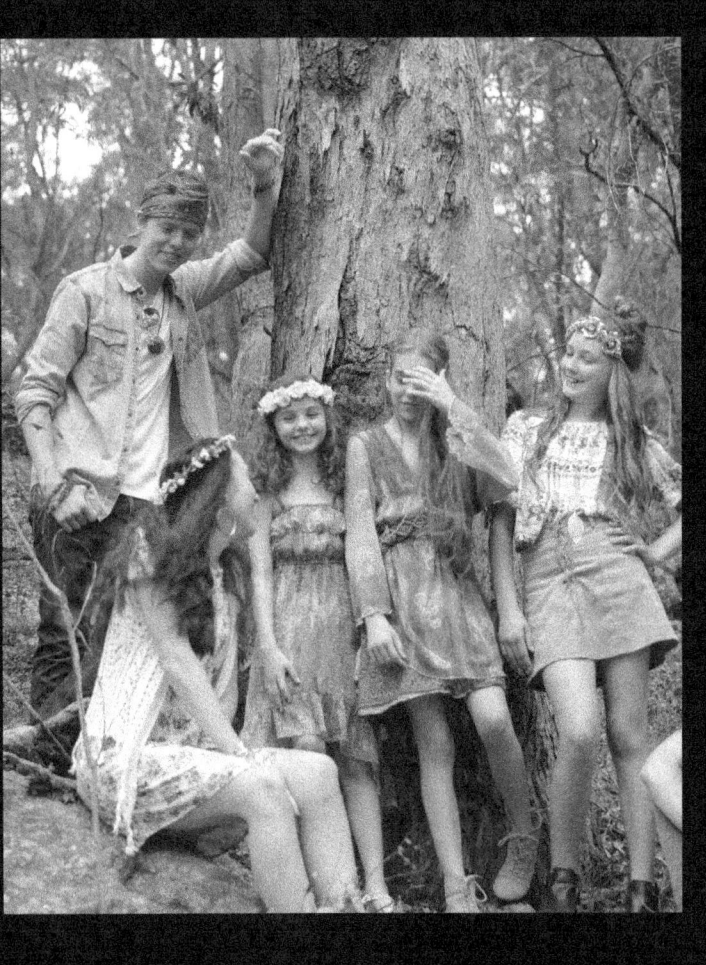
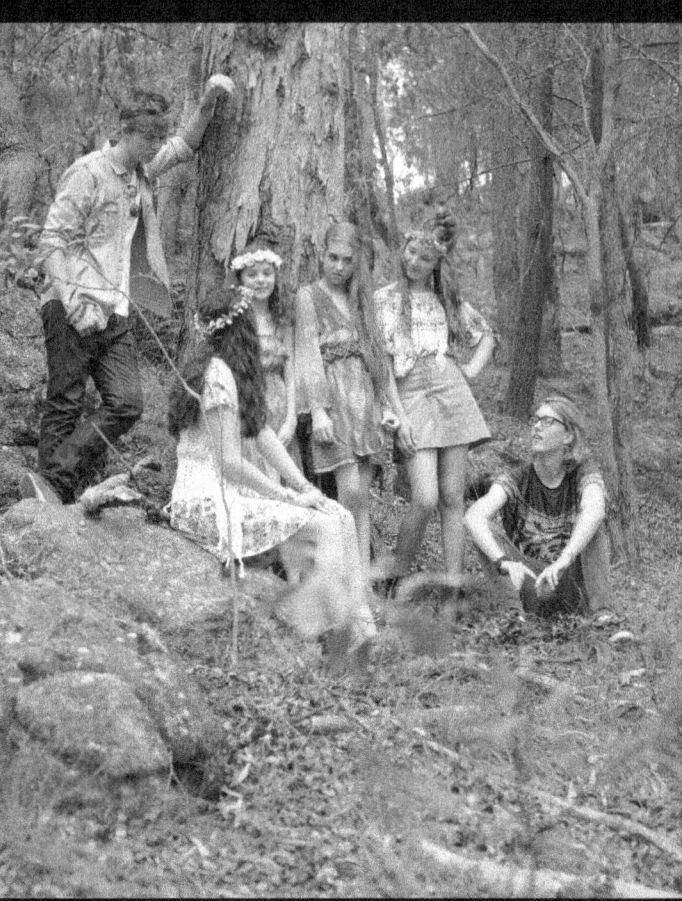
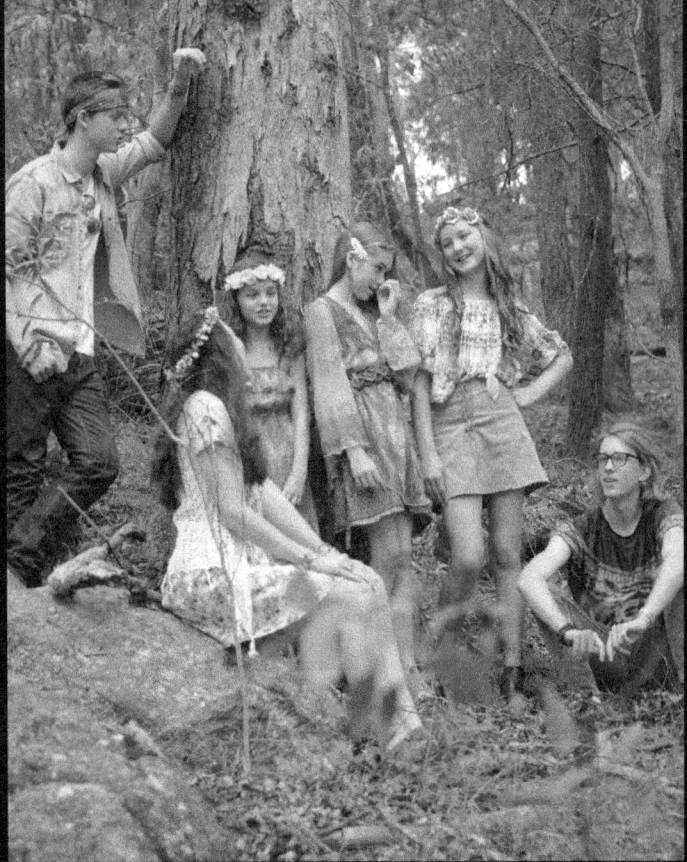
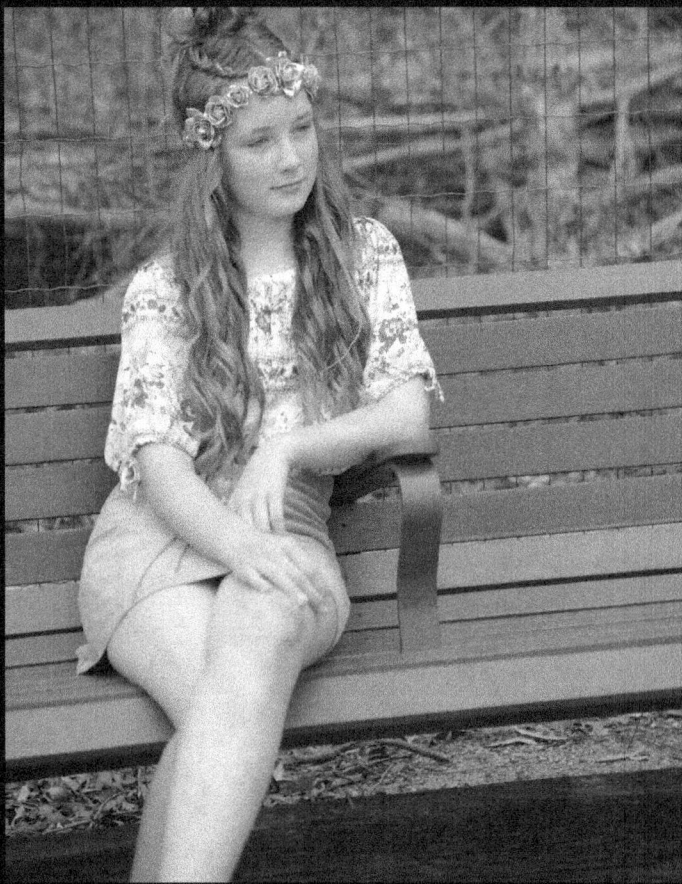

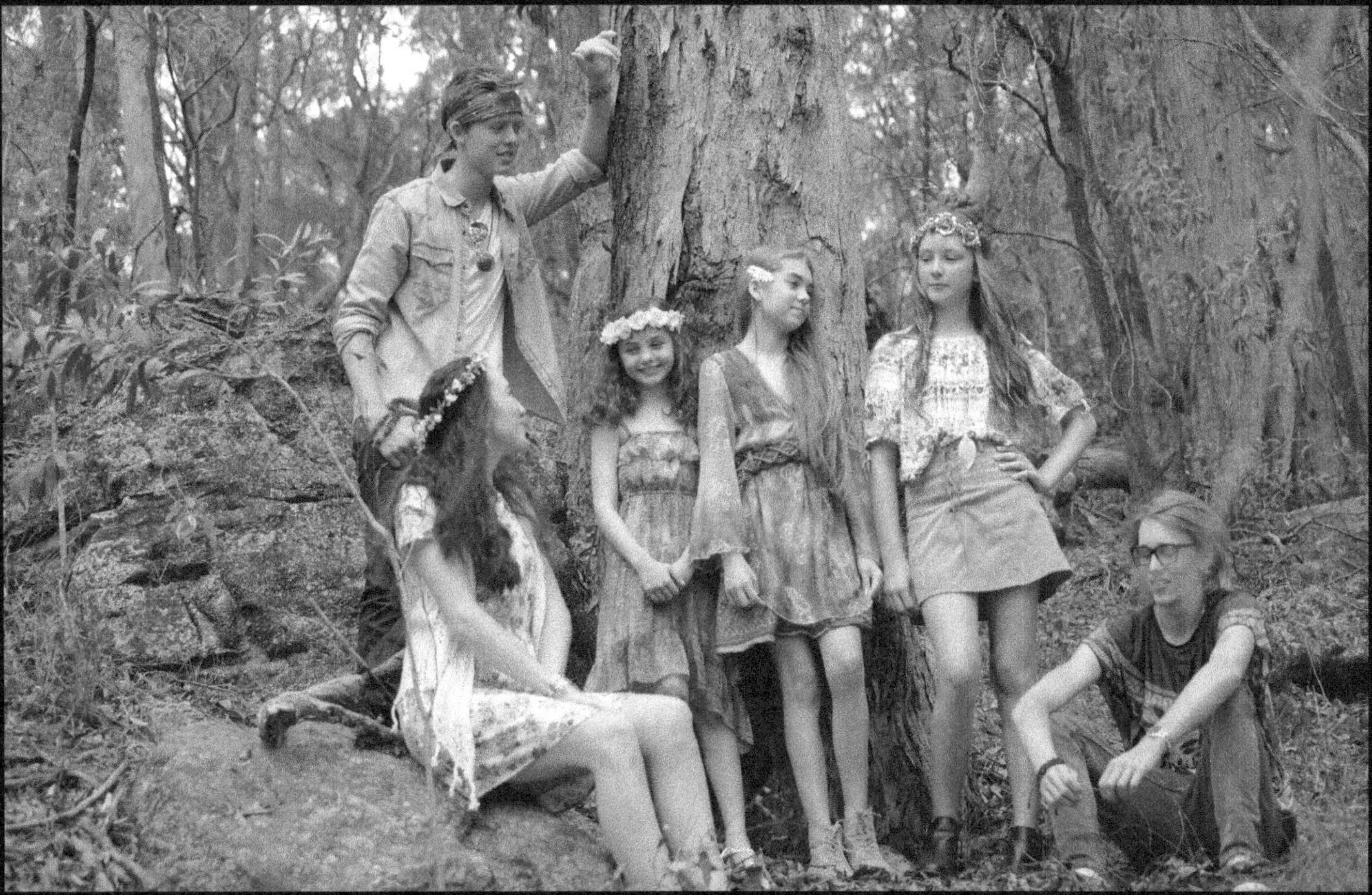

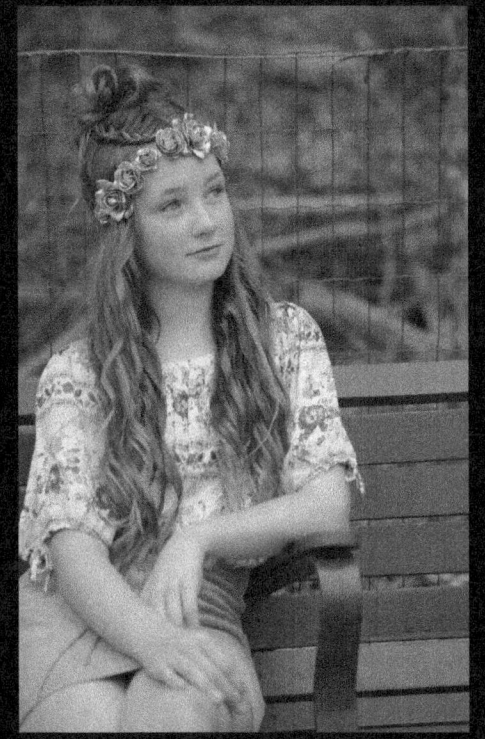
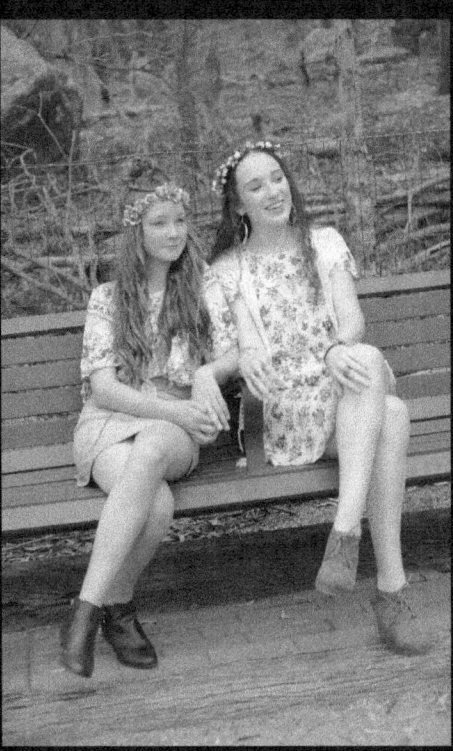
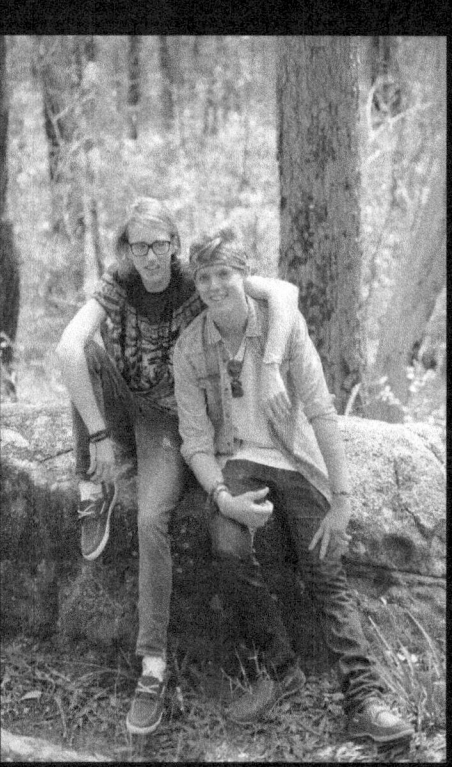

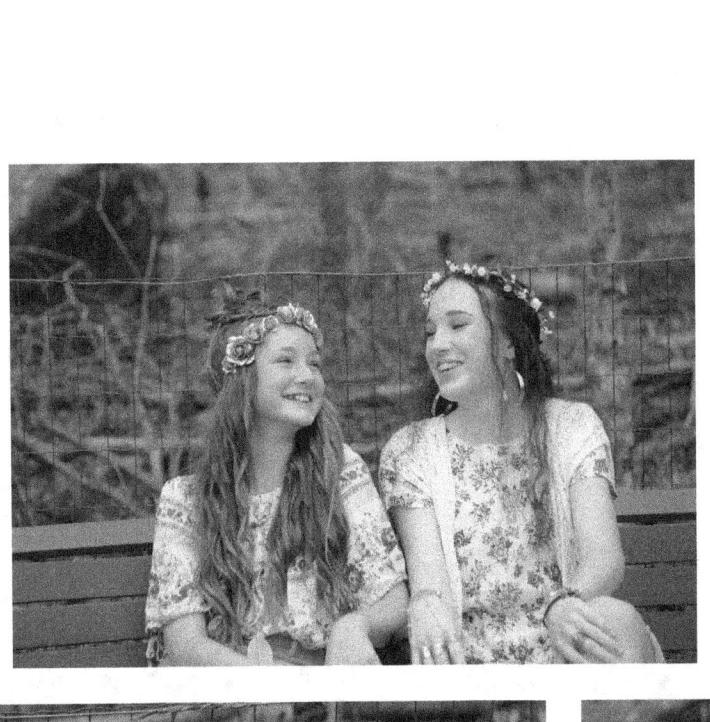

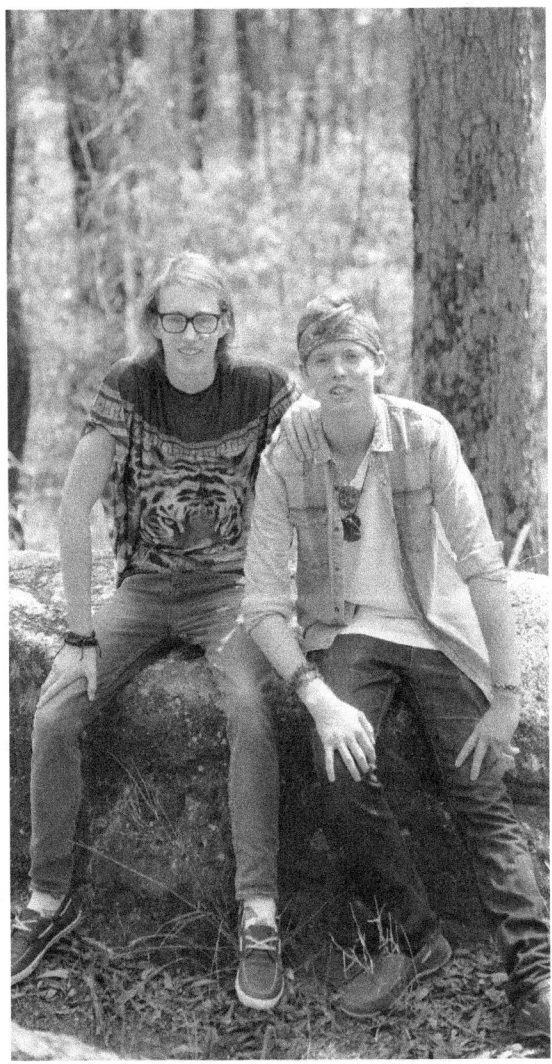

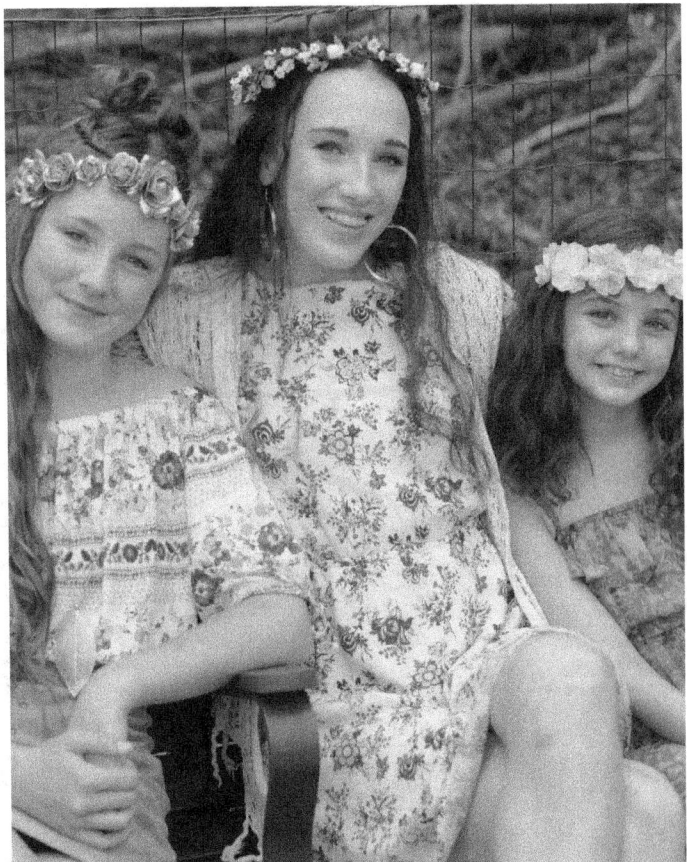

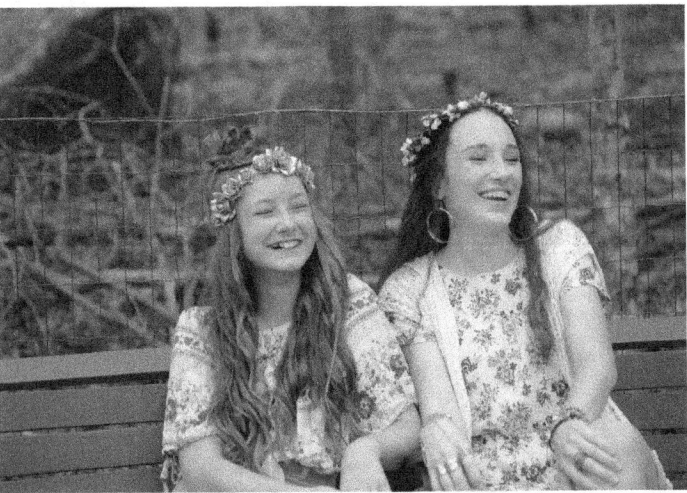

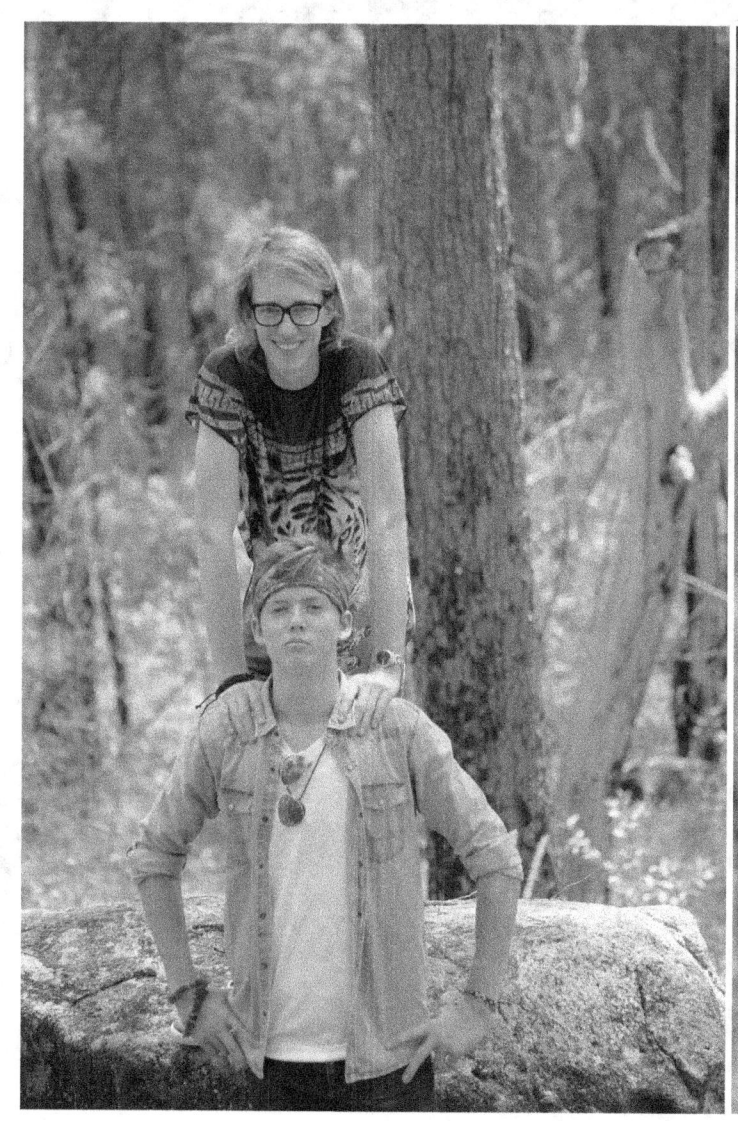
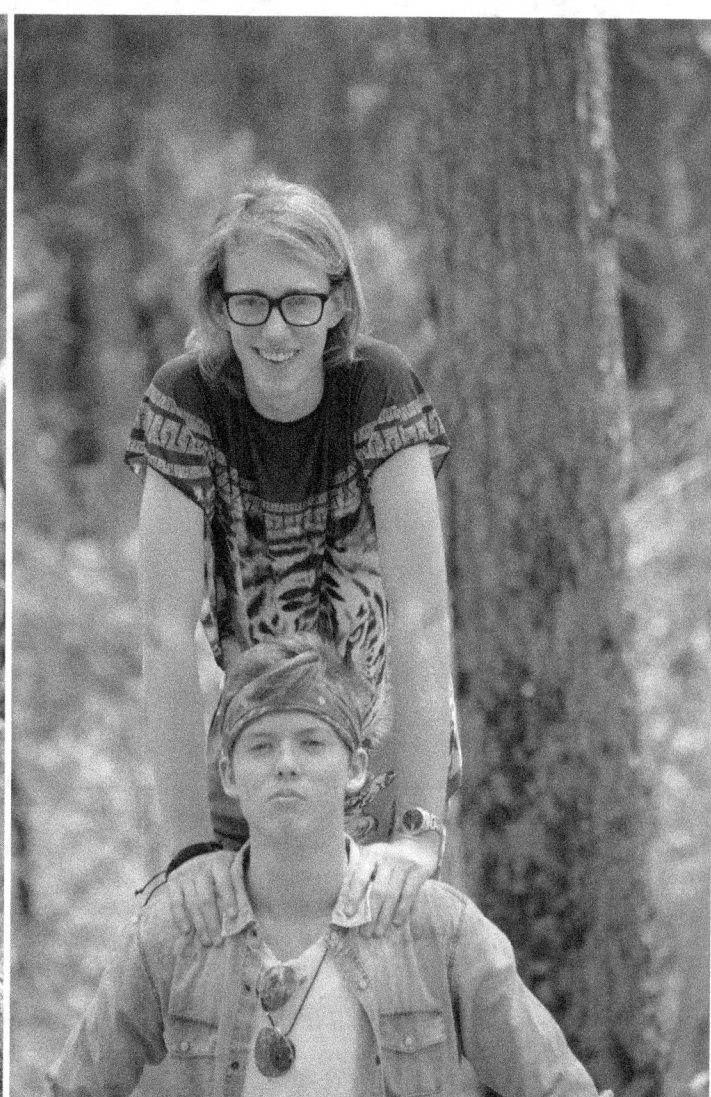
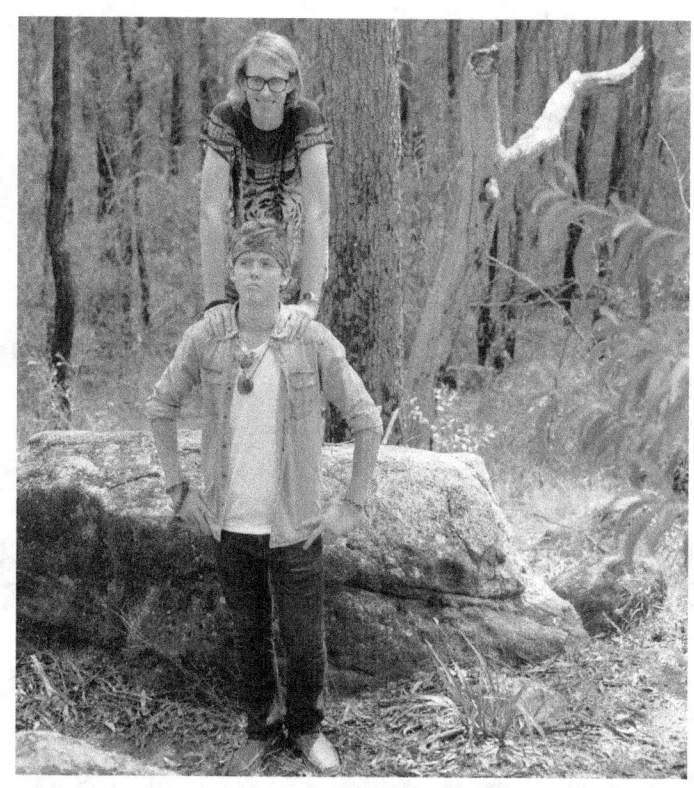
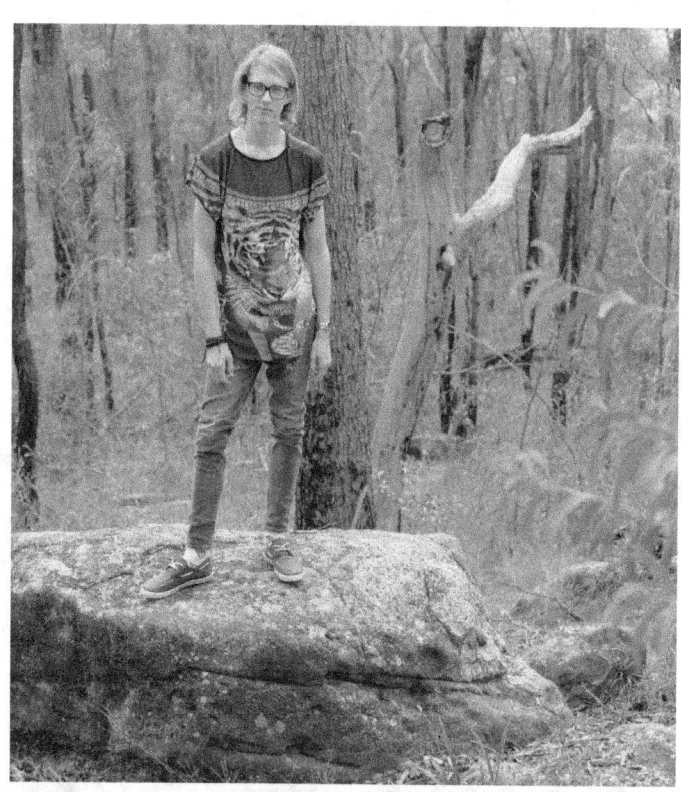

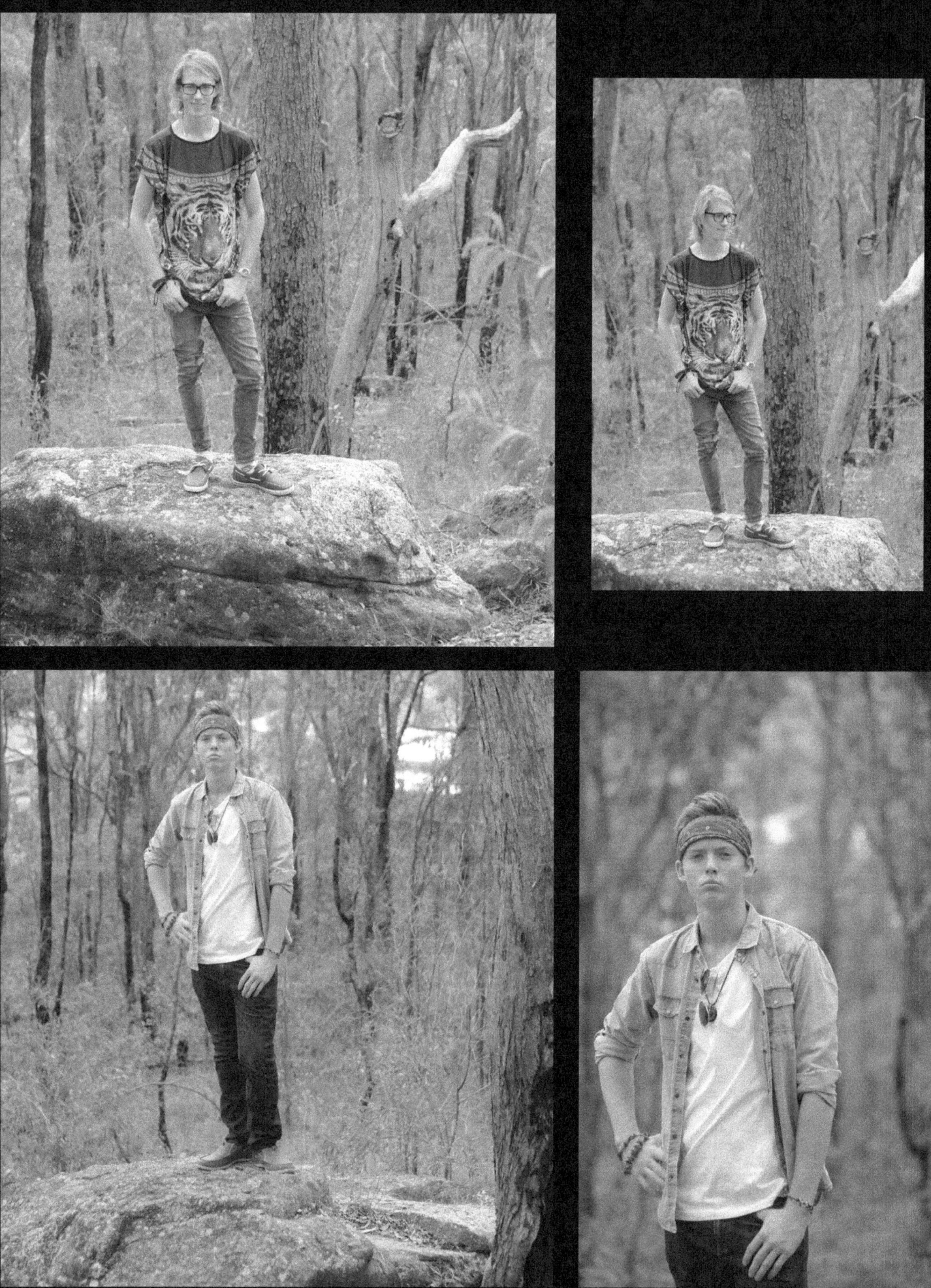

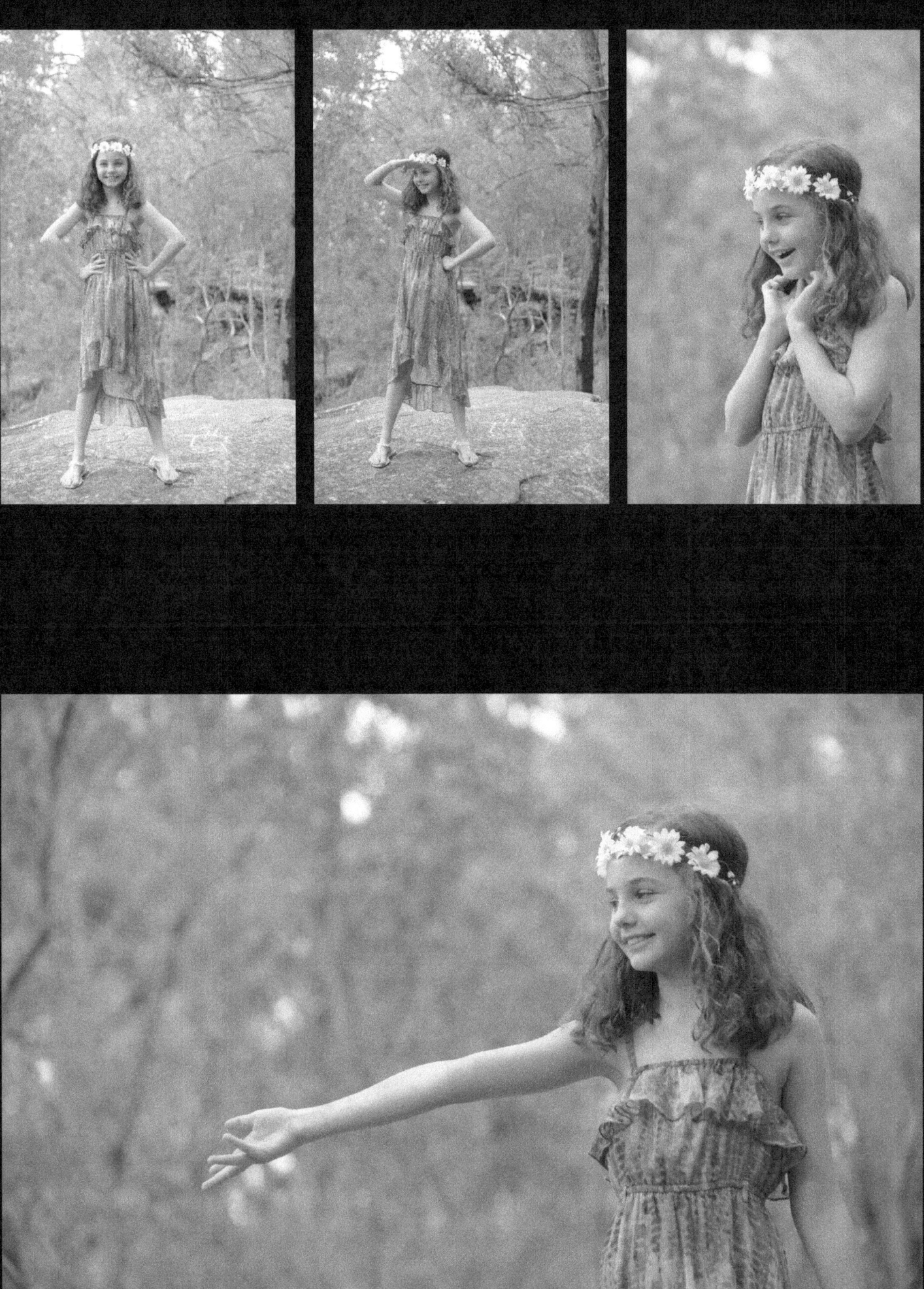

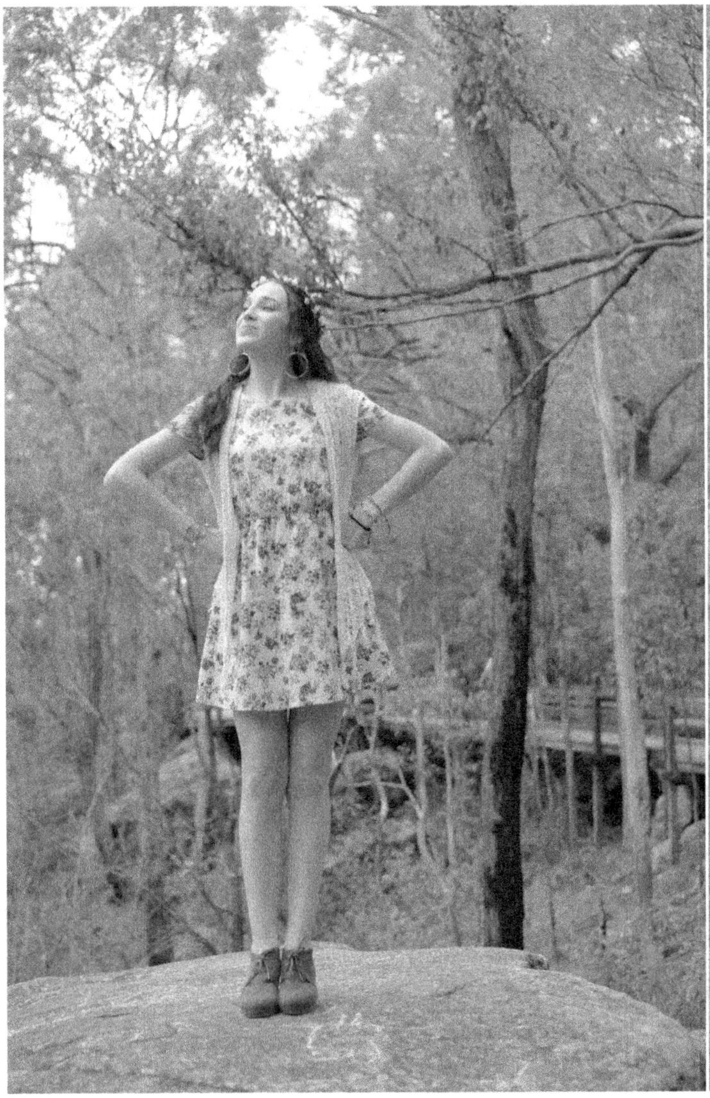

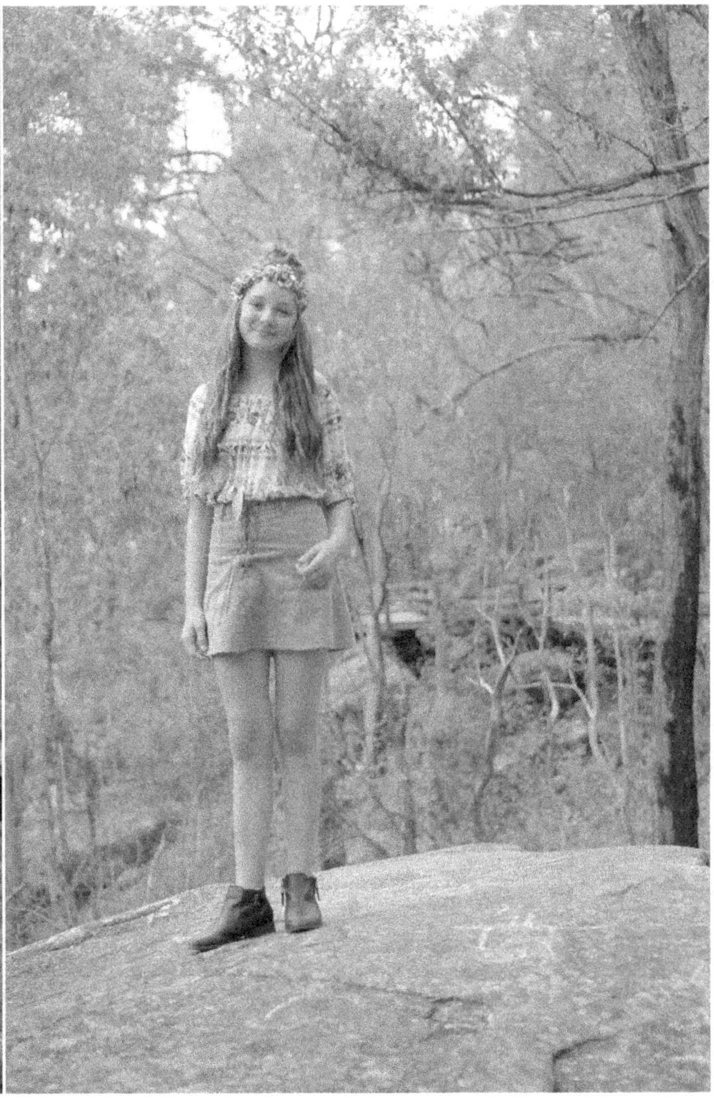

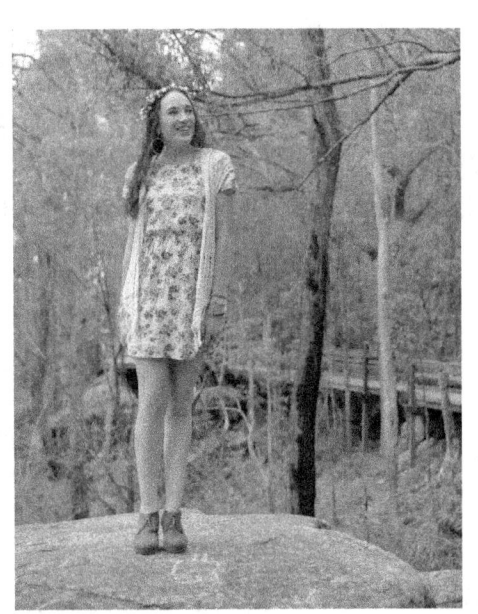
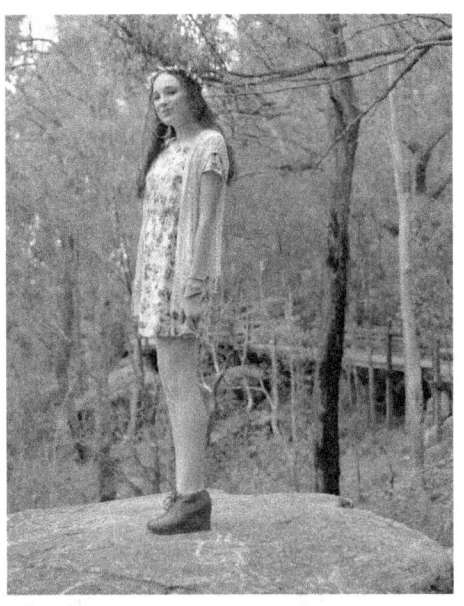
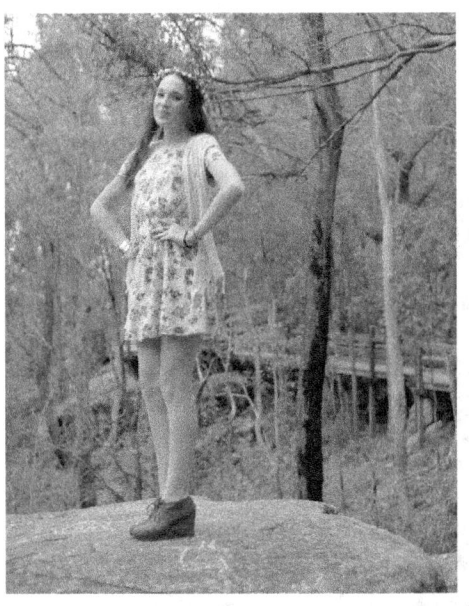

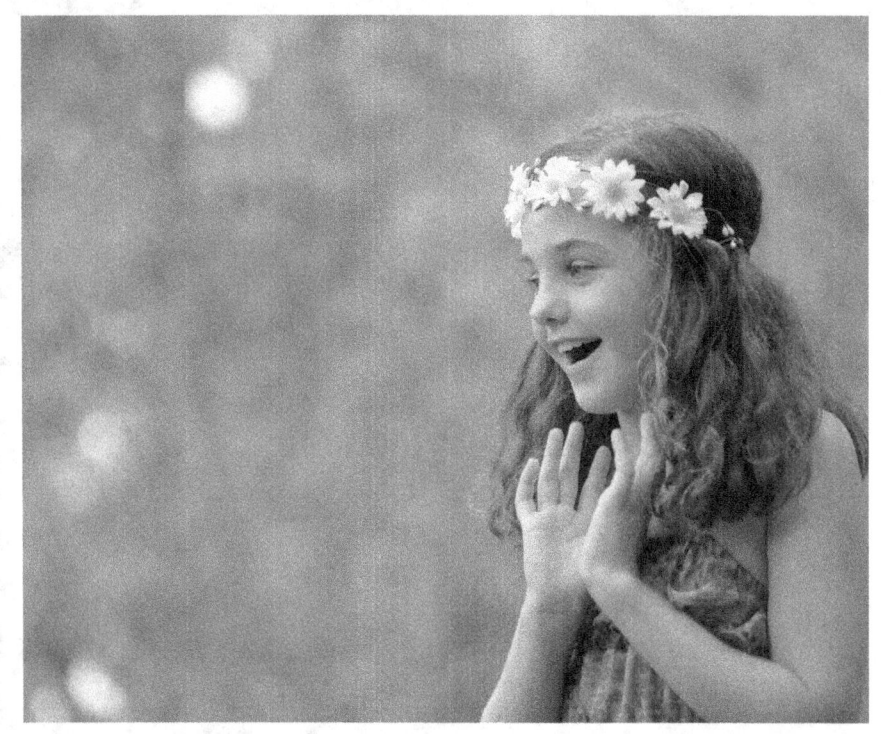

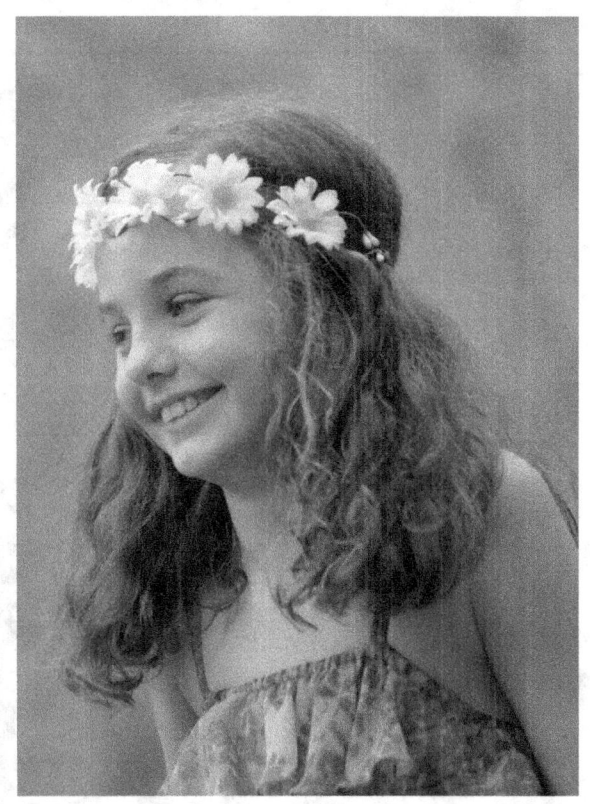

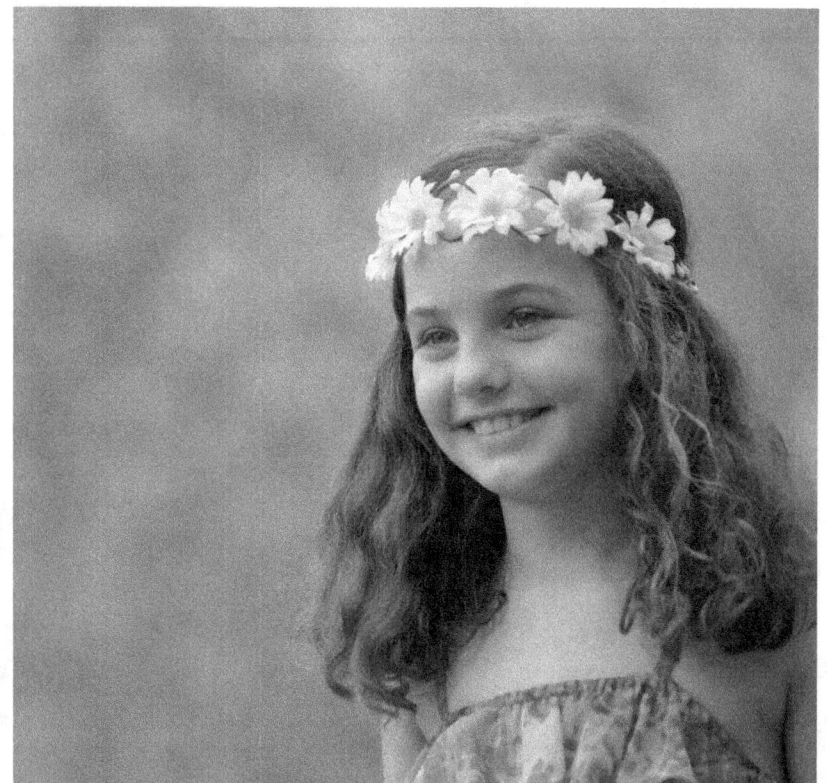

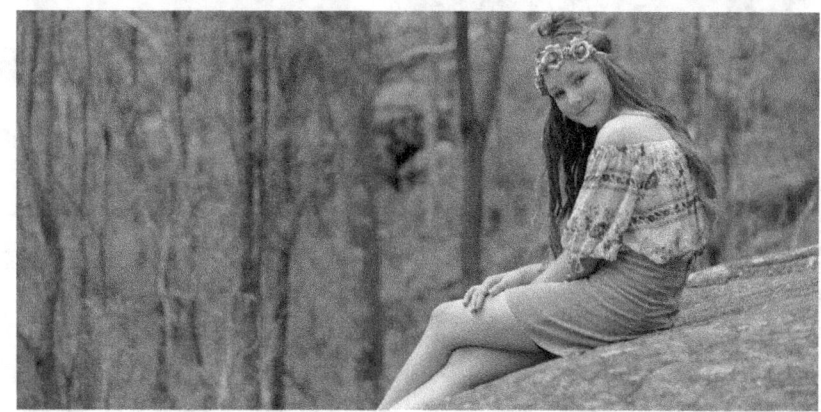

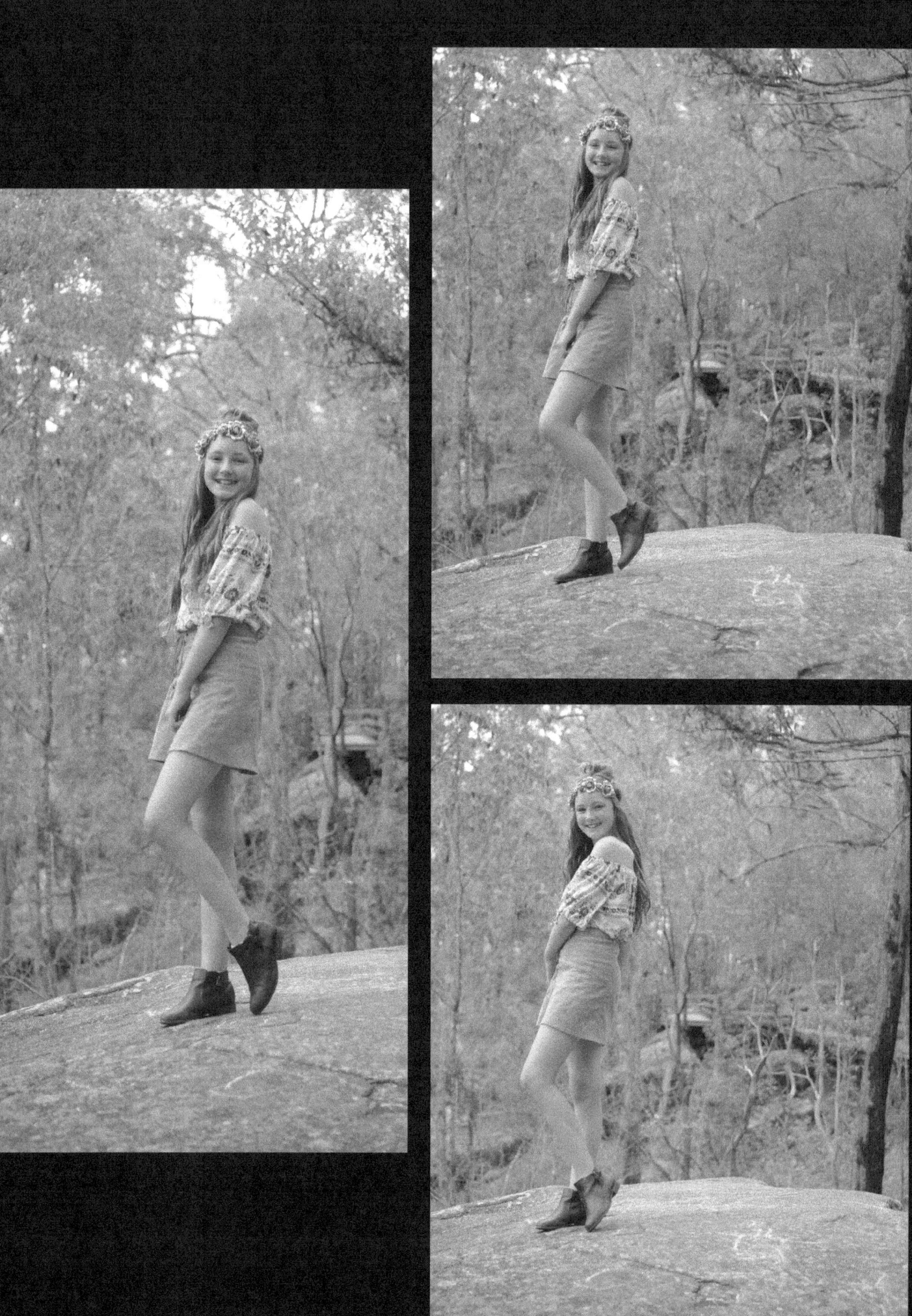

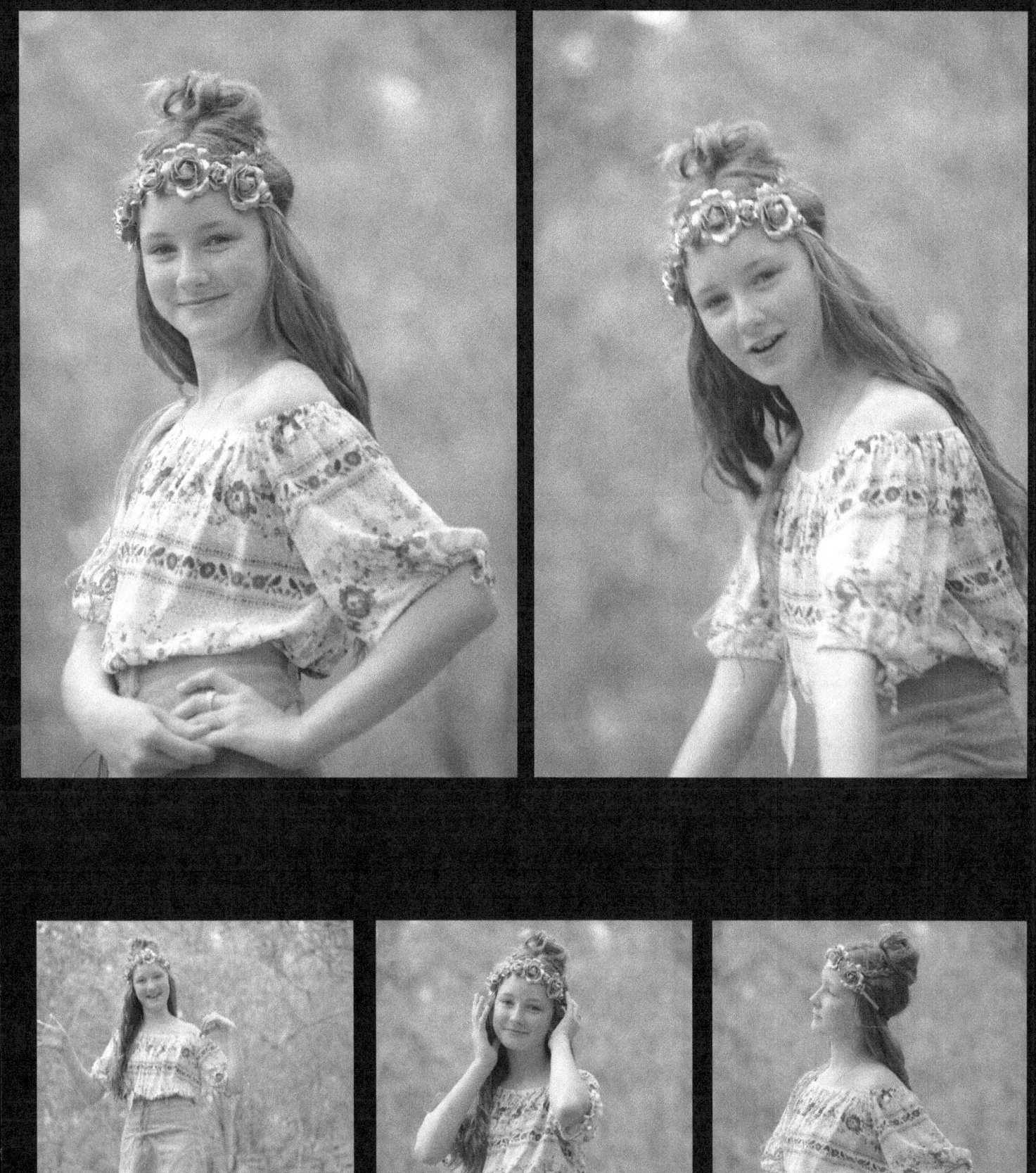

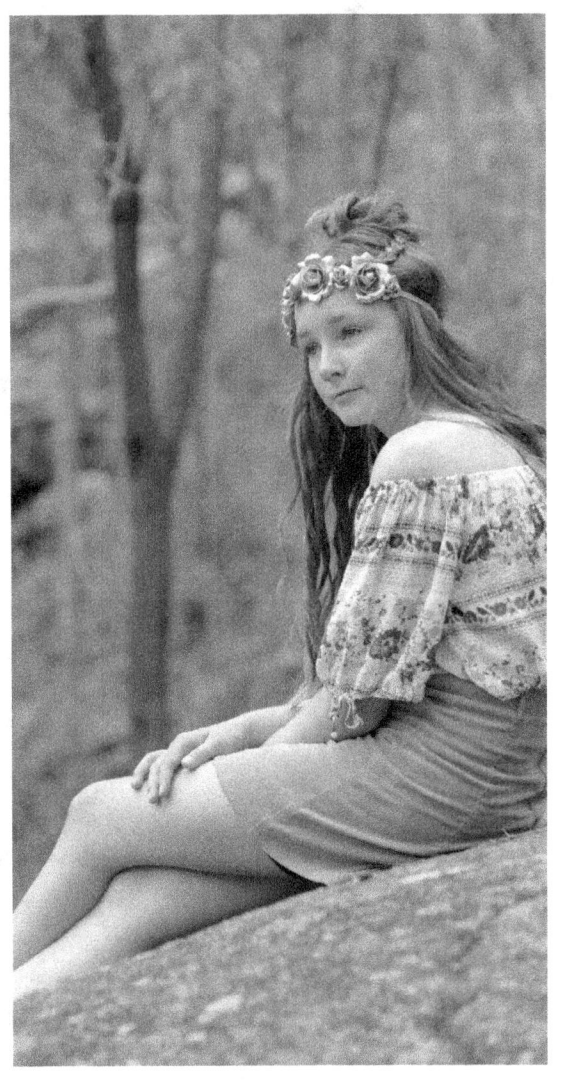

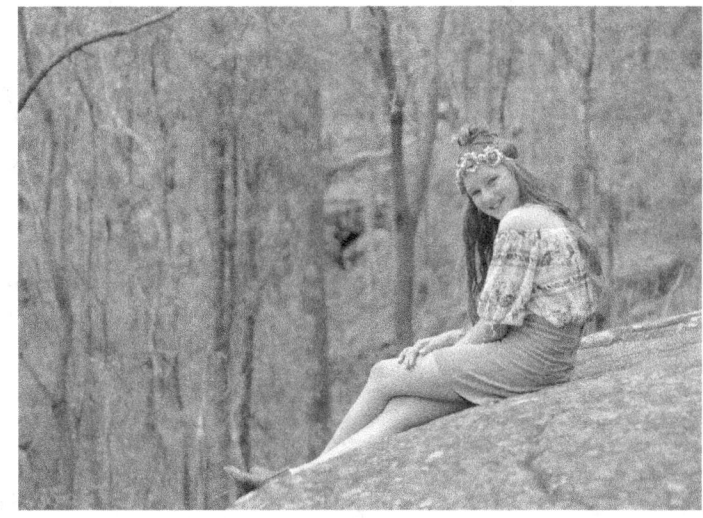

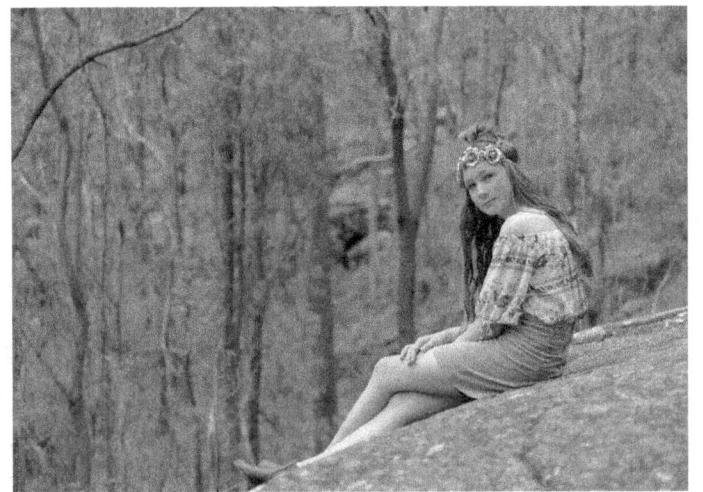

page 99

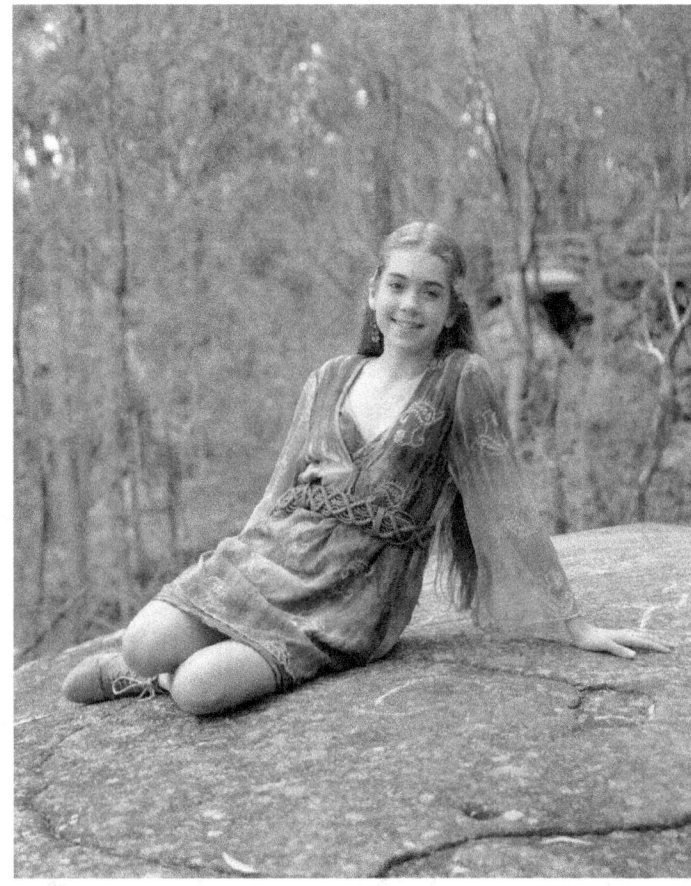

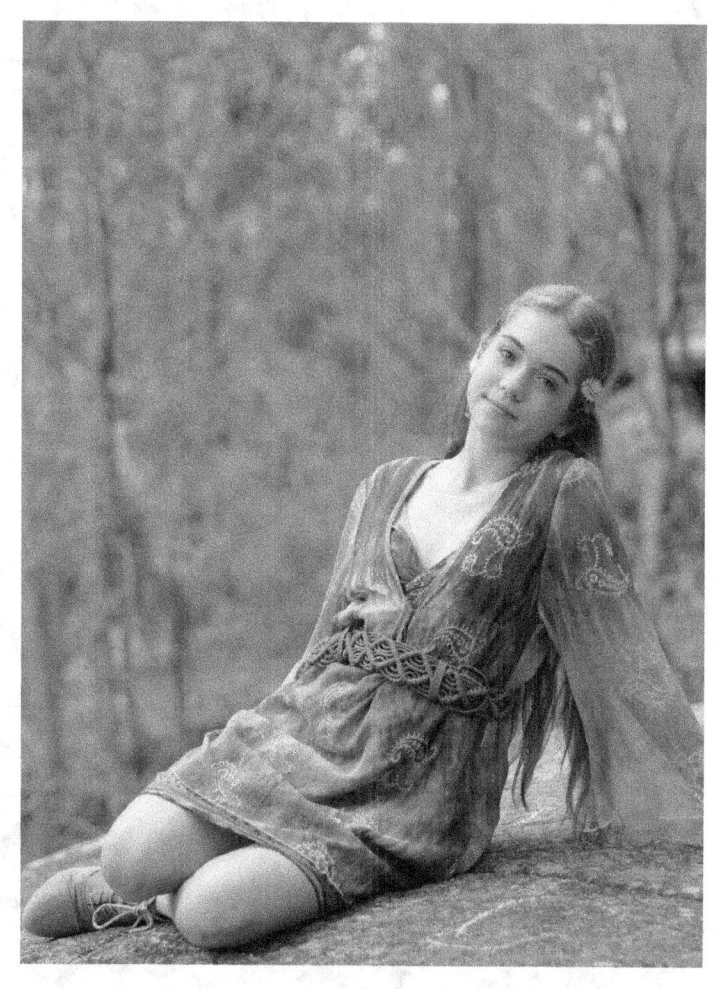
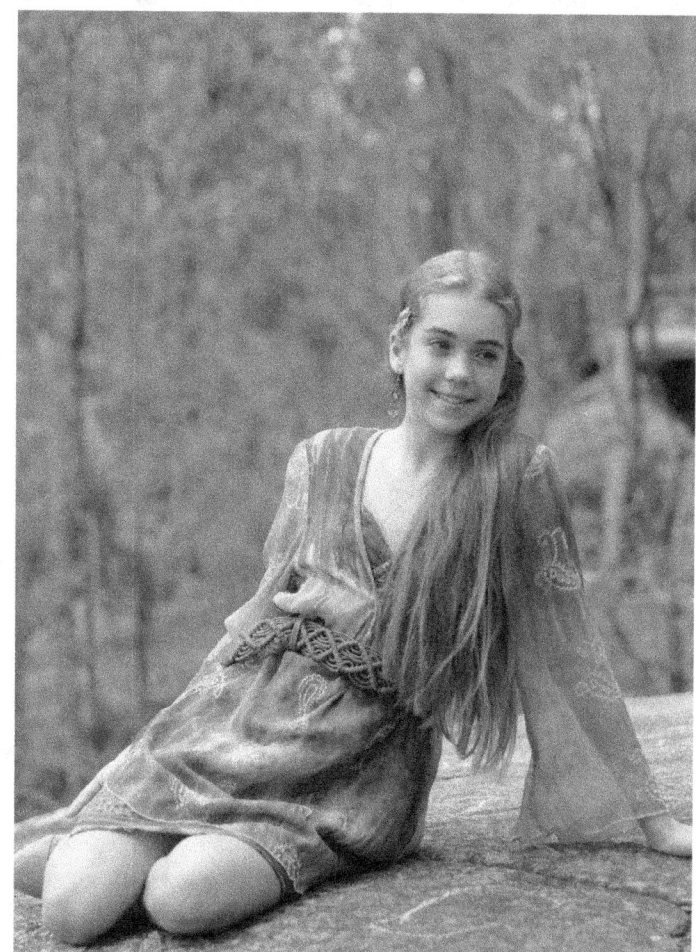
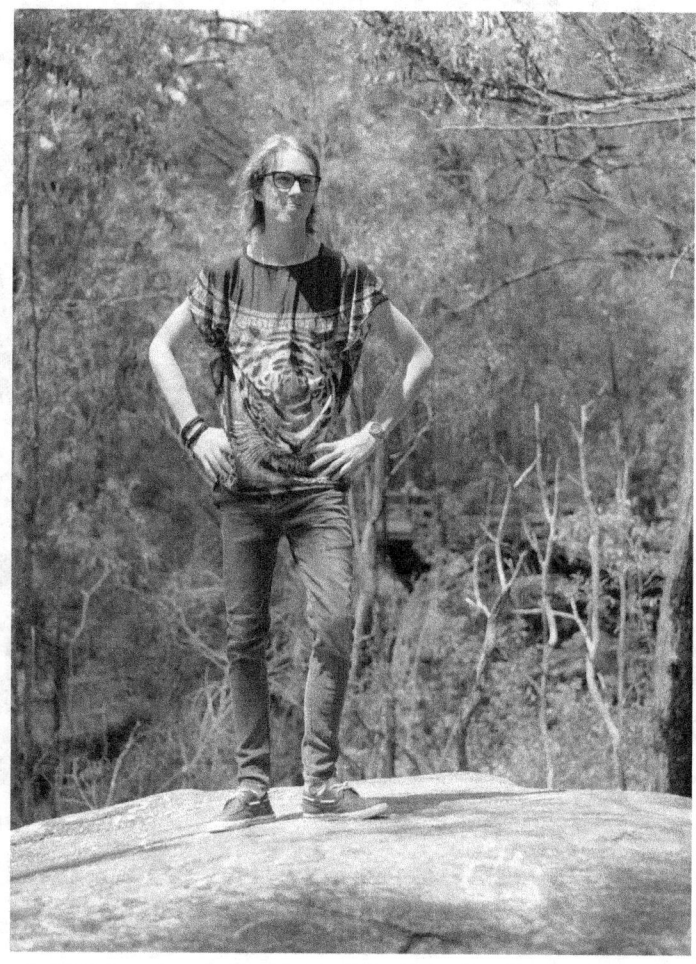
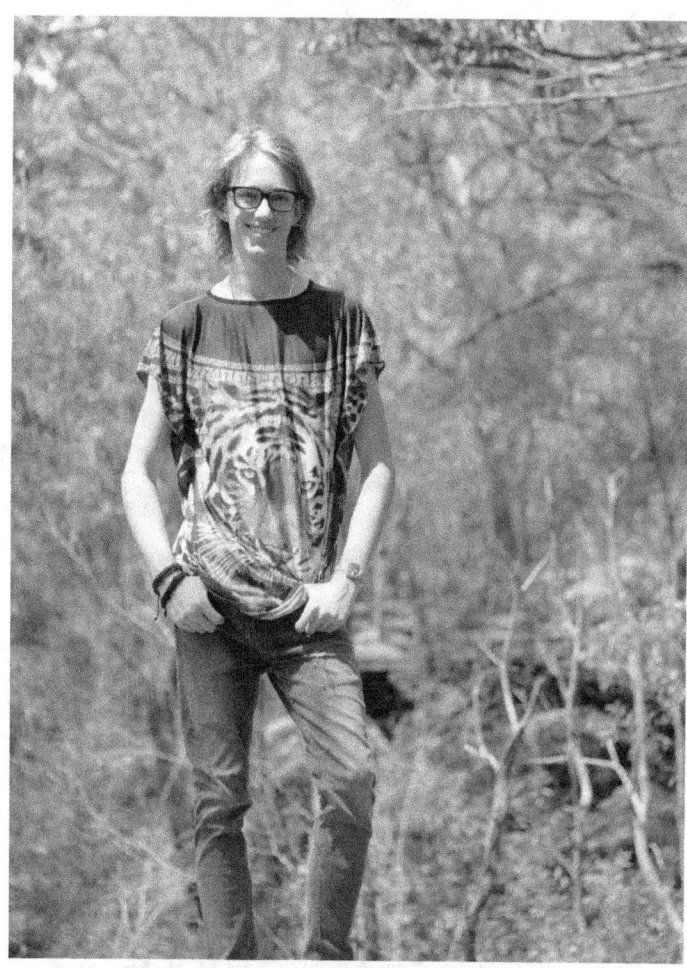

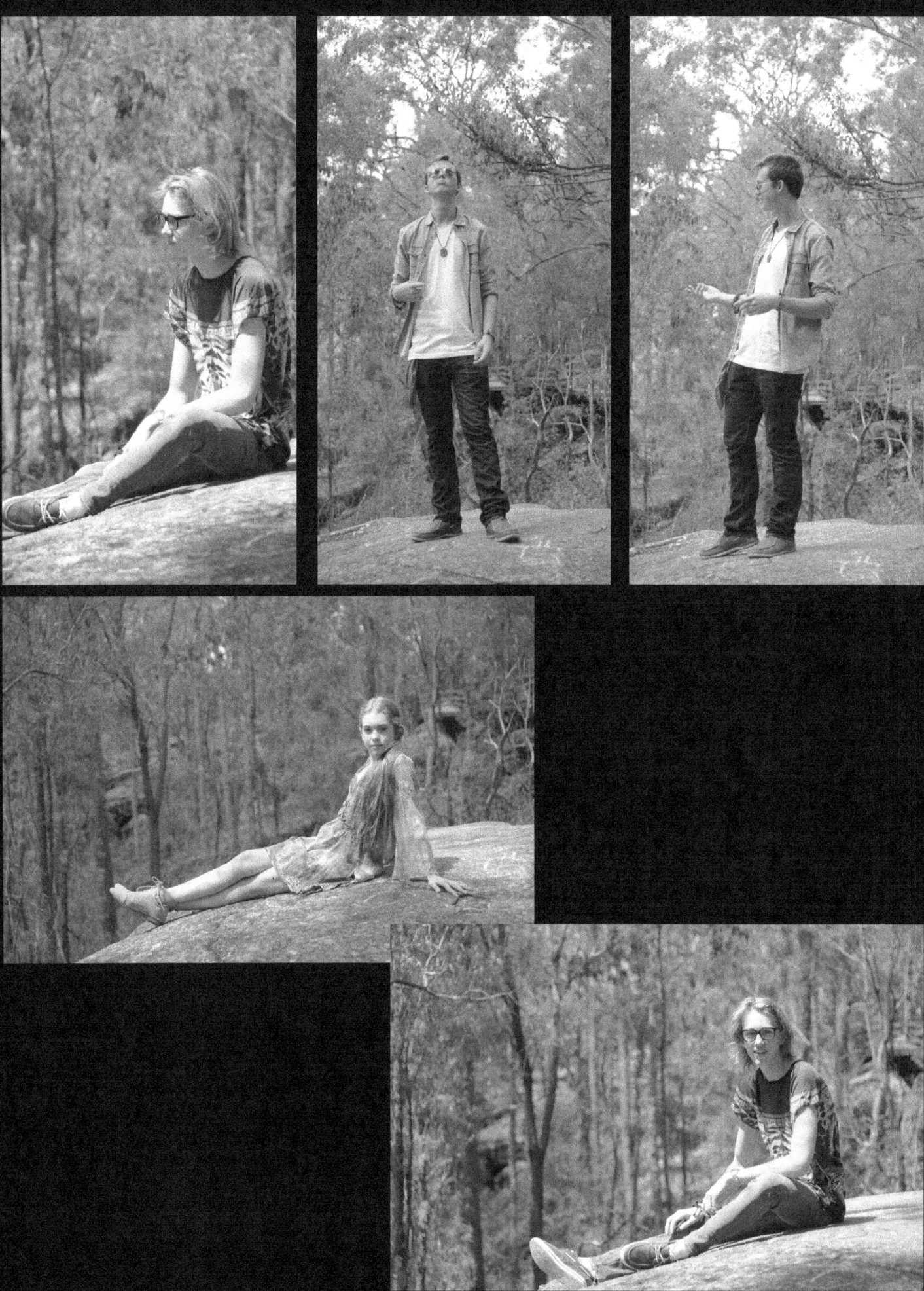

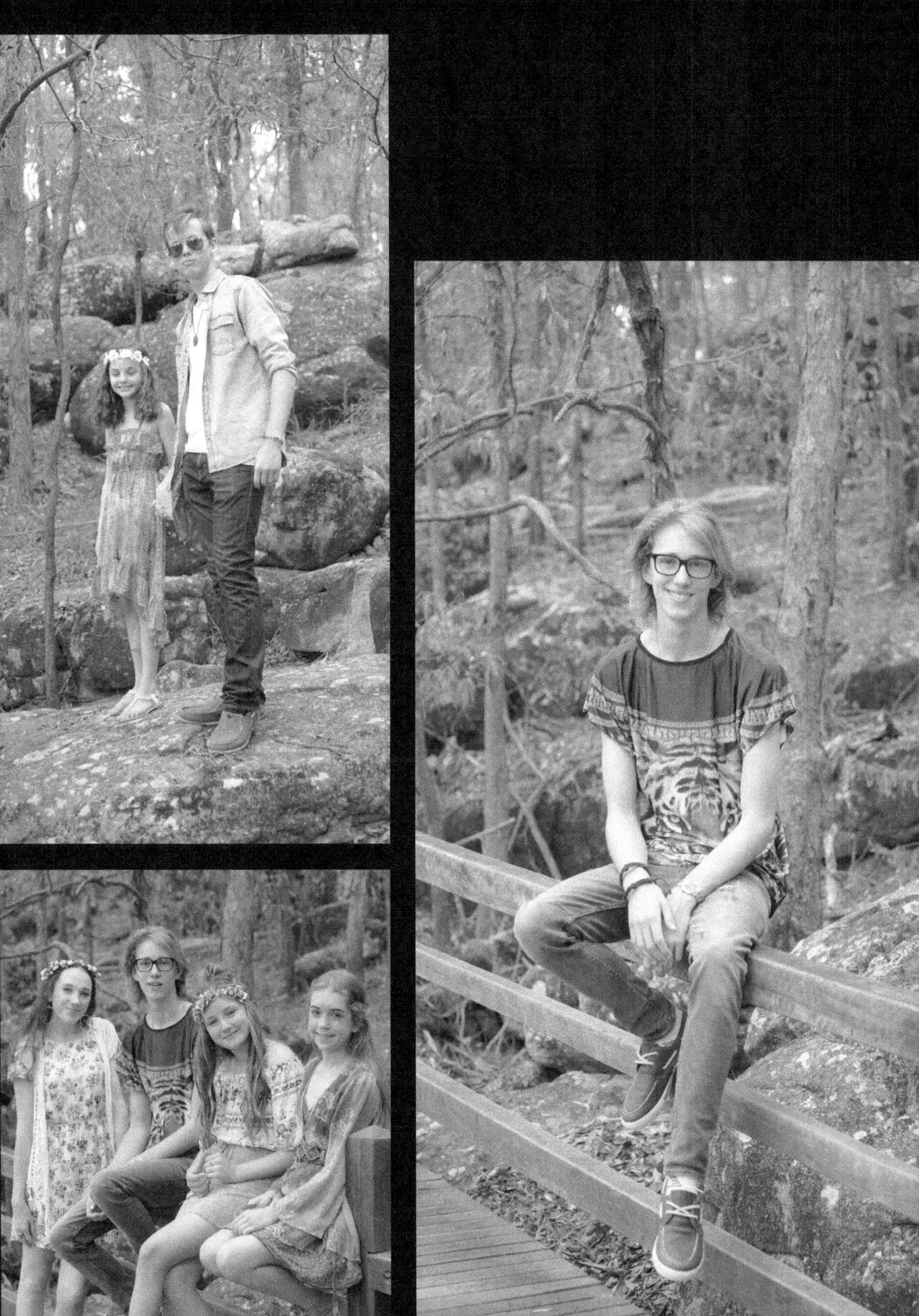

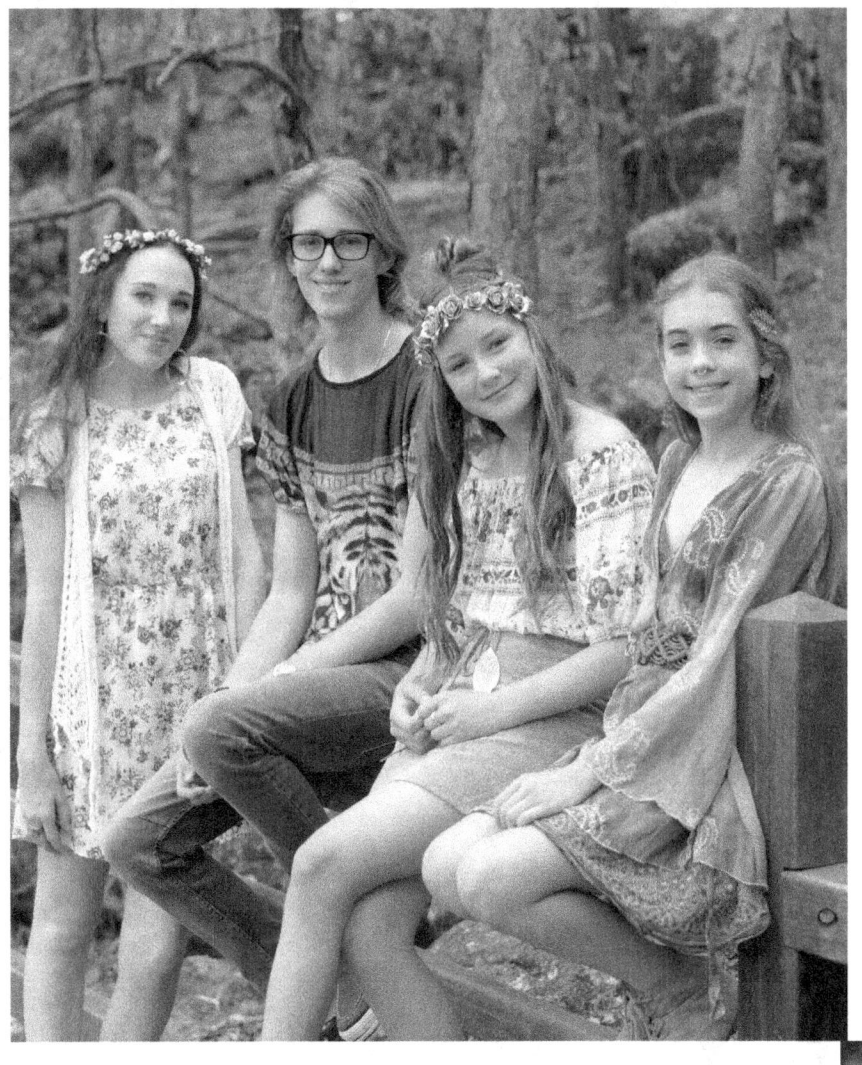

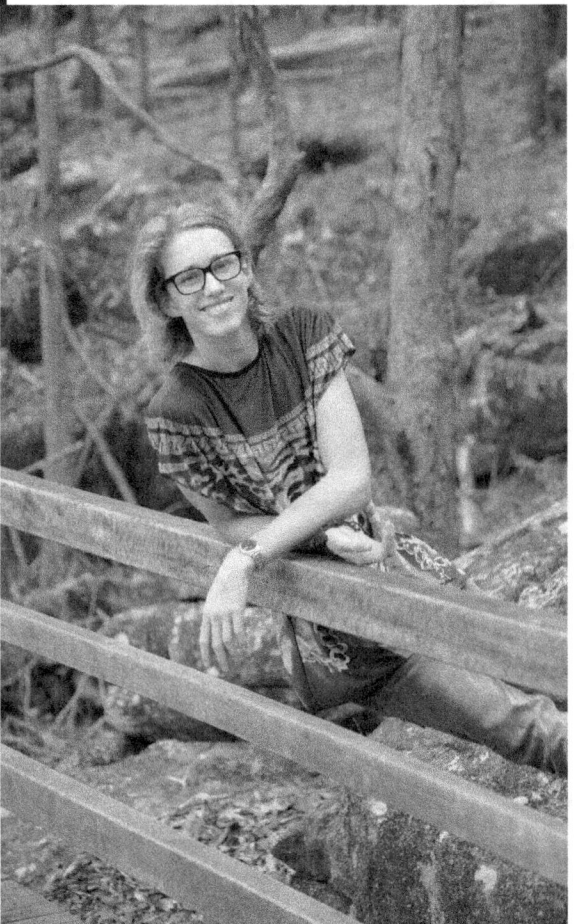

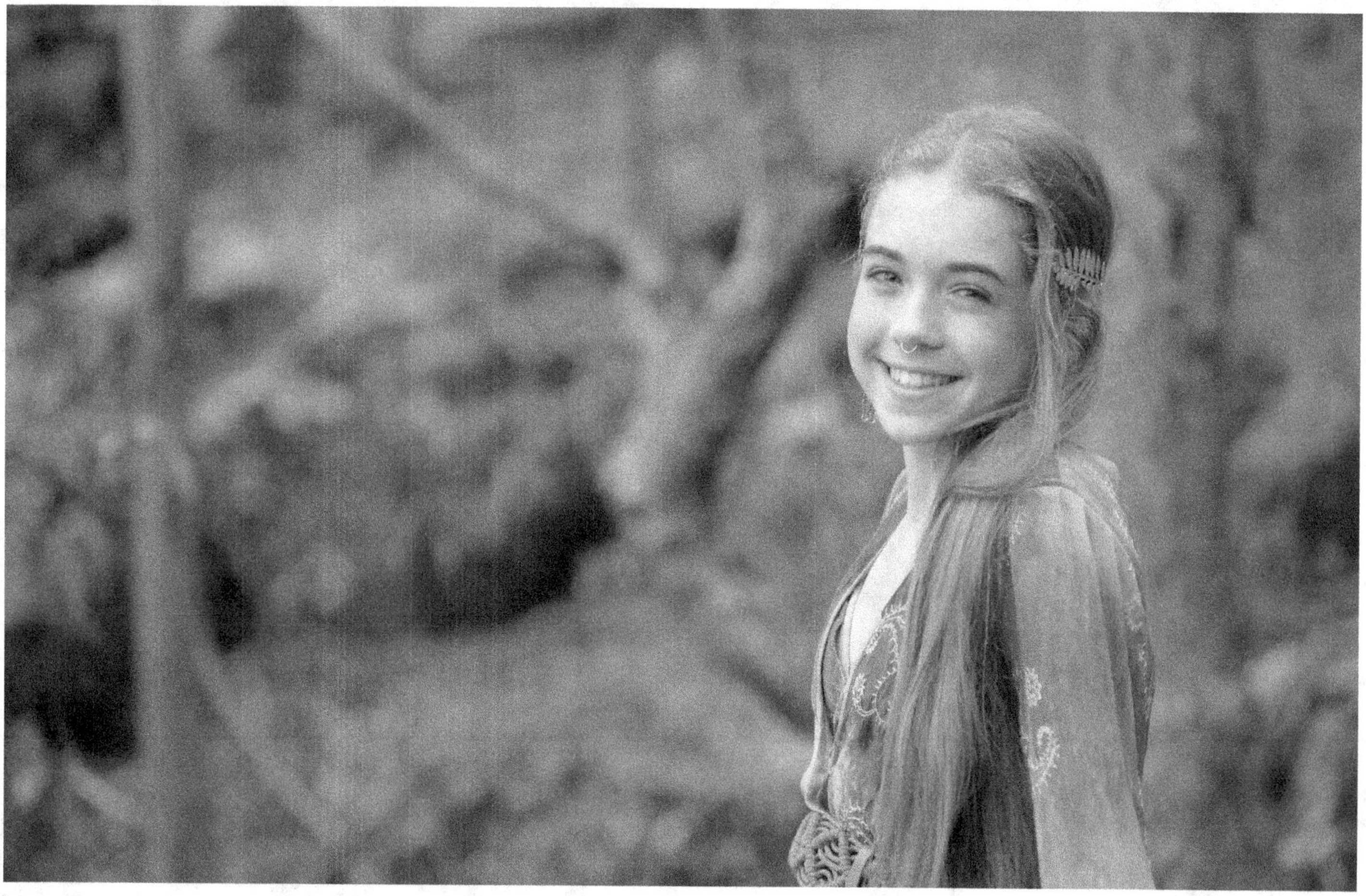

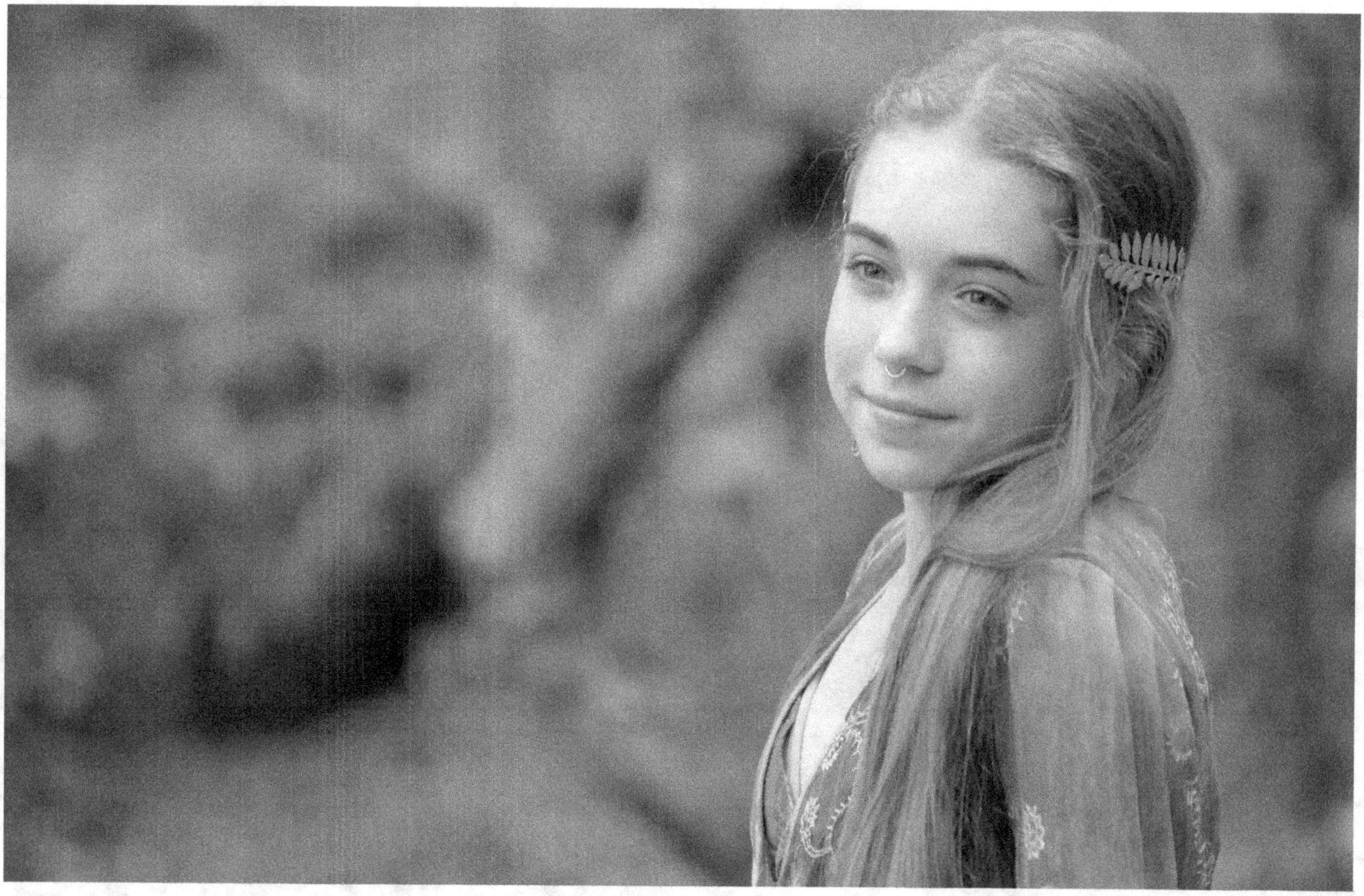

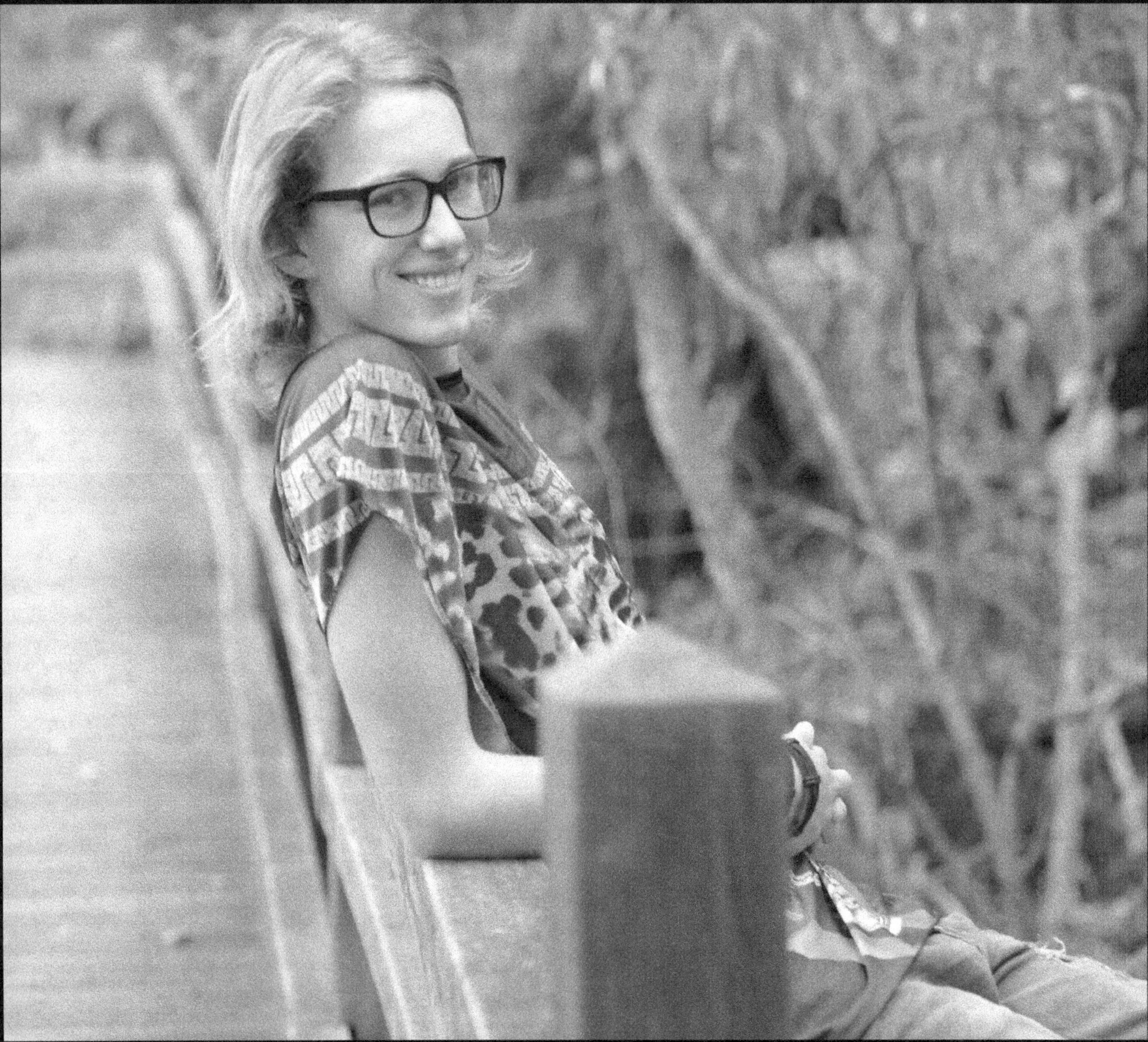

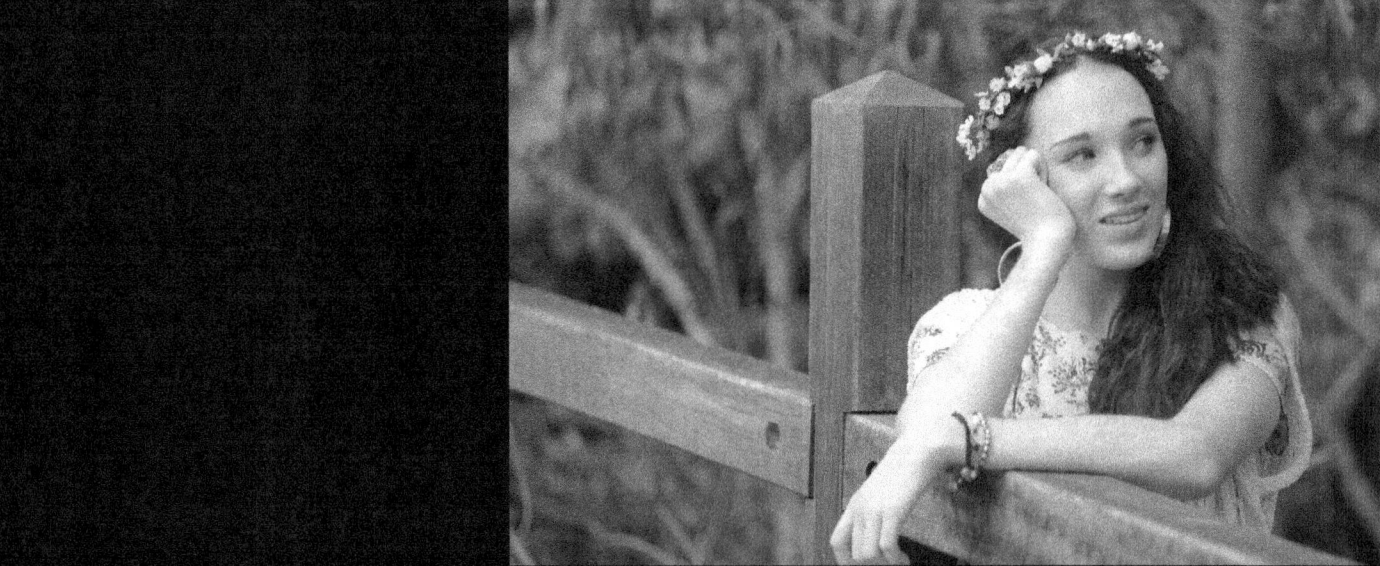

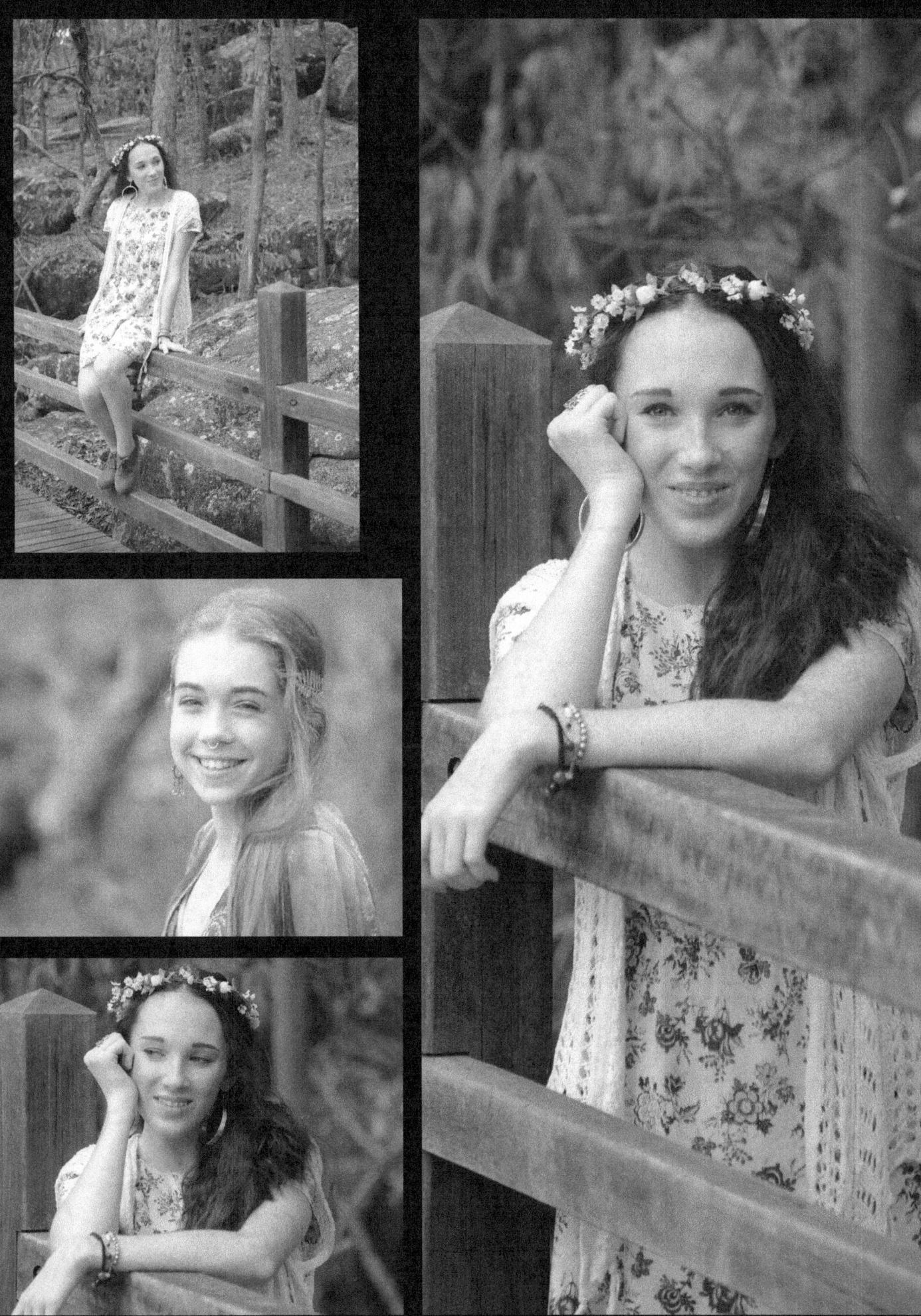

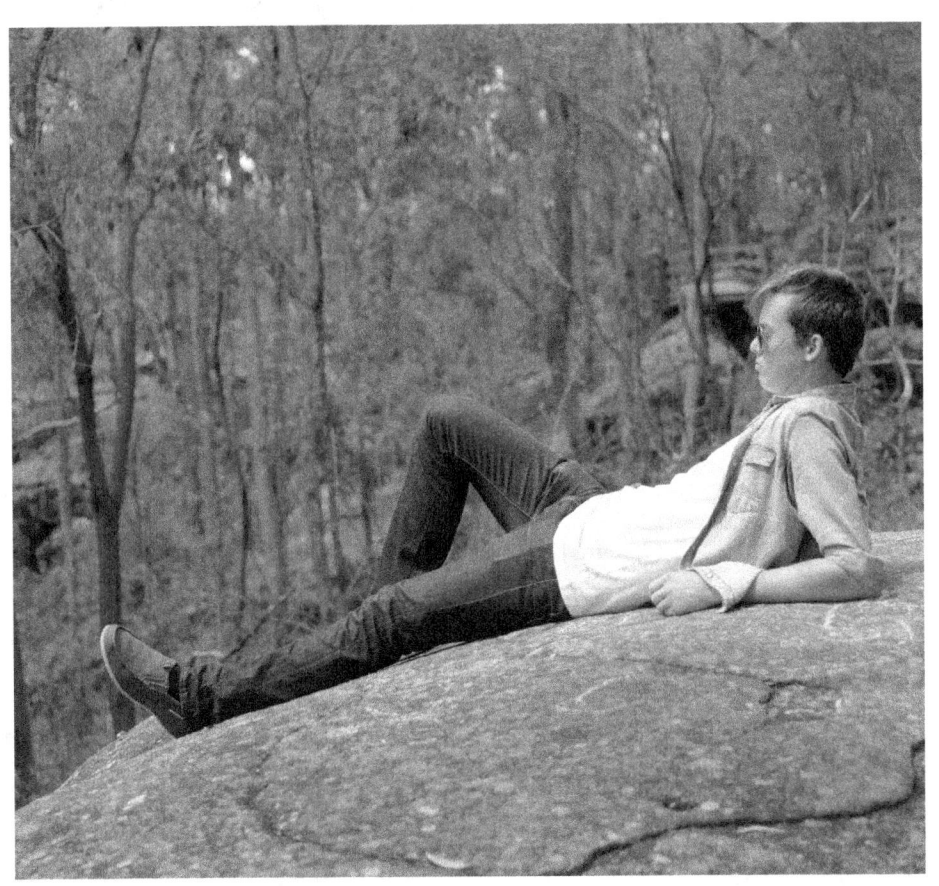

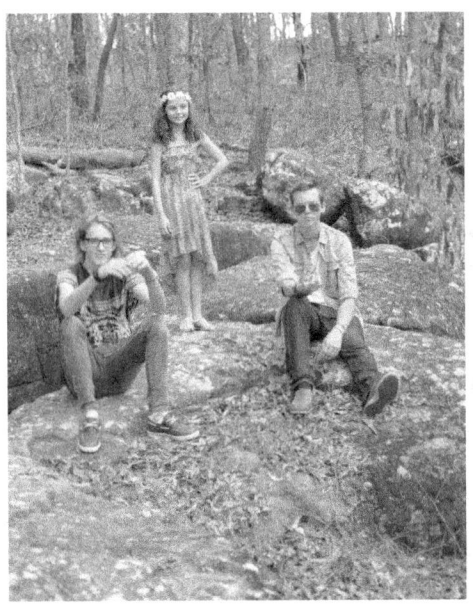

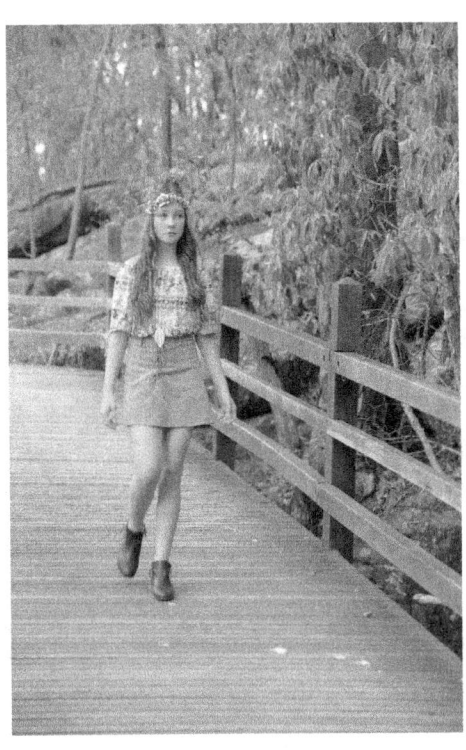

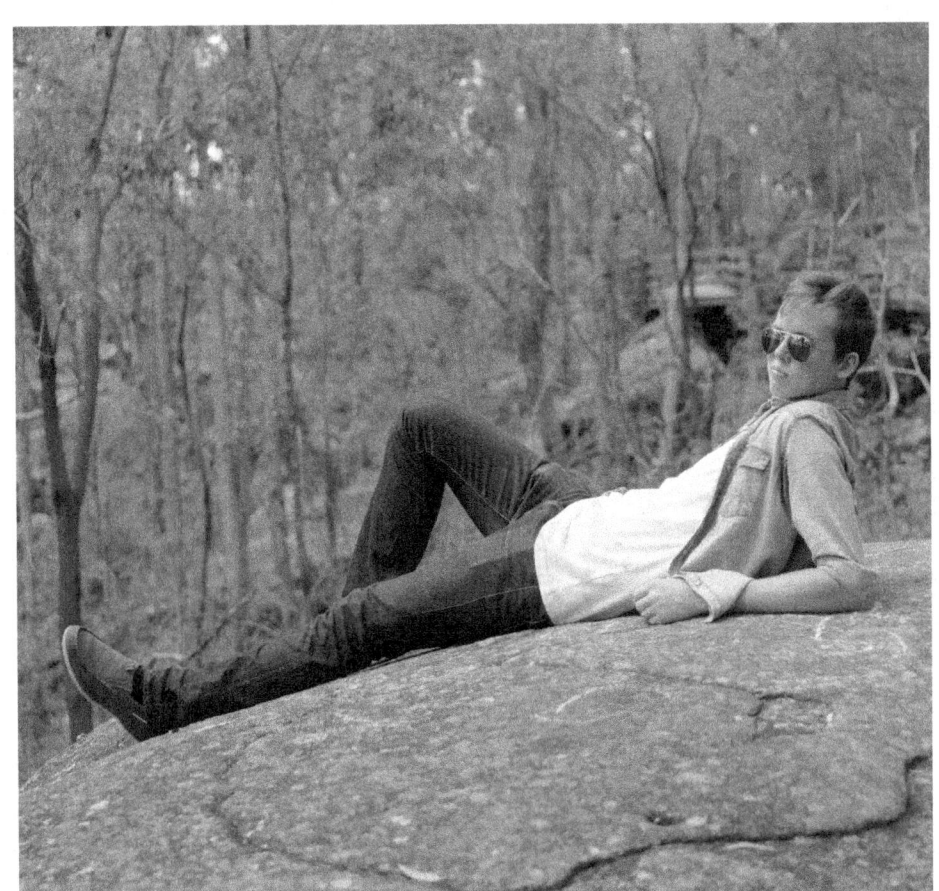

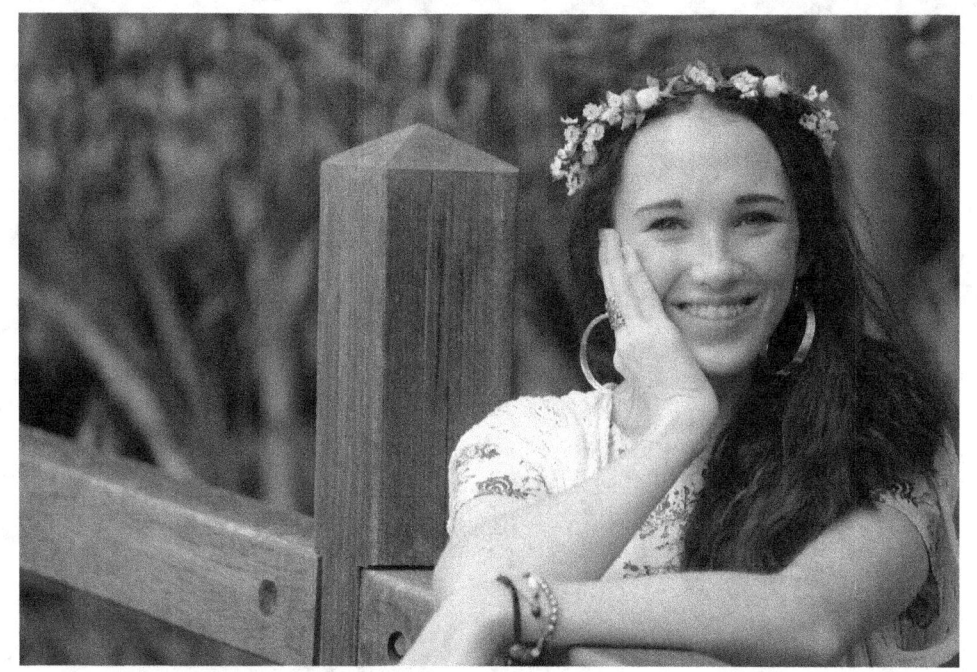

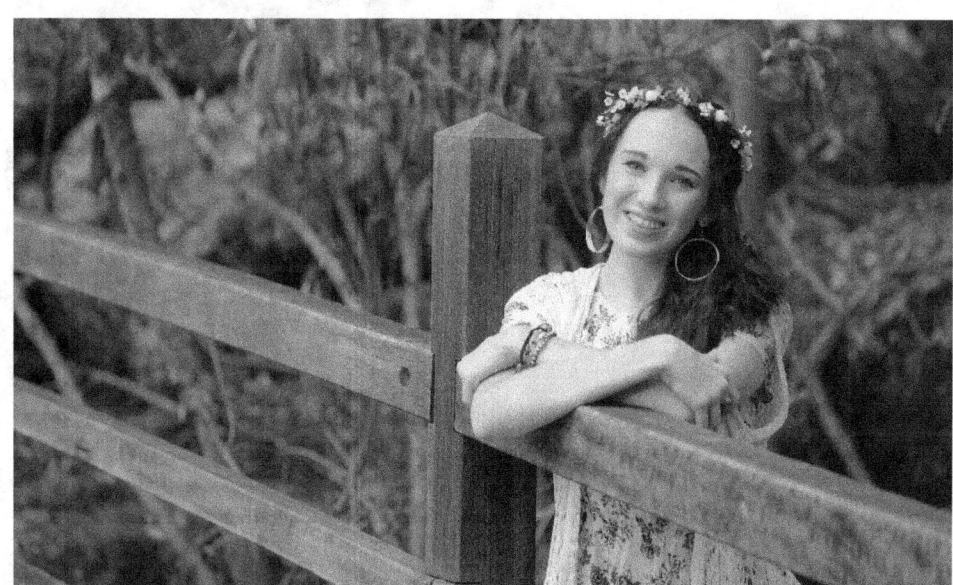

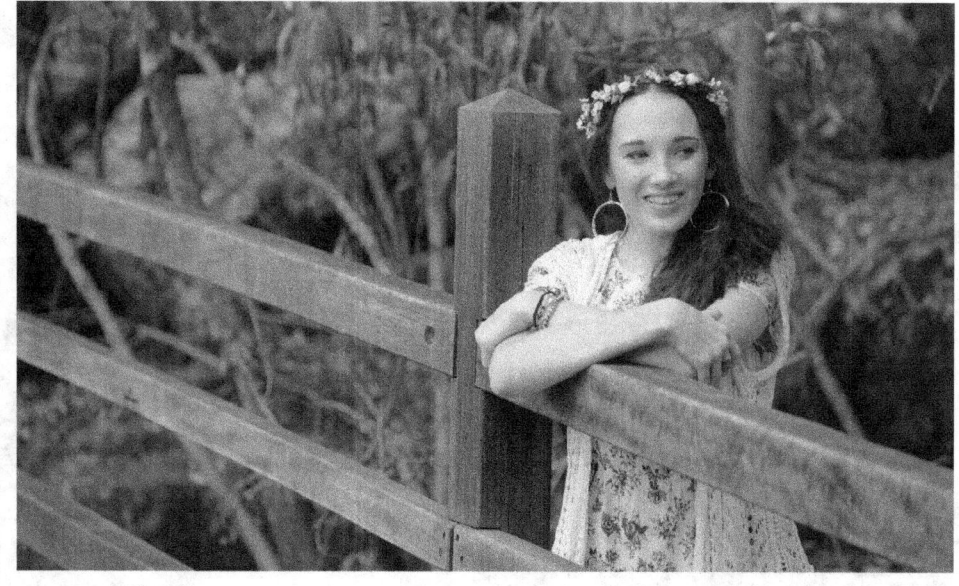

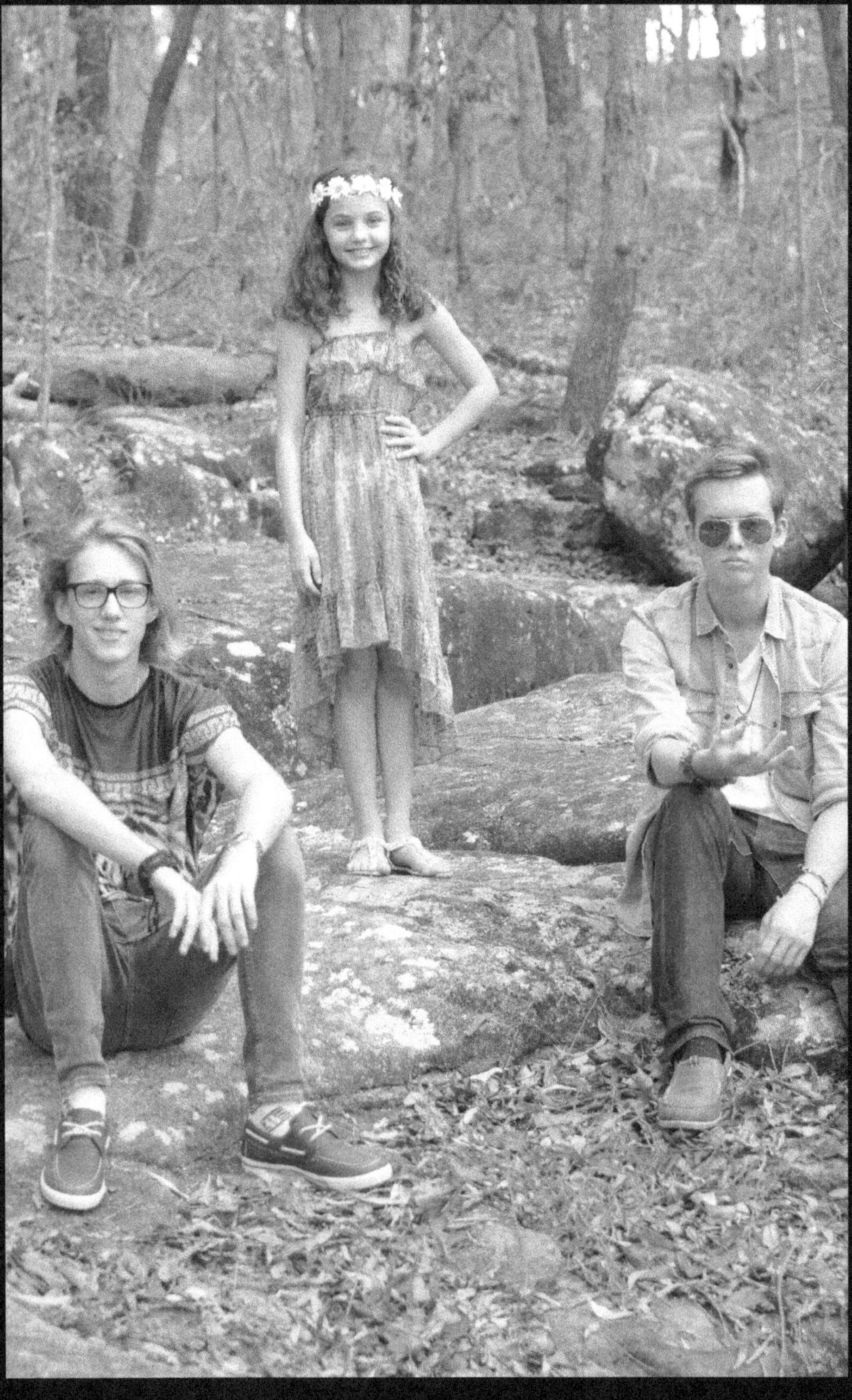

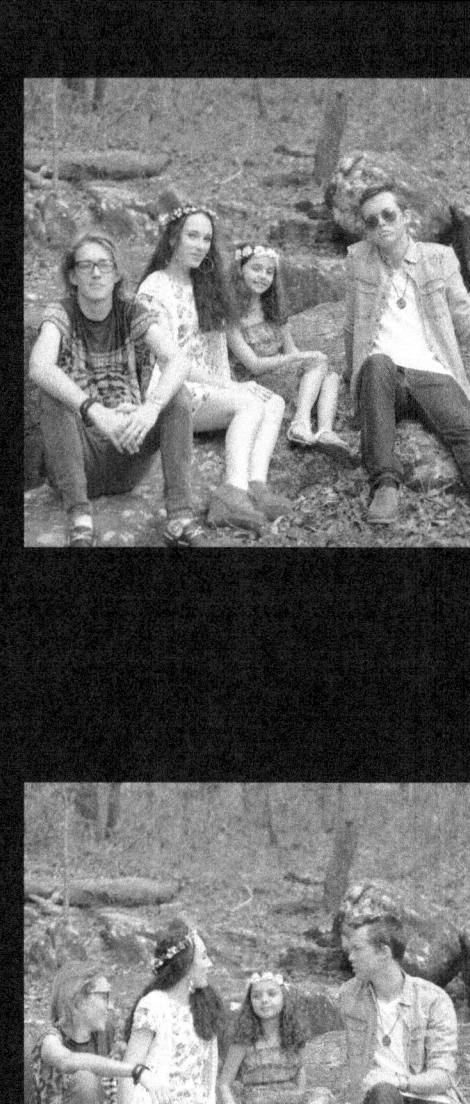
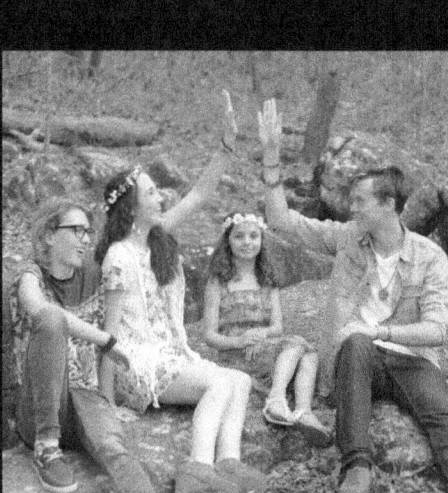

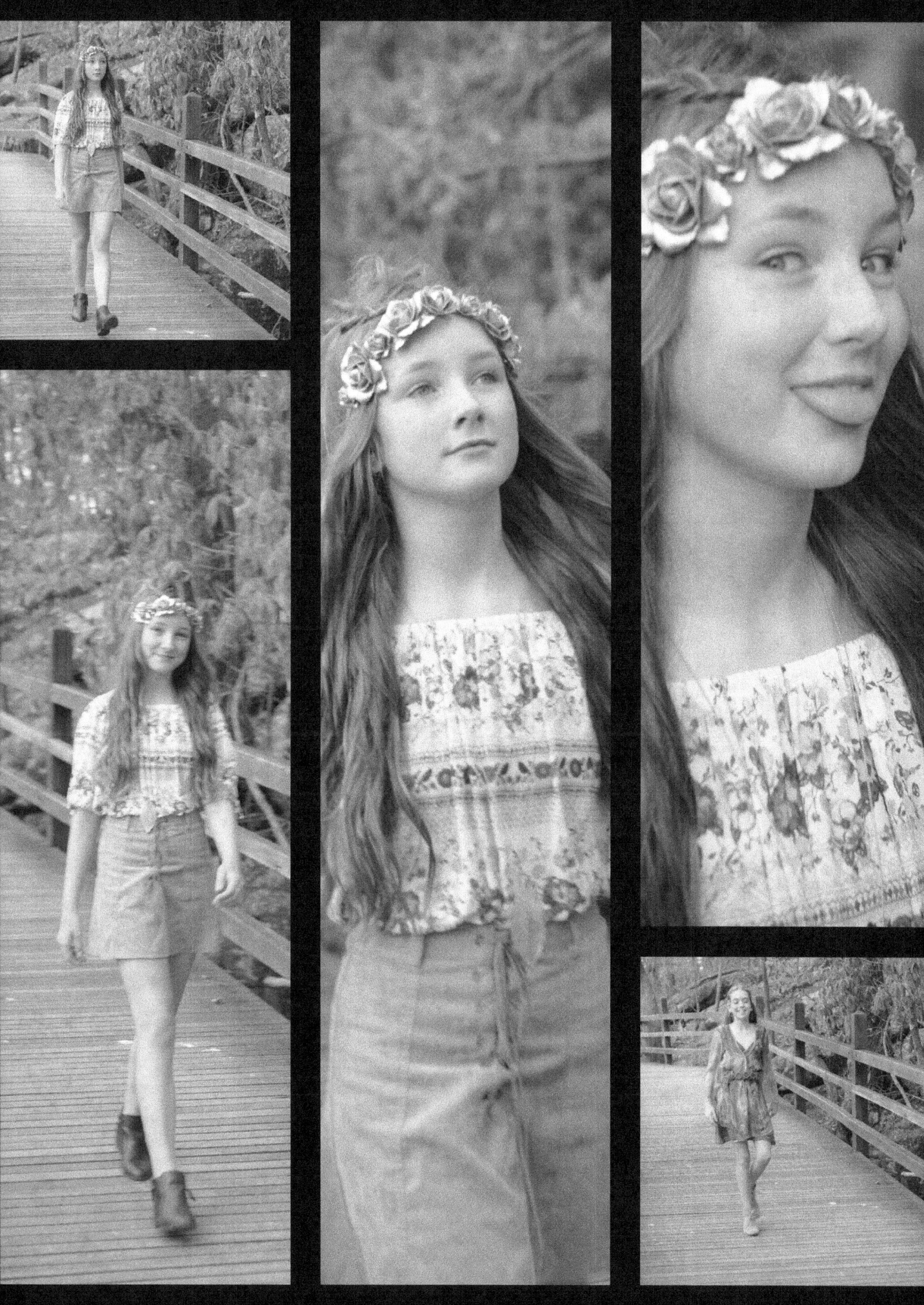

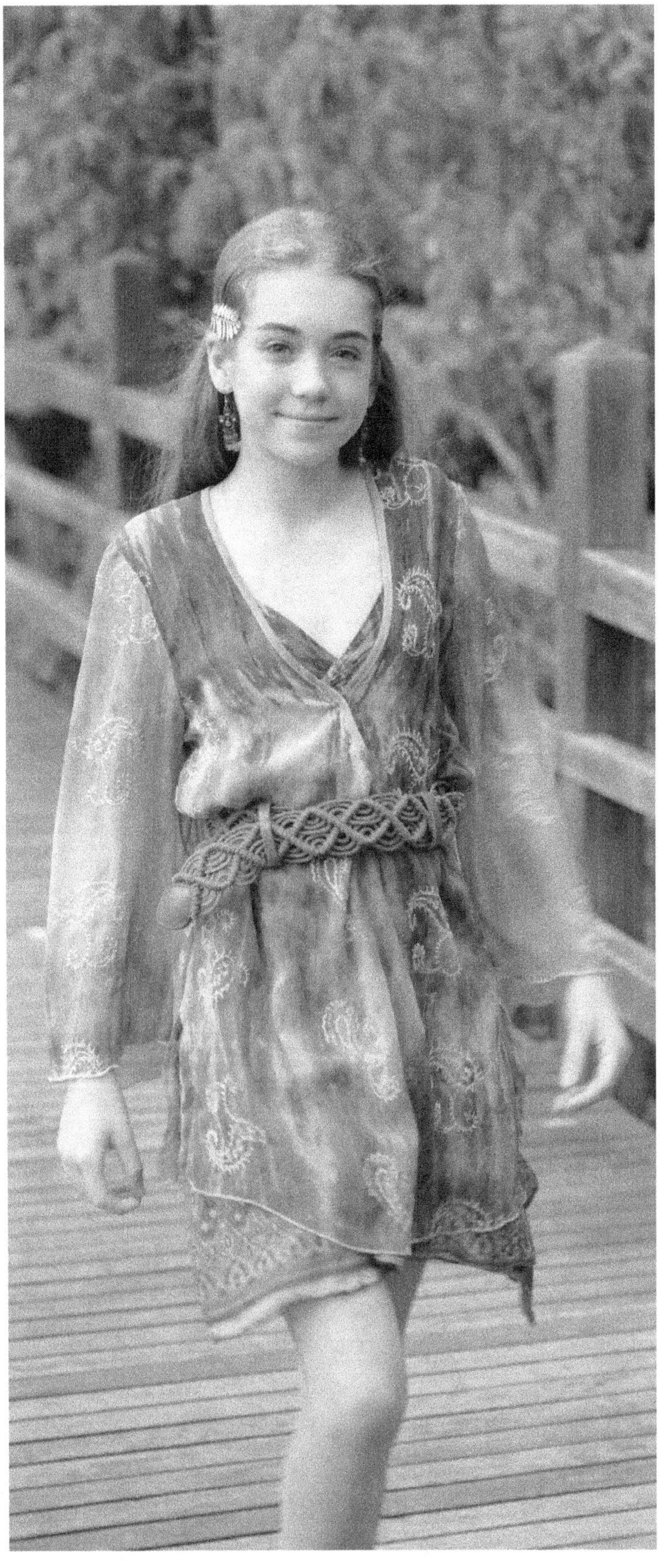

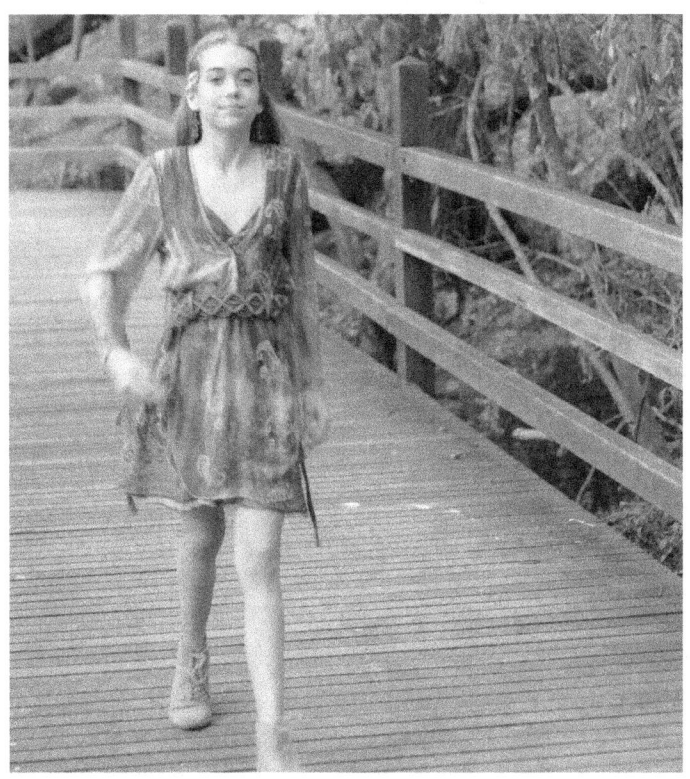

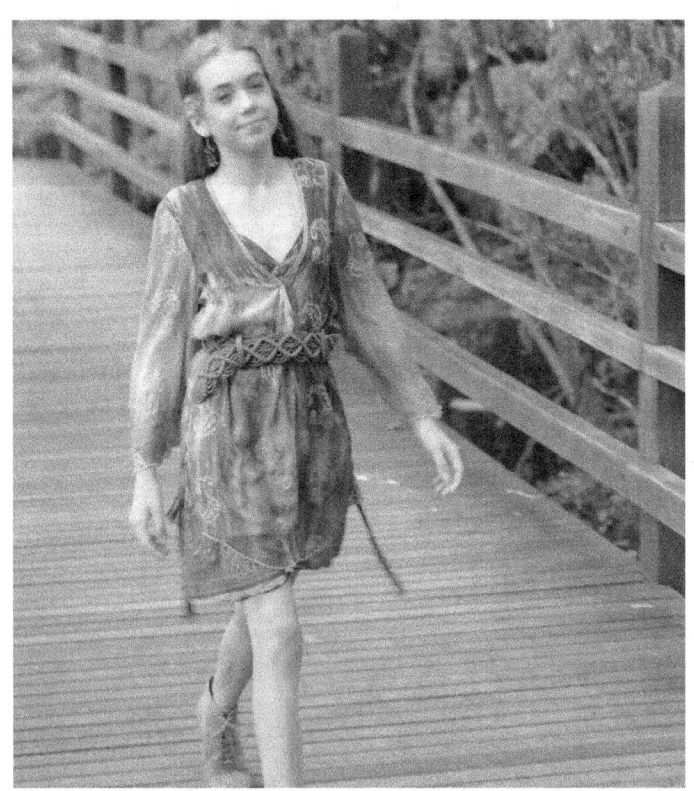

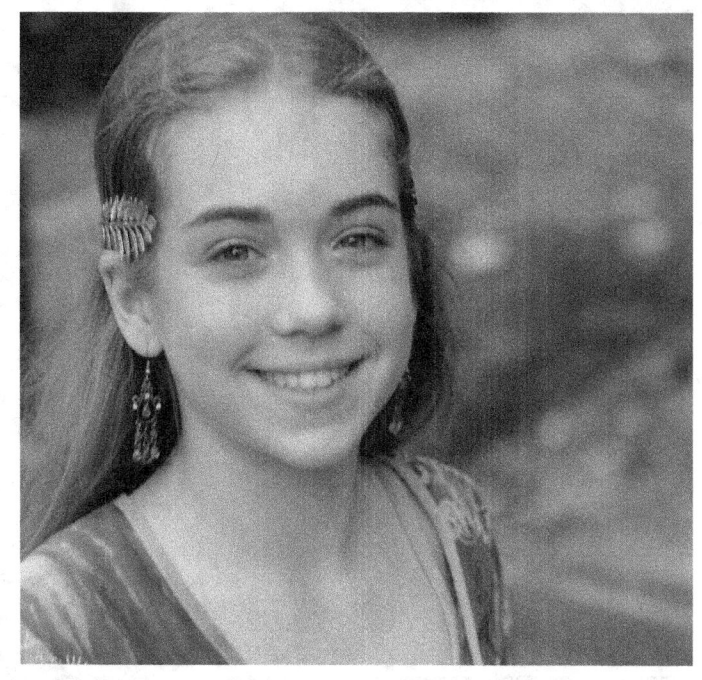

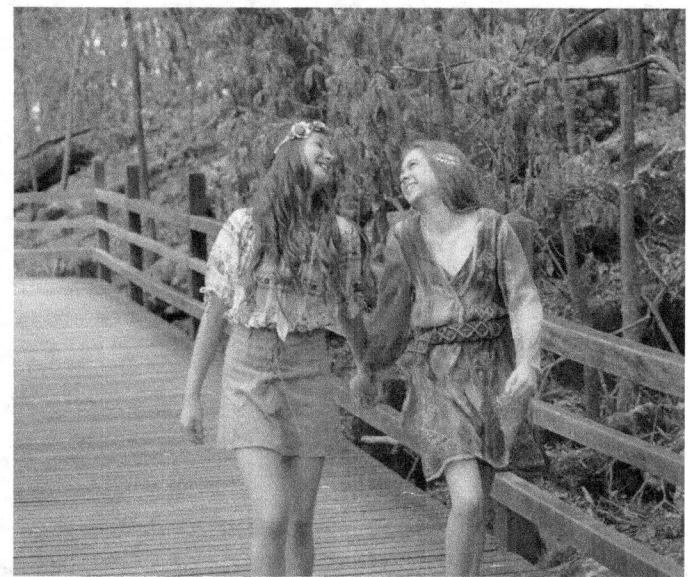

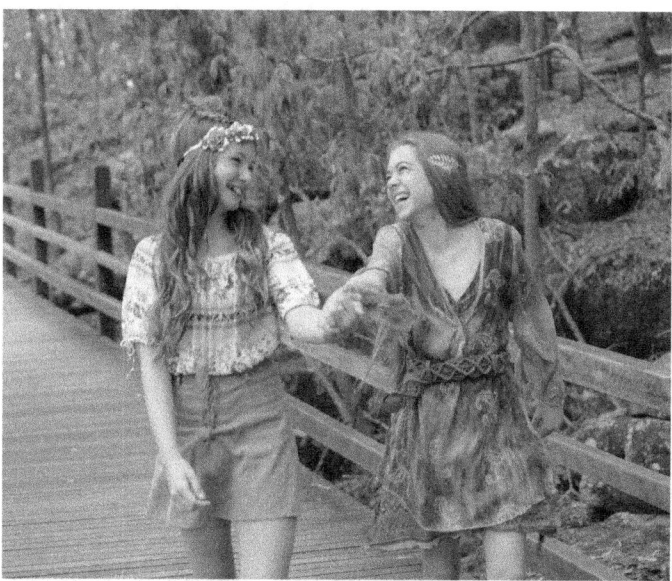

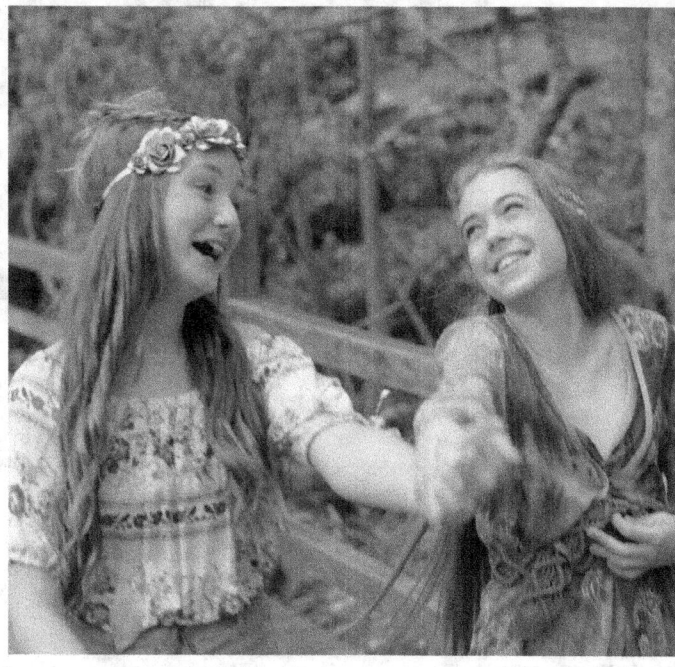

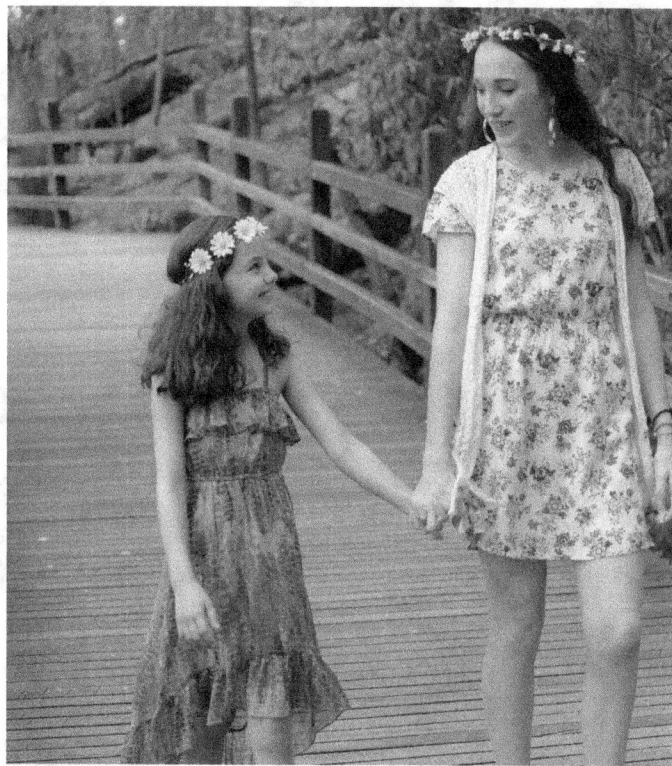

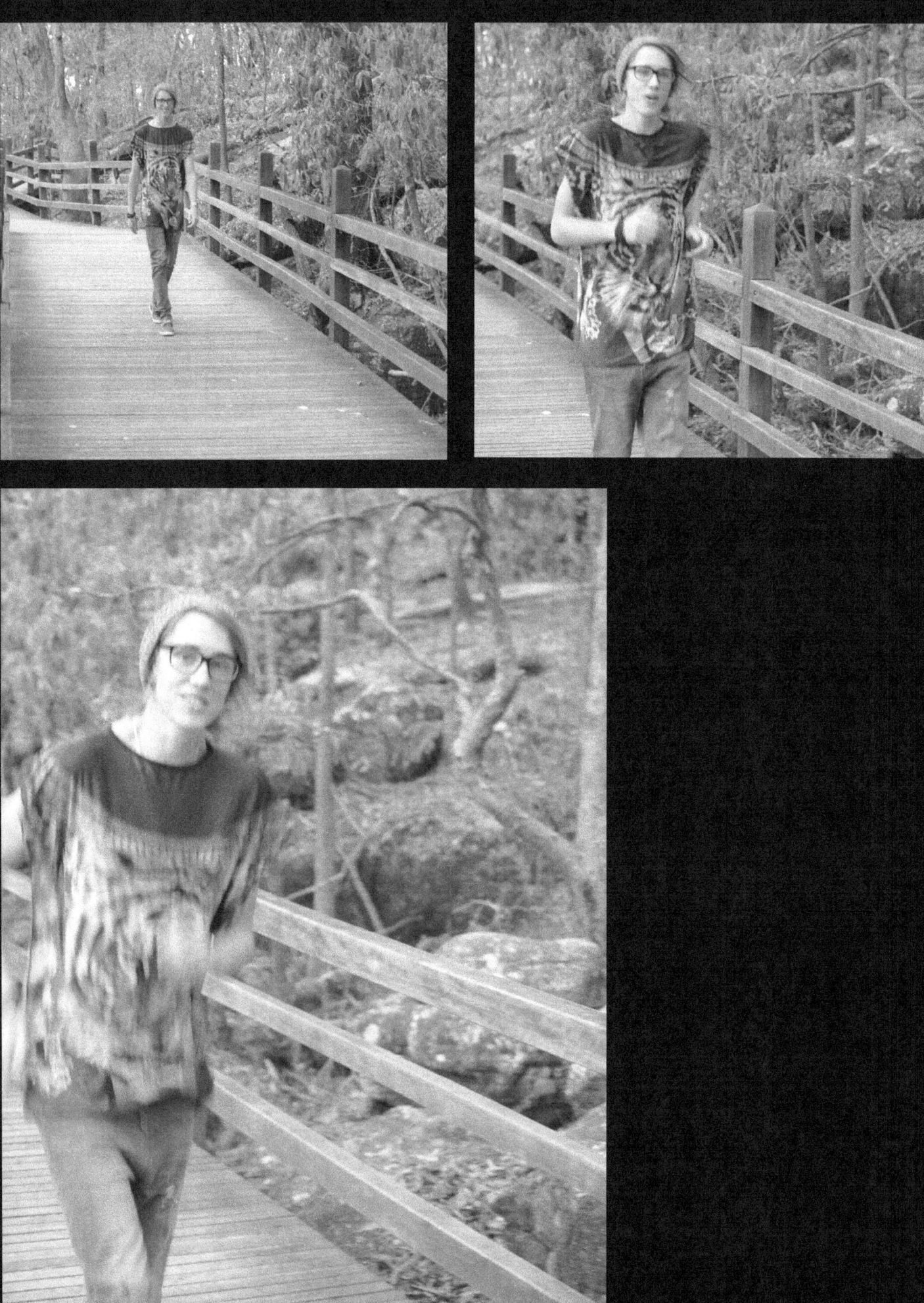

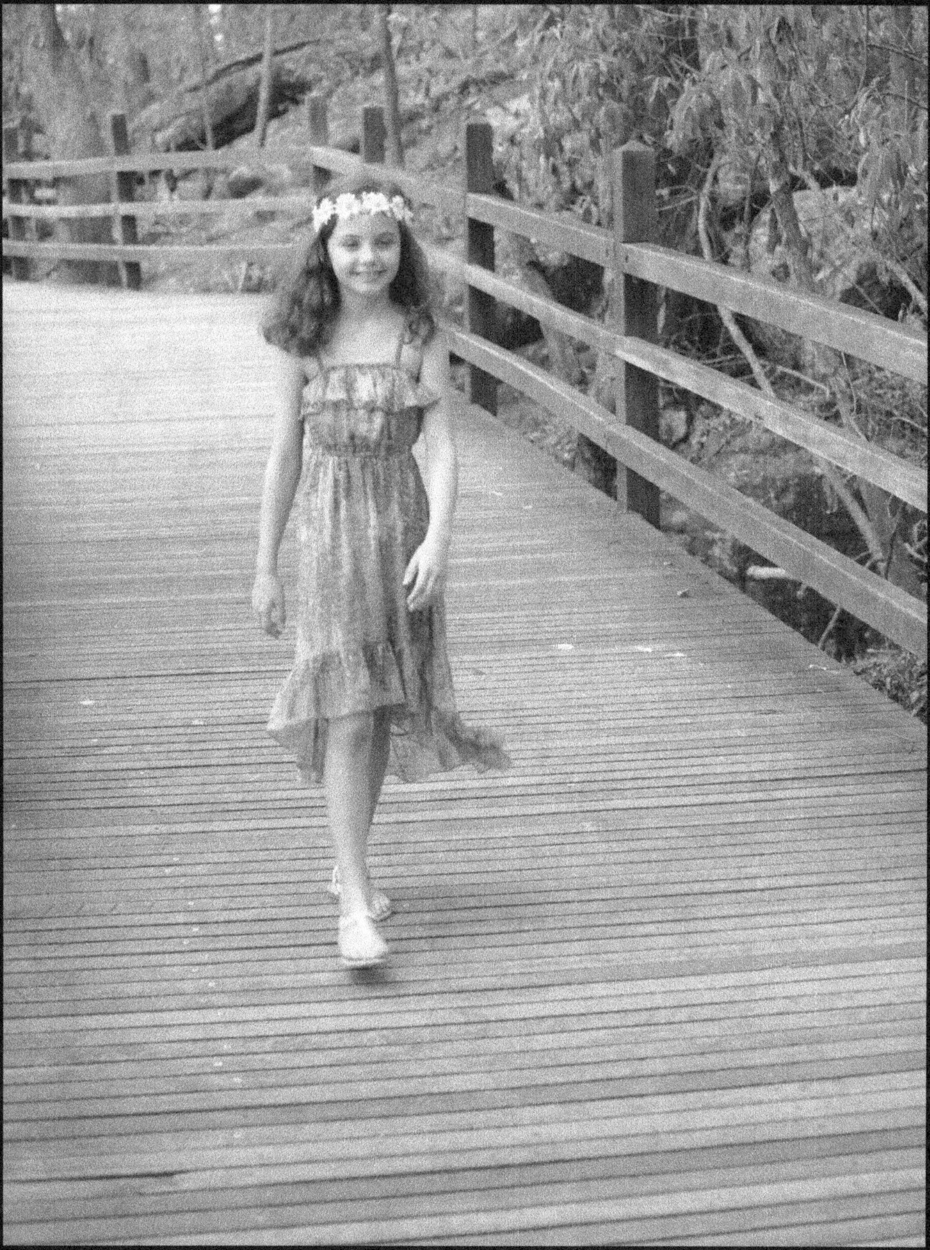

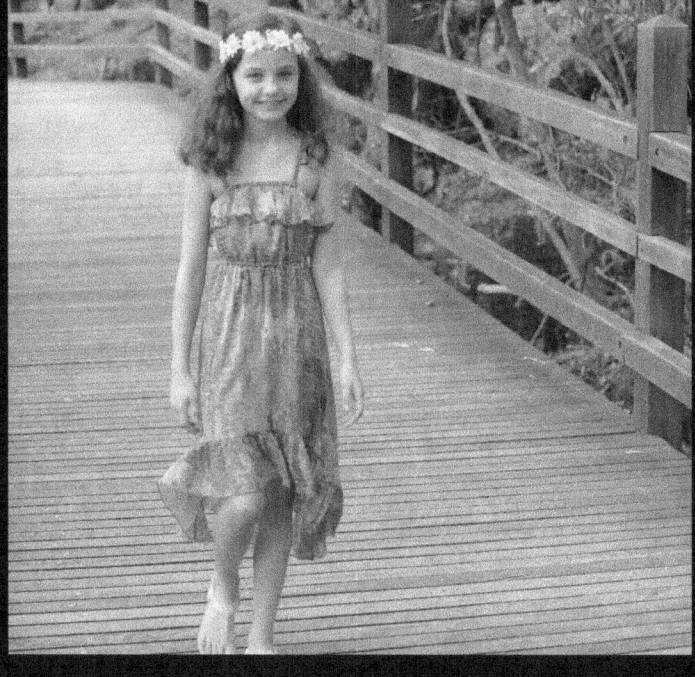
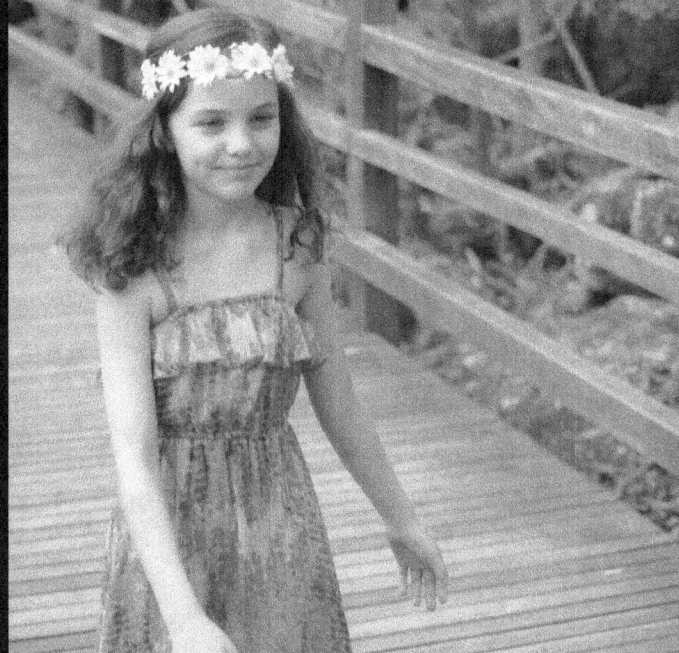

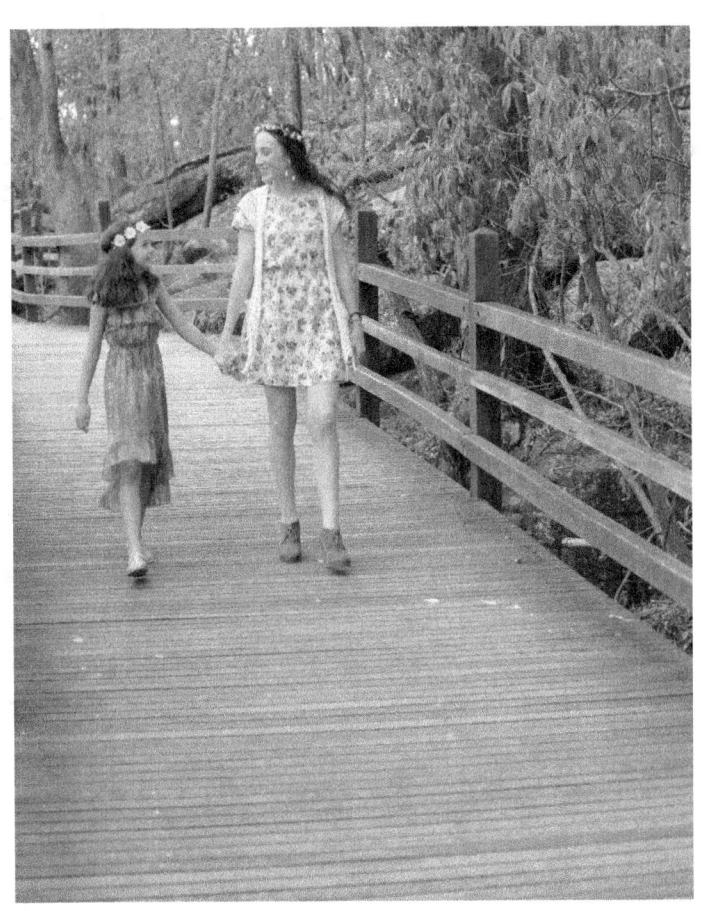 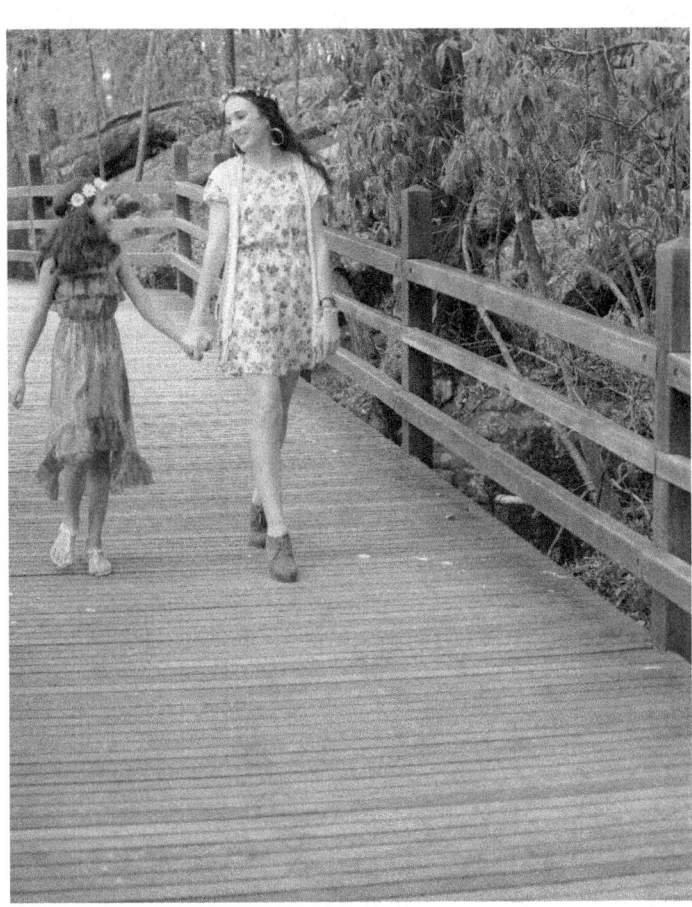

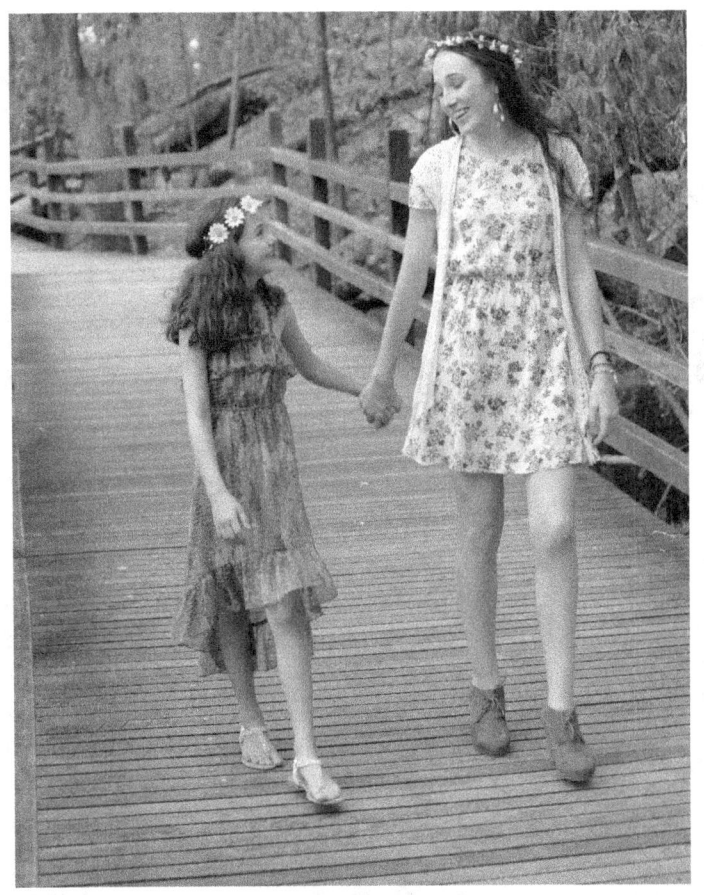 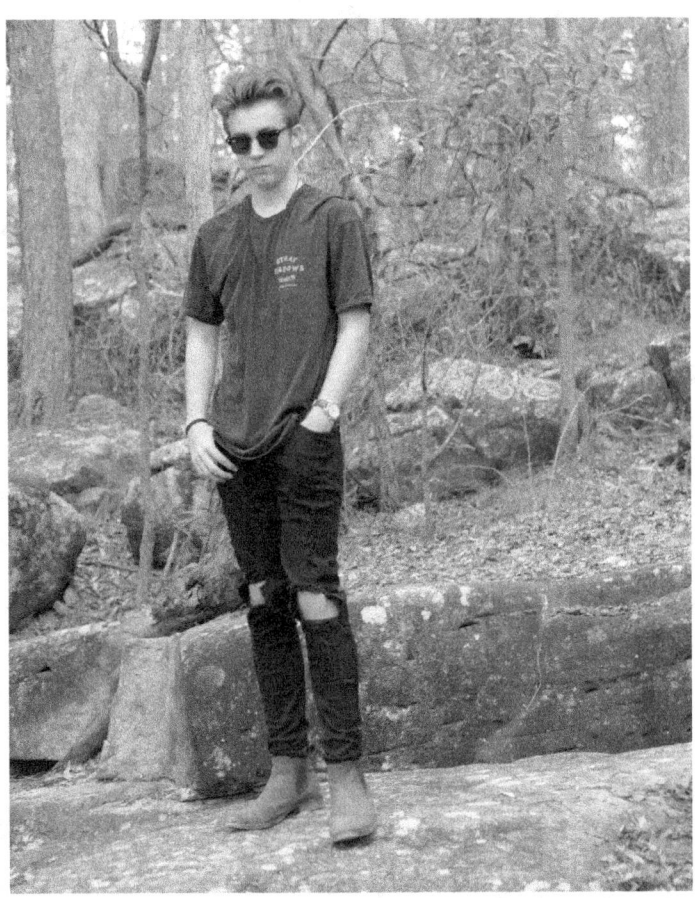

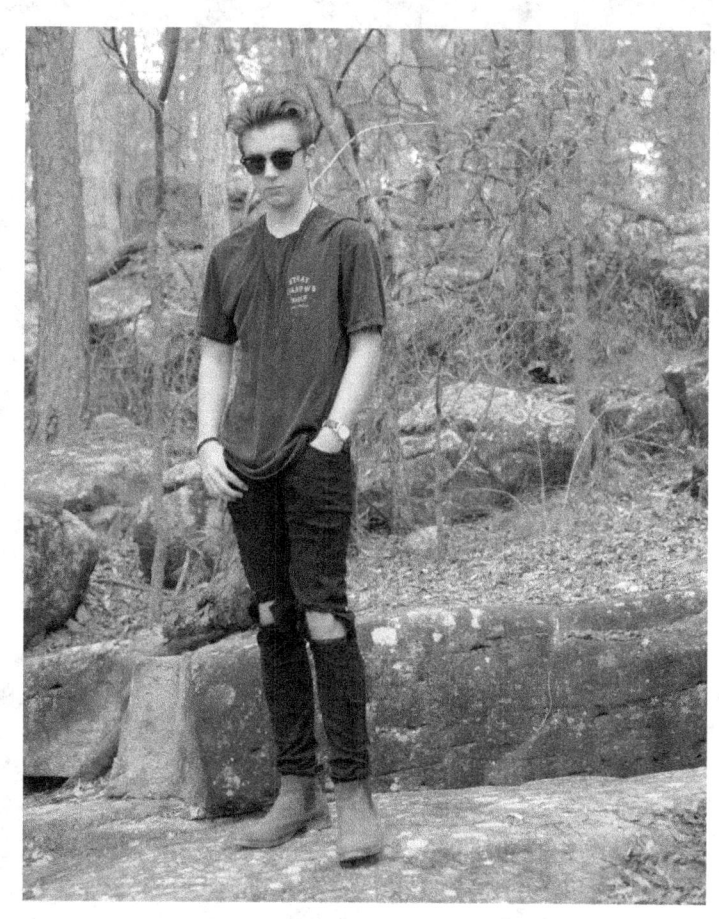
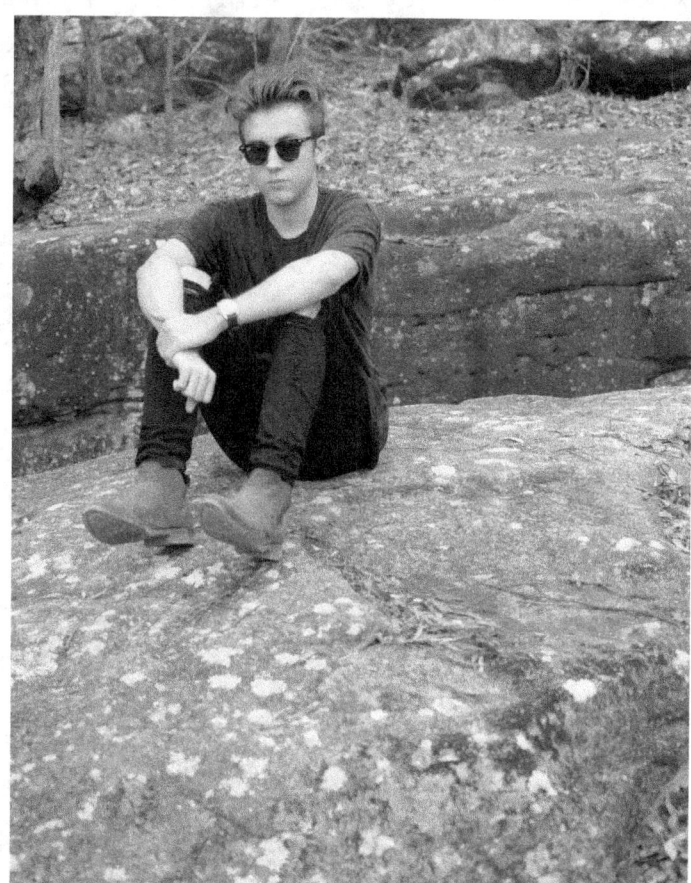
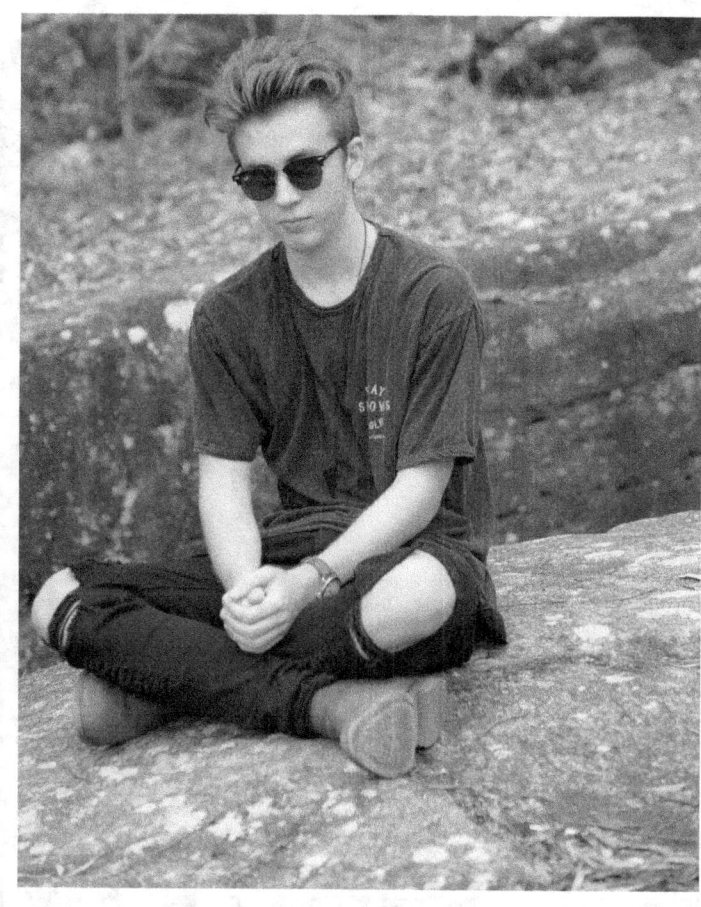
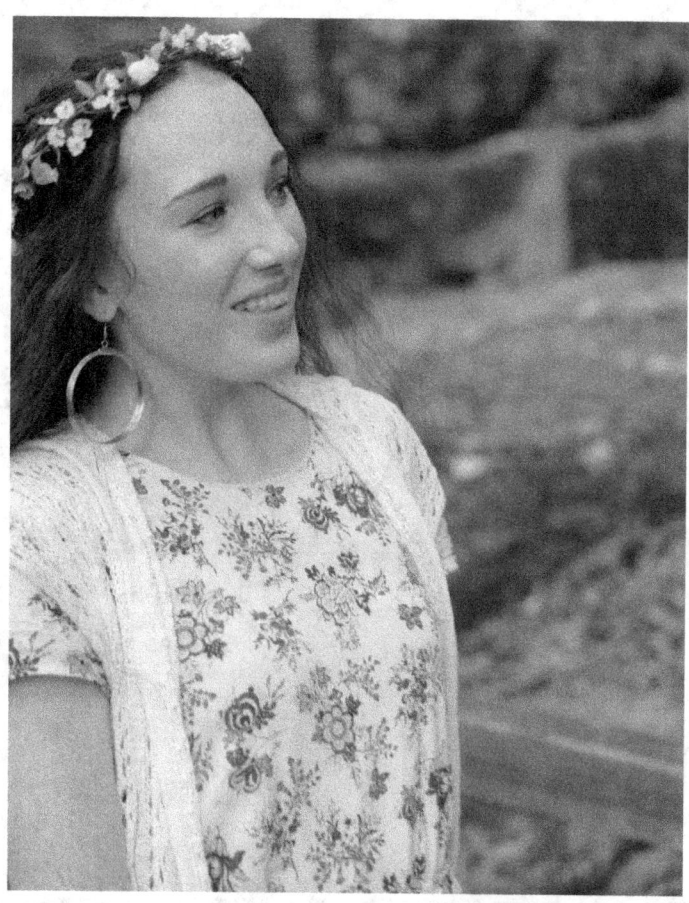

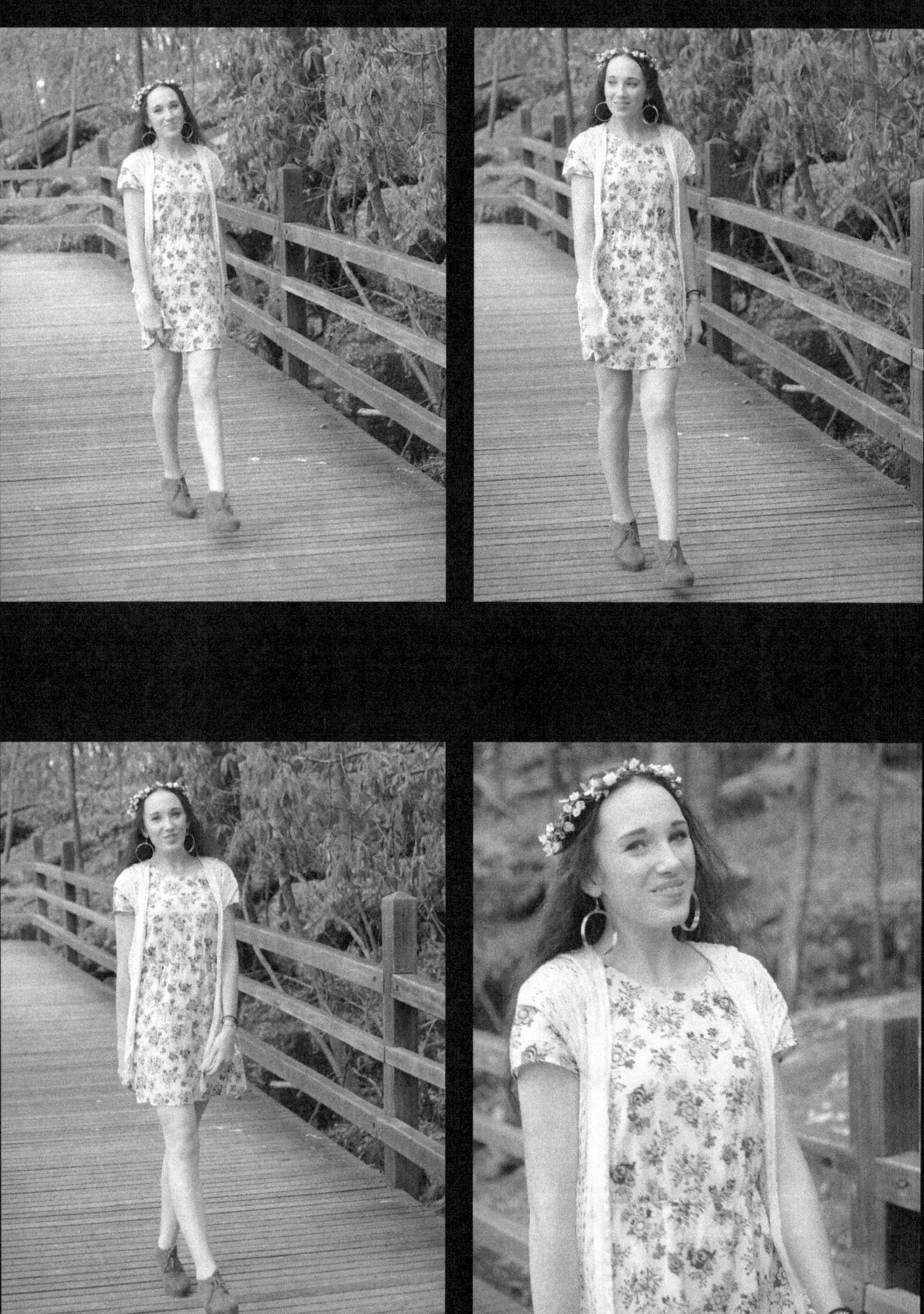

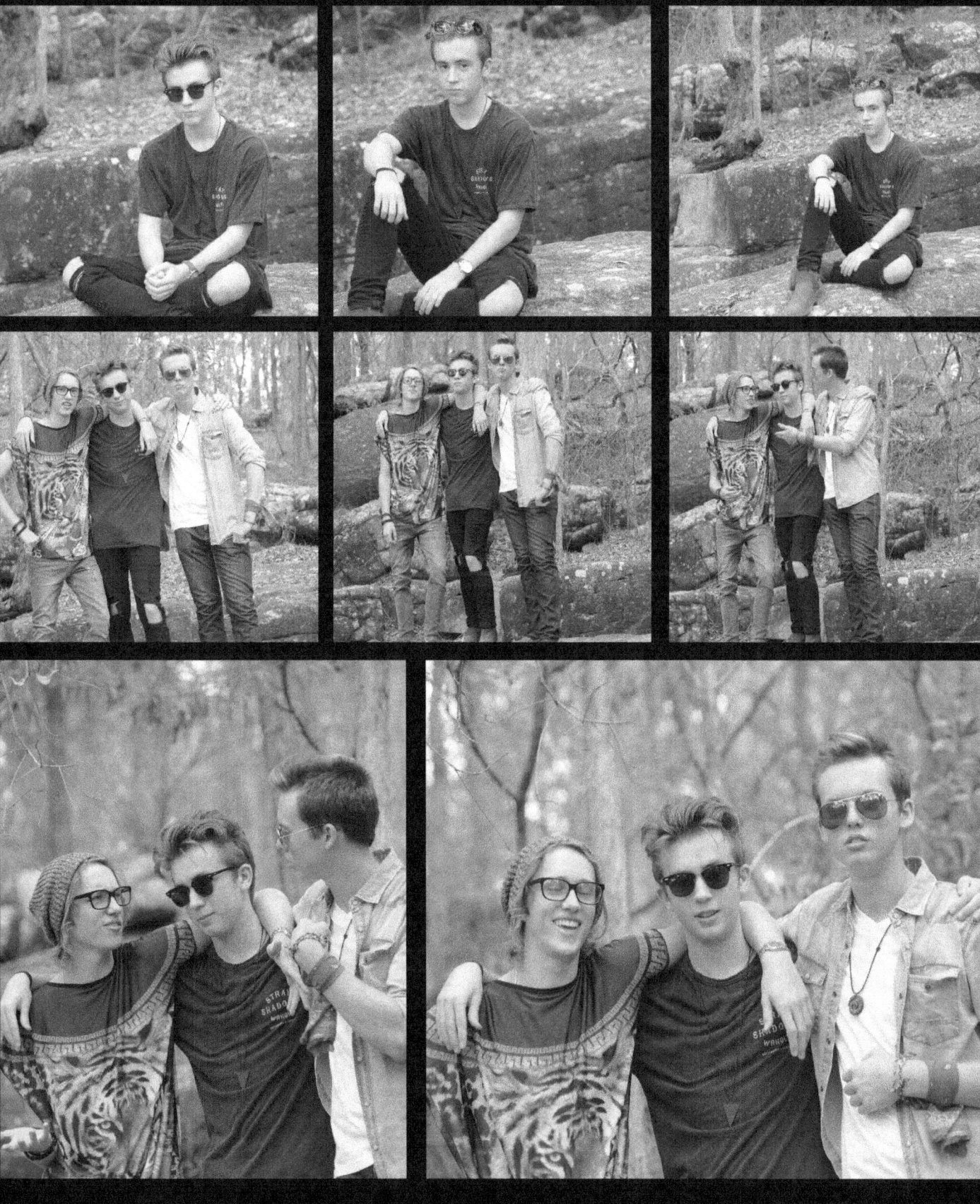

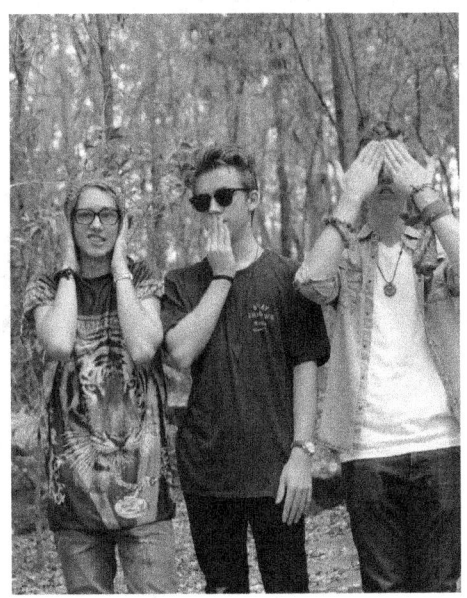
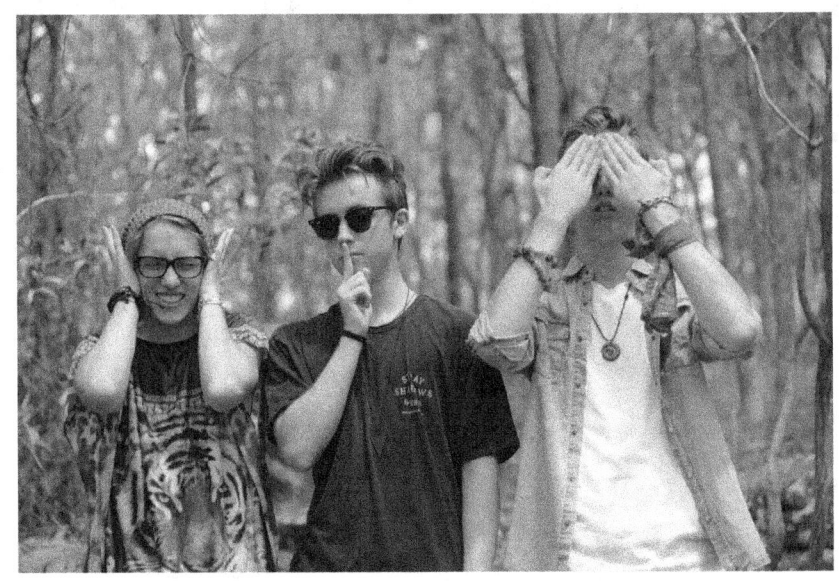
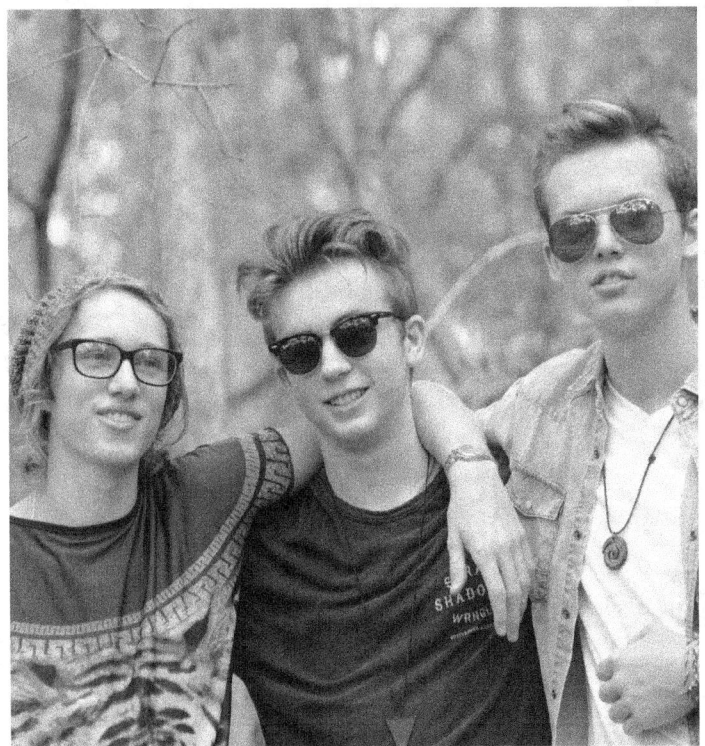
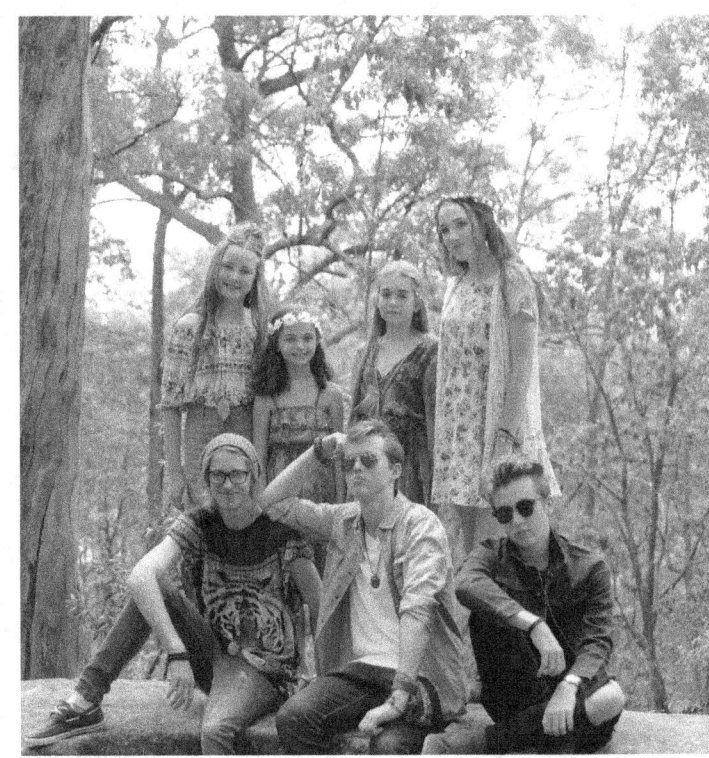
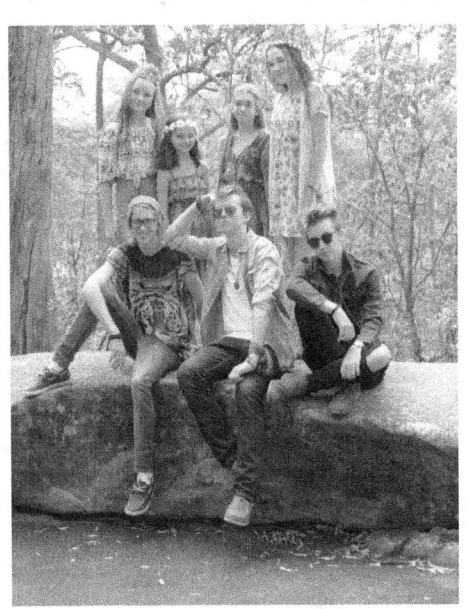
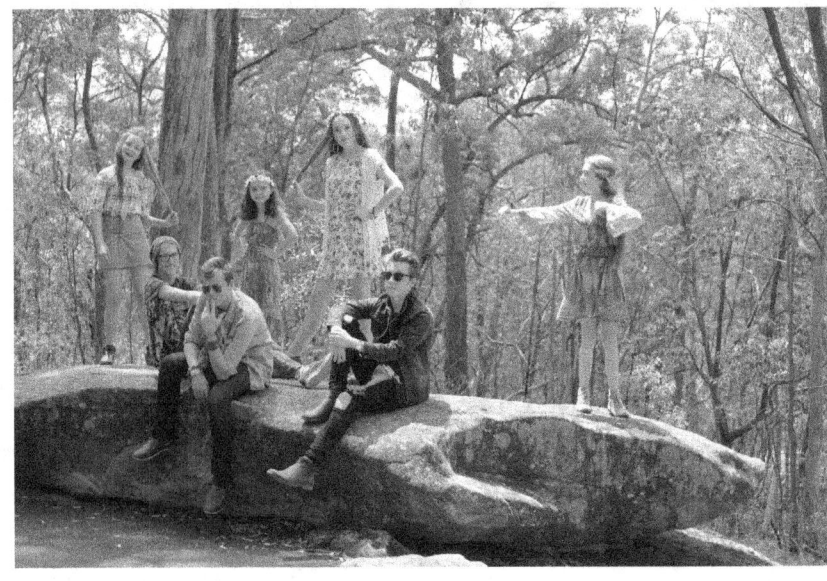

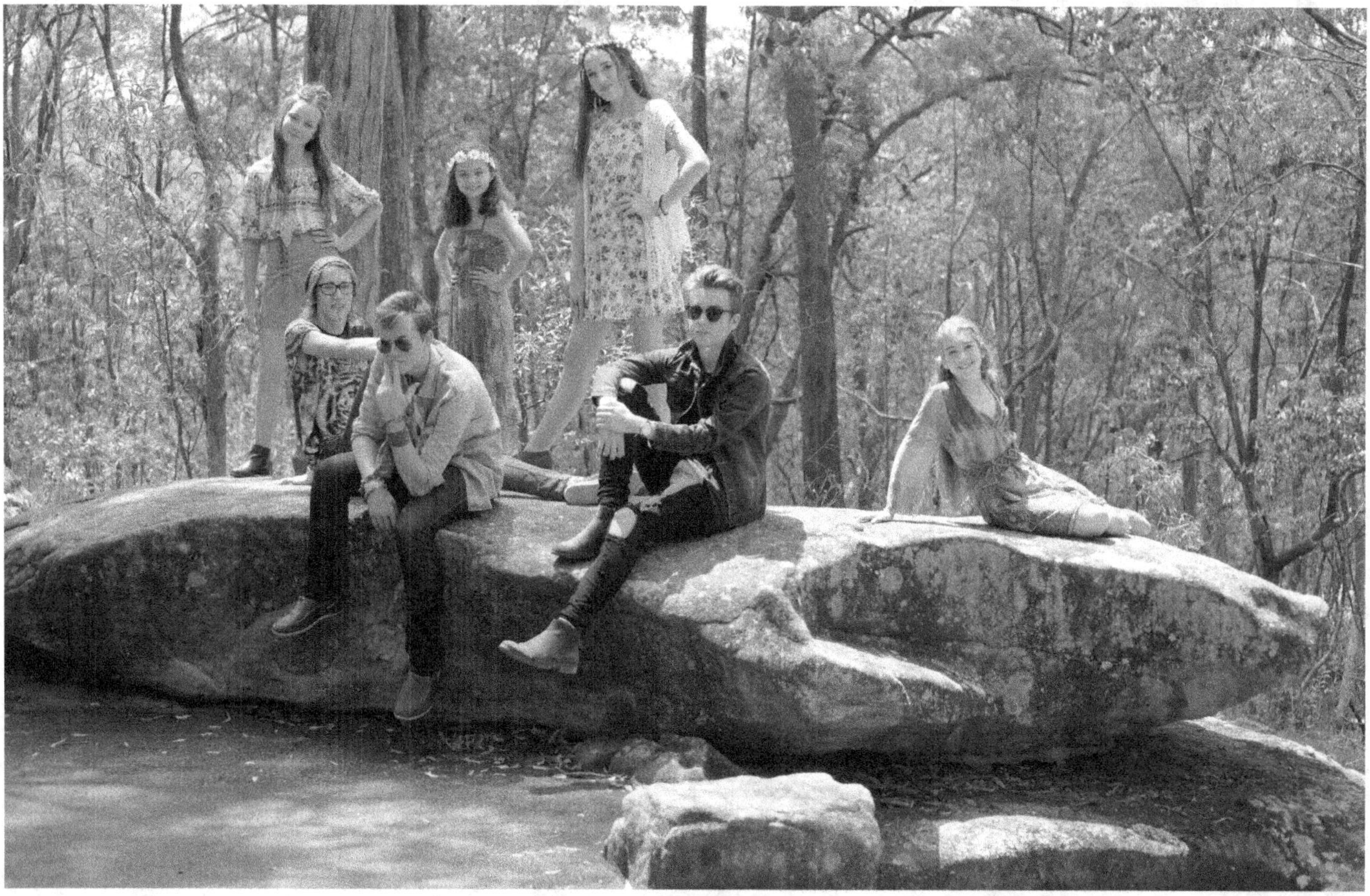

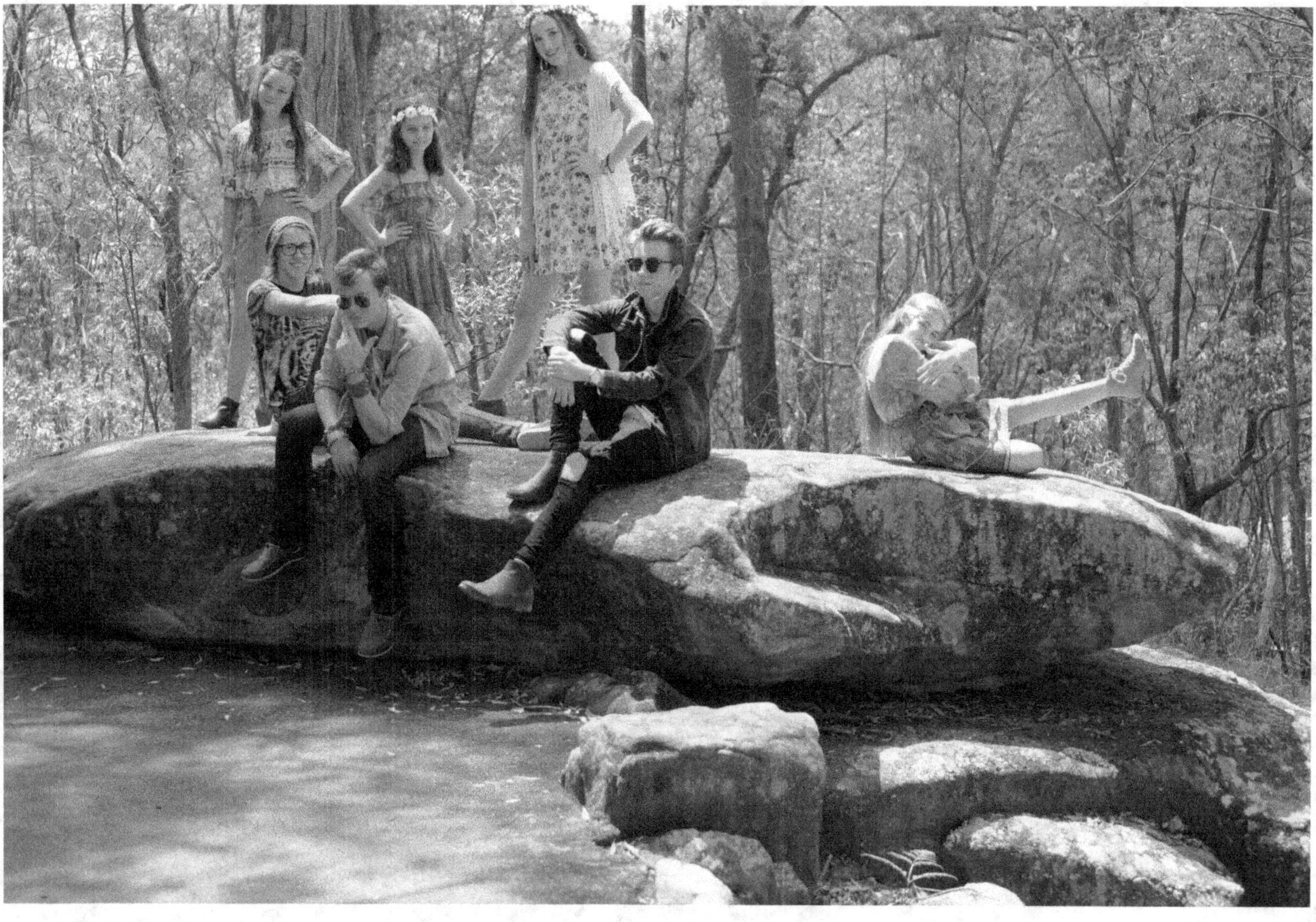

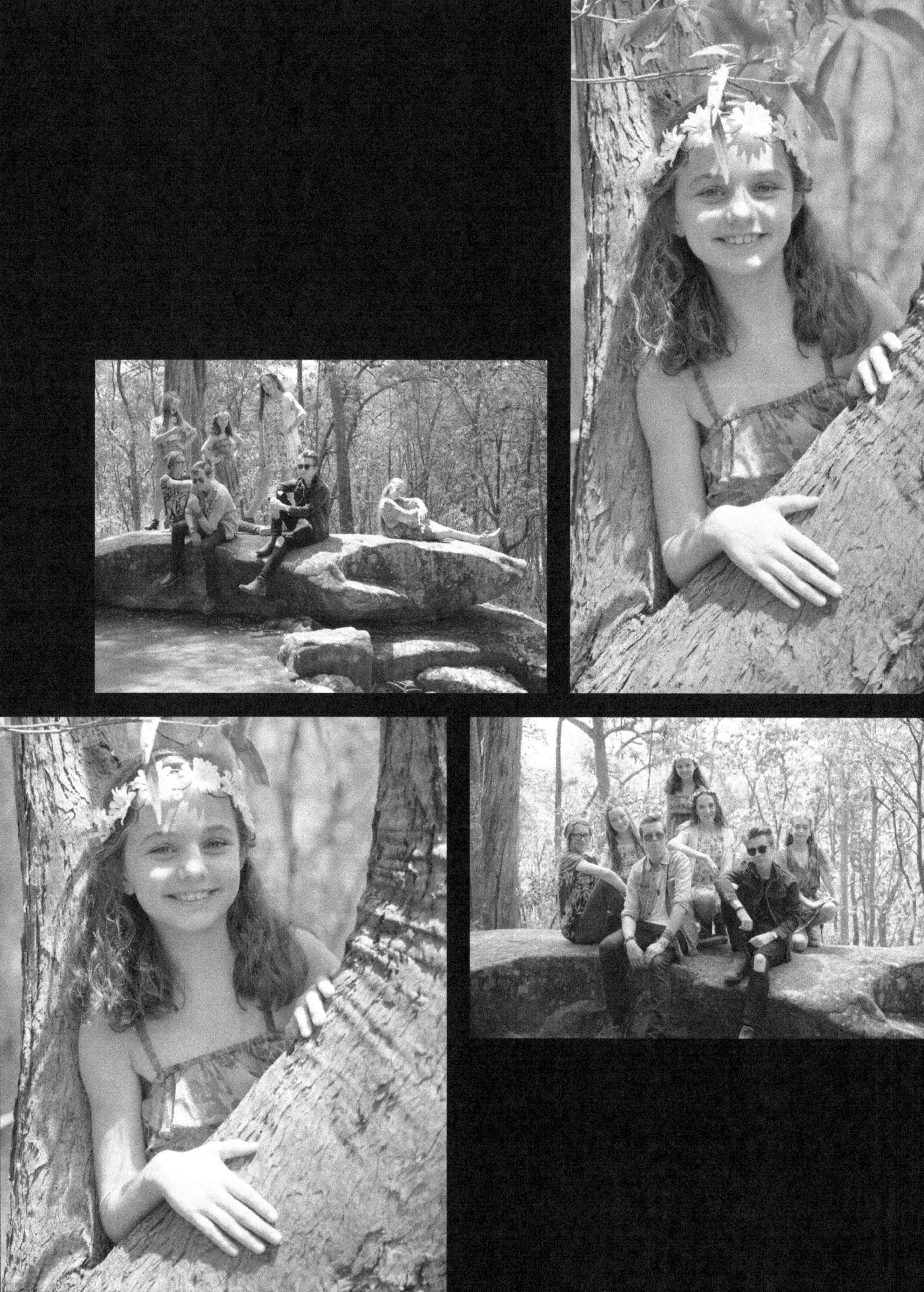

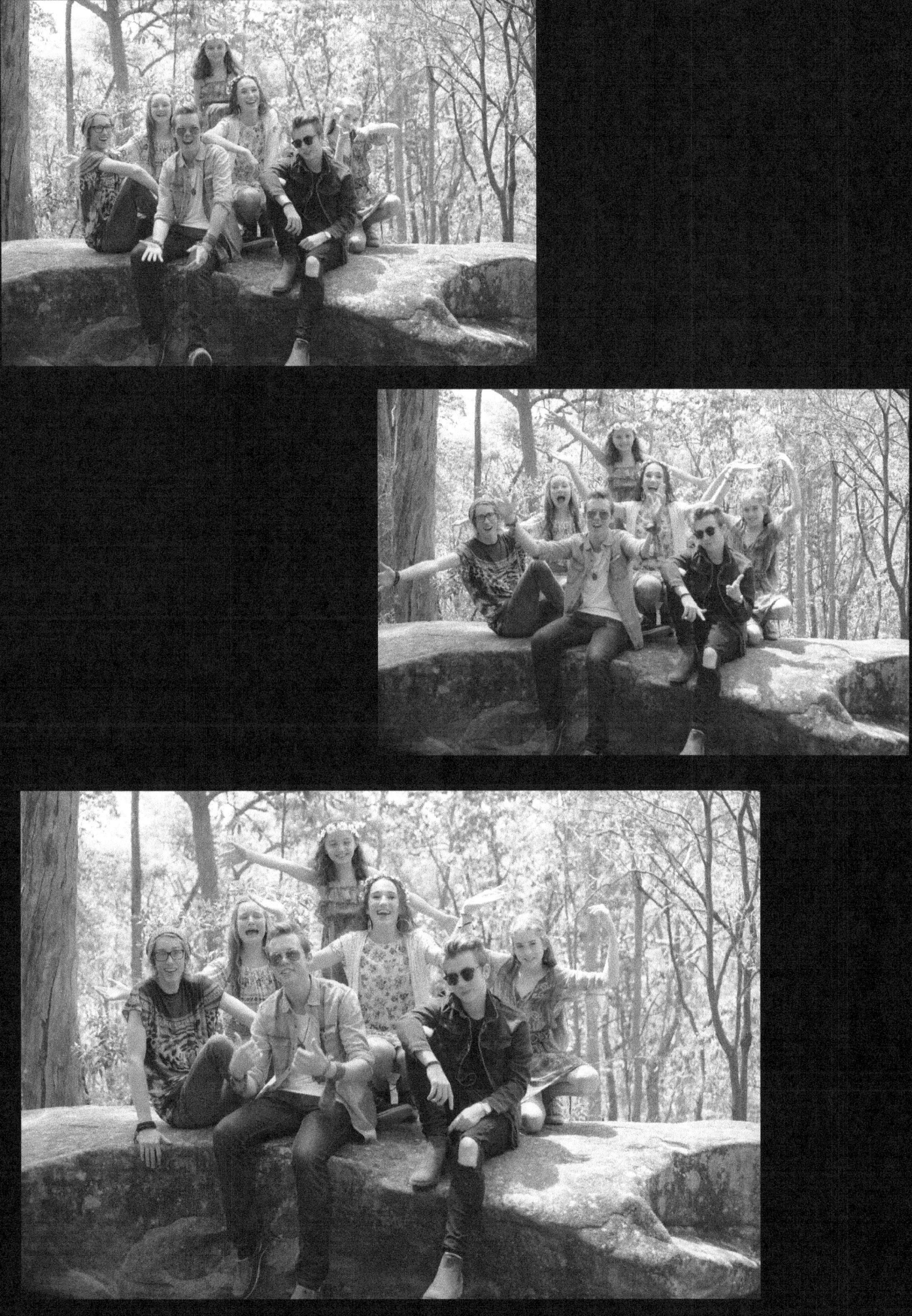

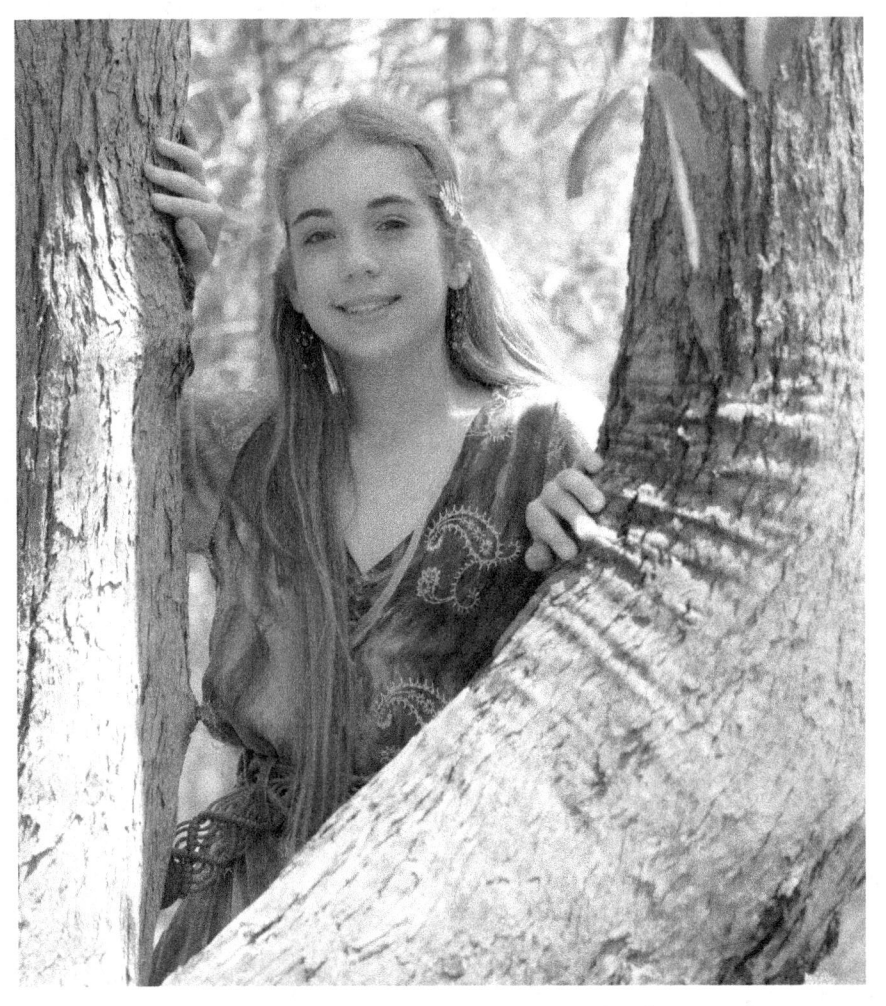
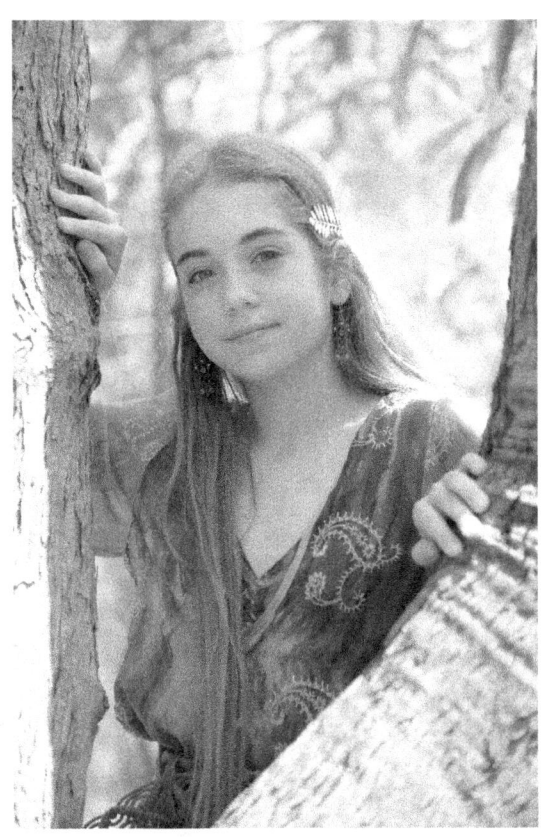
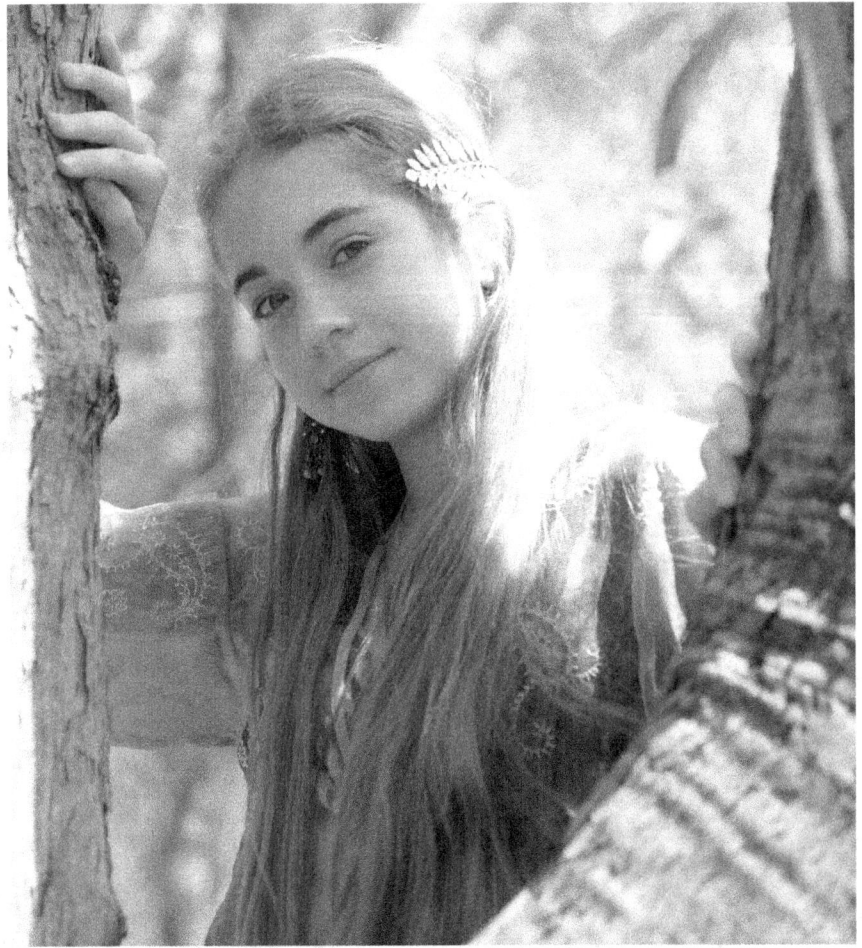
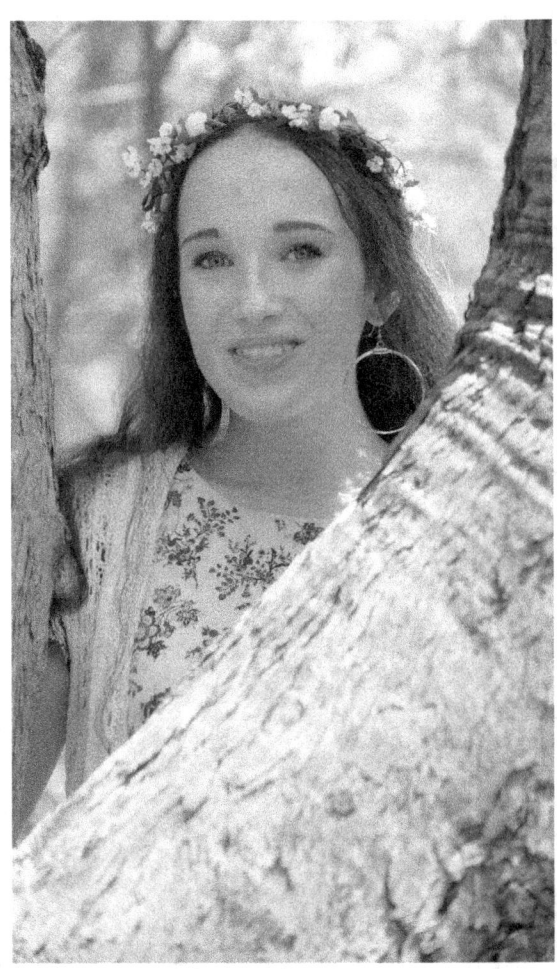

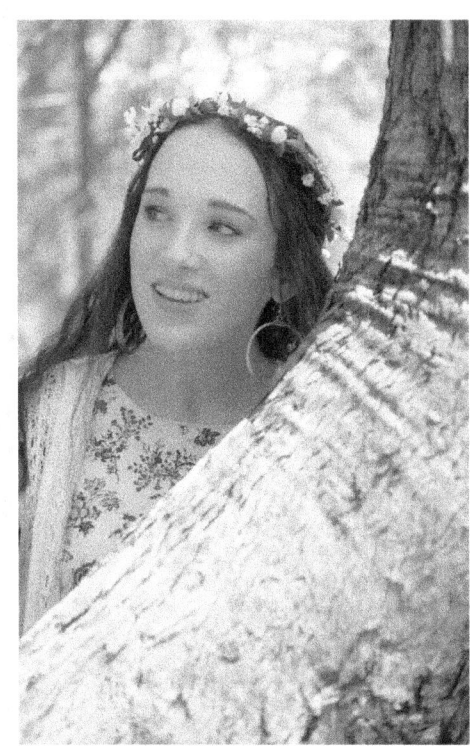
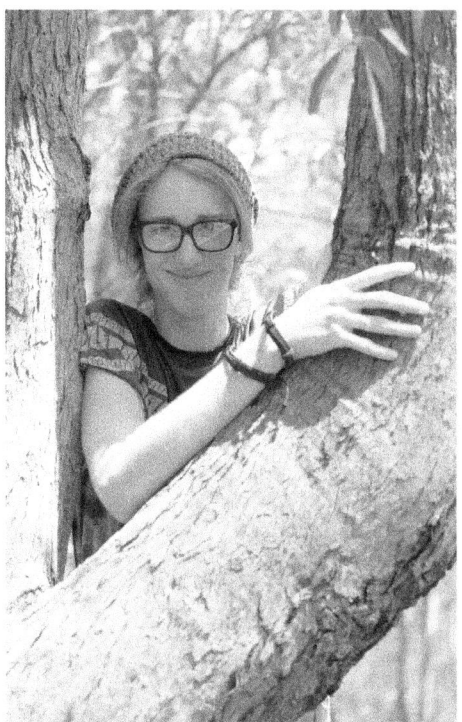
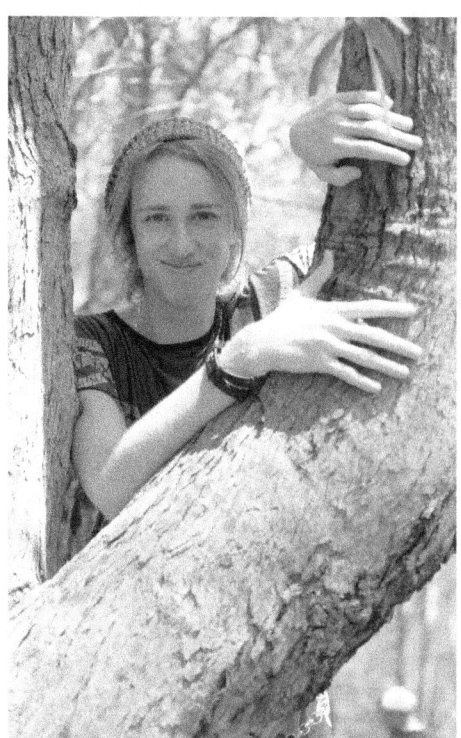

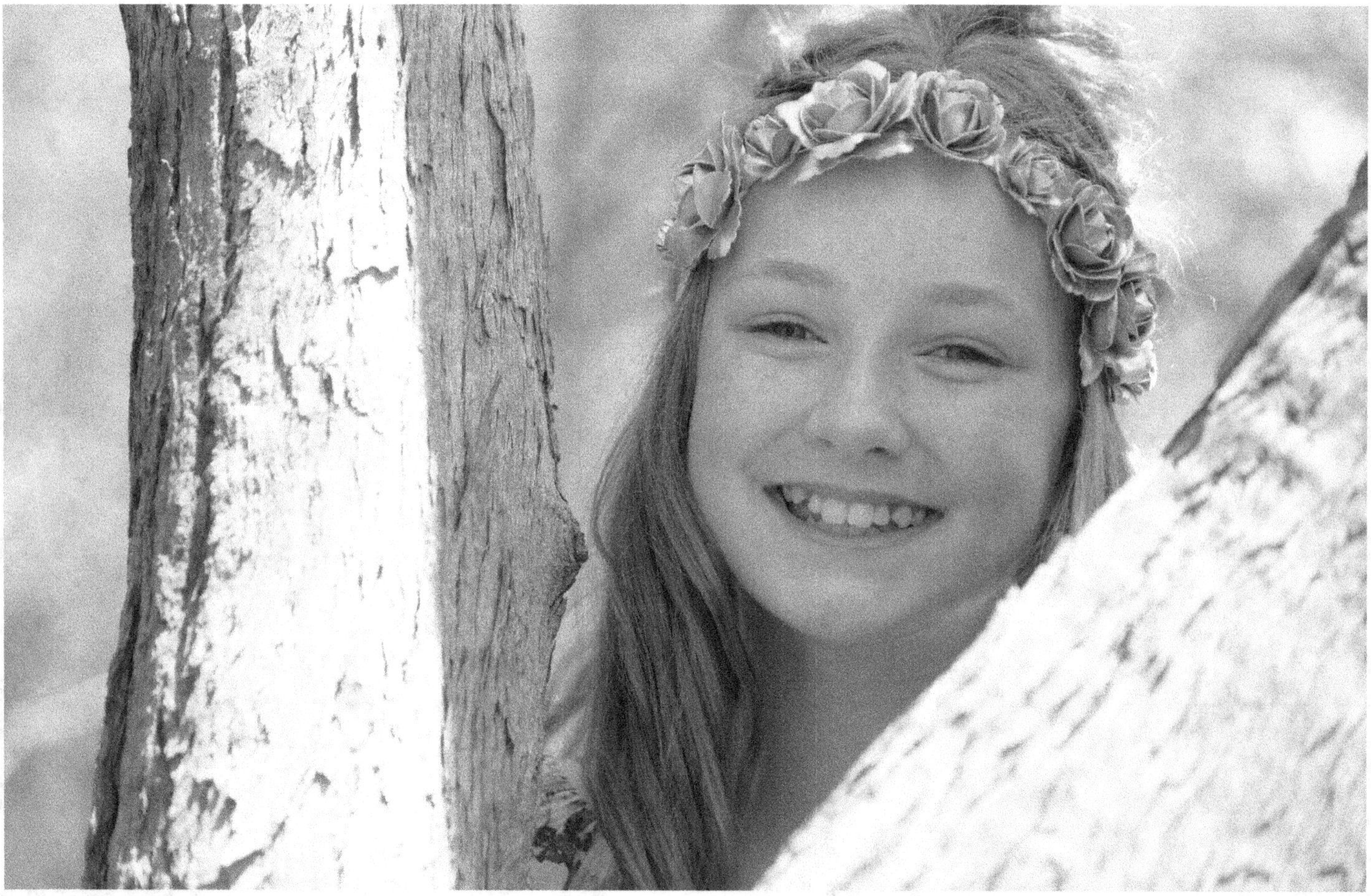

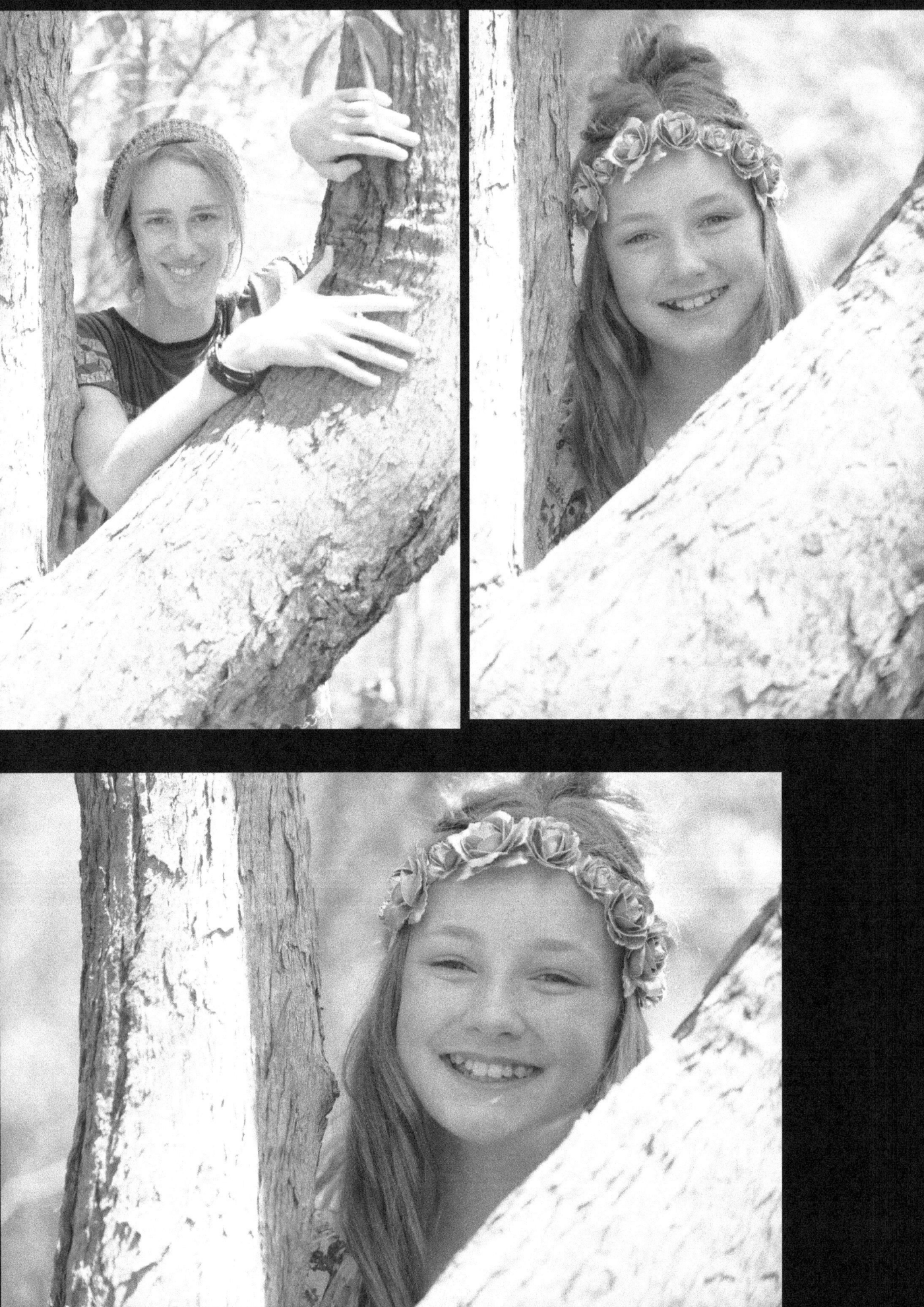

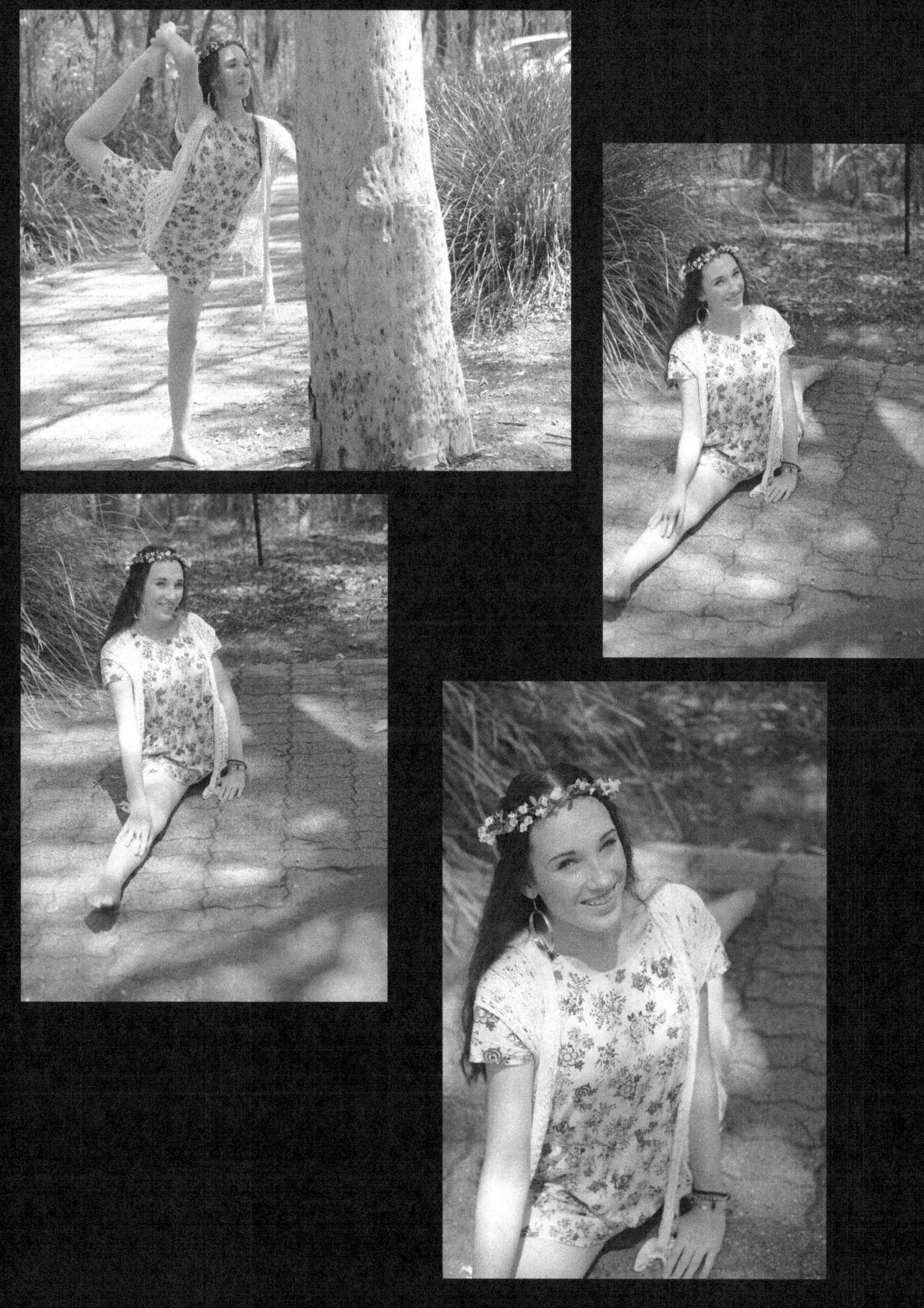

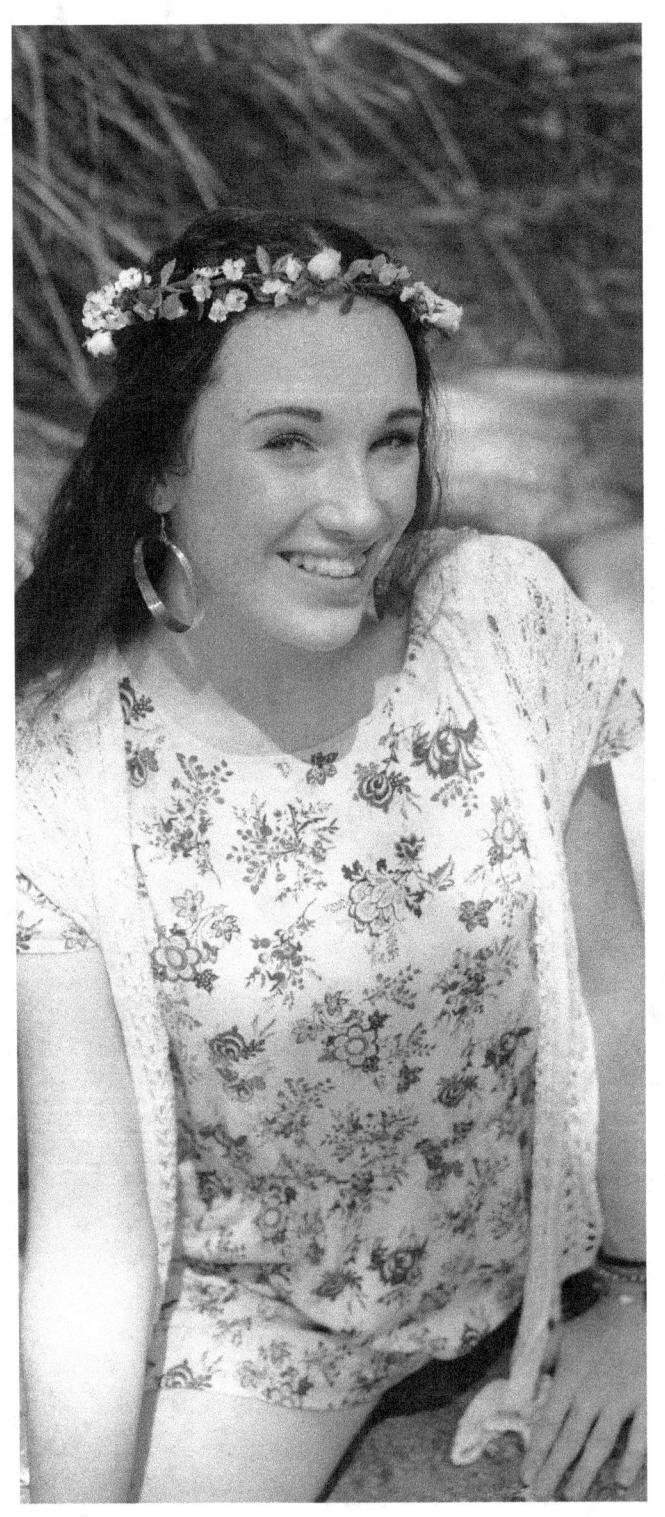
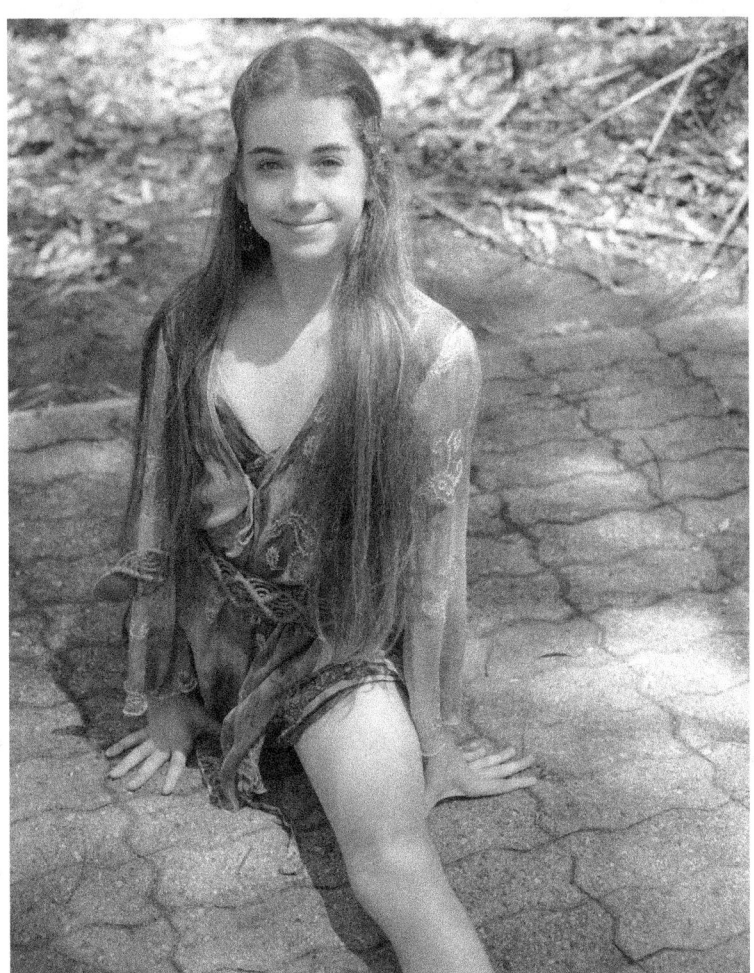
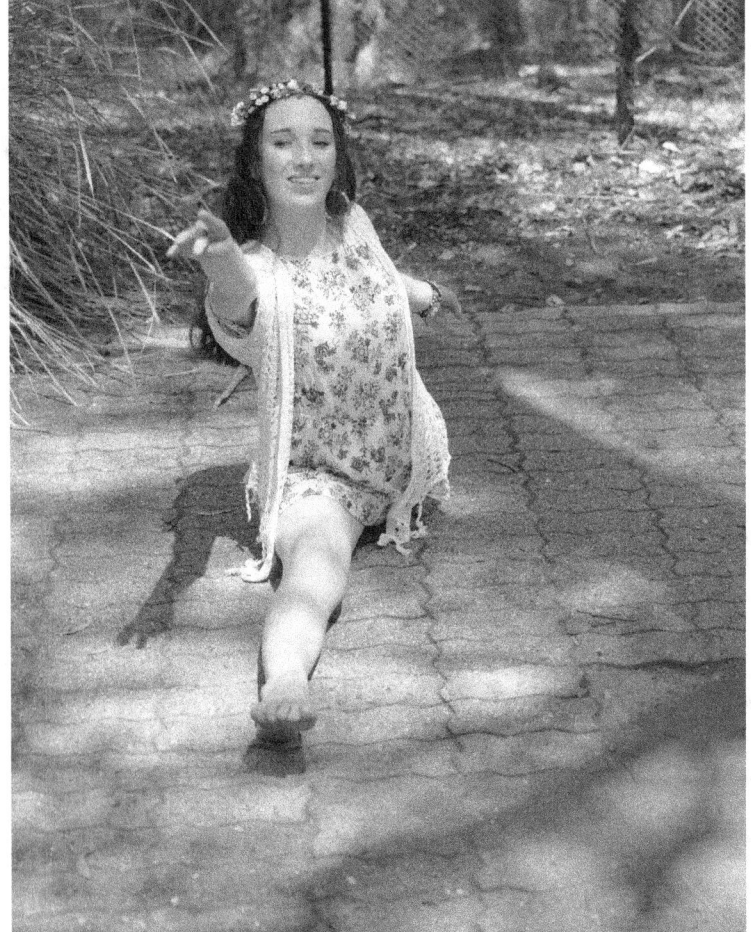

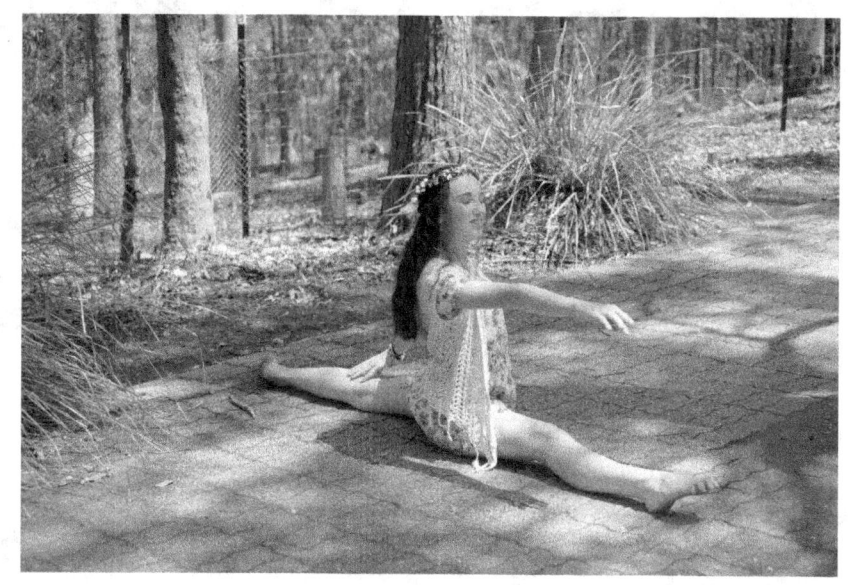

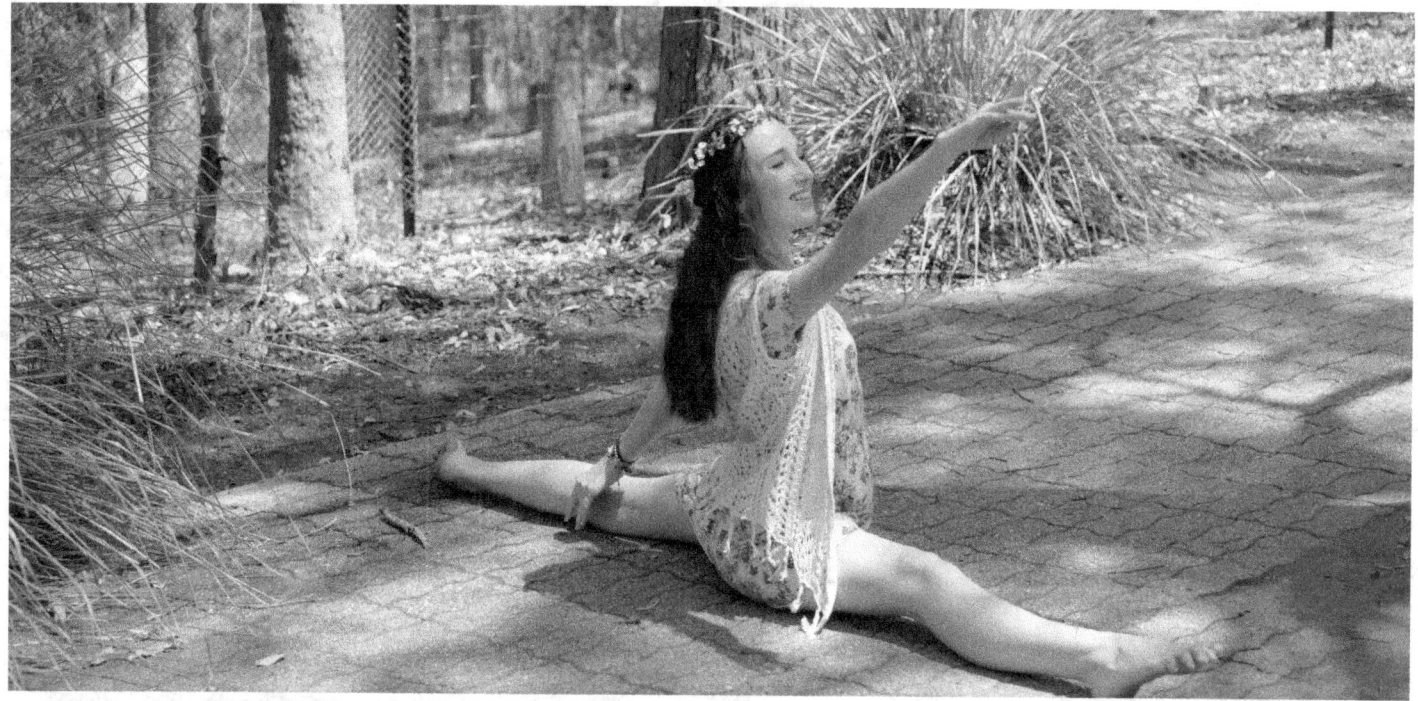

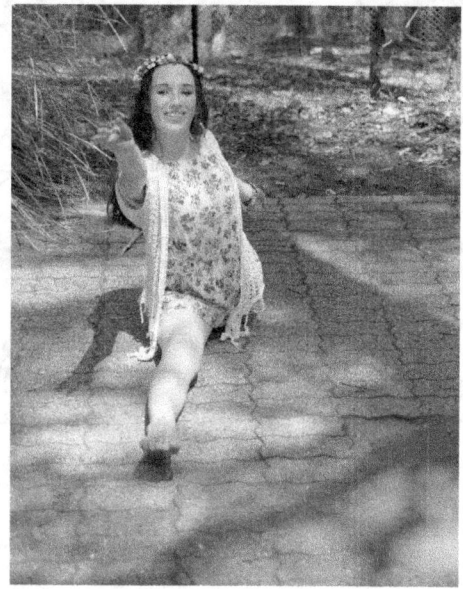
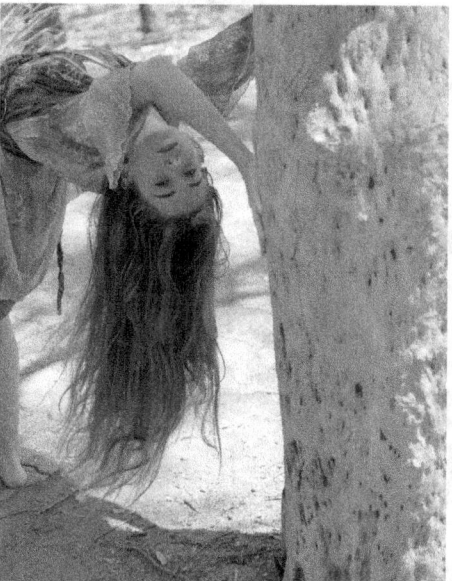
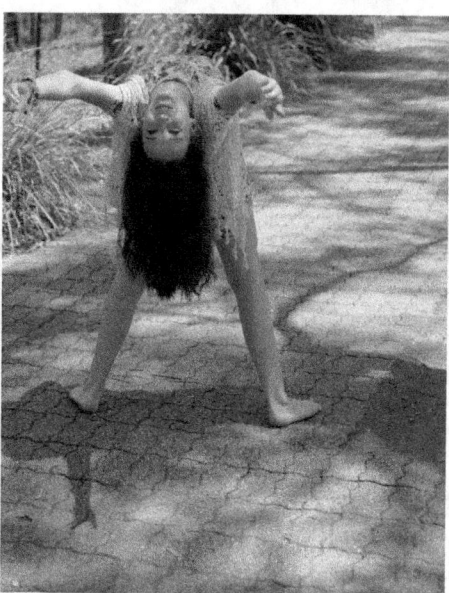

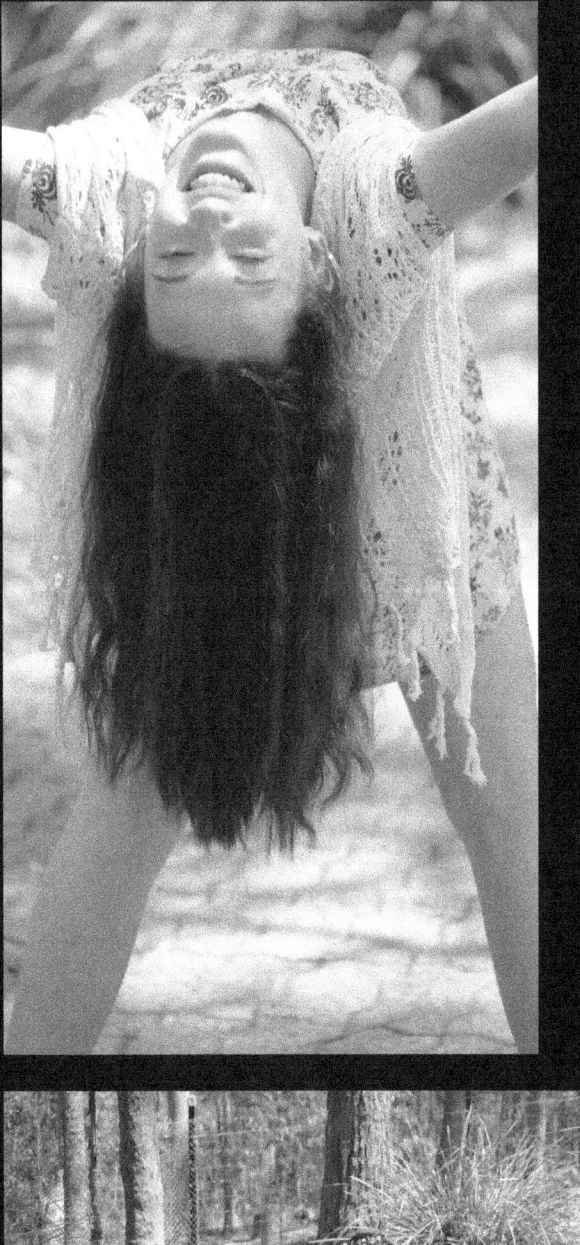
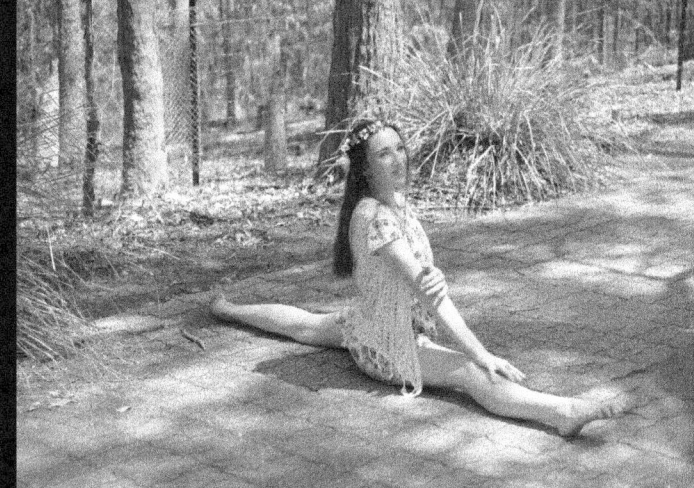
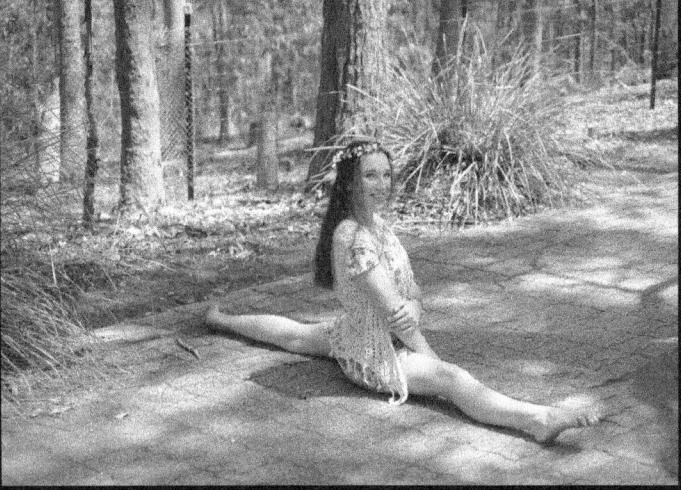
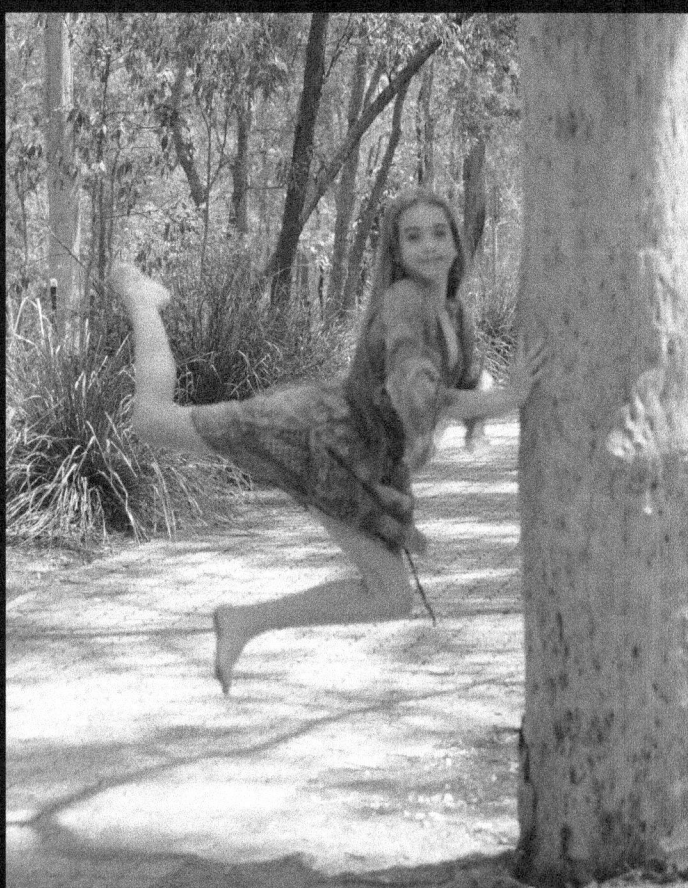

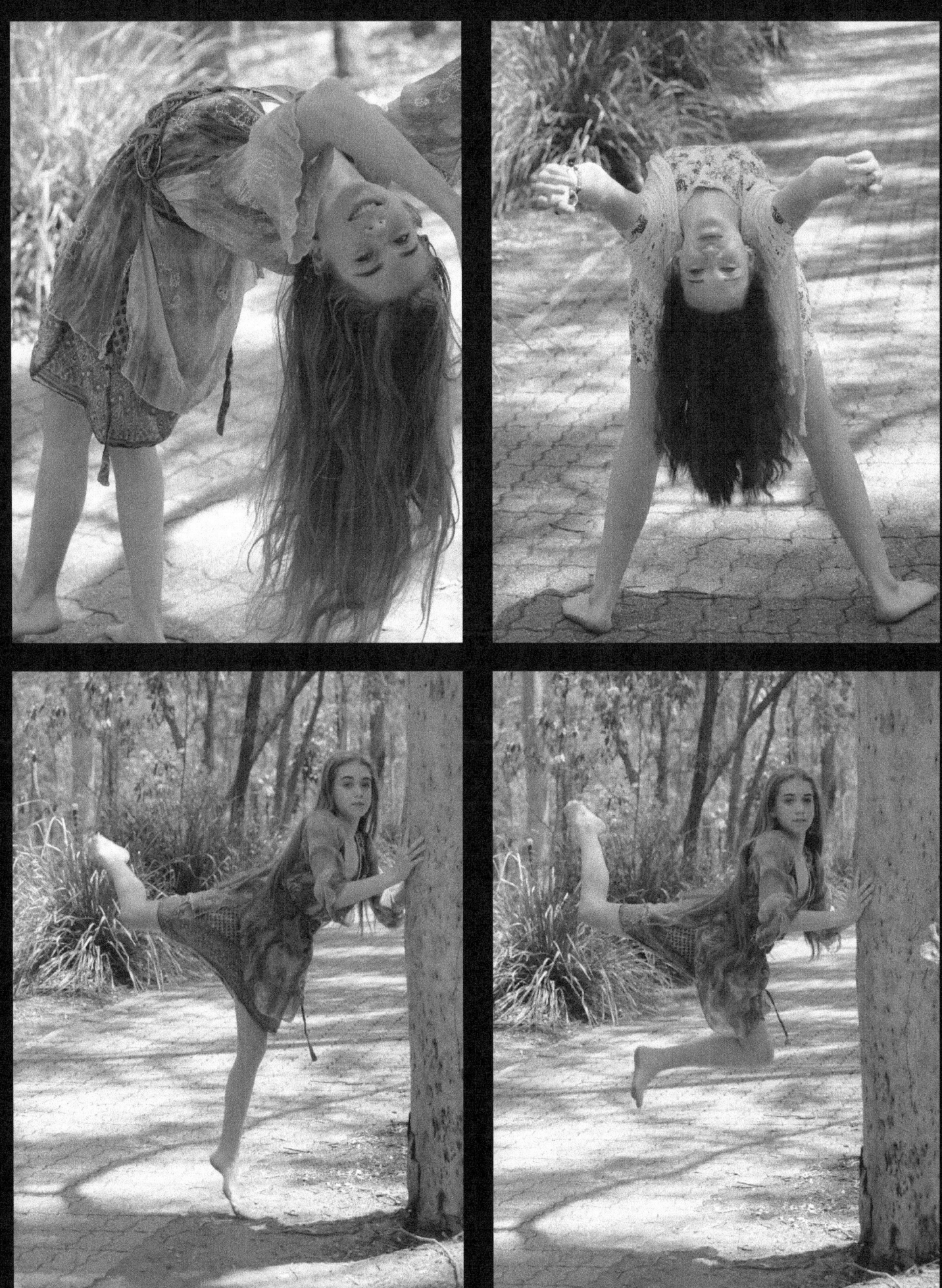

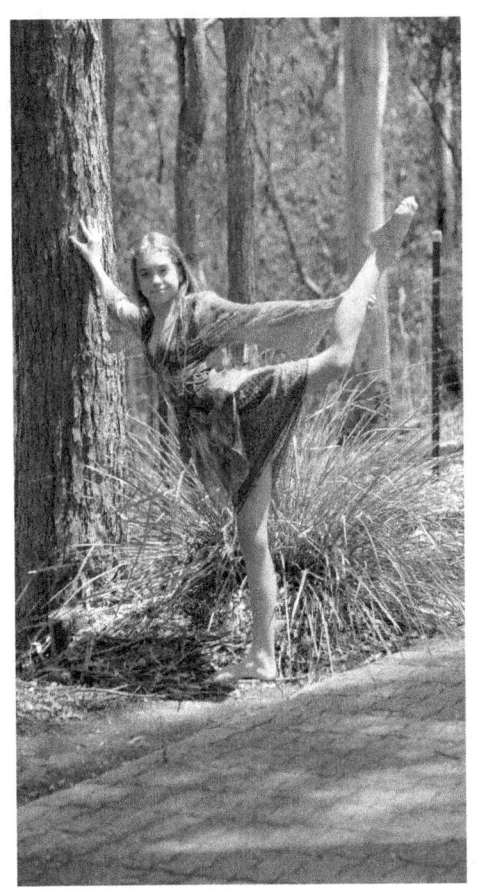 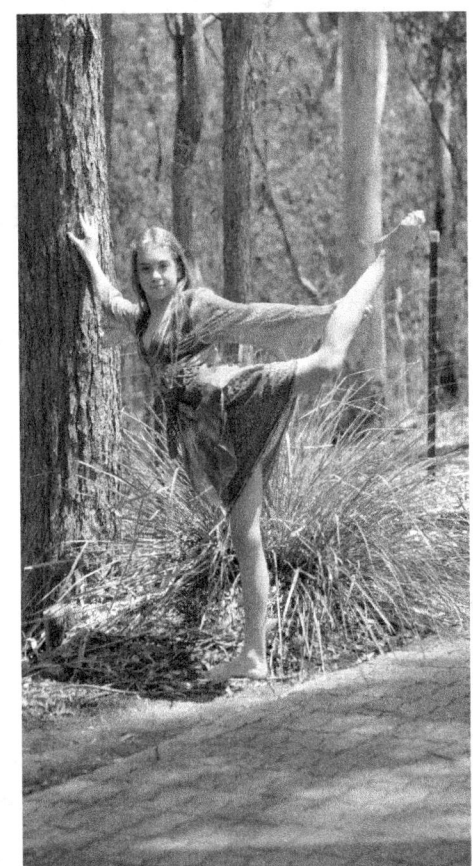 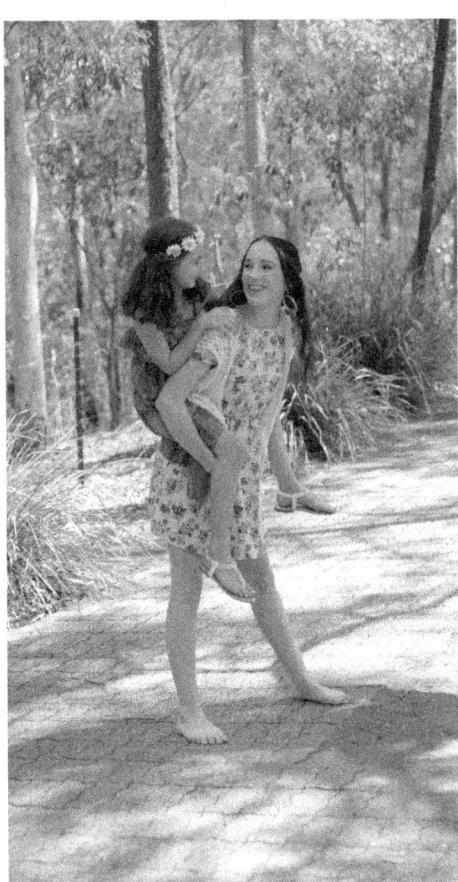

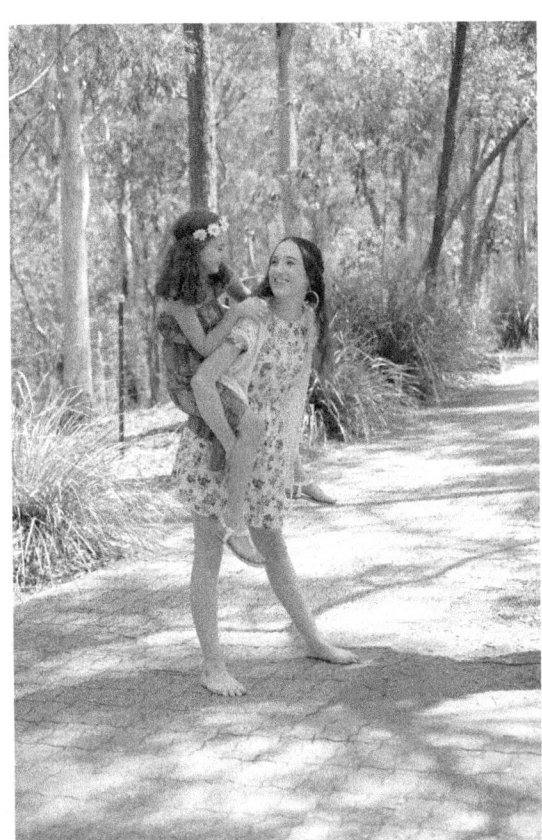 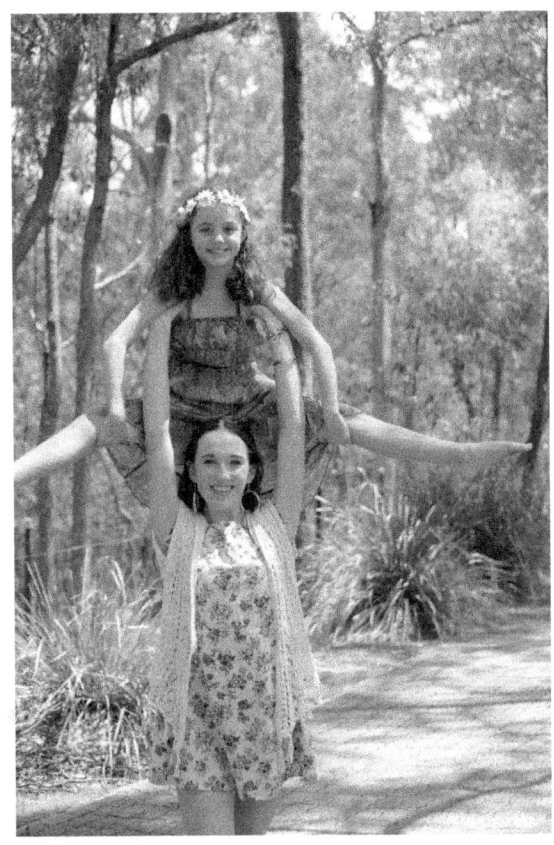

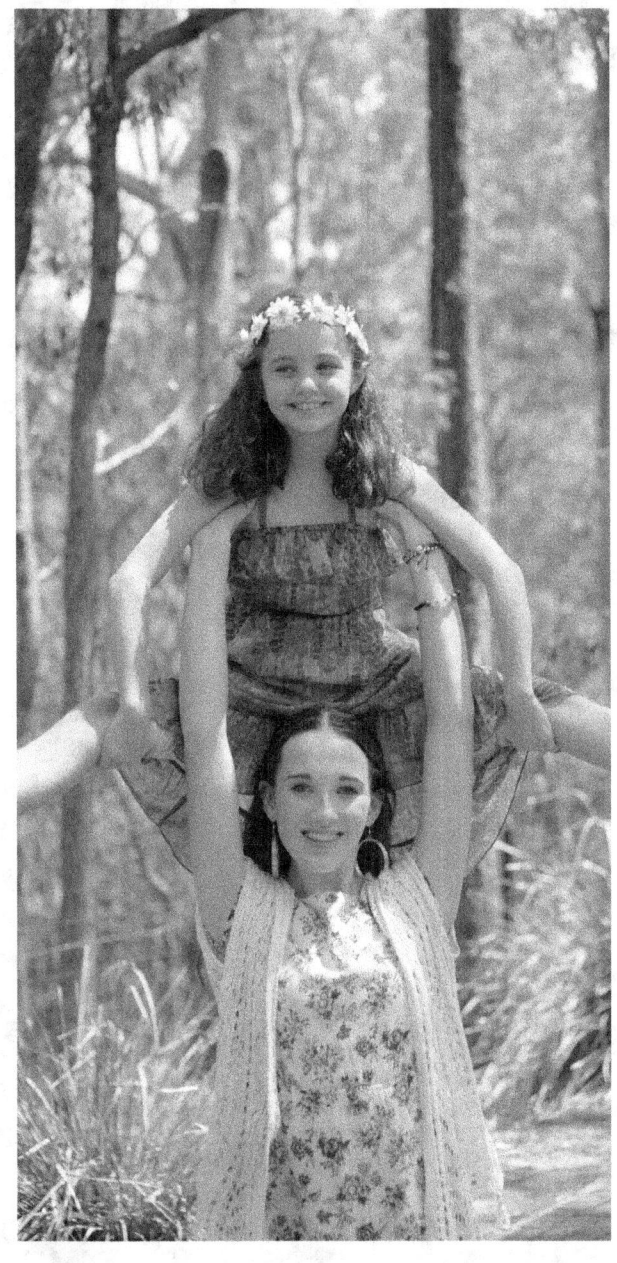

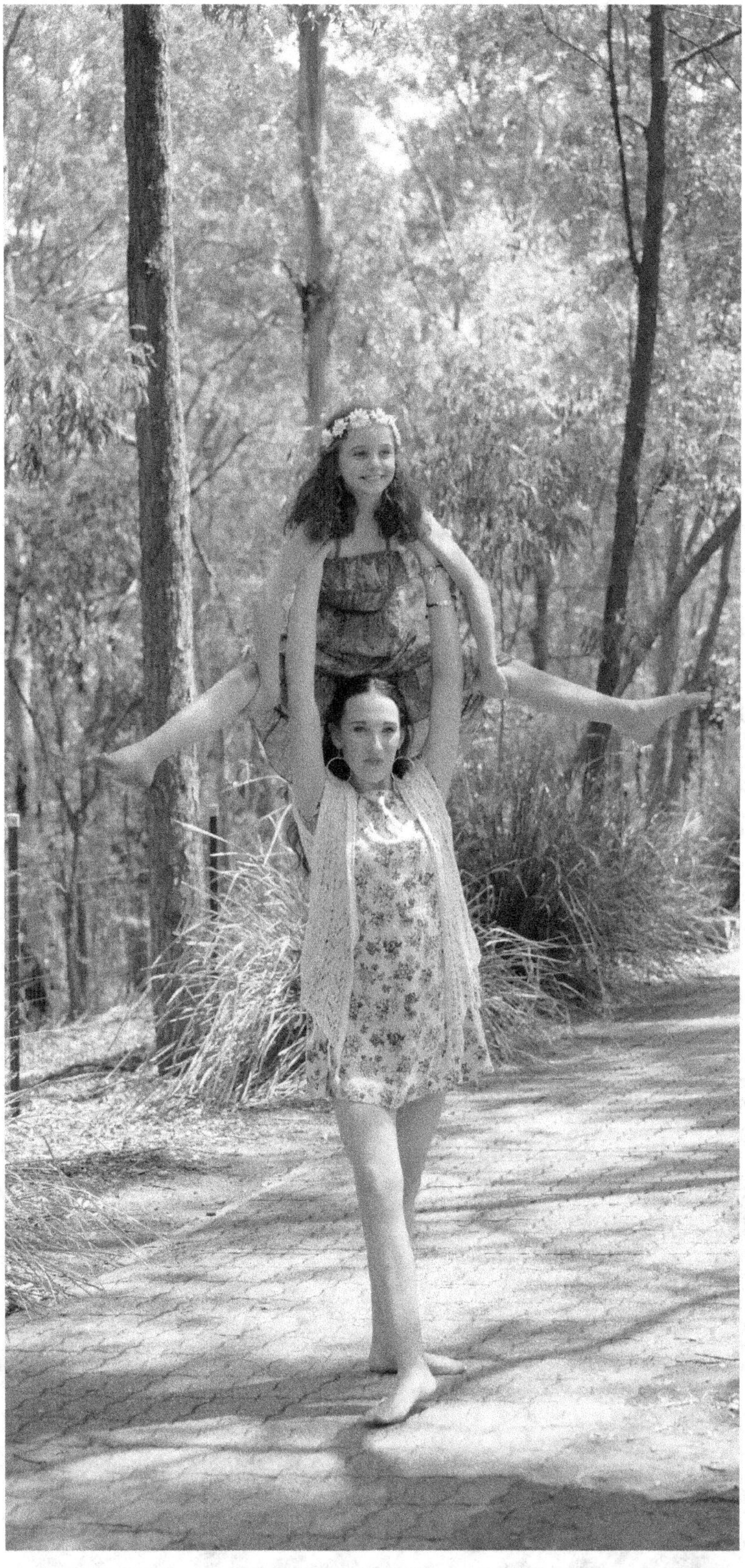

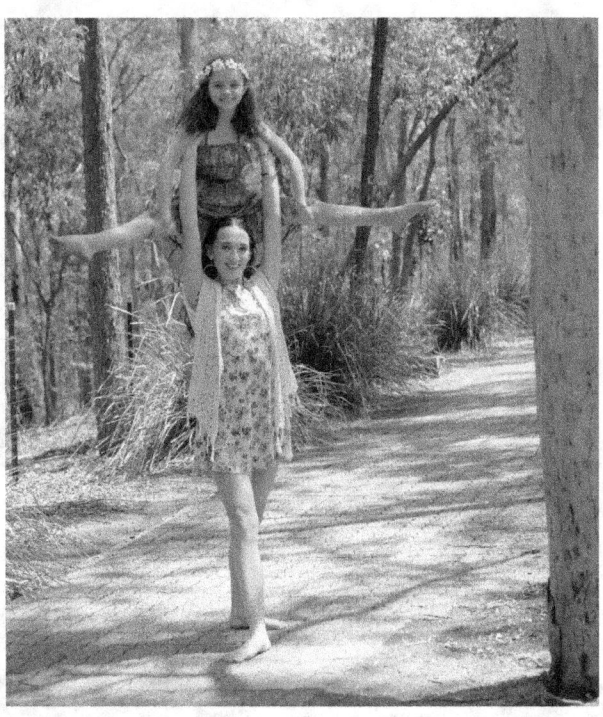

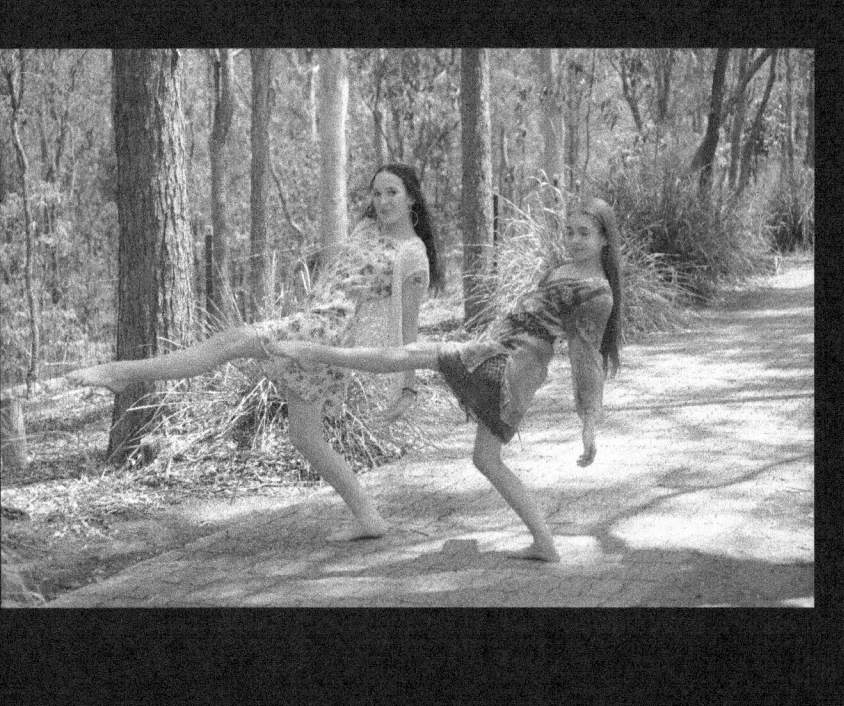

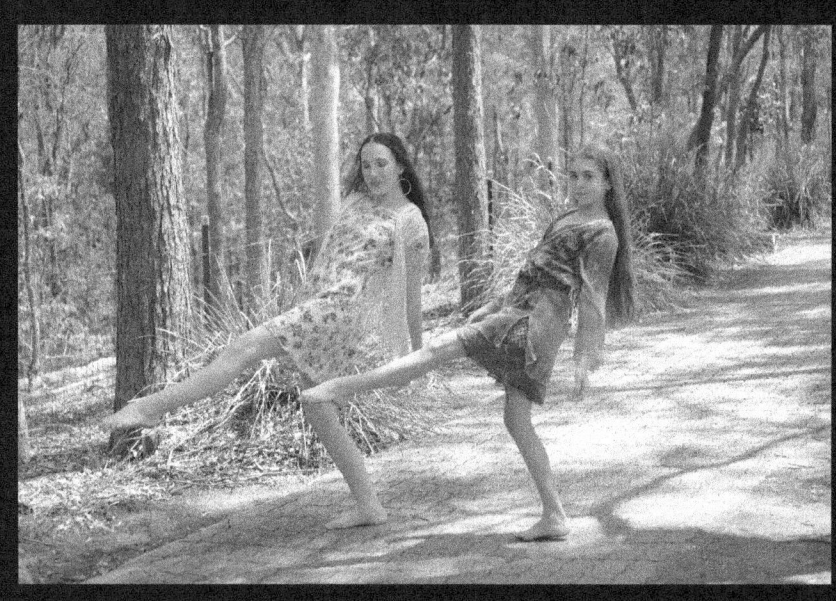

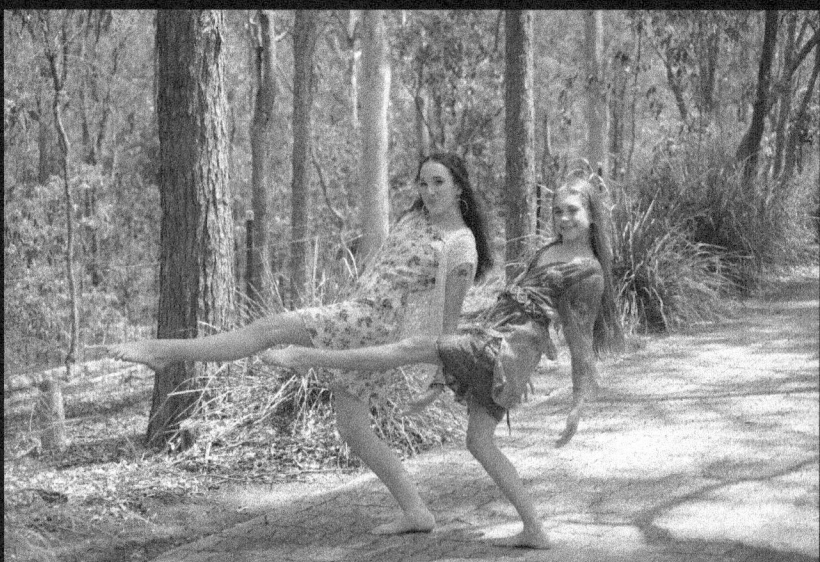

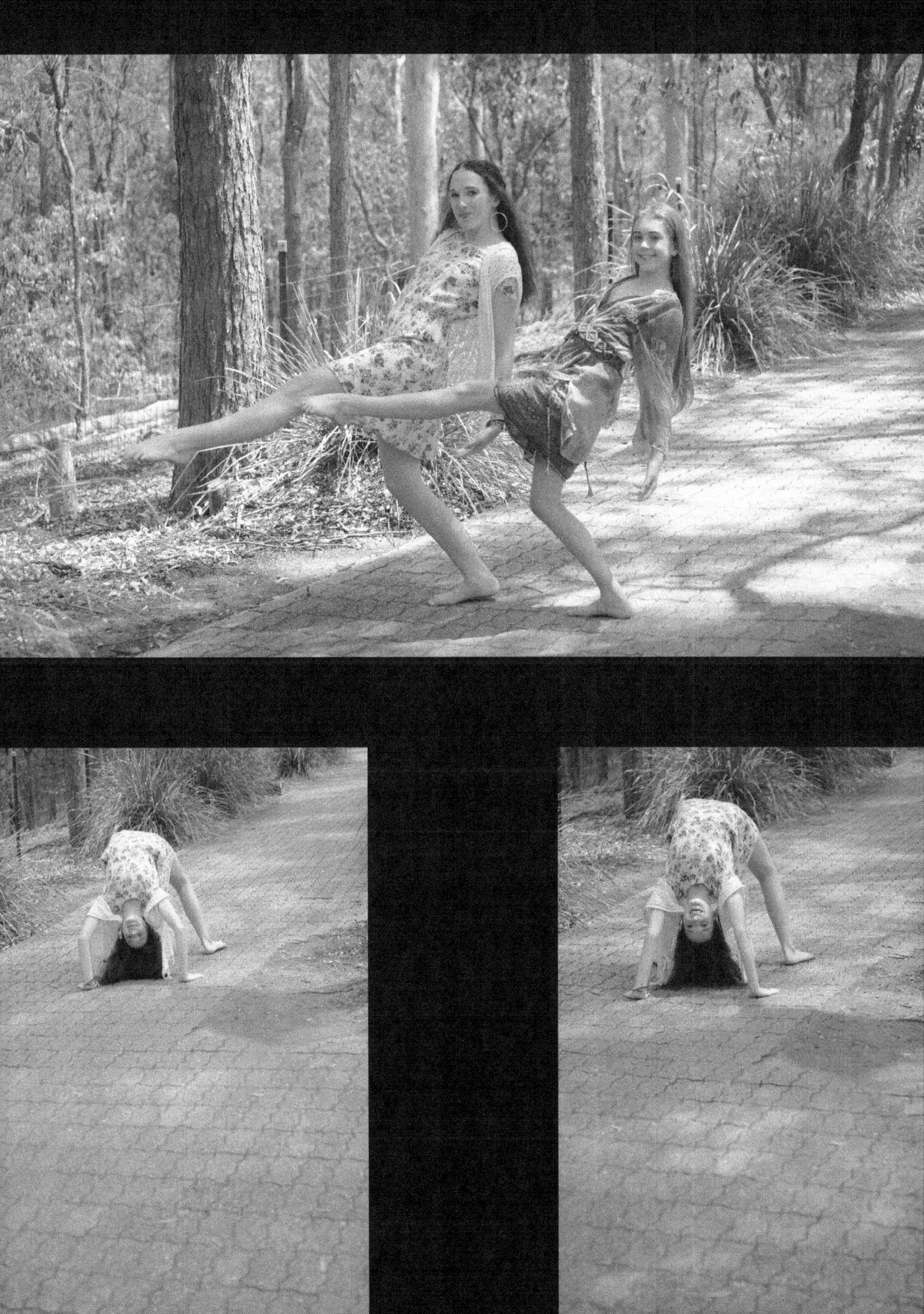

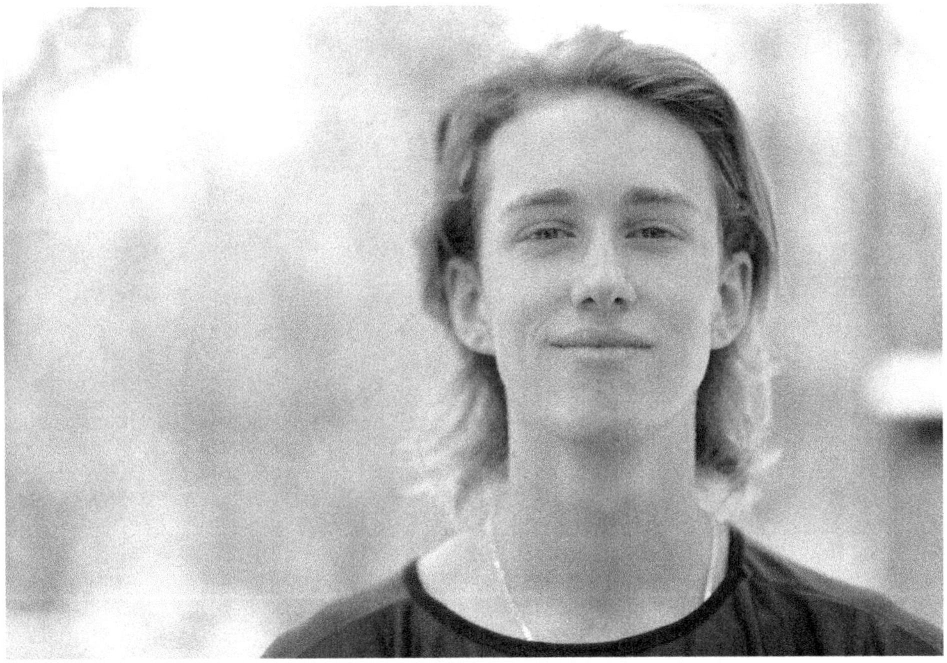

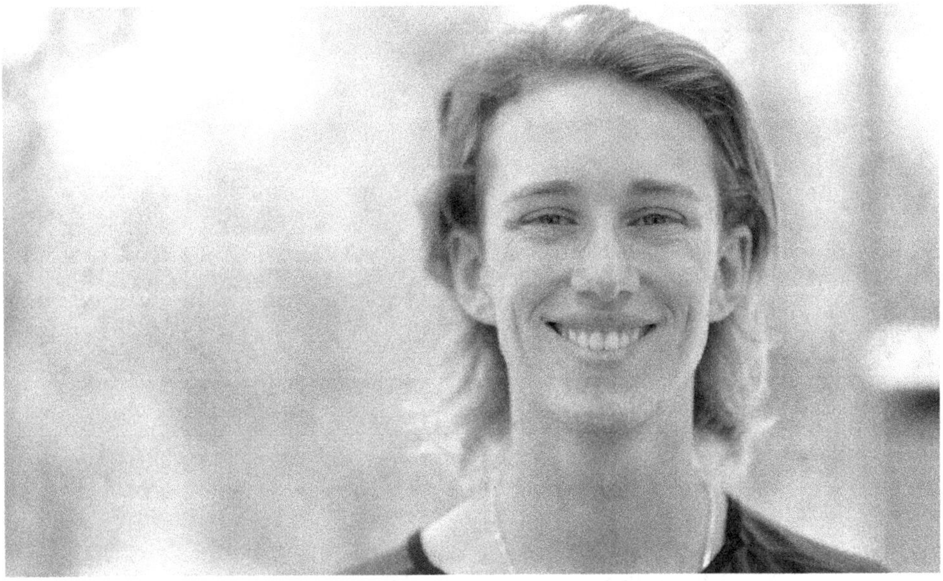

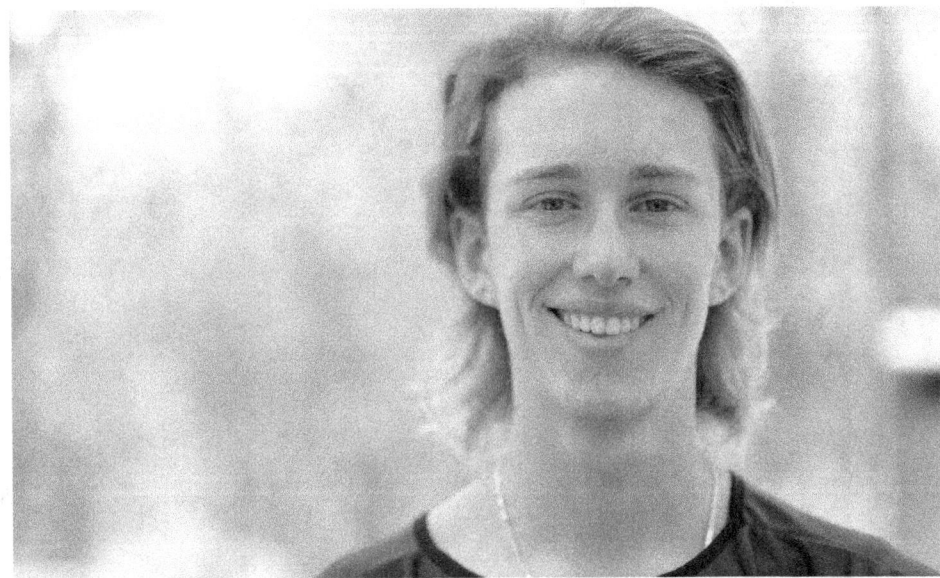

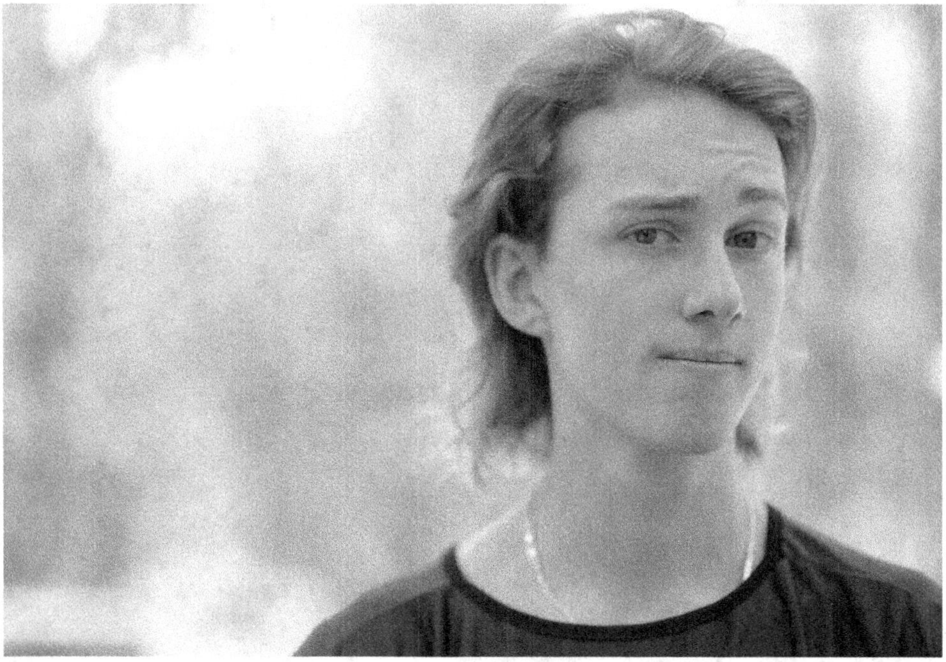

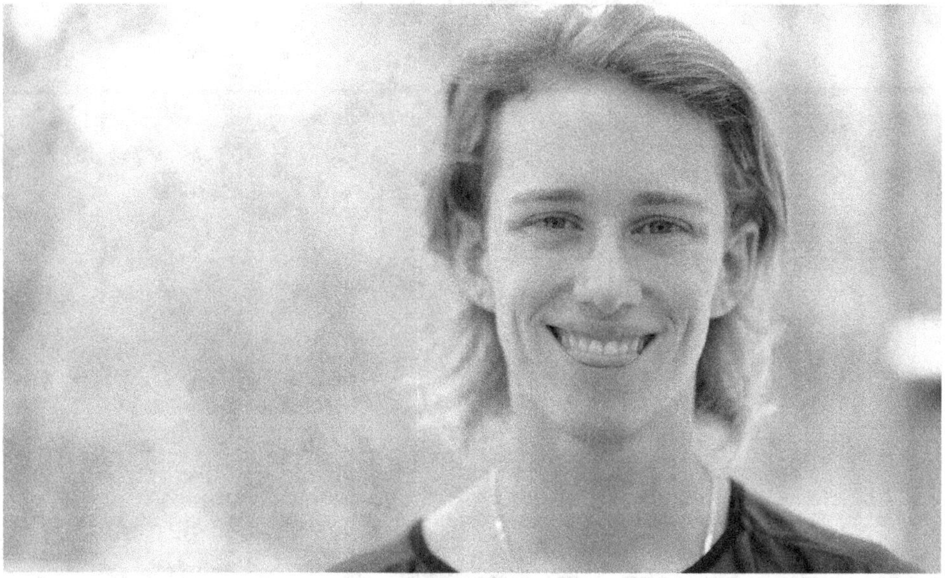

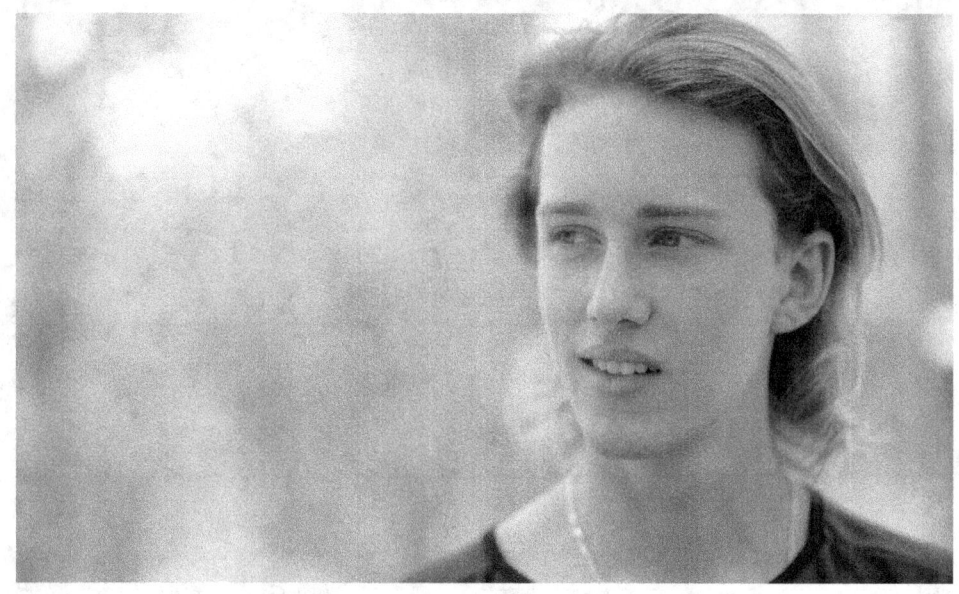

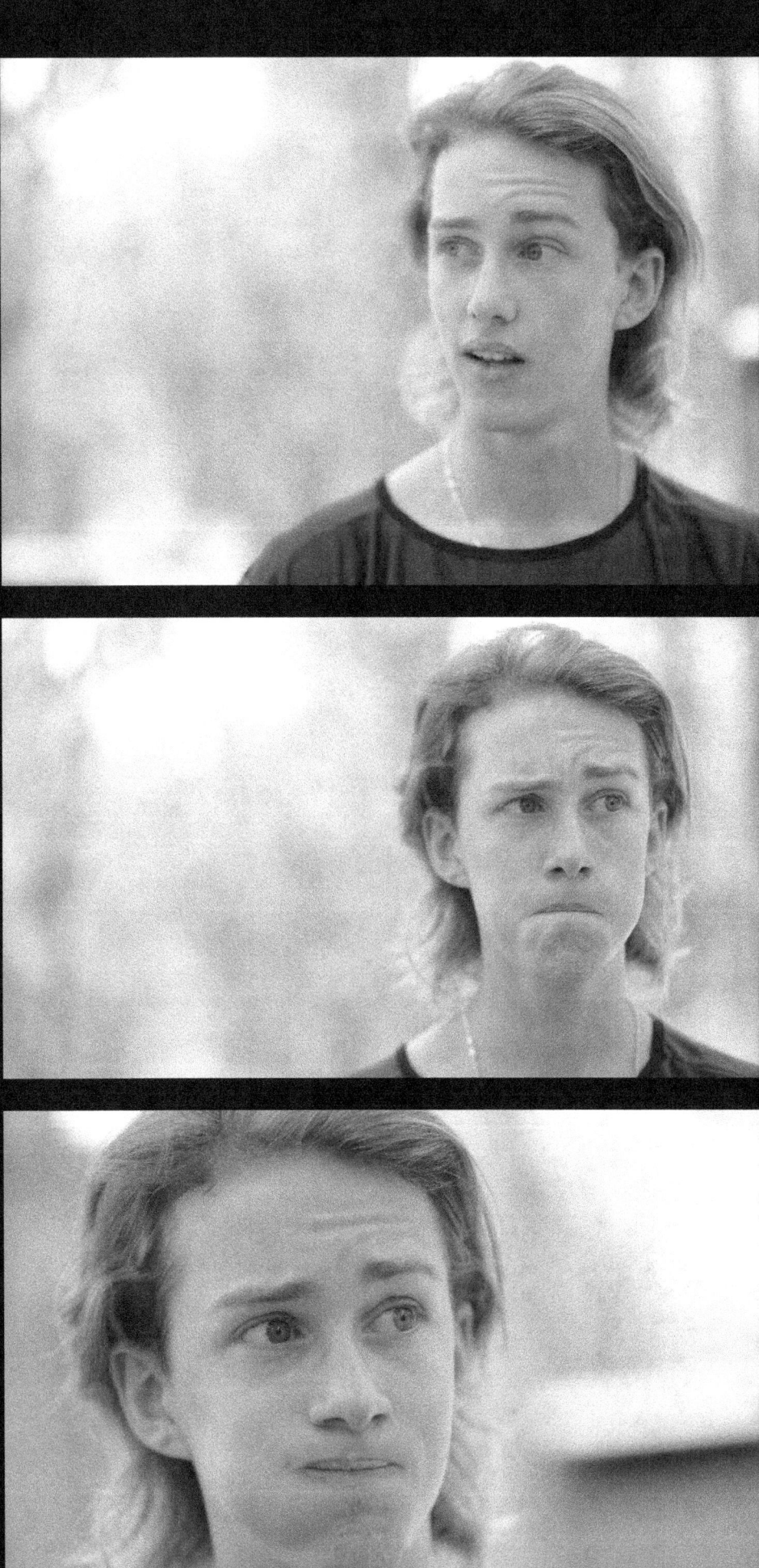

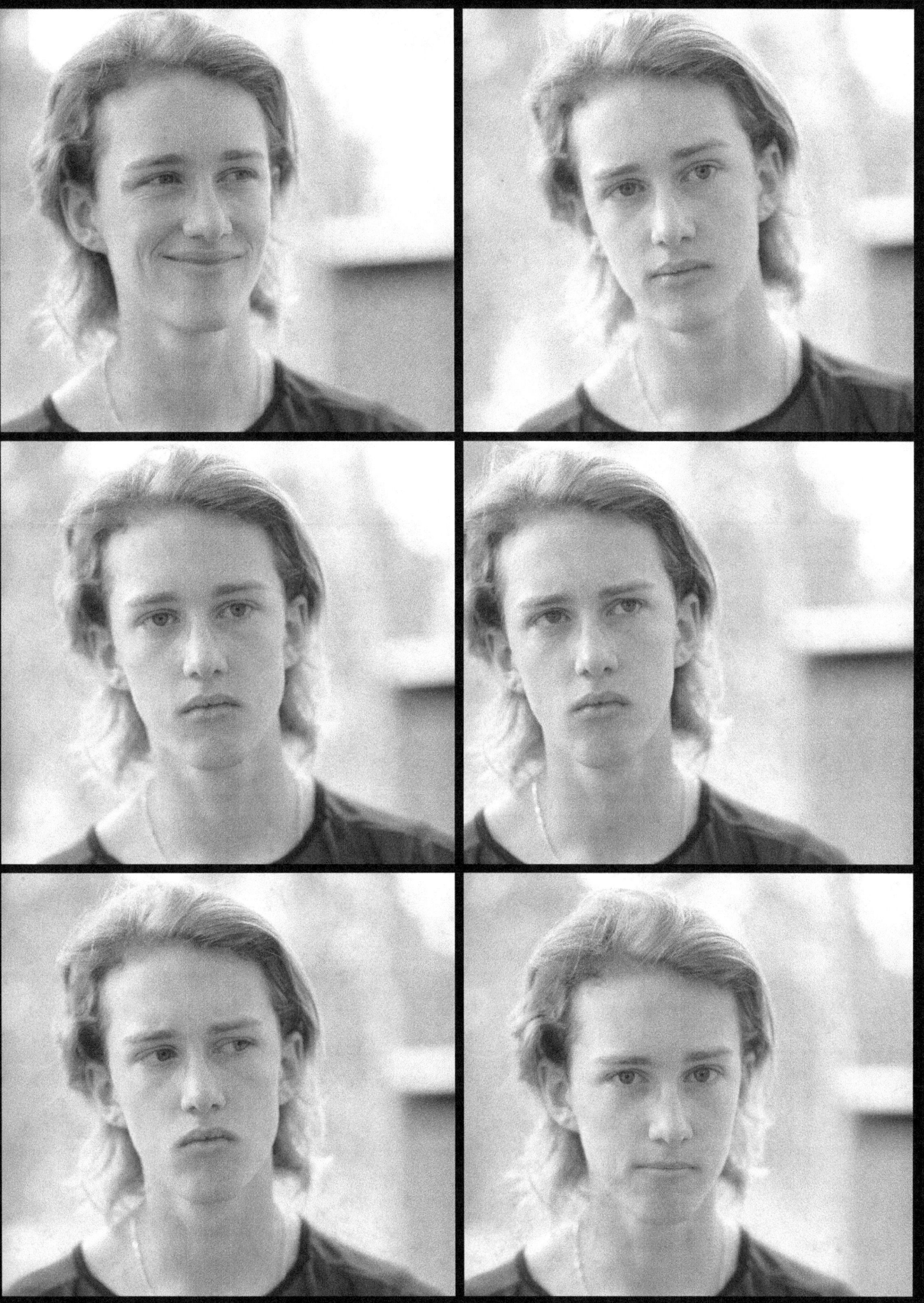

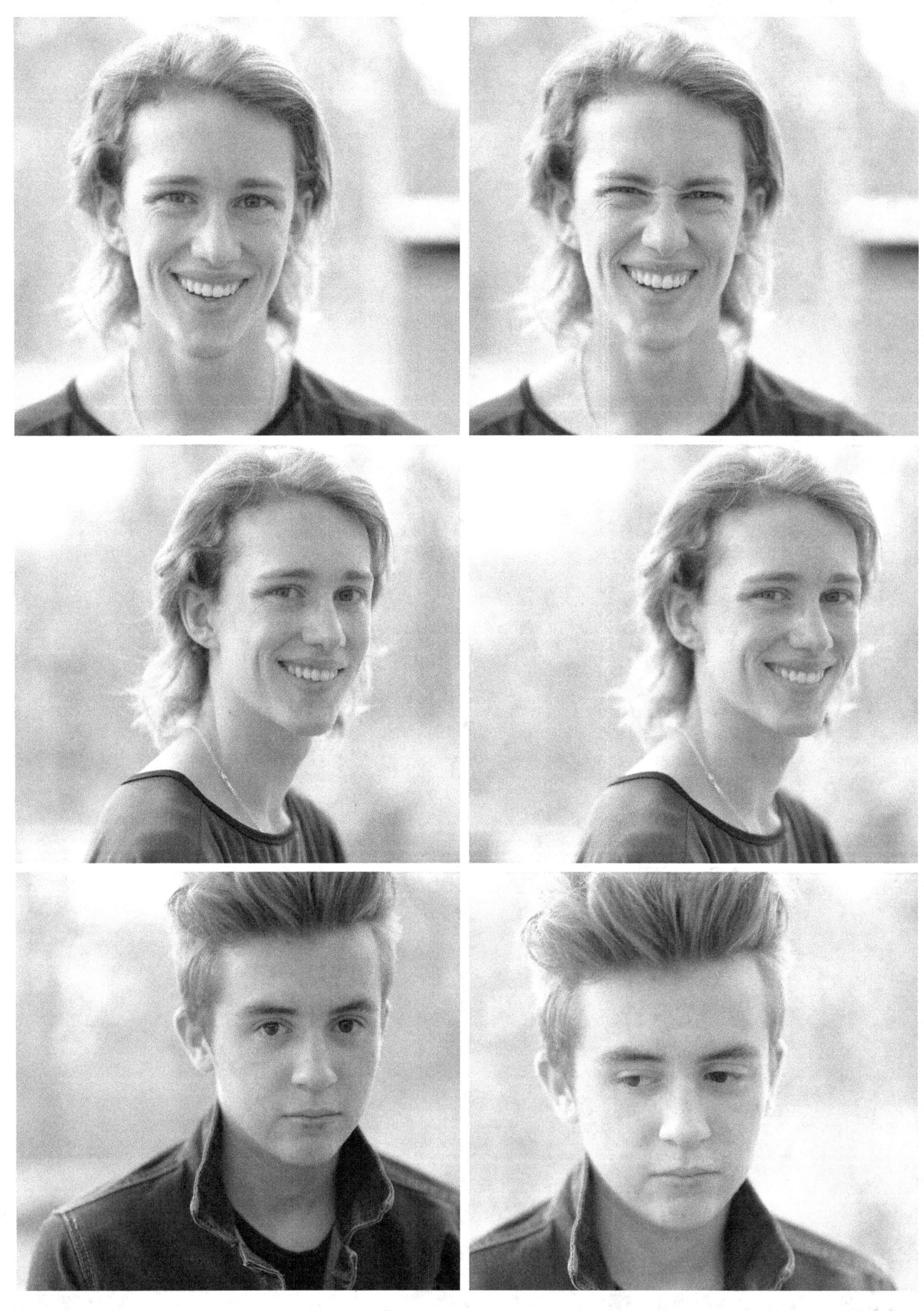

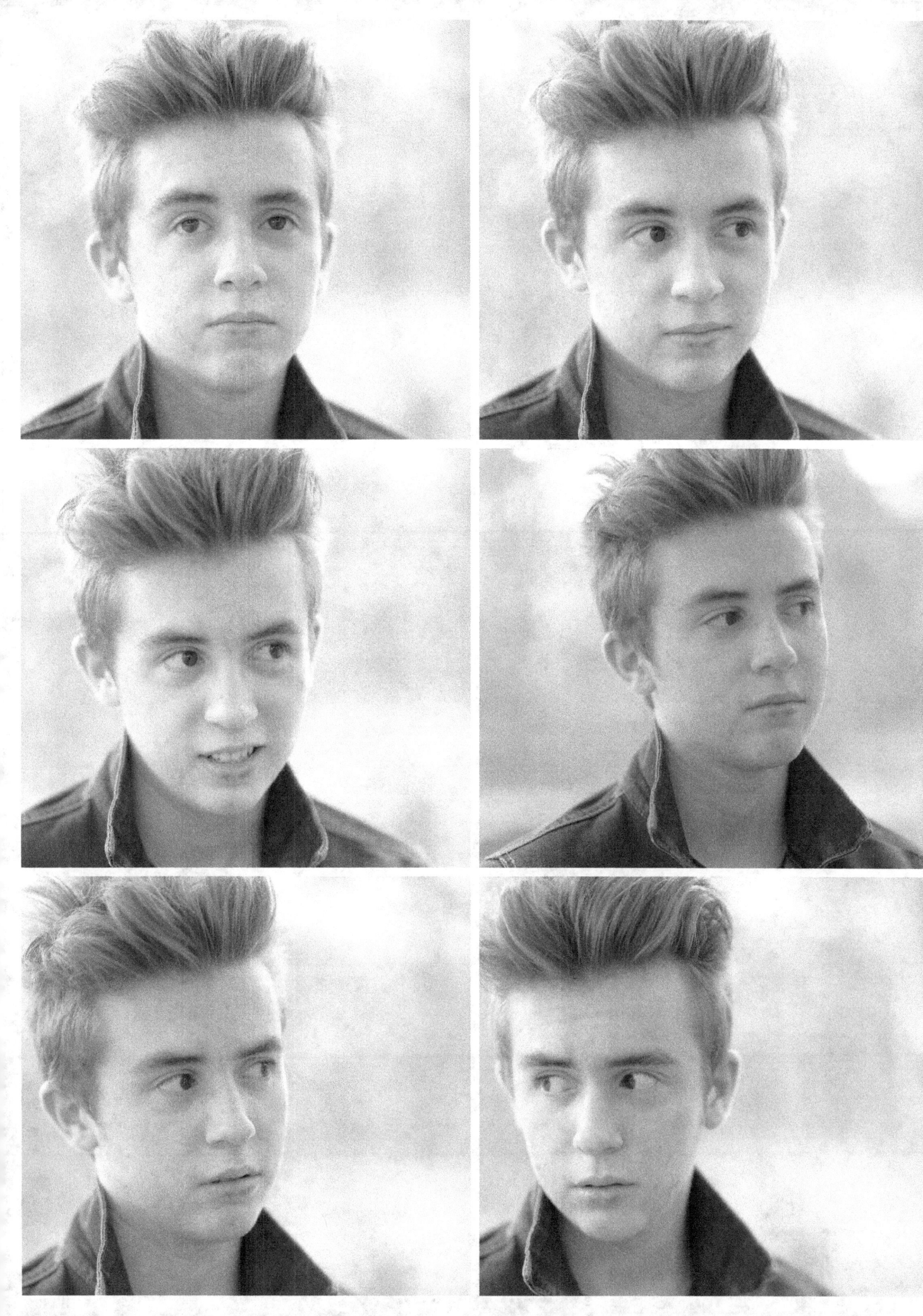

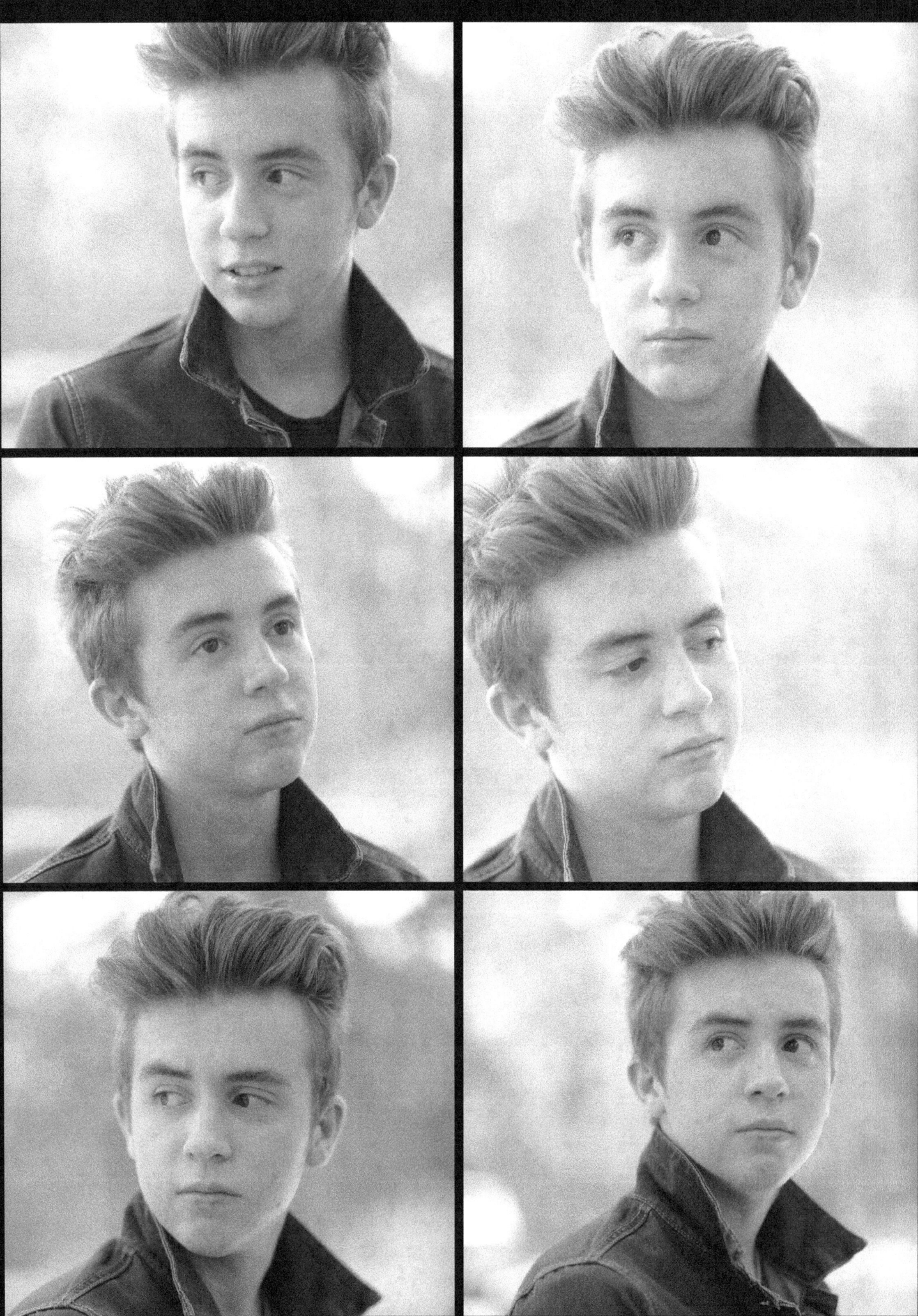

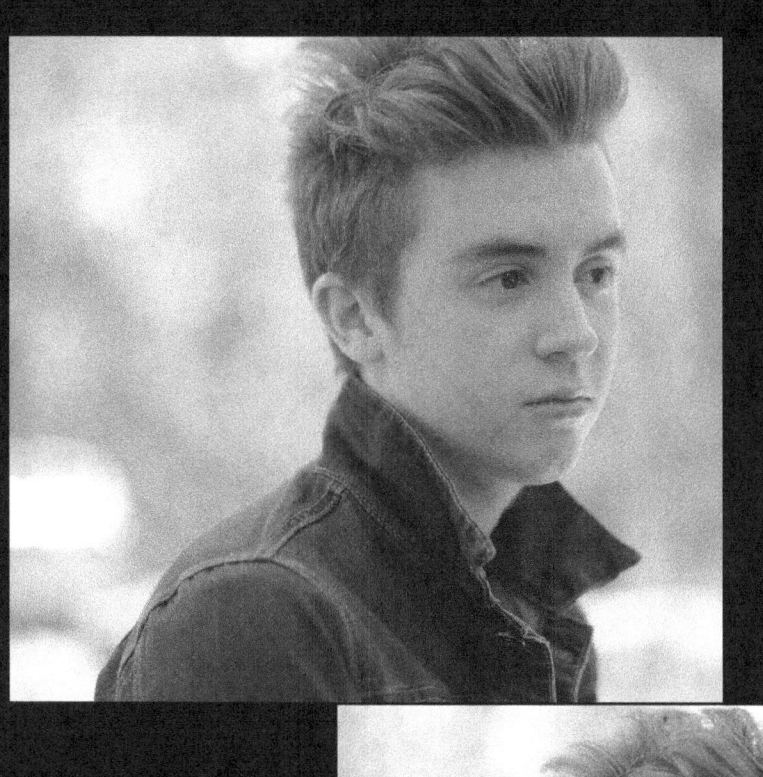

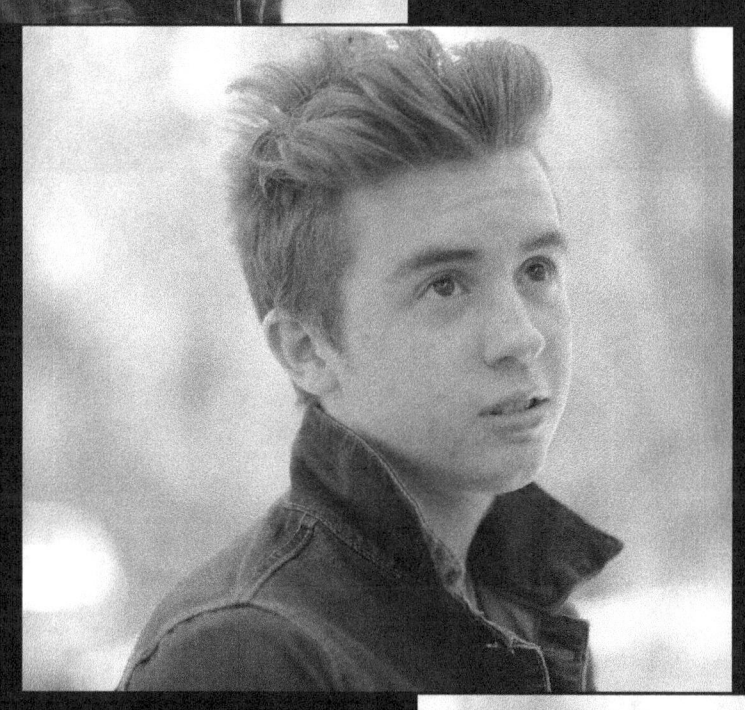

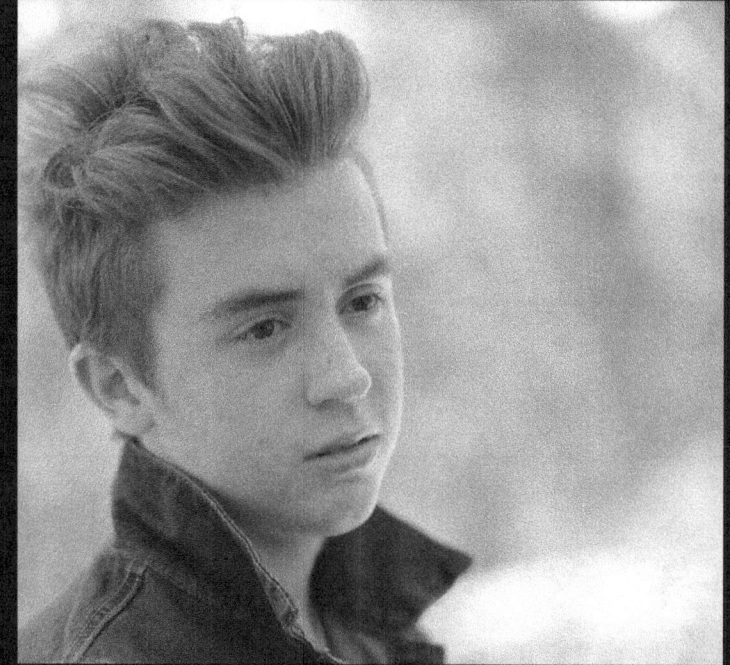